MW01040665

MUZZLELOADER MAGAZINE'S

THE BOOK OF
BUCKSKINNING VII

Edited by
William H. Scurlock

SCURLOCK PUBLISHING CO., INC. / TEXARKANA, TEXAS

EDITORIAL STAFF

EDITOR:
William H. Scurlock

ASSOCIATE EDITOR:
Linda Cook Scurlock

COVER PHOTOGRAPHY:
David Wright (Front)
K. Abercrombie (Back)

EDITORIAL ASSISTANT:
Cherry Lloyd

GRAPHIC DESIGN:
Cherry Lloyd

PUBLISHER:
William H. Scurlock

ABOUT THE COVERS

FRONT:
Dick Patton, longtime participant and leader of horseback rides in the West, prepares to mount up during a ride in the Pioneer Mountains of Montana in 1991.

BACK:
"October 12, 1836, ...our youngest had sobbed a peck of tears ever since departing Pittsburg. No song nor rhyme could raise those spirits 'til her momma bid me stop the team and unload the wagon down to the greatest trunk. Praise be that the puppet was there and not forgot."
Thanks to Conner Prairie, Fishers, Indiana, for their help in providing the historic atmosphere to bring these words to life.

ISBN #1-880655-05-5

Contents

Dedication

To the memory of Curly Gostomski. A great friend to us when we were just beginning. May we all be as helpful to newcomers.

Clothing of the Rocky Mountain Trapper, 1820–1840

by Allen Chronister and Clay Landry

Allen Chronister was born and raised in North Carolina, graduated from U.N.C. (Chapel Hill) in 1969 and from law school at George Washington University in D.C. in 1972. He moved to Montana in 1973 and has lived there ever since.

Chronister has published and spoken extensively about Plains Indian art and material culture. He is a contributing author to *Whispering Winds* magazine and has been published in *American Indian Art* and *American Indian Crafts and Culture*. He has spoken numerous times on Plains Indian and fur trade topics for the National Park Service (at Fort Union Trading Post National Historic Site), the Montana Historical Society and the Buffalo Bill Historical Center in Cody, Wyoming.

Being a Southerner by birth and having graduated from Texas A&M University with a master's degree in agriculture, most of his friends and relatives expected Clay Landry to settle near these very traditional origins. However, after a 1972 tour with the Army in Vietnam, he was assigned to a post in Colorado and found the clime and scenic vistas of the Rockies very captivating.

He and his wife, Jamie, now live in Columbus, Montana, which is located on the banks of the Yellowstone River and in the shadow of the Beartooth Mountains. An accomplished horseman, muleskinner and wilderness packer, Clay has organized and led several horse treks through the wilds of Montana and Wyoming into both the NMLRA and AMM Western rendezvous.

"We have enough broken-down legends without creating any new ones."
—Charles E. Hanson

Defining and understanding the clothing worn by the Rocky Mountain trapper in the rendezvous era is a difficult task. Misconceptions, misinformation and the absence of reliable information have led some to portray the trappers dressed as Philadelphia bankers, while others have festooned themselves with animal hides, furs, bones and skulls more befitting extras in a barbarian horde movie. The purpose of this chapter is to present and analyze much of the available historical information on the clothing worn by the trappers in the Rocky Mountains in the 1820-1840 period. Our focus is on the Euro-American who lived and worked in the field and whose primary occupation was trapping beaver. These men were generally called "trappers" or "mountaineers" at the time, and since the term "mountain man" did not come into general use until after the rendezvous period, we will avoid using it here.

It is important to remember that trappers were not the only "class" of people in the 1820-1840 West. Native Americans (both indigenous and displaced Eastern tribesmen), post traders and engages, traders and trappers operating out of the Southwest, "Canadians," and voyageurs each had their own more or less distinctive styles of dress. These other styles were influenced by national origin, occupation, personal preference and the fur trade social status. Our focus is solely on the trappers.

While particular dress styles did not begin or end precisely on the focus dates, this period encompasses the heyday of the rendezvous and of beaver trapping in the inter-mountain west. A great deal of myth and unsupported lore surrounds the trappers' clothing, and it is essential to separate truth from fiction. The primary sources are few: the surviving firsthand accounts of people who were among the trappers before 1840; the early paintings of Alfred Jacob Miller; and fur trade business records. Beyond these sources, reliable evidence on trappers' clothing is scarce.

There are literally thousands of pages of American Fur Company (AFC) records and other period fur trade business records that contain a wealth of relevant information. Some of this information has been available on microfilm for several years, but much of it is just now appearing in that form. None of these records are easy to access even on microfilm, and there is a tremendous amount of clothing information yet to be uncovered. The records we primarily used are those of the AFC's St. Louis operations and those of Nathaniel Wyeth's Fort Hall. Both contain detailed inventories of goods as well as records of transactions with individual engages, clerks, free trappers and native Americans.

We have also relied on Alfred Jacob Miller's paintings. They are a good source of primary information if they are understood and are used carefully. Miller attended the 1837

Horse Creek/Green River rendezvous on the commission of Scottish nobleman William Drummond Stewart. While this association resulted in the only paintings of trappers done from life before 1840, Miller's work is also the product of two romantic imaginations. "Miller saw everything through the romantic's eyes—he was a romantic, both in terms of painting and in what he read and how he saw" (Tyler 34). His patron, Stewart, had a similar orientation:

Stewart's trip was a nobleman's adventure full of Indian maidens, buffalo hunts, long evenings of western tales, and feats of horsemanship by Europeans and Indians alike.... Stewart and his chosen artist, Miller, were not interested in the literal view of the West—they did not intend to make maps or engrave prints of the flora and fauna. (Tyler 51)

While on the trail and at the 1837 rendezvous, Miller completed perhaps as many as 80 field sketches that would become the basis of his later finished paintings. The field sketches were usually very small (5 by 4 inches or 6 by 5 inches) works in watercolor wash over pencil. These paintings were "simple and expressive" and were "spontaneous, loosely painted, and delightful" (Tyler 54, 60).

The 1837 field sketches probably represent most closely what Miller actually saw at the time. His later oils and watercolors were based on the field sketches, supplemented "with imagery and remembered images when he returned to the studio" (Tyler 54). Miller returned from the rendezvous to

his studio in New Orleans and immediately set about completing paintings for Stewart. He had moved on to Baltimore and had finished and displayed 18 paintings by the spring of 1839. He spent the 1840-1841 period in Scotland at Stewart's Murthly castle finishing paintings at Stewart's direction. Stewart closely oversaw the Murthly paintings, frequently requesting changes and additions. As Miller himself said: "[W]oe to the Indian who has not sufficent dignity in expression and carriage for *out* he must come" (Tyler 51).

After completing Stewart's commission, Miller returned to Baltimore and continued to paint the same Western subjects for the next 30 years. During his career he completed multiple paintings of many of the scenes that originated in the field sketches. (See Tyler 209-370 for a complete catalog.) In later versions of the original 1837 scenes there are sometimes signifigant (for our purposes) changes made in the details. Whether done for Miller's purposes or Stewart's, these changes most likely represent Miller's disposition to romanticize what he had seen.

Differences between some of the field sketches and later paintings based upon them can be demonstrated. The original field sketch of Joe Walker and his Indian wife shows a clean shaven Walker wearing a floral beaded Red River-style shoulder bag and plain, fringed hide clothing (Parke-Bernet 12). In the later (some done as late as 1858-1860) and better-known versions of the scene, Walker looses the floral bag and gains a beard and painted stripes on his hide trousers (Tyler pl. 81; 289-290). In *Picketing the Horses—At Evening,* shown on

This 1837 Miller field drawing, *Picketing the Horses—At Evening,* is loaded with a variety of good detail. The two men in the middle front are depicted wearing knee breeches and have bare feet, while the man in the eared hood is drawn with full-length trousers. Suspenders and a fall-front panel can be seen on the pantaloons of the man driving in the picket pin. Only the man holding the horse is shown with a fringing down the arm of his frock. Both tents in this original sketch are wedge style while in later drawn versions they were changed by Miller to tepees.

the previous page, the two central figures in the 1837 version are barefoot and wearing plain knee breeches (Tyler pl. 38). In the later (c. 1858-1860) finished painting of the same scene, a number of details are altered and the two central figures are wearing fringed long trousers and moccasins (Tyler 220; DeVoto, *Across* pl. XLIII) The differences in both of these scenes are critical to an analysis of trappers' clothing.

While there is no absolute assurance that the original field works more closely record what Miller actually saw, that result is likely. Most of the surviving 1837 field sketches have been reproduced in the several books devoted to Miller, and one should consult them closely. (For example see: numerous plates in Tyler, including no. 32, 36, 42, 46, 63; DeVoto, *Across* pl. LXXVIII; Parke-Bernet 7, 11, 12, 19, 23, 25, 37, 46.) Using the Miller field paintings to supplement journal descriptions and other primary information helps to provide a relatively complete picture of trappers' dress, at least in the late 1830s.

A significant problem encountered in this research is the lack of documented specimens of clothing actually worn by trappers in the 1820-1840 period. This lack of specimens has led other historians and researchers to rely upon clothing specimens from the last half of the nineteenth century, sometimes with the knowledge that the specimen was owned by a man who had been a trapper before 1840. However, clothing owned by ex-trappers in the 1850s and 1860s is not a reliable indicator of what the same men wore 20 to 40 years before. Other sources of dubious value, which have nonetheless been relied upon, are buckskin military garments dating from the 1870s and clothing from the Canadian fur trade dating from the late nineteenth century.

The absence of reliable specimens has also led to use of the much more abundant surviving examples of native American clothing from the first half of the nineteenth century. While specimens of native American clothing from the West of 1820-1840 are rare, they are abundant compared to the almost total absence of surviving trapper clothing from the same period. Even though these elaborate dress and ceremonial garments may date to before 1840, there is little evidence that they have much relevence to the clothing of the field trapper.

Another factor that must be remembered is that less than a decade after the last rendezvous, the Rocky Mountain trapper and his appearance were already passing into legend. Rudolph Kurz, artist and journal writer at Fort Union about 1850, said of the engages there:

The "Mountaineer" costume, in which they array themselves in St. Joseph and St. Louis, they have made before their departure for the purpose of distinguishing themselves. Such suits of clothes are made up and sold at Fort Pierre. (Kurz 134)

A capote made with flap-covered pockets, a round crown felt hat adorned with a feather and a pipe, a cloth shirt, long fringed pantaloons/trousers and pucker-toe moccasins are worn by this "veteran" trapper in *A Rocky Mountain Trapper, Bill Burrows* by Alfred Jacob Miller.

While Kurz did not describe the "mountaineer costume," it was likely fringed hide coat and trousers. Such outfits appear repeatedly in paintings of mountaineers by Tait, Ranney, Deas and other artists in the 1850s and 1860s. (See *American Frontier Life* by Alan Axelrod.) The artist Carl Wimar was photographed wearing one in 1858 (Rick Stewart frontispiece).

The heavily beaded, quilled and fringed "frontiersman" and "scout" outfits of the 1860-1890 period carry on this tradition (Hanson and Wilson 28, 30; James Hanson, *Frontier Scout* 7-10, 24-28). However, this post-1840 material is not representative of trappers' clothing.

Trappers without Ammunition and in a Starving Condition near Independence Rock depicts the reclining trapper with fringed pantaloons, a fall-front panel, single suspender attachment, a neck scarf and a fringed buckskin coat.

Alfred Jacob Miller, Joslyn Art Museum, Omaha, Nebraska

This sketch, titled *Antoine Clement,* shows a buckskin frock fringed only at the shoulders, fastened with a thong tie and made with a welt in the seam of the sleeve. Could the collarless shirt worn underneath the coat be one of Fort Hall's "Guernsey frocks"?

TRAPPERS' SOURCES OF SUPPLY

A trapper in the West of 1820-1840 had several possible sources for clothing and other supplies. These may not have been "options" in that there were not necessarily several choices available at once. For most clothing items the sources of supply were limited.

The first option for a trapper was to bring his clothing with him from the settlements. Rocky Mountain trappers all came to the West from somewhere else, usually bringing clothing and equipment with them. In addition, the "jumping off" cities in Missouri were outfitting points that catered to individuals as well as larger commercial enterprises participating in the fur trade. As early as the 1820s, the availability of ready-made mens' clothing and shoes imported in quantity from the East (primarily Philadelphia or New York) were advertised in St. Louis in the *Missouri Republican* newspaper. In addition, traditional tailors also practiced their trade there (*Missouri Republican* 16 April 1822). There are several historical references, which will be noted later, to men purchasing their Western clothing in Missouri before departure to (and upon their return from) the West.

The records of the American Fur Company's St. Louis retail store for the 1820-1840 period preserve in precise detail the clothing purchases made by individual men. On June 4, 1831, for example, Michel Sicto, who was apparently bound for Fort Union, bought two hats, a frock coat, pantaloons, two pair of shoes, five handkerchiefs, a vest, four shirts, two pair of socks, one pair of boots and a pair of drawers (T: UMO Ledger B). In July, 1831, Jacob Halsey, a clerk, was issued (and charged for against his wages of $400 per year) two vests, a calico shirt, an "H.B. capot," a silk handkerchief, a pair of pantaloons, a pair of socks and a pair of brogans, all at the cost of $57.00 (R: Retail Store Ledger B: 200). On March 5, 1832, Fredrick Girard, apparently attached to the Upper Missouri Outfit (UMO), received five check shirts, two pair of fabric pantaloons, a pair of leather pants, a cotton handkerchief, a pair of shoes, four pairs of socks and a belt (T: UMO Ledger B).

The predominately fabric garments brought from the East often did not last long when worn constantly in the field. Asa Smith was one of a group of missionaries traveling to the 1838 rendezvous on the Popo Agie and then on to Oregon. He wrote his sister from Fort Laramie:

You would find me rather dirty & ragged for it is impossible to keep clean here & I wear out my clothes very badly. I calculate to get some leather clothes soon. They are better for riding on horseback and the labor we have to perform.

(Drury 147)

Not long after the last rendezvous, Francis Parkman traveled west wearing his "frock and trousers of civilization." These clothes wore out in about two months and were replaced with Indian-made "fringed buckskin frocks and trousers to match" (Parkman 252-253). In about 1850 Kurz compared the cloth clothing available at the AFC company store at Fort Union to buckskin clothes and found that the latter "are certainly more serviceable for life in the bush and on the prairie and serve as better protection against sun and mosquitoes when one is on horseback" (134).

In any event, both conventional fabric garments, as well as leather garments, were available for purchase or issue in Missouri and were worn and used by individuals participating in the fur trade.

A second option for the trapper was for him or one of his trapper associates to make his clothing in the field. There is historical evidence that trappers had the ability and materials to fabricate at least simple clothing. In the late eighteenth and early nineteenth century, complex clothing items such as leather breeches tended to be cut and sewn by specialist tailors and not by the ordinary housewife who might otherwise make much of the family clothing (Gehret 31, 93, 127). Therefore, except for the rare man with training as a tailor, it is not likely that most trappers would fabricate a pair of hide breeches unless forced by necessity.

Nevertheless, Osborne Russell's group bought a "large number of Elk Deer and Sheep skins...of the finest quality" from a group of Shoshone people they met in what is now Yellowstone National Park (Russell 27). Russell did not describe what they intended to do with these skins, but the variety of hides makes it probable that any intended clothing use included both moccasins and other clothing items. While there are some references to men making clothing in the field— such as on the Lewis and Clark expedition—most are very vague except for moccasins.[1]

The scanty evidence supports an inference that trappers did not regularly fabricate their own clothing in the field. Some things, like felt hats for example, had to be purchased and could not be made in the field.

A third option for a trapper was to obtain clothing from local Indians. Trappers commonly wintered and held their summer rendezvous with or near large groups of Indians, including Salish, Nez Perce and Shoshones and sometimes Utes (Gowans 76). There is evidence that trappers sometimes hired Indian women to sew garments for them (Porter 32; Field 142). These garments could have been tailored on Anglo-American or Indian patterns. At the same time, there is little evidence that trappers regularly obtained Indian-style clothing from the Indians, and local Indians were probably more important as a source of hides than of finished garments (Russell 27).

A trapper could also obtain his clothing from a supply train at the rendezvous. This was an expensive source and existing records show that the rendezvous supply trains brought a limited selection of clothing, especially in the early years (Morgan 151-152). Brigade trappers getting just a little over $100 a year (in 1827) could afford few major purchases (Morgan 172). Fabric shirts were the only clothing items commonly stocked in quantity, although the selection of goods

---

[1] (Moulton 2: 327, 4: 149, 5: 119, 6: 407; Sage 39)

Pierre by Alfred Jacob Miller, probably drawn from life at the 1837 rendezvous. Pierre is wearing fringed hide pantaloons with a strap under the instep of his foot, moccasins, vest and shirt and a long button-front fabric overcoat. His gun, pouch and horn, on separate shoulder straps, are leaning against the tree behind him. Note Pierre's short hair, clean shave and generally neat appearance.

apparently improved later in the period (Breun).

There are few surviving records of actual individual purchases of goods at rendezvous. Two accounts of purchases are *The West of William H. Ashley* by Dale Morgan, containing Ashley's sales in 1825, and Robert Campbell's 1832 account books, the original manuscript of which is held by the Mercantile Library Corporation in St. Louis, Missouri.[2] In neither set of records do men appear actually to be re-outfitting themselves at rendezvous with substantial durable goods. The existing records show that individual purchases of guns, clothing, horse gear and traps are rare. Most transactions deal in "luxury" items like alcohol, sugar, coffee, beads, knives, ribbon, bells, fish hooks and scarlet cloth. The surviving records indicate that most men bought trinkets at the rendezvous and made purchases of more substantial goods elsewhere. The same generally holds true of brigade trappers who purchased goods from the "company store" while in the field.

A trapper could also obtain clothing from a fixed post in the West. The larger trading posts like Fort Union, Fort Pierre, Fort Laramie and Fort Hall stocked a variety of ready-made clothing and often also had tailors on the premises. In addition, the AFC sometimes outfitted its rendezvous supply trains directly from trading posts (Gowans 75-76).

The records of the retail store at Fort Hall in the 1830s for example reflect numerous clothing purchases by individuals, many of whom are now well-known, including Osborne Russell and Kit Carson (Columbia, Ledger 1: 13-4, Ledger 2: 121). These purchases were sometimes one or two clothing items but were also often entire outfits of shirt, shoes or moccasins, pants and accessories. At Fort Hall, for example, on June 23, 1836, Dida, one of Wyeth's Hawaiian engages, bought a check shirt, skin pants, two pair of moccasins and a three-point blanket (Columbia, Ledger 1: 82). On March 13, 1836, Alexander Macon bought a check shirt, duck trousers and a green capote, along with blue seed beads, a pound of tobacco and an old fusil (Columbia, Ledger 1: 169). Nathaniel Wyeth, the founder of Fort Hall, in turn purchased moccasins

---

[2] All references to Campbell's account book are derived from the symposium paper by Raymond Breun. See Breun entry in Appendix A.

and other clothing from the Hudson's Bay Company's posts along the Columbia River in the fall of 1832 (Wyeth 28, 30).

Even with all of these supply possibilities, the clothing of the trapper was essentially simple. Contemporary descriptions usually describe only a single outfit of clothing, and seldom is there a reference to much spare clothing other than extra fabric shirts. Existing sales records support the information on spare shirts and additionally show that trappers often purchased several pairs of pantaloons or trousers. Ownership of a narrow selection of clothing was not unique to the trappers and is consistent with the apparel of the common working man of the late eighteenth and early nineteenth century. In the Eastern United States at that time a common farmer's clothing for a year was often as little as two shirts and two pair of pants, in addition to hat and shoes (Gehret 93).

Several original journal passages indicate that the trappers who penned them owned small stocks of clothing at the time being described. In 1834 William Marshall Anderson, upon his return from the West, was embarassed at eating in a tavern among "politicians, pedantic doctors and wise looking lawyers" while wearing only his dirty hunting shirt and greasy leather breeches (Morgan and Harris 221). Harrison Rodgers found himself in an almost identical situation at dinner at a California mission in 1826 (Smith 229). William Drummond Stewart describes his autobiographical character Edward Warren purchasing clothing for the West, and some extra shirts were his only changes of clothing (51).

We will now examine the primary items of clothing used and worn by the Rocky Mountain trapper in the 1820-1840 period.

FOOTWEAR

There were two footwear options for the trapper: moccasins, and manufactured shoes or boots. While shoes or boots could have been brought from the settlements and were available at rendezvous and from fixed posts, it is clear that most trappers wore moccasins most of the time.

Two general styles of moccasins were used. First, the ubiquitous moccasin of the northern Plains and mountain tribes before 1840 was the one-piece, side-seam style. Meriwether Lewis, while among the Shoshones in 1805, wrote:

The mockersons of both sexes are usually the same and are made of deer Elk or buffaloe skin dressed without the hair. sometimes in the winter they make them of buffaloe skin dressed with the hair on and turn the hair inwards as the Mandans Minetares and most of the nations do who inhabit the buffaloe country. the mockerson is formed with one seem on the outer

edge of the foot is cut open at the instep to admit the foot and sewed up behind. in this rispect they are the same with the Mandans. (DeVoto, *Journals* 216)

That same year Antoine Laroque described Crow moccasins "made in the manner of mittens having a seam round the outside of the foot only without pleat" (Laroque 81). About 35 years later, Rufus B. Sage stated that every mountaineer was proficient at moccasin making. He described the process as follows:

The process of shoe-making with [the mountaineer] is reduced to its most simple form. He merely takes two pieces of buffalo (or any other suitable) skin, each being a little longer and wider than his foot, particularly towards the heel; these he folds separately, and lays them parallel together with the turned edges; then, rounding and trimming the sides, to render them foot-shaped, with an awl and the sinew of buffalo or other animal, or small strips of thin deer-skin, ("whang,") he sews the vamps from end to end,—then after cutting a tongue-like appendage in the upper side, midway from heel to toe, and stitching together the posterior parts, his task is done. (155)

Side seam moccasins made of buffalo hide with the hair on the inside were probably used during the winter as described in the Lewis and Clark journals, quoted at left.

While side-seam moccasins required few skills to construct and were made by trappers in the field, trappers also sometimes obtained them from other sources. There are numerous references in the AFC and Fort Hall records to individuals buying single pairs of moccasins of unknown style. (See, for example, Columbia, Ledger 1: 89, 217, 275; American, UMO Ledger B: entry for Bennoil, 9 Oct. 1830.) In about 1812 one group of trappers traded an astounding 450 pairs of probably side-seam moccasins (as well as a quantity of furs, hides and meat) from a group of Cheyenne people (Luttig 100). Moccasins obtained "in bulk" like this could have been "one size fits all"—moccasins cut out and with the side seam sewn together but the heel seam left open. The purchaser then trimmed the heel to fit his foot length and sewed up that seam.

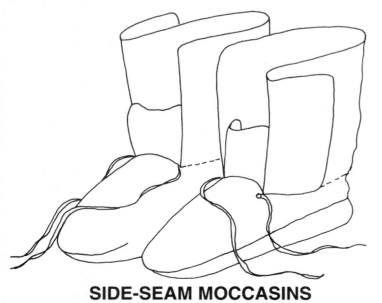

SIDE-SEAM MOCCASINS

PUCKER TOE

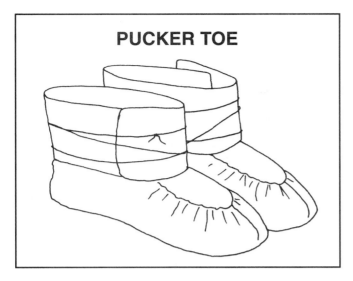

While no specific references have been found to trappers obtaining moccasins in this condition, it is the logical way to do it. Several pairs of Indian-made and decorated moccasins survive from the pre-1840 period, fully constructed but with no heel seam (Thompson 154-155).

Maintaining fresh moccasins could be a daunting task. By the time Lewis and Clark were portaging around the Great Falls in July 1805, Sgt. Ordway reported that the men wore out a pair of moccasins every two days (Moore 8). Under less strenuous conditions, moccasins would last longer, up to two or three weeks (Harrison et al. 76).

A second style of moccasin was clearly common among the trappers when Miller did his field sketches at the 1837 rendezvous (DeVoto, *Across* pl. LXXVIII). When the moccasin is clearly visible, a significant proportion of Miller's trappers wear a puckered front seam moccasin with an inset vamp (hereafter referred to as "pucker-toes"). While it is clear that many trappers wore pucker-toe moccasins in 1837, it is equally unclear where they came from.

While the pucker toe moccasin was used by native peoples over a wide area, it is not commonly associated with the Western tribes. Indian people from the Great Lakes, Northern and Eastern Canada, and the Eastern United States, as well as the Red River metis people all used this style of moccasin. In the early twentieth century, the Coeur D'Alene Indians in northern Idaho reported that although the one-piece, side-seam was the most common moccasin, they were familiar with the pucker-toe style. They stated that it "came in at a later date with the fur traders" and was called "white man's moccasin" or "Chippewa moccasin" (Teit and Boas 72-73).

Because this was not an indigenous Western moccasin style, it is unlikely that local Indians were a source. A possible source for these "Eastern" moccasins was the displaced Eastern Indians and the Canadians who figured prominently in the 1820-1840 Western fur trade (Swagerty 161-162). Significant numbers of Eastern Indians—especially Delawares and the Iroquois tribes—participated fully in the Western fur trade from an early date (see Ewers, "Iroquois" and Frisch). While these people sometimes worked as individual free trappers or engages, they often traveled in their own groups with their families. These Indian trappers from the East or their wives could have produced signifigant numbers of pucker-toe moccasins.

A last possibility is that the pucker-toe moccasins were

constructed by the trappers themselves based upon knowledge they brought with them from the East. While side-seam moccasins are slightly easier to cut out and construct, any trapper who could make side-seams could also probably make front seams if he knew the pattern. In sum, while it is clear that the trappers wore these moccasins in the late 1830s, their source remains a mystery.

It is clear that moccasins were available from trading posts in the West. While trading post inventories seldom include stocks of moccasins, retail sales records show that they were frequently sold. This probably means that they were made to order for the individual customer. Records of the American Fur Company's St. Louis retail store in the 1830s, as noted above, include multiple purchases of moccasins by individuals, usually just one or two pairs at a time. Similarly, the retail store records from Fort Hall in the 1830s, again noted above, reflect moccasin purchases, also usually one or two pairs at a time. Production of moccasins at Fort Hall is reflected in records of wages paid to men for "making moccasins" (Columbia, Ledger 1: 319). None of these entries, however, describe the style of moccasin being sold.

Either style of moccasin—side seam or pucker toe—could have been made from a variety of types of hide, although heavier hide was preferred for durability. While there are numerous references to deerskin and elkhide moccasins, a favored material (among trappers and Indians) was the dark

BROGANS

brown, heavily smoked buffalo cowhide taken from the tops of worn-out lodge covers. This material was lightweight, did not stretch and was not affected by wetting (Victor 55).

We have found no evidence that the two-piece Indian moccasin with the parfleche sole and soft hide upper was ever used by trappers (or anyone else) in the pre-1840 West. As noted above the prevalent native style in the west at this time was the one-piece, side-seam moccasin, and this remained true for many tribes until the latter stages of the nineteenth century. As late as 1910, the Hidatsa felt that the parfleche sole moccasin was a later style that they had learned from the Sioux and that their traditional moccasin was the one-piece, side-seam (Wilson 233.) The earliest known parfleche sole moccasins come from the southern Plains, where they were in use by about 1850 or slightly earlier (Ewers, *Indians of Texas* 184). They did not reach the northern Plains until as late as the 1860s (James Hanson, *Frontier Scout* 42)

We have likewise found no evidence that eighteenth century "shoepacs" or French-Canadian "beefhide" shoes or moccasins were used by trappers in the West in the period under

consideration (Klinger 25; James Hanson, *Voyager's* 16-17). The equipment for the Lewis and Clark expedition included a few pair of "ox hide Shoes," but their appearance is unknown (Thwaites 6, pt. 2: 278). However, because most references to "moccasins" in historical accounts do not specify style, we cannot categorically rule out the possibility that these two types were used.

While commercial shoes were available to the trappers before 1850, there is little firsthand evidence of widespread use. Lewis and Clark ordered only 20 pair of shoes for their entire expedition, and their journals mention construction and use of moccasins on a number of occasions (Thwaites 7: 242). All of Miller's figures at the rendezvous appear to be wearing moccasins. Warren Ferris said that in the 1830-1835 period all Indians and whites wore moccasins (286).

Ashley's accounts of sales to individual trappers at the 1825 rendezvous include no shoes or boots—or moccasins for that matter (Morgan 118-128.) Ashley sold twelve pair of womens' shoes and six pair of mens' shoes to "Gardner & Williams" (Morgan 127-28). Gardner was a free trapper who had been instrumental in convincing 23 of Ogden's men to desert the HBC with 700 beaver the month before. This same group apparently left the rendezvous for the Flathead country (Morgan 286-287). These events, plus the quantities of goods sold to Gardner and Williams make it likely that they were outfitting themselves with a stock of trade goods and not just goods for personal consumption. Besides, six pair of shoes would not go very far even in Gardner's group of 23 men. The interesting question is what did Gardner and Williams do with the womens' shoes, and why were they brought out to the rendezvous to begin with?

The list of trade goods that Ashley agreed to deliver to the 1827 rendezvous contained no shoes (Morgan 150-152). Robert Campbell's 1832 account book includes sales of a wide variety of goods but very few involving shoes and only one pair of "old boots." In addition, most of the shoe entires were for transactions that probably took place in Missouri before Campbell went west that year (Breun). Further, some references to "shoes" are ambiguous. Rufus Sage, for example, mentioned putting his "shoes" under his head while he slept, but later used the same term to describe one-piece, side-seam buffalo hide moccasins (144, 155). Antoine Laroque mentioned getting "a few pair of shoes made" at the Hidatsa village in October 1805 (Laroque 69). He later described Crow "shoes" as side-

seam moccasins (Laroque 81). It is probable that in both cases the authors intended "shoes" to mean "moccasins."

The records of the American Fur Company's retail store in St. Louis contains numerous references to sales of shoes to individuals, some of which have been noted previously. (See, for example, American, Retail Store Ledger B: entries for Miller, June 1831; Halsey, July 1831; Girard, 5 March 1832.)The Fort Hall records for the mid-1830s likewise include occasional sales of shoes to individuals, although the sales of moccasins are much more numerous. (See, for example, Columbia, Ledger 1: 205, 285, 317.)

The common civilian and military man's shoe in the 1820-1840 period was a low, straight-lasted brogan up to ankle height that tied with one to three sets of lacing holes (Charles Hanson, "Footwear" 2; Steffan 100, 111). These were also called boots, brogans and booties. Any reference to shoes in fur trade inventories, as well as any shoe worn by a trapper, was probably this brogan style. Fort Union, for example, carried "shoes," "brogans," and "boots" on its inventory in 1831 and 1832 and similar stocks were likely on hand at other American Fur Company posts (National).[3] Boots, shoes and brogans were repeatedly advertised for sale in St. Louis during the 1820s and 1830s in the *Missouri Republican*.

Trappers wore socks of some kind under their moccasins or shoes when they were available, even though Osborne Russell's classic description of trappers' dress states that "his hose are pieces of Blanket lapped round his feet..." (82). While references to socks in the historical journals are rare, fur trade business records paint a slightly different picture. The common stocking of the late eighteenth and early nineteenth century was either hand-knit or machine-loomed of linen, cotton or wool (Gehret 223). The trading posts regularly carried wool and cotton socks in inventory, and the retail store records at Fort Hall include sufficent sales of socks to indicate that they were a relatively common item.[4]

While this was the case at Fort Hall, it might not have been the same at other times and places. The Ashley lists of goods delivered to and sold at rendezvous do not mention socks (Morgan 118-128). The extensive inventory of goods sold by

---

[3] This National Park Service publication is compiled from the Choteau Collection—the papers, ledgers, etc. of the Choteau family—held by the Missouri Historical Society in St. Louis.

[4] (National 130; Columbia, Ledger 1: 7, 251, 363, Ledger 2: 52, 58, 112)

Robert Campbell to O'Fallon and Vandeburgh at Pierre's Hole in 1832 contains only two pair of socks. By contrast it contains other goods in quantity, including dozens of knives, 57 cakes of shaving soap, 20 gross of awl blades, 246 pounds of lead and 173 pounds of tobacco (Breun). Socks were probably an appreciated but not essential item.

We have found some evidence of other types of footwear in use by trappers. While there is some evidence of the use of boots in the pre-1840 West, references are rare. Among the many moccasin purchases at Fort Hall, for example, is Alexander Wade's July 1836 purchase of a pair of "thin boots" (Columbia, Ledger 1: 371). Fort Hall records also show, surprisingly, that "5 pairs Indian rubber shoes" were on hand there in 1834 and were later sold to individuals (Columbia, Ledger 1: 52). Robert Evans bought a pair on January 16, 1835, and John Baptiste Dushan bought a pair "for [his] wife" on January 7 (Columbia, Day Book: 65, 60). Rubber shoes may not be as rare in the 1830s as one may expect. "India Rubber Over Shoes" and "Gum Elastic" overshoes were available for sale in St. Louis by at least 1830 (*Missouri Republican* 2 Mar. 1830, 14 Dec. 1830). Missionary Sarah Smith, on the trip with her husband, Asa, as mentioned previously, recorded that she wore "India rubber shoes" during the trip (Drury 86). Although the appearance of these rubber shoes is not described, they might have been a type of slipper that could be worn over moccasins.

SHIRTS

Most trappers seem to have worn one or more common fabric shirts as the primary garment next to the skin. Dr. Rush's written instructions to Lewis and Clark for the health of the expedition admonished wearing a flannel (wool) shirt next to the skin (Moore 7). Among the articles purchased for the Lewis and Clark expedition were 45 flannel shirts, 20 "frocks" and 30 shirts (Thwaites 7: 242). The 20 "frocks" were probably the "fatigue frocks or hunting shirts" from Lewis' list of goods that he wanted and could have been the long, loose, closed-front military fatigue shirt. The 30 shirts were linen, while the flannel were wool. The party also carried 48 "calico ruffled shirts" in their store of Indian presents (Thwaites 7, pt. 1: 239). They still had at least one of these calico shirts in April 1806 when trying to purchase horses for the return trip east across the mountains (DeVoto, *Journals* 359). By the time the expedition reached the lower Missouri on its way home, many of the men had run out of cloth shirts, and the journals mention

trading "leather for linen Shirts and beaver for corse hats" just prior to entry into the settlements (DeVoto, *Journals* 471).

By contrast, Ashley's accounts of goods sold to trappers at the 1825 rendezvous contain no shirts, although there are a few entries for quantities of cloth sufficient to make a shirt (Morgan 118-128). Further, the list of goods Ashley agreed to deliver to the 1827 rendezvous contained no shirts, although it did contain common flannel, calico, domestic cotton and assorted thread (Morgan 151-152). Things may have changed by 1832, when Robert Campbell's account book contains numerous entries for linen, calico, (cotton) check, and flannel (including yellow flannel) shirts, as well as for cloth that could have been used for shirts (Breun). Likewise, the list of goods delivered to Bent, St. Vrain & Company at the Platte River in 1838 include several entries for flannel, cotton check, and cotton plaid shirts, along with significant quantities of yard goods that would have been suitable for shirt production. If these listings are representative, shirts were more common and available in the 1830s than in the 1820s.

The larger trading posts were generally well stocked with ready-made shirts. The first order of goods for stocking Fort Pierre in 1832 included 140 calico and flannel shirts (Schuler 90). Fort Union carried a large inventory and variety of finished shirts in the 1830s, including: red flannel—200 in 1834; pink (!) check—152 in 1834; and "fancy calico & bright colors"—260 in 1834 (National 131). Numerous shirts were purchased at Fort Hall, and John Denton, the same man who was paid for making moccasins, was also paid for making shirts (Columbia, Ledger 1: 319).

Miller's field sketches at the 1837 rendezvous show many trappers wearing fabric shirts, usually under hide coats. While not much of the shirt is usually visible, both solid color and very simple print fabrics are depicted (Tyler pl. 63; DeVoto, *Across* pl. LXXVIII). These paintings are corroborated by several historical journals. Warren Ferris said that while the trappers in the 1830s wore hide clothing, most of them also wore calico shirts (361-362). Osborne Russell stated that a trapper's dress included "a flannel or cotton shirt (if he is fortunate enough to obtain one, if not antelope skin answers the purpose of over and under shirt" (82). When Russell himself narrowly escaped a Blackfoot attack in what is now Yellowstone Park, he had only "trowsers and a cotton shirt" (Russell 106). When Charles Larpenteur arrived at Fort Union in 1833, he wore a "red flannel undershirt and a blue check shirt over that" (Larpenteur 43). William Drummond Stewart described the outfit that he purchased in St. Louis as containing "half a dozen coloured shirts" (51).

At the 1832 rendezvous in Pierre's Hole, flannel shirts cost $2.50 to $3.00 each. Cotton shirts were much cheaper, at $.75 to $1.25 each (Breun). Ready-made shirts at Fort Hall in the mid-1830s usually cost $3.00, and many were apparently made at the Fort's tailor shop (Columbia, Ledger 1: 381-82, Ledger 2: 78-9). At the AFC retail store in St. Louis at about the same

time, shirts were about $2.00 (Retail Store Ledger B: Halsey, July 1831).

On the rare occasions when no fabric shirt was available, trappers at least sometimes wore a hide shirt as the primary garment next to the skin. While the historical journals contain several references to hide "hunting shirts," these probably describe outer garments rather than garments intended to be worn next to the skin. Still, Russell's antelope skin undershirt, mentioned above, and other references to men dressed "entirely in deer skins, without a single article of civilized manufacture about them" leave little doubt that trappers sometimes did wear hide garments next to the skin (Townsend 66). Information on the construction and appearance of these leather shirts has not been found. There is one surviving square-cut, tailored buckskin shirt with anecdotal history to the American Revolution, and trappers may have occasionally worn something similar (Neumann and Kravic 243).

A garment that was well-known in the 1820s and 1830s, but not to reenactors, is the knit shirt similar to a light sweater. While the term "sweater" has not been found in any pre-1840 sources, it is clear that upper-body garments of knit material, probably wool, were available at that time. They were called "Guernsey frocks" and were advertised for sale ready-made in St. Louis as early as 1828 (*Missouri Republican*, 30 Sept. 1828). Guernsey frocks were commonly stocked and sold to trappers and others at Fort Hall in the 1830s. Peter, one of Wyeth's Hawaiian engages, bought a Guernsey frock and two deerskins for $8.00 on December 7, 1836 (Columbia, Ledger 1: 317). Bill King bought a Guernsey frock and a pair of leather pants on November 13, 1836 (Columbia, Ledger 1: 361).

Guernsey frocks were shirt-like garments made of knit fabric that originated as nautical wear in the early nineteenth century (Rutt 129-132). In the fur trade, they were priced more like shirts than coats and were advertised in the newspapers with the shirts, not the coats. Guernsey frocks might appear in some Miller works. His portraits of Antoine Clement show a collarless shirt-like garment with a buttoned opening at the neck, visible under his hide coat (DeVoto, *Across* pl. LXXXVII; Porter, illus. after 148). (While Clement shopped at Fort Hall prior to being painted by Miller, we have not yet found that he purchased a Guernsey frock there [Columbia, Day Book: 45].) A very similar garment appears on the central figure in *Trappers* under a hide coat and cloth shirt, although this is a late painting done about 1860 (Tyler pl. 79; 105).

COATS

We intend the term "coat" to describe a garment worn over the shirt (or shirts) as a primary outer garment but not to include heavy outer garments for cold weather wear. A number of pieces of evidence point to the fact that the common coat for most trappers was the "leather hunting shirt." That term appears repeatedly·in first-person accounts of trappers' dress, often in a context which indicates that it is worn over a fabric shirt. The journals of John Bradbury (1811), Harrison Rodgers (1826), James Ohio Pattie (1827), William Drummond Stewart (in *Edward Warren*), and Philip Edwards (1834) all describe the authors or trappers wearing leather or deerskin or "fringed" hunting shirts. Larpenteur described his own "cowskin coat" and "buckskin shirt" worn over two fabric shirts in 1833 (Larpenteur 43).

These references to the same garment over a span of 25 or so years establish it firmly in trapper use. The trappers' leather hunting shirt probably traces its heritage to the hunting shirt or "rifle frock" of the eighteenth century and after (Harold Peterson 222-223, James Hanson, *Longhunter's* 13-14). The journals almost certainly refer to the same fringed hide garment that appears repeatedly in Miller paintings of the 1837 rendezvous. (See Tyler pl. 32, 38, 42, 46, 50 and 63.) The Miller garments are open-front, mid-thigh length, simply tailored coats with short turned-down collars. In one close-up illustration of Antoine Clement, the hunting shirt is shown with heavy fringe around the sleeve-shoulder seam; a welted sleeve seam with no fringe; pairs of hide tie thongs for closure; and a small decorative scallop on all exposed hide edges (DeVoto, *Across* pl. LXXVII). Other Miller coats are fringed down the sleeves and around the hem. None are shown with buttons, pockets, cuffs, beadwork, quillwork and a high degree of tailoring. Most of the trappers in Miller's paintings are shown wearing the hide hunting shirt, usually over one or more fabric shirts. The hunting shirts are also usually shown open in the front and unbelted, although some leather belts with large knife sheaths worn at the back are shown over the hide garment (Tyler, pl. 38, 50).

These hide coats could have come from a number of sources. They were simply tailored, made from local materials (primarily buckskin), and most trappers could probably have produced their own. References to trappers making their own clothes have been noted.

Leather hunting shirts (and, as previously noted, other "Western" garments) were available ready-made in St. Louis and Independence, and at the larger trading posts in the West. William Drummond Stewart describes his outfit upon departure from St. Louis as including a "leather shirt over my cotton one" (51). Fort Union had two leather hunting shirts in its inventory in 1831 (National 131). The records of the American Fur Company retail store in St. Louis contain occasional

15

references to sales of leather or deerskin hunting shirts in the early 1830s. Alexis Fischer, an engage of Fontenelle and Dripps, bought a "deer skin hunting shirt" for $4.00 in February 1830 (American, T: UMO Ledger B, 94). It is unclear whether there was a difference between "leather" and "deer skin," but both terms are used in the records.

There are a number of highly tailored, highly decorated hide coats of probable Indian origin in museum collections with pre-1850 attribution dates (Jacqueline Peterson 80; Gilman 107). These coats carry a wide range of tribal attributions, and some are even attributed to ownership of men involved in the fur trade (Campbell coat with Blackfoot attribution in Jacqueline Peterson 80). There is little doubt that this style of elaborate coat was produced in the 1820-1840 period as a prestige item and that the primary production center was the Red River metis settlement (Harrison et al. 129; Heilborn 58). The metis women specialized in the manufacture of "fancy 'western' garments" for sale to Indians and non-Indians alike (Harrison 129)

We have found no evidence that these elaborate coats were worn by working trappers in the field. The common firsthand historic reference to use of a fringed hunting shirt, often also termed "greasy," does not seem to describe the tailored hide metis coats decorated with delicate quillwork. None of the elaborate coats are apparent in Miller's paintings. Even William Drummond Stewart, as he appears repeatedly in the Miller paintings, is wearing a simple hide coat, not an elaborately decorated one (Tyler pl. 42, 46). The fact that Robert Campbell, or some other high ranking personage in the trade, may have owned one of these coats (probably for wear around St. Louis) does not transform them into working garments for the trappers.

While the deerskin hunting shirt was the trappers' primary coat, fabric coats were worn as well. In 1805 Antoine Laroque reported Indians who possessed "corduroy jackets and trousers" allegedly taken from white trappers. (Laroque 39). Nathaniel Wyeth, traveling through Montana in 1833, complained that he "got a wet jacket" trying to ford a river (Wyeth 56).

The 1831 Fort Union inventory listed four blue frock coats, and in 1834 the Fort had eight "French" coats in stock in green, blue, brown and drab and 28 "roundabouts" (short jackets) in blue cloth and cordoury (National 132). While these garments may have been stocked for sale to the engages at the Fort, Miller's paintings (generally the later ones) occasionally show trappers wearing a simple cloth coat, usually blue (Tyler pl. 112). The surviving rendezvous supply records and inventories do not include frocks or coats, although they do sometimes include capotes. Perhaps more significantly, the records of cloth purchases by individual trappers show that they seldom bought more than a yard or two. Further, the cloth they purchased, often shirt material or "Indian stroud," was not appropriate for a coat (Morgan 118-129).

The records of the American Fur Company retail store in St. Louis contain few sales of coats to anyone who appears to be a trapper. Similarly, the Fort Hall records that reflect a large volume of clothing contain very few sales of coats. Capt. Thing bought a Beaverteen coat for $6.75 on August 3, 1836; on May 4, 1837, Mr. Lean (?) bought a fustian coat for $12.00; on October 6, 1837, one of the Kanakas (Hawaiian engages) named Pig bought a "cloth jacket" for $8.00 (Columbia, Ledger 1: 89, Ledger 2: 122, 124). (Capotes cost $20 to $25 during the same period. See, for example, Columbia, Day Book: 43.) During the same period, the tailor shop at the Fort was regularly making "Chief's coats" and "Indian coats" (Columbia, Ledger 2: 107). While these were probably intended for trade or gifts, the same tailor could have made coats for the trappers.

The most unusual coat located during this study was an "India rubber coat" that was sold in June 1836 at Fort Hall for $10.00 (Columbia, Ledger 1: 116). The appearance of this garment has not been determined.

There is very little evidence that trappers wore the Indian poncho shirt ("war shirt"). The numerous references to fabric shirts and to "hunting shirts" almost certainly describe traditional Euro-American garments and not traditional Indian garments. None of the trappers in Miller's paintings seem to be wearing Indian-style poncho shirts. At the same time, there are a few references that might describe pull-over, Indian-style shirts. Meriweather Lewis shortly after meeting the Shoshonis stated that he wore an "over shirt being of the Indian form..." (DeVoto, *Journals* 199). Osborne Russell referred to occasional use of antelope skin "over and under" shirts of unknown form (82). Larpenteur wore a "buckskin shirt" of unknown form over his flannel and blue check shirts (Larpenteur 43). William Drummond Stewart records wearing a "leather shirt" of unknown form over his cotton one upon departure for the West (51). While Meriwether Lewis' reference is clear, the others are completely ambiguous and are insufficient to prove that trappers wore Indian-style poncho shirts.

CAPOTES & OVERCOATS

There are repeated references indicating that trappers used hooded open-front overcoats made of blankets or of blanketing material. These were called capotes or "cappos" at the time and were available ready-made or made to order in St. Louis and Independence, at the rendezvous and at fixed posts. The records of Fort Hall in the mid-1830s include a number of purchases of blanket capotes. These seem to have been made at the Fort's tailor shop most often in green but also in blue and white (Columbia, Ledger 2: 78-79, Ledger 1: 169, Day Book: 41, 43). The average price was around $20.00, making them relatively expensive, since, at about the same time, moccasins were $1.00, fabric shirts were $2.00 to $4.00, shoes were $4.00 and pants were $6.00 to $8.00.

Warren Ferris stated that while most trappers dressed in hide they wore "blanket 'capotes' (overcoats)" (362). Osborne Russell listed a "coat made of blanket" as part of the usual trapper's dress (82). William Drummond Stewart purchased in St. Louis an "overcoat of white Blanket with a hood" to wear to the West (51). John Kirk Townsend's party, preparing to go west with Wyeth in 1834, purchased "enormous overcoats, made of green blankets" for the trip (Morgan and Harris 221). Additionally, Miller's paintings show a number of trappers wearing them. His excellent sketch of Bill Burrows shows the trapper wearing a white blanket capote (DeVoto, *Across* pl. LXXVII).

The rendezvous-era capote differs from its modern counterparts primarily in its simplicity. Almost all early nineteenth century references to and representations of capotes are of simple, functional garments. Bill Burrows' coat, noted above, of light color blanketing with a single dark stripe appears to be a simple, boxy cut with flapped pockets. Fringe, beadwork, yarn top stitching, matching sashes and other decorative embellishments are totally absent and manufacturer's labels were not placed on blankets until well after the Civil War (Charles Hanson, "Trade Blankets" 10). Rev. Pond, who lived with the Eastern Sioux people in the 1830s, recorded that Indian women constructed capotes from blankets in a few hours (Pond 34). These were working garments and could not have been very fancy. Burrows' coat, discussed above, also lacks buttons, although it is possible that capotes manufactured in the East or at trading post tailor shops closed with buttons or hooks and eyes.

Fur trade records that refer to capotes (and to other articles of clothing and blankets) sometimes include the descriptive terms "N.W.," "Northwest," "H.B.," or "H.B.C." (American R: Retail Store Ledger B, McKenzie, Oct. 1830; Columbia, Ledger 1: 35). We have been unable to determine exactly what these terms mean. They could refer to the type of blanketing material, to the style and tailoring, or to the place of origin of the garment. "H.B." in the old records probably means "Hudson's Bay" (much later records sometimes write "H. Bay" or "Hud. Bay") and this has led some to assume that it designates a white blanket with multi-colored stripes— today's "candy stripe" (Charles Hanson, "Trade Blankets" 9). While this is a possibility, we have found no fur trade record expressly listing the multi-stripe or candy-stripe blanket. While the "H.B." designation might mean "candy stripe," there does not appear to be any real evidence to support the supposition.

There are several surviving capotes that probably date to before 1850 and that are the overcoat equivalent of the elaborate hide coats discussed above (Harrison 70). These garments are highly tailored like the hide coats, and often have contrasting color collars, cuffs and hoods decorated with beadwork, quillwork, or thread or moose hair embroidery. There is no evidence that the average 1820-1840 period trapper in the field wore or even owned this kind of garment. At the same time, it must be acknowledged that the many references to capotes in the fur trade records do not describe what they looked like.

It is also clear that some trappers wore overcoats of buffalo hide, probably cowskin tanned with the hair on. Warren Ferris stated that some trappers "made coats of their buffalo robes..." (362). These buffalo robe coats could also have been obtained from Indian people. Carl Bodmer painted an Assiniboine man at Fort Union in 1833 dressed in a buffalo robe coat worn with the hair inside (Hunt and Gallagher 201). This coat appears to be a simple, square-cut garment lacking a hood but apparently including a cape over the shoulders and is probably very similar to the coats referred to by Ferris.

LEGWEAR STYLE & MATERIALS

In the late eighteenth and early nineteenth centuries several kinds of men's trousers were worn and in vogue. This time frame includes the transition in styles from "breeches," a knee-length garment, to the full, ankle-length "pantaloons" and "pantaloons trousers." Historical definitions and a descriptive discussion of these various garments should provide a good foundation for understanding the clothing terminology used in the various fur trade journals and records of the early 1800s.

Trousers" of the late 1700s or early 1800s were generally ankle length, had un-tapered or straight legs ("stove pipe legs") and were usually considered sailor's or laborer's clothing (Churchill 762). In the late 1700s, farmers sometimes wore trousers as a protective covering over their breeches (Wright 68). During the early 1800s, the front opening of trousers, like breeches, was covered by a narrow, front fall closure. Usually made of duck, denim, wool, fustian, tow and other such sturdy fabrics, trousers were primarily intended as a work garment. A description of early trousers is detailed by Robert Parke's observation of farmers in Delaware County, Pennsylvania during his 1725 visit:

In summer time they wear nothing but a shirt and linnen drawers trousers, which are breeches and stockings all in one made of linnen; they are fine cool wear in the summer.

(Vaughn 76)

In many of the references and documents that we studied, the term "trousers" is also used very generally to describe all men's legwear. This loose application of the term sometimes makes exact interpretation of the journals or historical writings very difficult.

Overalls," also called "gaitered trousers," refers to a style of legwear very common to the Colonial military that buttoned at the ankle (Neumann and Kravic 50). This garment was quite similar to the style of pantaloons that was made with a strap under the arch of the foot. Another garment sometimes referred to as "overalls" were "sherryvallies." Worn on horseback to

protect dress clothes from mud or dust, this item buttoned up the side and was used to cover both breeches and pantaloons (Gehret 286).

Breeches" of the 1700s were a knee-length men's garment that fit snugly at the lower edges and had a buckled closure just at or below the knee (Worrell 112). As early as 1785 the knee buckles were deleted and the breeches were made to reach to the upper part of the calf. The slit closure was then fastened by buttons or tied with strings. This style of breeches fit somewhat tight in the legs, were baggy or loose-fitting in the seat and were tightened about the waist by means of a drawstring at the rear of the waistband. The front opening was a buttoned closure five to eight inches in width, referred to as a "narrow front fall" (Earle and Blom 766). Breeches were made from a variety of materials, including buckskin, duck, fustian or denim for work apparel and velvet or satin for evening or formal wear (Gehret 126-7). This garment held its popularity among the older gentry of the period. President Thomas Jefferson was described as wearing knee breeches as late as 1820 (Baumgarten 104). During the period from 1810 to 1820, breeches were made at various lengths, generally much longer than in the 1700s, coming down onto a man's calf. In order to fit under the new vests and short coats they also became higher in the waist (Worrell 125).

The term "pantaloons" refers to a garment in use from 1790 to 1850, originally made as close-fitting tights shaped to the leg and ending just below the calf. During the transition period, in which breeches were being lengthened to below the knee and calf-length, tight-fitting pantaloons were becoming fashionable, it seems that at least for a short time these two garments were of the same basic construction. Sometime before 1820 pantaloons were lengthened to the ankles, usually made with short side slits at the cuff and held taut in the legs by straps that passed under the foot (Gehret 284). The early versions of these garments were made with only one seam down the outside of the legs (Waugh 116). Pantaloons trousers, a garment of a slightly different cut, also became fashionable in the early 1800s and was described as a "hybrid, tight-fitting style but moderately loose from the calf down and without side slits. The bottoms were cut square or with the front hollowed out over the insteps" (Gehret 284). The word "pants" appears on the various fur company ledgers and in the mountaineer journals as a shortened form of the word "pantaloons."

"Drawers" or "under drawers," contrary to some commonly held misconceptions, are another lower body garment that was used by Colonial and frontier men since the late 1700s (Arnow 351). Made knee-length if worn under breeches and longer if used under pantaloons or trousers, the fabric of choice appears to have been wool flannel (Cunnington and Cunnington 105). A wool pair owned by Thomas Jefferson, c. 1790-1820, is knee-length and has a button-over, flap-front closure, i.e a fly front (Baumgarten 102). This construction style is consistent with other existing examples held in British museums that have been documented to the early 1800s (Cunnington and Cunnington 105).

From these descriptions of late eighteenth and early nineteenth century American men's legwear, one can conclude that during the early 1800s the words "trousers" and "pantaloons" generally referred to garments reaching from the waist to the ankle, either tight-fitting or loose about the legs and that "breeches" and "drawers" were shorter length garments that had a slit closure at or just below the knee.

Closing this opening by the use of ties or buttons caused the garment to fit tightly between the knee and the upper calf.

During the period of the Rocky Mountain fur trade, most of the trousers, pantaloons and breeches used by American trappers would have been constructed with a narrow, front-fall panel. The broad-fall front opening on men's pantaloons and trousers did not become vogue until the late 1830s and early 1840s. The single slit front opening covered by a narrow band of cloth called the "French fly," adopted in Europe in the late 1830s, was not generally accepted as fashionable for outer wear in the United States until the 1840s (Worrell 150; Brown). A narrow, flap-front opening similar to the covered French fly was in use to the mid-1700s until being replaced by the narrow panel, fall-front opening (Waugh 55; Johnson et al. 25). The development of front-opening designs in men's legwear of the Canadian Northwest, Mexico and Spanish California may differ from this historical chronology. The clothing styles of these areas are outside the scope of this presentation so these comments are not intended to encompass the legwear of the trappers and mountaineers originating from those geographical locales.

Another important feature of the trousers, pantaloons and breeches of this time period was front pockets. Despite the campfire lore heard at many modern rendezvous, men's lower body garments were almost always constructed with nice deep front pockets. This point even applies to breeches or pantaloons made from buckskin. Extant samples of buckskin breeches incorporate the same construction features as cloth breeches, which include a narrow front-fall panel, front pockets and a watch pocket (Gehret 272). A fine pair of blue denim, narrow front-panel trousers, attributed to the early 1820s, also have pockets that are sewed into the waistband and lay in behind the fall front (Brown).

LEGGINGS

To assign a specific historical definition to the word "leggings" is very difficult because the term was a generalization used to describe a variety of protective leg coverings that differed primarily in length. The word "leggings" has been applied to both the knee length and shorter canvas or linen splatter dashes used by the Colonial armies (Neumann and Kravic 176), as well as to mid-thigh and full leg-length buckskin leggings. The term "gaiter" probably more appropriately describes the lower leg coverings that reached to just above the knee and were worn to protect breeches and stockings. When discussing the historical use of leggings by non-Indians, it becomes very apparent that one must very carefully differentiate between the various legwear styles that fall under this historically broad term "leggings." In his book on the Eastern longhunter, Dr. James Hanson warns the reader about this problem, "because it may not be clear in old descriptions as to how a man was dressed if he was wearing leggings" (*Longhunter's* 9). In addition to this descriptive problem surrounding the use of leggings by non-Indians, we must also point out that the leggings used and made by the Eastern and Great Lakes Indian people were much shorter than Plains Indians' leggings. Another interpretive pitfall with the word "leggings" in first-person journals and narratives is the automatic mental incorporation of a breech clout by many readers. As we discuss the many mountaineer accounts and fur trade records, it will become very obvious that many Euro-American trappers traded for and used Indian leggings as a protective covering for breeches or pantaloons. The acknowledgement by a Rocky Mountain trapper that he or his comrades wore leather or buckskin leggings *does not* necessarily imply the accompanying use of a breech clout.

The scantness of clothing items requisitioned by Lewis and Clark seems to infer that the expedition's limited clothing supplies were meant to supplement the clothing already owned by the party members and that Lewis and Clark intended to rely very heavily on clothing manufactured by the men from animal hides. The August 19, 1805, entry by Lewis states, "Some of the men who are much in want of leggings and mockersons I suffer to dress some skins" (Moulton 4: 149). The use of the word "leggings" in these journals lacks the preciseness needed to determine which category of legging was actually used. Were these full-length "Plains Indian-style" or the shorter "gaiter style"? Because the members of the Lewis and Clark expedition spent the first winter of their journey with the Mandan Indians, it is quite natural to assume that the leggings they constructed followed the Plains Indian pattern. However, the assumption that these men would make military gaiters or Eastern longhunter leather leggings, the styles with which they were most familiar, may be just as valid.

Much like the journals of Lewis and Clark, the extant accounts of Rocky Mountain trappers contain several comments about wearing and making leggings. In most of these narratives, the style and materials used to make the leggings and whether the trappers are wearing any other leg garments are not discernable.

Thomas James was a member of Manuel Lisa's detachment, lead by Andrew Henry, which attempted to establish a trading post at the Three Forks area of the Missouri River. James' comment on leggings, written on his 1810 trip to the Missouri River headwaters, is quite typical of the comments found in the trapper journals:

We had caught a few beaver skins in route from the Gros-Ventre village, and were employed ourselves in making moccasins and leggings and in killing game which was very plenty all around us. (17)

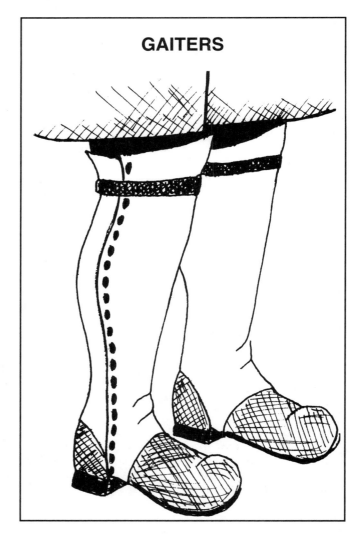

GAITERS

In recording a description of the leggings worn by the Indian men of the Konza (Kanza) tribe, the official journalist for the Stephen Long expedition in 1819, Edwin James, said they were "a pair of leggings, made of dressed deer skin, concealing the leg, excepting a small portion of the upper thigh" (91). He later records that, among a variety of food items, some of the men in his expedition traded with these Indians for moccasins and leggings (95). While the Long group was not fur traders or trappers, this passage does indicate that whites heading west purchased and used the long style of Indian legging. It also provides information on the style of leggings purchased from this same Indian tribe by the men in John Kirk Townsend's party, who were traveling to the 1834 rendezvous (Townsend 38).

In relating the as-yet-unsubstantiated 1825 story of his rescuing General Ashley from drowning in the Green River, Jim Beckwourth stated, "I threw off my leggings and plunged in" (Bonner 58). He also tells of killing two Crow Indians with "shotguns loaded with buck-shot," and "One of them wore a fine pair of buckskin leggings which I took from him and put on myself" (Bonner 77). This is definitely an account of a trapper wearing Plains Indian-style leggings. In another action-filled Beckwourth story, Jim and another trapper, called Le Blueux, were trapped by the Blackfeet in a grove of willows near a river. In preparing to slip into the water and escape, Jim told Le Blueux to "bind your leggings and moccasins around your head," (Bonner 130). Free trapper James Ohio Pattie also refers to wearing buckskin leggings in 1825 when he described his own dress, "My head was surmounted with an old straw hat. My legs were fitted with leather leggings, and my body arrayed in a leather hunting shirt, and no want of dirt about any part of the whole" (66).

On his first expedition to California in 1826-1827, both Jedediah Smith and his head clerk, Harrison Rodgers, maintained journals. Rodgers also kept the trading ledger, called a "day book," which, much like the books used by other traders and the fur trade forts, gives a listing of the items purchased from the company's trade goods by all of the party members. This system listed the dollar amounts of debits and credits under each man's name, with purchases of goods recorded as a debit and the value of furs brought in as a credit. In one of the few trading records that specifically give the kind of leather used in making a pair of leggings, Rodgers' day book for September 21, 1826, shows that John Gaiter received "1 pair of sheep skin leggings" for a debit of $1.50 (Smith 208-210).

In his novel about trapper life in the 1830s, William Drummond Stewart recounts the clothing to be worn on the trip to the mountains by the story's lead character, Edward Warren:

The kit that I selected from my baggage was...a leather belt,...and my leather leggings reaching half way up the thigh and tied to an inner sash, was to be the costume of the steamboat deck and the periods of halt. (51)

Stewart did not disclose whether the leather leggings covered pantaloons or breeches, but this is clearly a description of the long length Plains Indian-style leggings being worn over another leg garment. William Drummond Stewart was not the only Scottish nobleman to visit the American West. In 1835 Charles Augustus Murray was on a hunting expedition to the Pawnee country and his wardrobe "included...a pair of stout

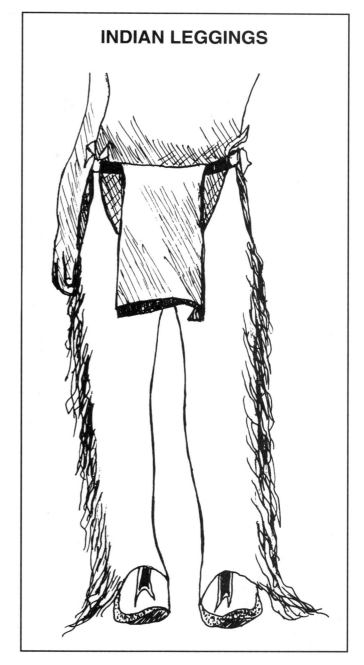

INDIAN LEGGINGS

corduroy breeches protected by buckskin leggings" (Merritt 19). Murray was a tourist, not a trapper or trader, however his choice and combination of hunting garments is further documentation of the types of clothing available and the functional needs encountered by all Rocky Mountain hunters and travelers. His specific use of breeches in combination with buckskin leggings is consistent with the comments of men who were trappers. The Alfred Jacob Miller 1837 drawing entitled *Trappers Starting for the Hunt at Sunrise* is the only Miller sketch that we could locate that shows a trapper dressed in leggings (Buffalo Bill 156). In this scene Miller depicted one of the mounted trappers wearing what appears to be fringed buckskin leggings, however the angle of the figures in the drawing permits no other conclusions.

BREECHES

Osborne Russell, who came west in 1834 with Nathaniel J. Wyeth's second venture, wrote a description of the trappers' dress, which included "a pair of leather breeches with Blanket or smoked Buffaloe skin, leggings, a coat made of blanket or buffaloe robe a hat or cap of wool (82). Despite the misplacement of the comma between the phrase "smoked Buffaloe skin" and the word "leggings," Russell is describing the use of leggings made from smoked buffalo or blanket, in conjunction with leather breeches. The combination of breeches and leggings, whether Indian or white man styles, correlates with the legwear mixture used by hunters, trappers and settlers on the United States frontier of the 1700s. Perhaps this description of "smoked" leather or blanket leggings relates to the effect of water on the garments from the trappers' routine of wading in beaver streams. Joe Meek indicates a very practical approach, obviously gained from wading many icy cold streams, in the following explanation:

In the spring when the camp breaks up, the skins which have been used all winter for lodges are cut up to make moccasins: because from their having been thoroughly smoked by the lodge fires they do not shrink in wetting like raw skins. For the same reason, when spring comes, the trapper is forced to cut off the lower half of his buckskin breeches, and pieces them down with blanket leggings, which he wears all through the trapping season. (Victor 55)

Following these instructions to alter a pair of knee-length breeches would result in a garment that is wool, or blanket material, from the mid-thigh down to the ankle. In the Alfred Jacob Miller 1837 drawing of two trappers setting beaver traps in a pond, the men are depicted wearing leg-length, fringed leather garments while wading in water to a depth of just below their knees (DeVoto, *Across* pl. XLVII). Because Miller departed Westport, Missouri, in April or May of 1837 and was back to the settlements by October of the same year, it is very doubtful that he ever personally witnessed the event depicted in this drawing (Ross XIX).

Leggings worn over buckskin or cloth breeches would have provided the trapper with a very versatile trapping garment combination. The leggings could be easily slipped off before wading in the stream, with the breeches then leaving the trapper's legs bare from the knee down. Any concern over wetting buckskin pantaloons, trousers or leggings would then be eliminated. The wool leggings mentioned by Osborne Russell, when worn over leather or cloth knee breeches, would also substitute quite well for the alterations described by Joe Meek. The combination of wool leggings and breeches would also serve as a useful and lightweight winter garment.

Like Russell and Meek, Marshall Anderson, a visitor to the 1834 rendezvous, makes reference to wearing "leather breeches." This reference to clothing comes near the end of Anderson's chronicle and is dated September 23, 1834, "I supped this minute at a tavern table, amidst village politicians, pedantic doctors, and wise looking lawyers—My dirty hunting shirt and greasy leather breeches seemed to offend their hyper-critical eyes and to curious olfactories—God help them" (Morgan and Harris 221). Anderson's choice of words would seem to indicate that he wore the knee-length leather garment. His description leaves the reader speculating as to whether the covering of his lower legs were stockings, Indian leggings or gaiters.

Visual documentation for the use of breeches by mountaineers is contained in *"Picketing the Horses—At Evening,"* which appears to be one of Alfred Jacob Miller's 1837 field sketches (Parke-Bernet 25). In this drawing two of the mountaineers are depicted wearing knee-length breeches and are shown with their legs bare from the knee down. In the later versions of this same event, Miller changed the trappers' leg garments to fringed pantaloons with a narrow front-fall panel. Miller's revision of the legwear in this sketch also adds to our skepticism about the accuracy of his drawing depicting trappers wading in beaver ponds while wearing full-length fringed leg garments.

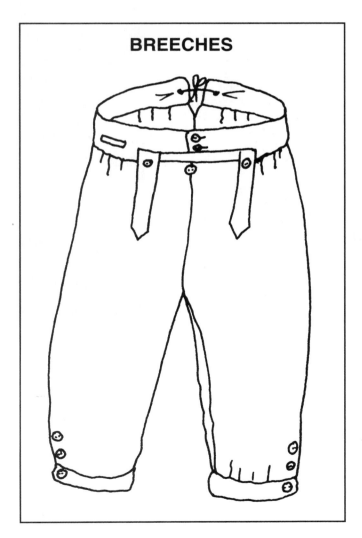

BREECHES

PANTALOONS & TROUSERS

Rreferences to pantaloons being used by fur men can be documented as early as 1813 with this excerpt from a letter to James Luttig, a clerk at the Upper Missouri trading post Fort Manuel, which reads, "I send in addition to the other articles a coat and pantaloons" (Luttig 130). Several ads from 1823 issues of the *Missouri Republican* also show that dry goods merchants in St. Louis were selling ready-made pantaloons of various fabrics (June 1823). At San Gabriel, California, on December 20, 1826, Jed Smith's clerk, Harrison Rodgers, includes a somewhat different pantaloons material in describing his clothing. Rodgers says, "all the clothing I have consisting of a leather hunting shirt, Blankett Pantaloons two shirts, pr of sock shoes and read cap" (Smith 229). Rodgers' choice of blanket pantaloons seems quite strange in light of the Mojave desert crossing just endured by the Smith party. The use of the word "blanket" instead of "wool" would seem to imply a garment fabricated in the field from a blanket rather than the manufactured product obtained through the company stores. If this sentence is loosely punctuated, as was very typical in old journals, and there should be a comma following the word "Blankett," Rodgers was merely reporting that his small wardrobe included a blanket. The material used to make his pantaloons is then open to speculation.

Documentation indicating the availability of ready-made cloth trousers, pantaloons and breeches in the Rocky Mountains can also be used to support the supposition that the trappers had the option to trade for conventionally styled and constructed legwear. The 1832 records of the American Fur Company's Fort Union disclose that "bourgeois" Kenneth McKenzie's requisitions list included pantaloons made from the following fabrics: "common blue cloth, cassinett, and Russia duck" (National 132). The American Fur Company's ledgers for the Upper Missouri Outfit records selling duck pantaloons to free trapper William Miller in 1831 (T: Ledger B 186). An invoice of goods that were shipped up the Missouri River to Fort Union shows that "50 pair of sattine (sateen?) pantaloons and 20 pair of Russia duck trousers" were received in 1834. This same record also has "common blue cloth, cassinett, summer, and Russia duck pantaloons" being ordered in the spring of 1832 and leather pantaloons listed in the Fort Union account books of 1836 (National 132).

Pantaloons of various materials were also a very big item at Nathaniel Wyeth's Fort Hall in the mid-1830s. During the years 1834 to 1837, the fort's two ledgers and day book list

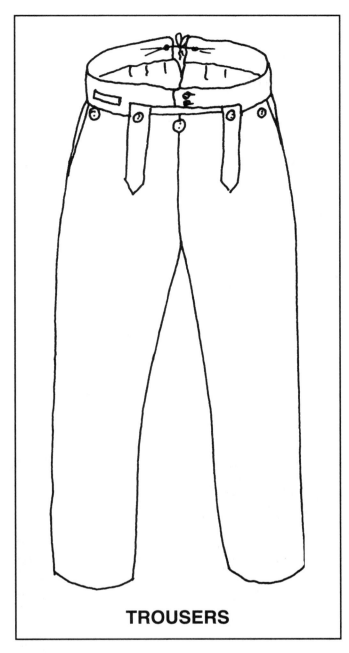

TROUSERS

"Kit" Carson. The 1837 ledger shows a debit to Carson of $8.00 for "1 pr cord pants" purchased while he was at the rendezvous with the Fort Hall contingent. Corded fabric is defined as "a heavy woolen or cotton and woolen fabric woven with a raised cord or ridge running in the warp of the fabric" by Florence Montgomery in *Textiles in America 1650-1879* (205). A February 1835 entry reveals that Kit outfitted himself by trading one of his mules and a trap for a long list of goods and clothing. This list included "1 pr Sattinet pants, 1 check and 2 gingham shirts" but had no leather or buckskin garments (Columbia Ledger 2: 46, 121, Day Book: 97).

Robert Campbell's account book records a very extensive list of goods "sold to O'Fallon and Vandeburgh by Robert Campbell on the Teton Fork of the Columbia River and under the three Teton mountain July 25th 1832" (Campbell 66-71). This $3491.50 worth of goods traded at the Pierre's Hole 1832 rendezvous lists only "2 pr Russian Sheeting pantaloons" and a total of 27 flannel shirts. The lists of the trade goods delivered to the 1837 rendezvous by William Sublette included, "105 pairs of satinet pantaloons and 25 pairs of duck," while the 1836 Sublette records show that "22 corduroy trousers" were sent west to rendezvous in that year. While we have not been able to study all of the inventory listings of the early fur trade forts and goods brought to the Rocky Mountain rendezvous, this information does indicate that the common trapper, camp keeper or trader had access to some ready-made cloth and leather pantaloons or trousers.

In 1832 Zenas Leonard and several other trappers were wintering on a section of the Laramie River that lies west of Laramie Peak, located in present-day south central Wyoming. The winter turned very severe, with very deep snow, causing most of their animals to die and the trappers to attempt a southern escape to Taos. In describing their preparation for the winter journey, Leonard says, "We had not even leather to make snow shoes, but as good fortune would have it, some of the men had the front part of their pantaloons lined with deer skin, and others had great coats of different kinds of skin, which we collected together to make snow shoes of" (26). This passage is the only instance that we have found where trappers are documented wearing cloth pantaloons that are lined with buckskin, rather than covering the cloth pantaloons with a pair of buckskin leggings.

In his dramatic account of a life-threatening clash with the Blackfeet Indians in present-day Yellowstone National Park, Osborne Russell comments on his dress thus:

...but [were] almost destitute of clothing I had on a par of trowsers and a cotton shirt.... (106)

Russell does not say if the trousers were cloth or buckskin and, while he earlier used the term "breeches," he now uses the word "trowsers." Unless he is using the word "trousers" in a general sense, a literal interpretation of these passages would mean that Russell possessed both knee-length leather breeches and ankle-length trousers. Either of these garments would provide satisfactory wear when covered by the smoked buffalo skin or blanket leggings that are included in his list of garments. Since Osborne Russell was employed at Fort Hall in the mid-1830s, his use of the word "trowsers" could be a direct reference to the elkskin or cloth trousers that were purchased by a few of the Fort Hall trappers.

Working in the trade from 1833 to 1872, most of that time for the American Fur Company at Fort Union, Charles

several trapper purchases of "leathern pants," "skin pantaloons," "Sattinett pants," "cord pants," "cotton duck pants," "cordroy pantaloons," "mixed cloth pants," "duffel pants" and "Indian leather pantaloons" (Columbia Day Book, Ledgers 1, 2). We are not completely sure of the difference between "leather pants" and "Indian leather pantaloons." We speculate that the latter garment was made in the style of typical leather pantaloons with the addition of fringing. These fringed, tight-legged, buckskin garments made with stirrups under the foot were probably very similar to the pantaloons depicted in many of the 1837 Miller sketches.

The references to trousers in the record of trapper purchases at Fort Hall consist of the December 1834 purchase of "1 pr elk-skin trousers" by John Bull and Peter Thompson and the "duffel trousers" that cost a trapper named Rice $6.00 in November of 1837 (Columbia Day Book: 41, Ledger 2: 155).

The Fort Hall records also furnish some interesting information on the trading habits of the famous Christopher

Larpenteur writes of possessing both leather pants and cloth pantaloons. In November, 1833, he records being "dressed in cowskin pants, cowskin coat, buckskin shirt,...This great suit was intended to last my time out" (43). Charles had signed an eighteen-month engagement as a common laborer with Sublette and Campbell but was promoted to clerk at the 1833 rendezvous because he was the only sober man in camp. When Sublette and Campbell sold out to the American Fur Company (AFC), Charles went to work at Fort Union for the "King of the Upper Missouri," Kenneth McKenzie. He must have been aware of his new employer's high standards of dress, as he wrote:

I must remark here that my dress was a little improved. I happened to have a pair of gray cassinette[5] pants which I had brought from the states, and held seldom worn; that and my clean blue check shirt and my old cap were the only dress I possessed on entering Fort Union. (56)

The fact that he was able to discard his leather garments in favor of cloth once employed as an AFC clerk gives a good indication of the difference in clothing serviceability required by clerks versus laborers. Charles Larpenteur was not a trapper, but the fact that he attended the 1833 rendezvous and worked at Fort Union makes his comments on dress pertinent to this discussion. Larpenteur's comment about expecting the hide suit to "last my time out" indicates that these garments had a minimum life expectancy of eighteen months and may denote a general attitude of the mountaineers toward the longevity of buckskin clothing.

In addition to Osborne Russell, Nathaniel Wyeth's second trapping party to the Rockies in 1834 included a young physician by the name of John Kirk Townsend. The journal kept by Townsend on this trip provides a very informative narrative about day-to-day life with a fur trade caravan. On March 24, 1834, he relates his first preparation for the upcoming trip. "He.[Capt Wyeth] accompanied us to a store in the town, and selected a number of articles for us, among which were several pairs of leathern pantaloons" (Townsend 11). Both Townsend and Marshall Anderson traveled west in

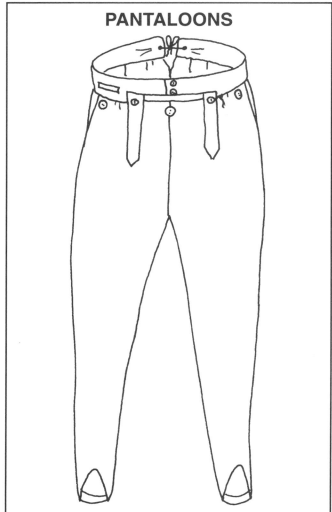

PANTALOONS

1834, yet Anderson chose to wear leather breeches while Wyeth selected leather pantaloons for young Townsend. Another garment is added to his mountain dress when, on May 20, Townsend states, "We remained with them [Kaw Indians] about two hours, and bought corn, moccasins and leggings in abundance" (38). The initial purchase of the ready-made leather pantaloons and the later addition of the Indian leggings could indicate that the two garments were being worn in combination, yet Townsend never offers any further elaboration. Townsend's revelation that Wyeth had to select certain articles of clothing for the greenhorn travelers strongly infers that articles like "leathern pantaloons" and "blanket coats" were specialty items more familiar to the men of the fur trade than the ordinary citizenry of the time. The ability of the Wyeth party members to purchase these articles from the retail stores of the Missouri River settlements would seem to indicate that there existed a continuous demand for this style of clothing.

William Drummond Stewart offers another depiction of the trappers' dress when he relates a fictional encounter by Edward Warren, the lead character of Stewart's novel, with "Ole" Bill Williams while enroute to the 1833 Horse Creek rendezvous. Stewart writes, "...the third was tall even as he sat, his long legs crossed under him were covered with shining leather pantaloons, once fringed and of natural length: the fringes now few....this was Bill Williams the divine" (95). This is the first account that actually describes fringed leather

---

[5] Cassinette was defined as a fancy dress fabric with a diagonal twill, the warp of cotton, the weft of fine wool and used primarily for making summer wear (Montgomery 193; Gehret 278). This fabric and other items of clothing made from it appear on many of the fur trade ledgers and invoices.

pantaloons, indicating a hybrid garment resulting from the combination of fringed buckskin, Indian-style leggings and white man's long pants or pantaloons. We suspect that the "Indian pants or pantaloons" that show up in the Fort Hall trade ledgers were the same item or of similar construction as the fringed pantaloons Stewart uses in his description of Bill Williams. It is quite interesting to compare this passage with the description of Captain Stewart's actual garments:

Captain Stewart made several modest purchases in St. Louis before his departure. He bought a thick woolen capote that cost twenty dollars, a pair of stout pantaloons and two heavy shirts to last him until they came to the Indian country. There, Campbell assured him, those fine seamstresses, the Crow women, would make him shirts of the finest tanned deer skin, properly smoked so that they would remain soft even after being wet. (Porter and Davenport 32)

One of Alfred Jacob Miller's 1837 sketches, entitled *Free Trappers without Ammunition and in a Starving Condition at Independence Rock,* clearly shows a mountaineer wearing fall- or panel-front pantaloons or trousers (Ruxton 74-75). In this scene the fall front is easily seen but the entire garment's style of construction is not discernable. Another field drawing of the same vintage, entitled *Bill Burrows,* shows a veteran trapper dressed in a long, fringed, leg garment (DeVoto, *Across* pl. LXXVIII). The drawing lacks definition in the waist area so it is difficult to positively identify the garment. The absence of a breech clout seems to narrow the possibilities to either fringed pantaloons or leggings worn over breeches. In two other works, *Pierre* and *Trappers,* all the men are in sitting positions and are wearing fringed buckskin coats, therefore the fronts of the pants are not visible (Parke-Bernet 3; Ross 29). However, the clearly visible bottoms of their moccasin feet show that they are wearing fringed legwear made with stirrup straps that pass under the instep of the foot. This fact, plus the close-fitting nature of the garment that Miller drew, would lead to the conclusion that most of the trappers in these works are wearing fringed buckskin pantaloons made to fit tight in the legs, with a narrow, fall-front panel and stirrup straps under the foot.

DRAWERS

Contrary to the theories espoused at many modern rendezvous reenactments, trappers did have available and use underwear. The fact that shirts, during the period being studied, were considered an undergarment and made with long tails in order to wrap under and around the loins has been documented by several historians (Gehret 101). The use of drawers by the mountaineers of the Rocky Mountain fur trade can also be documented.

James Baird and Robert McKnight were two of the fur men who attempted to open trade between Santa Fe and St. Louis in 1812 (Hafen 3: 29). Although their efforts resulted in a nine-year stint in a Mexican prison, after their release Baird stayed in the country of the Gila and trapped for two seasons. In November of 1826, while in El Paso, he took sick and died. The inventory of his belongings, taken on November 4, 1826, includes a "small valise containing pantaloons, 2 pr flannel drawers" and many other items of clothing (Documentos). Flannel must have been the fabric of choice for drawers because it shows up in several other historical records. In 1828 a St. Louis newspaper contains ads for various dry goods, listing "Drawers, fine and common, white and red flannel" being carried by John & E. Walsh Company and "Linen, flannel and cotton drawers" available from the Baltimore Clothing Store (*Missouri Republican* Sept. 1828). The records of the American Fur Company's Upper Missouri Outfit have the famous fur captain Andrew Dripps purchasing "2 prs white flannel Drawers" in March 1833 (T: Ledger B 186).

The trade ledgers and records of Nathaniel Wyeth's Fort Hall also contain a great many transactions concerning drawers. This garment seems to have been quite popular with Captain Wyeth's imported Sandwich Island trappers, referred to, both in the fort ledgers and Wyeth's journal, as "Kanakas." On the same day in August 1836, two trappers listed as "Issac (Kanaka)" and "Jack Fowler (Kanaka)" each purchased "1 pr flannel drawers" (Columbia, Ledger 1: 355, 357). In June of that same year, trapper Paul Ritchardson traded for "1 pr Canton flannel drawers" (Columbia, Ledger 1: 469). The 1836 records for the "Tailors Shop" at Fort Hall list "floor cloth Drawers" as one of the items being manufactured. One of the trapping brigade leaders, Joseph Gale, was charged $3.00 for his "green floor cloth drawers" in January 1836, while Nathaniel Wyeth was charged only $1.32 for the same garment (Columbia, Ledger 2: 4, 30). One of the trapper inhabitants of Fort Hall, more familiar to present-day readers because of his book *Journal of a Trapper,* Osborne Russell is recorded as purchasing "1 pr woolen Drawers" on January 25, 1835 (Columbia, Day Book: 80).

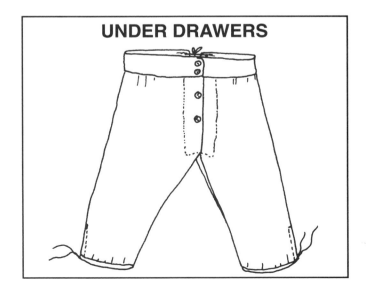

UNDER DRAWERS

BREECH CLOUT & LEGGINGS

Few other issues create such instant and polarized arguments among historians and buckskinners than the issue of whether the white Rocky Mountain trapper wore the Indian breech clout and leggings. The debate centers on the argument that white Euro-American trappers reared in the Eastern society dominated by "Puritan" morals and strict class distinctions would consider immoral and decadent a man who adopted "savage" customs or dress. While there is ample evidence that some fur men lived by the convictions of polite society, there are also enough journal and diary comments about "white men desiring to look like Indians" to question the idea that *none* of the trappers would dress Indian. In addition to the moral and ethical concerns, there is the problem of determining just what garments a white trapper had to wear in order to "look Indian." Because there exists a comprehensive study of the "Puritan values" issue (Landry), the information presented in this discussion will only examine the probability that some of the Euro-American trappers may have adopted the use of breech clouts and leggings.

To establish whether there exists a precedent of whites wearing clout and leggings, we examined some of the journals and published accounts from the United States of the 1700s. Joseph Doddridge, who was raised on the then-western frontier of Pennsylvania and Virginia, recorded the following description of the early Ohio River settlers during the 1770s:

On the frontiers, and particularly amongst those who were much in the habit of hunting, and going on scouts and campaigns, the dress of the men was partly indian and partly that of civilized nations,...A pair of drawers or breeches and leggings were the dress of the thigh and legs; a pair of moccasins answered for the feet much better than shoes. (91)

It seems that civilized society's concepts of propriety in dress had not spread to the Ohio settlers, for Doddridge further stated:

In the latter years of the Indian war our young men became more enamored of the Indian dress throughout, with the exception of the matchcoat, the drawers were laid aside and

the leggings made longer so as to reach the upper part of the thigh. The breech clout was adopted...the young warrior [young white man] instead of being abashed by this nudity was proud of his Indian like dress. (92-93)

Nicholas Cresswell, a wealthy Englishman, who spent most of 1774 to 1776 traveling beyond the Cumberland Mountains and in the country surrounding the Ohio River, had an observation similar to Doddridge. His journal contains the following entry on Saturday, June 10, 1775:

These people [the woodsmen] behave very kind to me, I believe there is but two pair of breeches in the company, one belonging to Mr. Tilling and the other to myself. The rest wear breechclouts, leggings and hunt shirts, which have been washed only by the rain since they were made. (82-83)

A review of the journals written on the Lewis and Clark expedition reveals two instances where the men are referred to as dressing Indian. The first is recorded by Sergeant Ordway on April 11, 1805, when he says, "the day [was] verry warm. Some of the men worked naked. only a breech cloth" (Moore 8). Captain Clark documents the second instance on August 17, 1805, when he comments that he discovered "Drewyer" (George Drouillard) among the Shoshoni "dressed like an Indian" (DeVoto, *Journals* 202). Sergeant Ordway's specific description of the men on this militarily conducted expedition wearing breech clouts would seem to indicate that men of the less disciplined fur trapping brigades would have just as readily adopted this "uncivilized" mode of dress.

Considering the comments about the white Eastern United States frontiersmen and the men of the Lewis and Clark expedition wearing breech clouts and leggings, we should not be too surprised with fur trapper James O. Pattie's comment of January 1, 1827:

We appeared before the Alcaide clad not unlike our Indian friends; that is to say, we were dressed in deer skin, with leggings, moccasins and hunting shirts, all of this article, with the addition of the customary Indian article of dress around the loins, and this was of red cloth, not an article of which had been washed since we left the copper mines. (109)

This passage specifically describes the white trappers in Pattie's New Mexico trapping venture wearing leggings and a red breech clout. The acknowledgement of this style of dress by a participant in the early years of the fur trade, plus the documented use of these same garments on the frontier of the 1700s and in 1805 by Lewis and Clark's men, gives strong indication that for some Euro-Americans the perceived immorality of such garments was not a concern.

William Ashley's diary and records of fur trading transactions during the early 1820s offer a wealth of detailed information on the goods and items that were available to the Rocky Mountain trapper. His trading account ledgers of the July 1825 rendezvous do show a "Brech Cloth" for $2.50 being charged to "John B. Lou alessa" (Morgan 122). There are also charges to "T. Vergel & Issc Gilbredth, Mr. E. Provo, Labontee, Adams, Logan, Bell & able, Mr Lolo, and Mr Monteaus Bill" for various types of cloth. Most received "Scarlet and Blue cloth," yet "Flannels" and "Chochenelle" (cochineal) are also listed (Morgan 118, 119, 124). However no ready-made clothing is included. Another very detailed itemization of goods is contained in the 1826 contract requiring General Ashley to deliver goods to the firm of Smith, Jackson and Sublette at the next year's (1827) Bear Lake rendezvous (Morgan 151-152). Here again, there is no reference to clothing of any kind, only to scarlet, grey and blue cloths at four to six dollars per yard, and common flannels, calicos and domestic cotton. These listings cover the supplies brought to the first three rendezvous (1825, 1826 and 1827) and point out the fact that, for the first few years in the mountains, there is no record that the Ashley men ever received any assembled garments. Even when they had the opportunity to order their goods a year ahead, as in the case of Ashley's contract with SJS, they evidently saw no need to request breeches, pantaloons, trousers or shirts.

Another transaction recorded in Harrison Rodgers' day book records that on the "Siskadee Octr 5th 1826" Abraham Laplant, one of Jedediah Smith's men, received a $2.50 credit "By differnce in Breach cloths" (Smith 210). Evidently Laplant had exchanged a breech cloth for a less expensive one. The cost difference in the two clouts could have been attributed to the type of cloth, with some kinds of cloth trading for $6.00 per yard and others $3.00 to $4.00 per yard. While the Laplant and Alessa trade/purchase of breech clouts, along with the sheepskin leggings bought by John Gaiter, indicates that the Smith and Ashley men traded for leggings and breech cloths, these transactions do not prove that these items were worn at the same time by any one individual.

Wyeth's rendezvous caravan of 1834 brought west the first group of Oregon-bound missionaries. Under the leadership of the Reverend Jason Lee, this group of "greenhorns" joined the rendezvous supply train for safety reasons. A layman in the Lee party, Philip L. Edwards, made this comment after observing the mountaineers at the 1834 rendezvous:

Here is the hardy mountain veteran who has ranged these wilds for more than thirty years...who has been in the country from his youth, whose connections and associations with the natives have identified his interests and habits with theirs....To form an adequate conception of their apparel, you must see it. A suit of clothes is seldom washed or turned from the time it is

first worn until it is laid aside. Caps and hats are made of beaver and otter skins, the skins of buffalo calves, etc....You will perhaps recollect to have seen in the "far west" of our United States, the buckskin hunting shirt and leggings gracefully hung with fringes along the arms and sides. But I am sure you have never seen the tasty fashion of fringes carried to perfection. Here they are six or seven inches long and hung densely on every seam, I believe, both of the hunting shirt and leggings. Indeed their weight is a great burden. (Morgan and Harris 32)

Mr. Edwards' comparison of the Rocky Mountain trappers' fringed buckskin leggings and hunting shirt to the similar garments worn by the Eastern frontiersman indicates that long fringing was unique to Western buckskin clothing. His observation seems also to infer that long fringing was an important fashion feature to the mountaineers. This extra long fringing may have been one of the mountaineer clothing traits that caused other fur trade participants to state that many of the trappers tried to "look Indian." Had the trappers been adorned in breech clouts surely Mr. Edwards' religious nature and indignation would have elicited comments on more than just the length of the fringing.

The 1838 rendezvous, held on the Popo Agie River located in present-day south central Wyoming, was the intermediary destination for another group of Methodist missionaries. While

their writings do not contain specific information on the mountaineers' dress, these visitors left very informative descriptions of the trappers' behavior and attitudes. Myra Eells records in her diary on July 6, 1838:

Last night twelve white men came, dressed and painted Indian style and gave us a dance. No pen can describe the horrible scene they presented. Could not imagine that white men, brought up in a civilized land, can appear to so much imitate the Devil....About noon, the white men and Indians gave us another dance. (Drury 2: 100)

Another lady in this party was Mary Walker, and she records her impression of this same event:

The same musick scalp, etc. Their faces were painted. White men acted like Indians. It is said that many of the white men in the Mts. try to act as much like Indians as they can & would be glad if they really were so. (Drury 2: 100)

Concerning the arrival of Bridger's trapping party, Sara Smith said, "Their appearance was rude & savage, were painted in a most hideous manner" (Drury 3: 94). It is very obvious that these lady missionaries were repulsed by the "savage" nature and appearance of the mountaineers. Unfortunately, other than paint, they did not say what aspect of dress made the trappers "look Indian." The Indian dancing and face paint may have been something done by the trappers just to impress the "greenhorns," who were easily shocked by such behavior.

Dr. Frederick A. Wislizenus, a German physician on a tour of the West, attended the 1839 fur trade rendezvous near the junction of Horse Creek and the Green River. Dr. Wislizenus published a book that included this comment about the trappers he met at the rendezvous:

of these rangers of the wilderness, and their appearance in camp was strikingly characteristic. (59)

This passage seems to say that all free trappers' "strikingly characteristic" dress included some articles of Indian dress because these men felt complimented if mistaken for an Indian brave. We wonder about the inherent dangers in the Rocky Mountains of being mistaken for an Indian rival by both whites and Indians. With most tribes disposed to trading with white traders, it does seem that recognition as a white man would

In manners and customs, the trappers have borrowed much from the Indians. Many of them, too, have taken Indian wives. Their dress is generally of leather. The hair of the head is usually allowed to grow long. (87)

While his description of the trappers' dress lacks specifics on items of clothing, Wislizenus's opening remark concerning the trappers "borrowing much" in the way of "manners and customs" from the Indians coincides with the remarks of the missionary women. We strongly suspect that fringed leather clothing and long hair were the traits sufficient for most of the Eastern visitors to put a man in the "looks Indian" category.

Washington Irving's book about the fur trapping adventures of Captain Bonneville during the early 1830s contains some hints on the kinds of apparel that would give a trapper the Indian look. While describing the differences in lifestyles and methods of commerce between "free trappers" and company men, Irving credits Captain Bonneville with providing this information:

You cannot pay a free trapper a greater compliment than to persuade him you have mistaken him for an Indian brave; and in truth the counterfeit is complete. His hair suffered to attain great length,...or plaited neatly and tied up in otter skins, or parti-colored ribbons. A hunting shirt of ruffled calico of bright dyes, or of ornamented leather, falls to his knee: below which, curiously fashioned leggings, ornamented with strings, fringes, and a profusion of hawks' bells, reach to a costly pair of moccasins....Such is the account given by Captain Bonneville

have created a friendly reception from most Indians and all of the mountaineers. Indeed the Fort Union bourgeois in 1851, Mr. Denig, cautions that "if he is a white man in the Indian garb of a different tribe he runs far more risk of being killed, because he may not be recognized in that disguise as a pale face" (Kurz 134).

Another image of these "rangers of the wilderness" is portrayed in a latter Irving passage:

The wild dress of the Free trappers, their leggings, blanket and cloth caps garnished with fur and topped off with feathers....weather bronzed complexions, gave them the look of Indians rather than white men. (166)

If, as Irving portrays, the free trappers were heavily inclined toward Indian dress, it does seem somewhat strange that neither description includes the mention of a breech clout. This point brings to the surface the fact that Washington Irving was not present for the events described in Captain Bonneville's story but rather wrote the book based on the information contained in Bonneville's journal. Because the journal has never been found, it is very difficult to know how much Irving embellished these descriptions. The fact that we could find no published contemporary comments to the contrary, either by Bonneville or any other participant in these events, would seem to indicate that the essence of Irving's descriptions are correct. We therefore suspect that the group of Euro-American trappers most likely inclined routinely to wear clout and leggings were those who carried the proud label of "free trapper."

HEAD GEAR

The mountaineer hat style of choice, and the easiest to document, is the round crown, broad-brimmed, wool felt hat. The Ashley records of 1825 show that trapping brigade leaders Gardner and Williams ordered and received "2 doz naped Hats" (Morgan 127). In a reverse of fashion, William Drummond Stewart refers to a "Broad-Brimmed un-napped white hat" being worn in 1833 by the lead character in his novel (51). The word "nap" refers to the small fibers, in this case wool, that stick out of the fabric and give it a fuzzy appearance. John Kirk Townsend gave the best description of these hats when he says that "white wool hats with round crowns fitting tightly to the head, brims five inches wide,..." were among the clothing items selected for him by Nathaniel Wyeth just prior to their 1834 trek to rendezvous (11). The 1832 requisition records of Fort Union include orders for "mens' black wool hats" as well as the white hats described by Townsend. An inventory list of Fort Union for 1834 shows "90 Black fur hats, 24 Black wool hats and 48 drab wool hats" on hand in the post stores (National 132). This same inventory lists "black cloth caps," which indicates that the "black fur hats" were probably fur felt with full brims. "Caps" were probably made with only a bill ("peak") or no brim at all. "Drab" is a word that appears quite often in the original trading ledgers and inventories. While it usually refers to an undyed cloth of a grey-beige color (Montgomery 224), in this case "drab" probably refers to the color of the wool felt used to make these hats.

These same Fort Union records have "red woolen hats" being ordered in 1831 and also show "36 red silk hats" in inventory in 1834 (National 132). The 1835 trade ledger of Fort Hall shows that William Dempsey and hunter Antoine Godar each bought "1 Red Cap" for $1.00 (Columbia Day

Book: 72). While these records indicate that red caps/hats were available to trappers, the actual trades involving this item indicate that red hats and caps were primarily intended for the Indian trade or desired by the many rivermen and voyageurs who frequented Fort Union. The 1838 inventory for Fort Union

includes "2 doz tri-cornered hats," which were out of fashion by that time. We have found no evidence of trappers wearing tricorns, and the ones at Fort Union were probably for the Indian trade or for wear by the laborers or clerks who lived at the fort.

Osborne Russell included a "cap of wool, Buffaloe or otter skin," in his listing of a trapper "outfit" (82). The problem with this passage as well as with the descriptions of several other fur trade journalists is the wide range of head gear that is described by the word "cap." For instance, an extant example of a fur cap is made much like a modern winter cap, complete with ear flaps and visor, while the wool or blanket hoods depicted by Miller and Rendisbacker are also referred to as "caps" (Hanson and Wilson 2: 3). Without more defining terminology, we cannot be certain of the style to which Russell is referring. A very simple cylinder-shaped fur cap, such as the ones depicted by the 1850s artist William Ranney, could also fall under Russell's description of buffalo and otter-skin caps (Axelrod 98). As an even further complicating factor, we have found what appears to be the same item referred to as both a hat and a cap. The 1831 Fort Union requisition invoices noted above include "Scotch woolen hats," while the American Fur Company's St. Louis 1831 ledgers show Colin Campbell, the interpreter, purchasing "1 Scotch Cap" (American R: Ledger B).

Charles Larpenteur included a "Wolfskin cap" in his list of personal clothing. Some readers may think that Larpenteur's wolfskin cap included the entire animal's skin, much like the full-hide caps so popular among modern rendezvous participants. This is extremely unlikely because he later states that upon going to work at Fort Union as a clerk for McKenzie his dress included "my old cap" (Larpenteur 43). It is just not probable that Kenneth McKenzie would have permitted one of his clerks to carry on the business of the mighty American Fur Company wearing a full-hide wolf cap. Based on all of the accounts, journals and descriptions researched, we have found no evidence that any mountaineers wore a complete animal hide for a head covering.

The Irving/Bonneville description of the head gear worn by the free trappers was not animal skins but rather "cloth caps garnished with fur and topped off with feathers" (Irving 166). This may be a reference to wool or blanket hoods like the ones seen in the Alfred Jacob Miller drawings or could also refer to round crown, cloth caps made with leather visors (forage caps) and then decorated with fur or feathers. In a narrative from the 1834 rendezvous, which is very similar to Russell's, Philip Edwards gives some additional information about the trappers' hat and cap decorations:

Caps and hats are made of beaver and otter skins, the skins of buffalo calves, etc. Some of these are fantastically ornamented with tails and horns. These ornaments may be badges of distinction, for aught that I know...." (Morgan 32)

This head gear sounds very much like the horned, ermine-covered fur hats worn by the men of many Plains Indian tribes, and Edwards may have seen some of the free trappers wearing

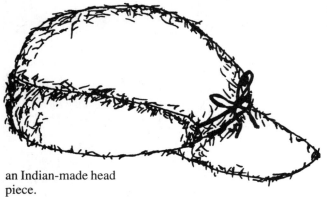

an Indian-made head piece.

Several of the Miller spot sketches, one entitled *Approach of a Band of Sioux* for example, show a flat-crowned hat on both William Drummond Stewart and some of the trappers (Tyler pl. 59). Millers' field drawings, such as *Pierre*, also show many of the trappers' round crown hats adorned with one or more feathers.

The 1834 to 1837 Fort Hall ledgers also include trades involving felt hats at $3.75 each, with one 1835 transaction showing that Joseph Gale purchased "1 yd silk webbing for Hat band" (Columbia Day Book: 55). The April 1836 ledger also includes a transaction in which both Captain Joseph Thing and a Kanaka trapper called Dick purchased "Chinook hats" (Columbia Ledger 1: 353). These were a tightly woven hat of grass or reed, also referred to as "basketry hats," made by the Chinook Indians of the West Coast. One design was very similar to the dish-shaped, Chinese workman's hat, while another was also made dish-shaped with the addition of a lobed and pointed shaped fixture on top (Robin Wright 84-85). It is doubtful that these hats had any utilitarian purpose for the trappers since only two are in the records. We also found them included in a list of Indian trade goods at Fort Vancover, the prominent Hudson's Bay Company post, and Captain William Clark records purchasing a hat from Chinook Indians made of "Splits & Strong grass" on November 21, 1805 (Rickman 189; DeVoto, *Journals* 291).

In 1836 the tailor shop at Fort Hall starting making an item called an "Indian cap," and 75 were made between February and April of that year. From the list of yard goods purchased by the tailors shop during the same time period, it would appear that these articles were made from wool cloth and ribbon (Columbia Ledger 2: 107). We have yet to determine just what these caps looked like and whether they were intended for trade with the Indians or for use by the trappers working out of Fort Hall.

It is possible that the Fort Hall "Indian Caps" were the eared hoods drawn by Alfred Jacob Miller in 1837. In a caption for his painting entitled *Trappers*, Miller wrote that the trappers often manufactured "peculiar caps" to replace the felt hats that were either worn out or lost (Ross 29). The hoods in this drawing do not show the pronounced ears or horns like the ones on the hood of a central figure in the 1837 Miller sketch *Picketing the Horses—At Evening*. In several other Miller drawings of a later vintage, he depicts these hoods with shorter ears and includes bunches of feathers as adornments (*DeVoto, Across* pl. XXXVII, XLV). Similar cloth hoods were worn by Indian people of the Great Lakes region and Canada throughout the first half of the nineteenth century (Feder 31; King 17). Cloth hoods could have been an item adopted by the American trappers from the Canadian half-breed or Indian trappers who

worked for Hudson's Bay Company. Exactly when the style of cloth hood depicted by Alfred Jacob Miller became popular with the Rocky Mountain trappers is not clear. The ones seen and painted by Miller may well have been an 1837 rendezvous fad.

Another interesting item listed in the ledgers of Fort Hall is a "water proof hat." Trapper John Bull and two Kanakas named Pig and Peter each purchased "1 water proof hat" for $6.00 on October 6, 1837 (Columbia Ledger 2: 108, 112, 114). We have been unable to determine the appearance of these hats or the material used to make them. They could have been made from a heavy duck oilcloth or tarred straw like the ones used by the sailors of the period. With only three of these hats showing up in the ledgers it would be very easy to categorize them as something unique or a novelty. However, an ad carried in a March 1827 St. Louis newspaper for "Black and white water proof hats: Also a few doz. of Shelmenllhes' superior water proof" indicates that these hats were readily available to all of the fur companies and may have been used by trappers from the very early years of the fur trade (*Missouri Republican* Mar. 1827).

The use of bandannas or silk scarfs as head coverings has been mentioned by other authors (Hanson and Wilson 1: 6). Like many other aspects of mountaineer dress this adaption is probable but none of the journals or art work from the period provide any documentation for this usage. This manner of head covering may have been more favored by the river men or engages than by the Rocky Mountain trapper. Artists of a later vintage such as Kurtz and Ranney, both from the 1850s, seem to be the main pictorial sources of bandanna head coverings.

HOODS

Drawing by Ronald Kil

VESTS & OTHER ACCESSORIES

Only one of the many journals or narratives studied for this project mentions the wearing of a vest or waistcoat. In this category of clothing, the first-person accounts differ somewhat from the fur trade ledgers and inventory records, because the actual trade documents indicate that vests were carried by the trading posts and purchased by many of the trappers.

The 1826 estate inventory of James Baird includes "1 vest" among the deceased trapper's personal effects (Documentos). From this description it is impossible to know anything about the style, cut and cloth used in making this vest. Some

information about the various fabrics used to make vests in the early 1800s can be garnered from the dry goods ads contained in the St. Louis, Missouri, newspapers. For example, two different dry goods merchants in 1828 advertised vests from a variety of fabrics. Deavers Emporium carried "ready made vests of silk, velvet...valentia, Marselles of various patterns," while the Walsh Company had vests made of more common fabrics such as "black and blue cassamere, cassinet and Swansdown" (*Missouri Republican* May, Jan. 1828). While "vests" were regularly offered in the 1820s and 1830s, none of these ads mentioned "waistcoats." This could indicate that the longer-bodied waistcoat was no longer on the cutting edge of fashion or that the word "vest" was used to describe both the short and long garments.

In 1834 John Kirk Townsend indicates that he wore a waistcoat, stating that "we cast away all our useless and superfluous clothing....such things as spare waistcoats" (66). If he was actually wearing a vest, then Townsend was using the word "waistcoat" as a generalization, which was directly contrary to the usage of the St. Louis newspapers. Townsend's calling the items that he was throwing away "spare" would seem to indicate that any waistcoats beyond the one that he was wearing were not needed. Was his characterization of an extra waistcoat as "superfluous clothing" a general sentiment of the trappers who were Townsend's traveling companions towards this garment in particular or clothing in general?

The 1830 trading records for the Upper Missouri Outfit of the AFC show that Kenneth McKenzie purchased "1 winter vest" for $1.34, which would have been wholesale price to the factor of Fort Union. These records also include charges for vests to AFC employees Colin Campbell and Michael Siuto; $4.00 and $6.00 respectively. Fort Union's clothing inventories for 1834 include "12 vests in black bombazine and 2 black cloth double breasted vests." "Vests of bright and lively colors" as well as "grey and drab" were ordered in 1832 from the AFC stores in St. Louis to replenish the Fort Union supplies (National 132).

Nathaniel Wyeth's August 1834 list of "Goods Remaining at Fort Hall uncashed" contains "3 striped Worsted Vests, 3 Velvet vests and 6 in sattinets" (Columbia Ledger 1: 45-46). Swansdown and valentia vests also appear on the 1836 trade records of Fort Hall, when Joseph Thing and W. Leun each purchased "1 Valentia vest" for $5.00 and the Kanaka trapper Pig chose a "Swansdown vest" for $4.00 (Columbia Ledger 2: 112, 146, 156). The day book for 1834 also shows Joseph Thing, a fur brigade captain, purchasing "1 silk vest" for the discounted price of $1.85 while "Capt Walker" (John Walker) is charged $3.75 for "1 vest" (Columbia Ledger 1: 89, Day Book: 39). Benjamin Sloat was charged $5.00 for "1 woolen vest" in March of 1836 while Paul Ritchardson received a 25 percent discount for the same article because it was "taken while on a hunt" in June of the same year (Columbia Ledger 1: 464, 469). We also know that at least two of the partners of the trapping group "Collins, Briggs, Schwan, & Wade" wore vests because of the June 1836 ledger entry following the four men's names that says "following goods for trade used trapping at this appointment .. 2 thin Vests @ $5" (Columbia Ledger 2: 31). Nowhere in the records of Fort Hall did we find the word "waistcoat" (Columbia).

Vests were also available in several popular styles. The Fort Union entry that refers to double-breasted vests makes an obvious reference to style, and 1820s newspaper ads mention

vests with "rolling and falling down collars" (*Missouri Republican* May 1828). Another term used to describe vests with long wide collars is "Shawl collared Vests" (Rickman 145). A verification that the shawl style vest was used by the men of the mountains can be seen in the 1837 sketch *Pierre* by Alfred Jacob Miller. This field sketch shows the young half-breed trapper wearing a vest made with large collars underneath his fringed buckskin coat.

Bandannas and handkerchiefs of several fabrics were also part of the well-dressed mountaineers' attire. In addition to providing the trappers with an item of fashion importance,

Gardner & Williams per their order" (Morgan 120, 127). The firm of Smith, Jackson and Sublette also included "hand kerchiefs assorted at one dollar fifty cents each" in their requisition for goods to be delivered by Ashley at the 1827 rendezvous (Morgan 151). Based on the number of references to particular colors and fabrics in the trade records, black silk was probably the handkerchief fabric and color most available to the mountaineers.

Robert Campbell's ledgers of the trades made at the 1832 rendezvous include some very famous fur men. Under the heading "Rocky Mountain Furr Co." is the line "1 Blk Silk

these neck scarfs had a very utilitarian function. Just like the cowboys and ranch hands of today, mountaineers and early travelers through the harsh Western climes used bandannas and handkerchiefs to protect their faces from blowing dust, rain and snow. Samuel J. Parker, one of the missionary travelers who visited the 1835 rendezvous, said that "our silk handkerchiefs over the face provided protection against the dust" (61). A comment from the journal of Warren A. Ferris, recorded in 1830, leaves little doubt that he and his fellow trappers used this item. Ferris says that "the snow and hail melted and froze again on our hair, eye-brows, and neck cloths" (83). The 1837 sketch by Miller entitled *Trappers in a Starving Condition and without Ammunition near Independence Rock* provides visual documentation and verification of Ferris' remark about use of neck cloths by trappers. In this drawing the trapper being held up by his friend is wearing a neck cloth in the style of the day, i.e. under the collar of his shirt and knotted in the front.

There are many records of famous trappers and fur brigade captains purchasing handkerchiefs and bandannas. The day book ledger of the Jedediah Smith trapping party shows that Capt. Smith himself purchased "1 Black silk handk" in 1826. A member of the same party, Manuel Eustavan paid $3.00 for "1 black silk hand," while Abraham Laplant and James Reed must have purchased similar items, probably made with cotton, because the entry under their names reads, "to 1 handerchief $1.00" (Smith 208, 211, 213). The William Ashley records from 1825 also include "Black Silk Hks" as part of the list of goods purchased by Gardner & Grey, and "1 gr [gross] Black silk hks" are listed in the "Memorandum of goods for Messers.

Hdkf to Fraeb [Ole Frapp] for $3." A few pages later is recorded "Thomas Fitzpatrick to 2 Hdkfs @ $2 ea." In the later pages of Campbell's account book is an extensive list of goods sold to the AFC captains O'Fallon and Vandeburg that includes "18 Blk silk hdkfs 1.50 —$27.00" (Campbell 53, 63, 66). Evidently wholesale price on the silk handkerchiefs was $1.50 because "ole Frapp" paid twice that for his purchase. The price for silk handkerchiefs was apparently the same whether in the mountains or St. Louis, because the 1831 AFC St. Louis retail ledgers list a charge of $3 to clerk Jacob Halsey for "1 silk hdkft" (American R: Ledger B 200).

Some very unique neck adornments show up in Nathaniel Wyeth's Columbia River Fishing and Trading Company 1834 inventories of "cashed" and "uncashed" goods left at Fort Hall. The uncashed items included "6 neck stocks, 36 cotton Hdkfs, 13 silk do [Hdkfs], 24 silk in Black and 24 do do comforters". The Fort Hall records include several references to "comforters." These were often listed with or near neckwear and were probably neck garments similar to a scarf or bandanna, possibly made of a knitted wool fabric. Webster's Dictionary defines "comforter" as a "long narrow, usually knitted, neck scarf." The 1834 records show that trappers Charles Neybo and Lewis Boseley each purchased "1 comforter" for $1.00 (Columbia Day Book: 34).

The list of "cashed goods" also included "1/2 doz neck stocks," so the Fort Hall inventory of neck stocks totaled twelve (Columbia Ledger 1: 45 46). Stocks were a pre-shaped band that fastened at the back of the neck with either ties or buckles. They were made from either horsehair or buckram, which provided some stiffness, and were covered with velvet, satin or silk arranged and cut so that no seams showed (Waugh 118). The scarf or cravat was then tied over the stock in a manner fashionable to the period. That neck stocks were not an item favored by the common trapper is verified by the Fort Hall trade ledgers, because the only men who are recorded making purchases of this item are the former sea captain Joseph Thing and Nathaniel Wyeth, the company founder (Columbia Ledger 1: 440, Ledger 2:4).

The Miller sketch *Trappers in a Starving Condition*, noted above, also includes a curious depiction of the next item to be discussed. The trapper wearing the neck cloth is also drawn with one suspender or "galluses" draped over the left shoulder and connected to a button on the right side of the fall front opening of his pants. Anyone who has ever had to hold up their trousers with only one suspender can attest to the effectiveness of this opposite front/back attachment. Miller's unusual depiction of the opposite sides attachment of one suspender, strongly suggests that he drew something that he actually observed.

The ledgers and records of the fur trade do not contain an abundant amount of suspender purchases by trappers. This seems to indicate that suspenders were an item that most trappers could easily manufacture from commonly available materials. The Fort Union records show two dozen suspenders on hand in 1834 and the AFC Upper Missouri Outfit ledgers show that the fort's booshway Kenneth McKenzie purchased a pair of "knitted suspenders" in July of 1831 (National 130; American R: Ledger B 200). The Fort Hall records use another term for suspenders when the Kanaka trapper Pig and a man named Rice were each charged $1.00 for "cotton braces" in October of 1837 (Columbia Ledger 2: 112 155).

An advertisement from L. Deaver's Emporium of Fashion in a November 1828 issue of a St. Louis newspaper indicates that suspenders made from "worsted, web and cotton" were available for purchase. This same ad tantalizingly announces a new kind of suspenders called "Vanhorn's patent of Philadelphia, with springs, of various qualities" (*Missouri Republican* Nov. 1828). While later newspaper ads refer to these as "patent suspenders" we have not found any references to patent suspenders in the fur trade records, journals and ledgers that we have examined.

Leather belts are another clothing accessory item that was commonly used by the trappers of the Rockies. The Campbell accounts show men purchasing belts and scabbards jointly with several transactions from 1832 listing "1 belt and scabbard $1.50" (Campbell 30, 34, 67). Most of the time heavy leather belts were worn outside the hunting frock or capote to hold these coats closed. Alfred Jacob Miller did many drawings that show the trappers wearing belts around the outside of their buckskin frocks and usually include a knife sheath located in the middle of the man's back (Ross 208). Pantaloons and breeches of the period did not have belt loops and were intended to be held up by braces or suspenders (Gehret 297). The addition of leather or wool leggings would have required the

trapper to wear either a belt or a sash on his waist in order to tie off the thongs used to hold up the leggings. William Drummond Stewart's earlier quoted reference to wearing both a sash and a leather belt allude to each article's separate function.

Various references to trappers trading for sashes appear in the Fort Hall ledgers. On January 14, 1835, Lewis Boseley was given $10.00 credit by the company for "1 sash pd in exchange for Horse (while trapping)" (Columbia Ledger 2: 64). With most sashes selling for $4.00 to $6.00, Boseley's sash must have been somewhat special to command a $10.00 price. A list of general expenses for April of the same year includes "3 Red Sashes" and Nathaniel Wyeth is charged $2.00 (wholesale price) for "1 crimson sash given to Ant. Godar" in a February 1836 entry (Columbia Ledger 2: 2, Ledger 1: 33). Red or crimson must have been the sash color of choice, because another crimson sash was bought by Thomas McKay for $6.00 on the same date as Wyeth's purchase. A ledger entry for "1 broad scarlet belt" in 1837 could be describing a different style of sash or merely referring to a red leather belt (Columbia Ledger 1: 114).

Like many other articles used by the Rocky Mountain trapper, sashes were also an Indian trade item. While our documentation proves that trappers purchased dual culture trade items, such as sashes or breech clouts, it does not conclusively prove that the trappers used these items. Whether the motivation for such purchases was to trade with an Indian or acquire an item for personal use is usually not discernable from the trade records. Supplementing trade ledger information with descriptions from journals or personal narratives and art work from the period usually assists in delineating the Indian/white man usage of many dual trade items.

WHAT DOES IT ALL MEAN?

Distilling thousand of pages of journals, fur trade records and other information into simple "rules" is difficult. Our experience has been that additional research in primary sources almost always produces additional information. The thousands of pages of fur trade records that we have not yet examined probably hold a wealth of additional information on the clothing of the trappers. Much of the information that we found confirmed many of the conventional wisdoms but at the same time much was new. There is suffcient evidence to add underwear drawers and knit fabric shirts to the wardrobe of the average trapper. The "mystery" of where the trappers' fringed hide trousers came from and what they looked like has been answered, at least to some extent. The view that the average trapper substantially re-outfitted himself at the rendezvous is called into doubt.

Some of the new material, particularly evidence of isolated items or practices, needs to be used with caution. Few reenactors portraying trappers would appear at rendezvous in the helmet and curass of the Queen's Lifeguard, even though it can be conclusively proven that Jim Bridger dressed that way at the 1837 rendezvous (DeVoto, *Across* pl. LXXV). Many, however, pattern their clothing and equipment upon similarly slim evidence. Reenactors, for example, should not begin wearing rubbers over their moccasins based upon the five pairs of rubber shoes that were sold at Fort Hall in the 1830s. While that would certainly be a convenient way to confront a wet modern rendezvous, the historical basis is just too thin. Reenactors should go beyond being satisfied with a single historical reference to authenticate something everyone already does. A more historically based goal is to develop a well-founded understanding of the clothing and equipment the average trapper was most likely to use.

We would like to dedicate this chapter to Charles E. Hanson, Jr. in honor of his almost single-handed effort and leadership in applying competent research methods to the study of the American "mountain man."

APPENDIX A: WORKS CITED

American Fur Company. Fur Trade Ledgers, 1802-1871. 74 vols. Microfilm ed. St. Louis: Missouri Historical Society, n.d.

Arnow, Harriette Simpson. *Seedtime on the Cumberland.* New York: Macmillian, 1960.

Axelrod, Alan, ed. *American Frontier Life: Early Western Paintings and Prints.* New York: Abbeville Press, 1987.

Baumgarten, Linda R. "Jefferson's Clothing." *The Magazine Antiques* 144.1 (July 1993): 101-104.

Bent, St. Vrain & Company. "Inventory of Merchandise, Utensils, Buffalo Robes, Furs and Livestock Formerly Belonging to Messrs. Sarpy & Fraeb Delivered Messrs. Bent, St. Vrain & Co. at Platte River." 1838. Copy of manuscript held by authors, location of original unknown.

Black, Francis. "The Canadian Capote." *Museum of the Fur Trade Quarterly* 27.3 (Fall 1991): 4-13.

Bonner, Thomas. *The Life and Adventures of James P. Beckwourth.* Lincoln: University of Nebraska Press, 1972.

Breun, Raymond. "What Money Tells Us—Robert Campbell's 1832 Account Book." Fur Trade Symposium. Pinedale, Wyoming, Sept. 1992.

Brown, William. "Clothing of the Early 1800s." Fur Trade Symposium, Montana Centennial Rendezvous. Red Lodge, Montana, July 1989.

Buffalo Bill Historical Center. *The West of Buffalo Bill.* New York: Abrams, 1974.

Churchill, Amos. "Something Concerning the General Customs of the People 60, 50 and as Late as 40 Years Ago." *Vermont Historical Gazeteer.* Ed. A.M. Hemenway. Claremone, NH: Claremont Manufacturing, 1877.

Columbia River Fishing and Trading Company. Fort Hall Accounts, 1834-1837. 3 vols. Microfilm ed. Portland, OR: Oregon Historical Society,

Cresswell, Nicholas. *The Journal of Nicholas Cresswell 1774-1777.* London: J. Cape, 1925.

Cunnington, C. Willet, and Phyllis Cunnington. *The History of Underclothes.* New York: Dover, 1992.

DeVoto, Bernard. *Across the Wide Missouri.* 1947. New York: Bonanza Books, 1957.

—, ed. *The Journals of Lewis and Clark.* Boston: Houghton Mifflin, 1963.

Documentos de Cuidad Juarez. "Intentario y Manifesta los Muebles y Estado...de Anglo Americano Santiago Baires." Microfilm ed. Reel 50/0427. Texas Western College, El Paso, n.d.

Doddridge, Joseph. *Notes on the Settlement and Indian Wars.* Pittsburgh, 1912.

Drury, Clifford M. *First White Women over the Rockies.* Glendale, CA: Clark, 1966.

Earle, Alice Morse, and Benjamin Blom. *Two Centuries of Costume in America.* 2 vols. 1903. Rutland, VT: Tuttle, 1971.

Ewers, John C. "Iroquois in the Far West." *Red Man's West.* Ed. Michael S. Kennedy. New York: Hastings House, 1965.

—, ed. *The Indians of Texas in 1830.* Washington, D.C.: Smithsonian Institution, 1969.

Feder, Norman. *Art of the Eastern Plains Indians.* New York: Brooklyn Museum, 1964.

Ferris, Warren A. *Life in the Rocky Mountains.* 1940. Denver: Old West Publishing, 1983.

Frisch, Jack. "Iroquois in the West." *Handbook of North American Indians, Northeast.* Ed. William Sturtvant. Washington, D.C.: Smithsonian Institution, 1978.

Gaede, Fredrick, and Bryce Workman. "Notes on Point Blankets in the Military Service." *Museum of the Fur Trade Quarterly* 15.2 (Summer 1979): 1-5.

Gehret, Ellen. *Rural Pennsylvania Clothing.* York, PA: Liberty Cap Books, 1976.

Gilman, Carolyn. *Where Two Worlds Meet.* St. Paul: Minnesota Historical Society, 1982.

Gowans, Fred. *Rocky Mountain Rendezvous.* Provo, UT: Brigham Young University Press, 1976.

Hafen, Leroy, ed. *Mountain Men and the Fur Trade of the Far West.* 10 vols. Glendale, CA: Clark, 1965-1972.

Hanson, Charles E. Jr. "The Legacy of Edward Warren." *Museum of the Fur Trade Quarterly* 22.3 (Fall 1986): 7-14.

—. "Some Additional Notes on Trade Blankets." *Museum of the Fur Trade Quarterly* 24.1 (Winter 1988): 5-11.

—. "Some Thoughts for Buckskinners and Others." *Museum of the Fur Trade Quarterly* 14.2 (Summer 1978): 1-3.

—. "Some Thoughts on Footwear." *Museum of the Fur Trade Quarterly* 27.3 (Fall 1991) 2-3.

—. "Trade Goods for Rendezvous." *Book of Buckskinning V.* Texarkana, TX: Rebel, 1989.

—. "The Trader's Dress." *Museum of the Fur Trade Quarterly* 25.1 (Spring 1990): 1-5.

Hanson, James A. *The Frontier Scout and Buffalo Hunter's Sketch Book.* Chadron, NE: Fur Press, 1980.

—. *Voyager's Sketchbook.* Chadron, NE: Fur Press, 1981.

—. *The Longhunter's Sketchbook.* Chadron, NE: Fur Press, 1985.

Hanson, James A., and Kathryn J. Wilson. *Mountain Man's Sketch Book.* Vol. 1. Chadron, NE: Fur Press, 1981.

Harrison, Julia. *Metis.* Calgary, Canada: Glenbow-Alberta Institute, 1985.

Harrison, Julia, et al. *The Spirit Sings.* Toronto: McClelland and Stewart, 1987.

Heilborn, Bertha. *With Pen and Pencil on the Frontier in 1851.* St. Paul: Minnesota Historical Society Press, 1986.

Hunt, David C., and Marsha Gallagher. *Karl Bodmer's America.* Omaha, NE: Joslyn Art Museum, 1984.

Irving, Washington. *Adventures of Captain Bonneville.* 1837. Portland, OR: Binfords and Mort, 1986.

Jackson, Donald. *Letters of the Lewis and Clark Expedition with Unrelated Documents, 1783-1854.* Vol 1. Urbana: University of Illinois Press, 1978.

James, Edwin. *From Pittsburgh to the Rocky Mountains 1819-1820.* 1822-23. Golden, CO: Fulcrum, 1988

James, Thomas. *Three Years among the Indians and Mexicans.* 1846. Lincoln: University

Larpenteur, Charles. *Forty Years a Fur Trader on the Upper Missouri*. 1898. Lincoln: University of Nebraska Press, 1989.

Leonard, Zenas. *Adventures of a Mountain Man: The Narrative of Zenas Leonard*. 1839. Lincoln: University of Nebraska Press, 1978.

Luttig, John C. *Journal of a Fur-Trading Expedition on the Upper Missouri 1812-1813*. New York: Argosy-Antiquarian, 1964.

Luzader, John. "Clothing of the Fur Trade Era." Fur Trade Symposium, Montana Centennial Rendezvous. Red Lodge, Montana, July 1989.

Merritt, John I. *Baronets and Buffalo: The British Sportsmen in the American West 1831-1881*. Missoula, MT: Mountain Press, 1985.

Missouri Republican, 1822-1833. Missouri Historical Society, St. Louis.

Montgomery, Florence. *Textiles in America 1650-1879*. New York: Norton, 1984.

Moore, Robert. "The Clothing of the Lewis and Clark Expedition." *We Proceed On* Aug. 1994: 4-13.

Morgan, Dale, ed. *The West of William H. Ashley*. Denver: Old West Publishing, 1964.

Morgan, Dale, and Eleanor Harris, eds. *The Rocky Mountain Journals of William Marshall Anderson—The West in 1834*. 1967. Lincoln: University of Nebraska Press, 1987.

Moulton, Gary, ed. *The Journals of Lewis and Clark*. 7 vols. Lincoln: University of Nebraska Press, 1983-1991.

National Park Service. *The Things of Life*. Buford, ND: Fort Union Trading Post National Historic Site, n.d.

Neumann, George C., and Frank J. Kravic. *Collector's Illustrated Encyclopedia of the American Revolution*. 1975. Texarkana, TX: Rebel, 1989.

Ordway, John. *The Journals of Captain Meriwether Lewis and Sergeant John Ordway Kept of the Expedition of Western Exploration 1803-1806*. Madison: State Historical Society of Wisconsin, 1916.

Parke-Bernet Galleries, Inc. *A Series of Watercolor Drawings by Alfred Jacob Miller*. Catalog no. 2436. New York, 6 May 1966.

Parker, Samuel J. *Journal of an Exploring Tour beyond the Rocky Mountains*. 1838. Ithaca, NY: Mack, Andrus and Woodruff, 1840.

Parkman, Francis. *The Oregon Trail*. 1849. New York: Penguin Books, 1983.

Pattie, James Ohio. *The Personal Narrative of James Ohio Pattie*. 1831. Lincoln: University of Nebraska Press, 1984.

Peterson, Harold. *The Book of the Continental Soldier*. Harrisburg, PA: Stackpole, 1968.

Peterson, Jacqueline. *Sacred Encounters*. Norman: University of Oklahoma Press, 1993.

Pond, Samuel W. *The Dakota or Sioux in Minnesota as They Were in 1834*. St. Paul: Minnesota Historical Society Press, 1986.

Porter, Mae Reed, and Odessa Davenport. *Scotsman in Buckskin: Sir William Drummond Stewart and the Rocky Mountain Fur Trade*. New York: Hastings House, 1963.

Rickman, David. *The Sutter's Fort Costume Manual*. Sacramento, CA: Sutter's Fort State Historical Park, n.d.

Ross, Marvin C. *The West of Alfred Jacob Miller*. Norman: University of Oklahoma Press, 1951.

Russell, Osborne. *Journal of a Trapper*. 1914. Lincoln: University of Nebraska Press, 1965.

Rutt, Richard. *A History of Hand Knitting*. Loveland, CO: Interweave Press, 1987.

Ruxton, George F. *Life in the Far West*. 1849. Norman: University of Oklahoma Press, 1979.

Sage, Rufus B. *Rocky Mountain Life*. 1846. Lincoln: University of Nebraska Press, 1982.

Schuler, Harold. *Fort Pierre Choteau*. Vermillion: University of South Dakota Press, 1990.

Smith, Jedediah S. *The Southwest Expedition of Jedediah S. Smith, His Personal Account of the Journey to California, 1826-1827, and Harrison G. Rodgers Daybook*. Ed. George R. Brooks. Lincoln: University of Nebraska Press, 1989.

Steffan, Randy. *The Horse Soldier*. Vol. 1. Norman: University of Oklahoma Press, 1977.

Stewart, Rick, et al. *Carl Wimar: Chronicler of the Missouri River Frontier*. Fort Worth, TX: Amon Carter Museum, 1991.

Stewart, William Drummond. *Edward Warren*. 1854. Missoula, MT: Mountain Press, 1986.

Sublette Papers. Missouri Historical Society, St. Louis.

Swagerty, William. "Marriage and Settlement Patterns of Rocky Mountain Trappers and Traders." *The Western Historical Quarterly* 11.2 (April 1980): 159-180.

Teit, James, and Franz Boas. *The Salishan Tribes of the Western Plateaus*. Washington, DC: Bureau of American Ethnology, 1928.

Thompson, Judy. *The North American Indian Collection, a Catalog*. Bernisches Historiches Museum, Berne, Switzerland, 1977.

Thwaites, Reuben Gold, ed. *The Original Journals of the Lewis and Clark Expedition*. New York: Dodd, Mead, 1904.

Townsend, John Kirk. *Narrative of a Journey across the Rocky Mountains to the Columbia River*. 1839. Lincoln: University of Nebraska Press, 1978.

Tyler, Ron. *Alfred Jacob Miller: Artist on the Oregon Trail*. Fort Worth, TX: Amon Carter Museum, 1982.

Vaughn, Alden. *America before the Revolution 1725-1775*. Englewood Cliffs, NJ: Prentice-Hall, 1967.

Victor, Frances. *The River of the West*. 1870. Missoula, MT: Mountain Press, 1983.

Waugh, Norah. *The Cut of Men's Clothes 1600-1900*. New York: Theatre Arts Books, 1964.

Wilson, Gilbert. *The Horse and Dog in Hidatsa Culture*. Anthropological papers of American Museum of Natural History. Vol. 15, pt. 2. New York: American Museum Press, 1924.

Wislizenus, Frederick A. *Journey to the Rocky Mountains in the Year 1839*. 1840. Glorieta, NM: Rio Grande Press, 1969.

Wood, W. Raymond and Thomas D. Thiessen. *Early Fur Trade on the Northern Plains*. Norman: University of Oklahoma Press, 1985.

Worrell, Estelle. *Early American Costume*. Harrisburg, PA: Stackpole Books, 1975.

Wright, Merideth. *Everyday Dress of Rural America 1783-1800*. New York: Dover, 1992.

Wright, Robin. *A Time of Gathering: Native Heritage in Washington State*. Seattle: University of Washington Press, 1991.

Wyeth, Nathaniel J. *Journal of Captain Nathaniel J. Wyeth's Expedition to the Oregon Country 1831-1836*. 1899. Fairfield, WA: Galleon Press, 1984.

Indian-Influenced Woodsmen of the Cane

by Ted Franklin Belue

Descended from a long line of Carolina Huguenots and Mississippians, Ted Franklin Belue has a deep love for the American frontier. In the early 60s at his grade school in Orlando, Florida, he read a book on Daniel Boone that he says "made me tremble." Firmly hooked, he spent the next five or six years scouting out libraries, lugging home armloads of books on Boone, Simon Kenton, Simon Girty, Shawnee Indians and Kentucky rifles, while vigorously avoiding math and grammar.

In 1978, married and broke, he moved to Kentucky and took a job from which he was soon fired, so for the next few years he trapped in the fall and winter, framed houses in the spring and summer and played bluegrass when he could. On a nostalgic whim, he bought a flintlock and a copy of *Foxfire V*. A year later he met Warren "Hawk" Boughton. Inspired, Ted returned to his roots. Soon, ears bored, nose ring in place and face painted, he was prowling the woods, scaring locals and risking getting shot.

Belue made his writing debut in MUZZLELOADER in 1990 and in 1993 joined the staff as a special features writer. To date he has had over fifty articles published in the academic and popular press. Besides MUZZLELOADER, his essays have appeared in the *Dixie Gun Works Blackpowder Annual*, *Muzzle Blasts*, *The Kentucky Explorer*, *Wildlife Art News*, *Bluegrass Unlimited*, *The Kentucky Encyclopedia*, *Filson Club History Quarterly* and Garland's *The American Revolution 1775-1783: An Encyclopedia*. In the summer of 1991, he worked for seven weeks as an extra in the movie *The Last of the Mohicans*. Ted lives in Murray, Kentucky, with Lavina Turbeville, his virtuoso wife, and teaches history at Murray State University.

During the mid to late 1700s European and American woodsmen dressing, living and acting like their Indian peers were a colorful part of life east of the Mississippi. For white hunters in the first far west, who were already seen as a breed apart by their more urbane contemporaries, "becoming Indian" was an easy, often logical step to take. A German touring western Virginia in 1750 was startled when he met "a kind of white people...who live like the savages." Such whites had a "half-Indian appearance" and were "nearly allied in disposition and manners to Indians" (Jordan and Kaups 2, 87).

Dubbed "marginal men" by 20th century historians, such native-influenced whites or persons of mixed-blood—whether traders, hunters or Indian agents—often played pivotal roles as interpreters or mediators. Some had skills useful to Indians, such as blacksmithing or the ability to make black powder or repair guns. Many marginal men—like Sir John Caldwell, William Augustus Bowles, Alexander McKee, Simon Girty and Louis Lorimier—rose to respected positions, passing easily between native and Anglo cultures (Calloway, "White Renegades" 43).

This chapter is written in two parts. Part one describes representative Europeans and their American Long Knife counterparts who lived on the cultural fringes in the Cumberland, Ohio Valley and the Middle Ground. Emphasis in part two focuses more on dress, accoutrements, trade wares, food and skills of the day. Readers will note that I omit the long hunter forays of the 1760s-1770s as they are discussed in other works, most notably *Seedtime on the Cumberland* by Harriette Simpson Arnow.

These days, what might inspire a reenactor to portray an Indian-influenced person of the frontier? Not to be dismissed is the lingering influence of the romantic notion of the "natural man." It was philosopher Jean-Jacques Rousseau (1712-1778) who argued that advances in civilization brought vice and the evils of class distinctions. Primitive man, he said, was "naturally good and free." Disciples of Rousseau saw Indians as "Noble Savages," native paragons of human purity. Daniel Boone's first biographer John Filson paid a debt to Rousseau in 1784 by portraying Boone as a "natural man." In 1826 James Fenimore Cooper in *The Last of the Mohicans* recast Boone as Nathaniel Bumppo, a noble "white savage" raised by the Delaware. Certainly the strong pull of such mythic images are lost on few, but there are other reasons besides romance for living history folks choosing to "go native."

For woodland wear a blend of European and Indian clothing is practical. An otter turban pulled over a silk scarf keeps the head warm. Linen shirts over leggings and belted at the waist let the body breathe. In snake country leggings can blunt a pit viper's strike. Dress can be as simple as a breechcloth and moccasins. But for those wanting to gird up their loins more fashionably, we have this glimpse of mixed-blood interpreter Andrew Montour, recorded in Pennsylvania on September 30, 1742, by Count Nicholas Zinzendorf:

Andrew's cast of countenance is decidedly European, and had his face not been encircled with a broad band of paint, applied with bear's fat, I would certainly have taken him for one. He wore a brown broadcloth coat, a scarlet damasken lapel waistcoat, breeches, over which his shirt hung, a black cordovan neckerchief decked with silver bangles, shoes and stockings, and a hat. His ears were hung with pendants of brass and other wires plaited together, like the handle of a basket....(Hanna 1: 223)

Such a fop might look odd prowling the Scioto for buffalo, but it does show how far one can go. The key to authenticity is research—context—influences. But this is not an essay on the art of interpretation and the like. I assume reenactors know their choices of personae are determined by specific Indian and Anglo societies, by available goods, food, guns and accoutrements, and other variables. Geography—where one was born, lived, explored, was garrisoned or was taken to as a captive—strongly influenced such factors and that is where we shall first look.

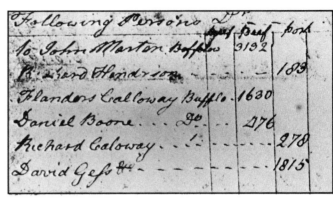

Rare, previously unpublished receipt from James Harrod to John Martin, Flanders Callaway and Daniel Boone for buffalo beef totaling 5,238 pounds. Richard Henderson, Richard Callaway and David Gass sold 2,276 pounds of pork. Circa mid-1770s (Draper 17J: 85). **Courtesy of the State Historical Society of Wisconsin, Madison**

TORIES & LONG KNIVES ON THE CUMBERLAND

The lands along the Cumberland had been known of for centuries. The Cherokee, Creek, Chickasaw and Shawnee claimed parts of the fertile country at one time or another. By 1673 Cherokee armed with Spanish guns were fighting other tribes for territory. Leading to the Cumberland from the Middle Ground was the Wabash, which flowed into the Ohio near Smithland, Kentucky, but the easiest way to Tennessee was from the south via the Great River. Whites were soon attracted to the country.

After the fall of Fort Loudon in 1760, the Cherokee requested that a British officer be sent to them as a token of trust. Volunteering for the job were two Virginians, Henry Timberlake and Thomas Sumter. Well-outfitted, the men paddled a canoe to the Cherokee towns by way of the Little Tennessee River. From there the whites trudged through what is now Greene County and pushed on up to Horse Creek. Timberlake wrote that the Indians' "dress is now become very much like the European; and, indeed, that of the men is greatly altered" (Williams 77). Besides ear slitting, tattooing and roaching their hair, the warriors wore "collars of wampum," silver brooches, bracelets and breast plates, breechcloths, European trade shirts, quilled moccasins and "a sort of cloth boots." A match-coat thrown over their shoulders completed their dress (Williams 75-77).

About 1766 Timothy De Monbruen first hunted in middle Tennessee. Joseph Guild, who knew him, described him as a tall, "athletic, dark-skinned man, with a large head, broad shoulders and chest, small legs, a high, short foot, and an eagle eye" (Guild 311). Flamboyantly dressed, the Frenchman wore a blue cloth hunting shirt, leather leggings and a red regimental weskit from his days back in the French and Indian War. On his head he wore a foxskin cap (Guild 310-13).

James Smith (1737-1812), a Pennsylvanian who hunted the Cumberland Valley in 1766, had once been a "white Indian." In May 1755 he was captured and marched to Fort Duquesne weeks before the July rout of General Edward Braddock. Amidst scalp halloos Smith saw the French and Indians returning from Braddock's defeat with "a great many bloody scalps, grenadiers caps, British canteens, bayonets, & etc. with them....[and] Indians in British officers dress with sash, half-moons, laced hats & etc" (12-13). A month later he was adopted by the Delaware. A brave yanked out his hair, leaving three tufts. Around the first two hanks was wrapped a "narrow beaded garter"; the third was braided and "stuck full of silver brooches" (Smith 14). An awl was jabbed through his septum and ears and he was fitted with ear and nose rings. Silver armbands were added, a wampum belt tied around his neck and then he was stripped and painted. After three young

"White Indian" Tony Gerard levels down on a buffalo in west Tennessee.

squaws scrubbed him free of his white blood in a river, Smith was led back to the village and dressed in "a new ruffled shirt...a pair of leggings with ribbons and beads, porcupine quills and red hair—also a tinsel laced cappo" (Smith 15-16). Finally his face was repainted and a shock of red feathers tied to his crown.

Renamed "Scoouwa," Smith lived with his Delaware kinsmen for about five years. His native skills later proved to be an asset. In 1763, as captain of an elite ranger unit, he dressed his men in "breechclouts, leggings, moccasins, and green shrouds....In place of hats we wore red handkerchiefs and painted our faces red and black like Indian warriors. I taught them the Indian discipline, as I knew no other" (106-107). In 1766 Smith, Uriah Stone, Joshua Horton and others explored the lands south of the Kentucky River on to the Cumberland and Tennessee Rivers, from Stone's River down to the Ohio" (Smith 114).

As the men headed west, Smith and Horton's slave, Jamie, hunted near the Tennessee River then headed to North Carolina. Their clothing was so outrageous that when they made it over the Blue Ridge they were jailed as suspicious characters. Jamie "had nothing on him that was ever spun. He had buckskin leggings, moccasins, and breech-clout—a bear skin dressed with the hair on which he belted about him, and a raccoon-skin cap" (Smith 117). After release Smith was dressed more suitably, in "an old beaver hat, buckskin leggings, moccasins, and a new shirt" (Smith 118).

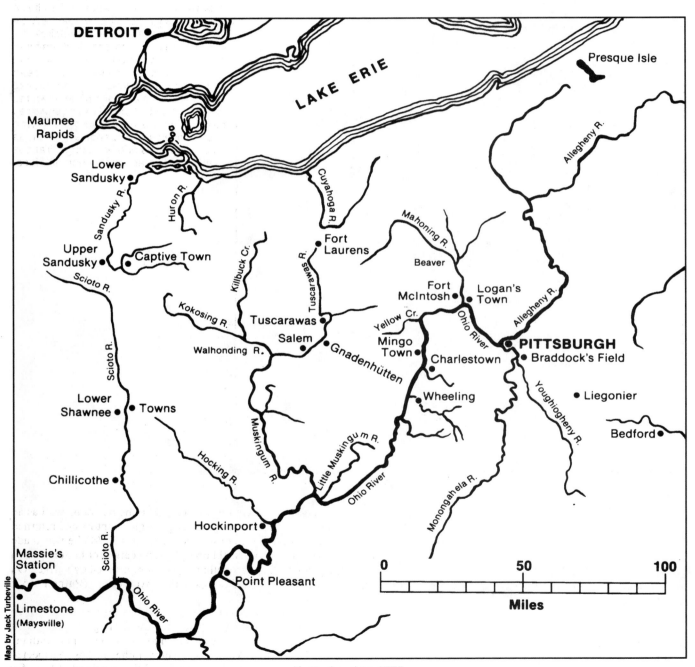

Kentucky, circa 1775.

In 1796 Joseph Wabun painted this watercolor, *Sauvage de la Nation des Shawanoes,* of a Shawnee in the Illinois country. This warrior's hair is roached, his ear rims slit and blue beads encircle his neck. His shirt and breech clout are blue, his blanket is white with a blue stripe and his scarlet leggings are European stockings with leg ties. Tufts of red-dyed deer hair in metal cones hang down the sides of his stockings. His finger-woven red wool garters have an indigo chevron pattern woven in. Armbands are silver, as are ear wheels and nose rings. Tattoos and vermilion adorn his head and face.

In the Old Southwest by 1780 a number of forts—Nashborough, Asher's, Fort Union, Bledsoe's, Stone's River, Mansker's, Buchanan's, Freeland's and Eaton's—gave refuge from the Creek, Chickasaw and Cherokee raids. In 1782 during a Creek attack on Kilgore's Station, braves seized Sam Martin and Isaac Johnson and took them to their towns. Few lamented the loss of Martin, a churlish Tory. In fact when Johnson escaped and told the locals that Sam was happy among the Creek most were glad to be rid of him. "Good riddance!" one declared. "Hope he will do them as much harm as he did us" (Putnam 156). A year later Sam—"elegantly dressed," sporting silver spurs and leading two fine horses—returned to Kilgore's. Many feared he was in league with the British-allied Creek,

because he had not only survived, but he had done well as an Indian trader, bore no grudge against his captors and returned in splendor! But Sam was no turncoat. In 1783 he was made an officer at Fort Nashborough. Ten years later he served as a spy during Captain Nathan Evers' forays on Obey's River. On March 10, 1794, he was killed by Indians (Putnam 156; Haywood 134-135).

Tory and land speculator, Bennett Belue was said to be "a romantic figure to young women just coming of age. He had lived among the Indians and may have been part-Indian" (Baldwin 192). When his wealthy father-in-law "suspected Indian ancestry" and in the mid-1770s disinherited him, for spite Belue took his wife and child from the Holston to

Kaskaskia. In 1779 he deserted his family, returned to Tennessee and hired on as a hunter for John Donelson's trip down the Cumberland. Donelson mentions "Ben Belew" in a journal entry on March 4, 1780 (Draper 11ZZ: 14). Belue returned to his native Wilkes County, North Carolina, and married but in 1785 he forsook his new wife for a Cherokee woman. Exploiting his influence with the Indians, Belue and fellow Huguenot John Sevier tried to bilk the United States out of thousands of acres of Tennessee country. On July 2, 1789, General Joseph Martin warned Patrick Henry that:

Bennett Belue, a man of infamous character...has collected a few of the fugitive Cherokees together, and forged a number of letters; setting forth that he is appointed by the chiefs of the Cherokees to do business for that nation, & has taken two Indians of the lower class with him to put a better face on his villainy; and has got a deed or lease from the Indians for a great part of their country. (Draper 1XX: 30-31)

Their scheme did not work. Undaunted, Belue next tried to swindle the government out of a chunk of west Tennessee. "Belue is now in the Chickasaw nation & claims all that valuable part of your purchase," Martin wrote to Henry on January 18, 1791. He had so swayed the Indians, that "should any person go there...their life might be in danger" (Draper IXX: 31). In 1792, a few days after some American soldiers were ambushed by Cherokee, Belue was spotted in Knoxville wearing "a coat appearing to be one of ye uniforms of ye Federal Regiment" (Baldwin 195). But Robert Welsh lodged Belue and his red men at his Natchez inn that August and said he "behaved himself as an honest man" (Potter 38). It was rumored that Belue died on the Natchez Trace a year later.

Other white Indians—like Alexander McGillivray, the Colberts, William McIntosh and William Augustus Bowles—played key, often conflicting roles in the southern Mississippi Valley. In Kentucky such men were also prominent.

HIE TO KENTUCKY!

Kanta-ke. Shawnee called it the Land of Great Meadows. Dragging Canoe, a Chickamauga Cherokee, once warned Daniel Boone that "there was a dark cloud over that country" (Lester 34). Reports from Christopher Gist and George Croghan in 1750 and 1765, however, portrayed the land that lay beyond the Blue Ridge as a paradise. Such tales Boone heard from John Findley, an employee of Croghan's, during his days as one of Braddock's teamsters.

Adopted by the Chalahgawtha Shawnee in March 1778, Sheltowee ("Big Turtle," as Boone was known to his native family) ultimately became America's first frontier hero and archetypal frontiersman. How did he dress? Accounts vary. But he must have dressed much like Michael Cassidy, Silas Harlan, Laban and Spencer Records and other woodsmen. In 1774 Boone was seen near the Holston wearing a buckskin hunting shirt "dyed black," most likely sewn from leather steeped in the tannin-based dye leached from a simmering broth of black walnut hulls. Thomas Rodgers was fifteen in 1791 when he saw Boone at Limestone after a hunt on the Big Sandy wearing a "linen hunting shirt and moccasins, the color of leaves" (Draper 19S: 168). Another saw him near Blue Licks dressed as "the poorest hunter" with his powderhorn, shot bag, rifle and hunting shirt (Draper 21S: 204).

To William Hickman, a Baptist preacher who came to Kentucky in 1776, such attire was hardly picturesque. "We

Col. Daniel Boon., by Chester Harding and James Otto Lewis. In September 1820 Lewis engraved this image from a portrait painted from life by Harding. Harding destroyed the painting in 1861, making this engraving the only full-length likeness of Boone extant. He is dressed in a caped and pleated buckskin hunting shirt. His hat is typical of tall hunting hats of about 1803. Boone, perennial longhunter, frontier hero and adopted brother to the Shawnee, became America's prototypical frontiersman. (Original engraving at Missouri Historical Society, St. Louis, Missouri.) Courtesy of Pathfinder Press

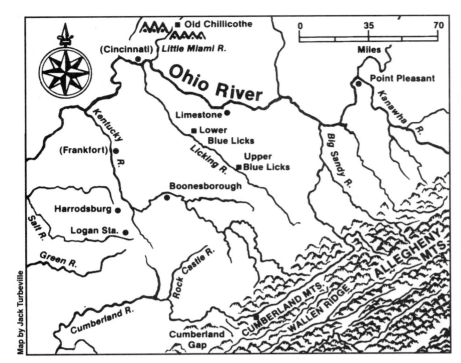

The eastern half of the *pays d'en haut*, the Middle Ground, circa 1778-1780, bordered by the Ohio and the Allegheny to the western tip of Lake Ontario.

got to Harrod's Town the 1st day of April, and a poor town it was in those days, a row or two of smoky cabins, dirty women, men with their britch clouts, greasy hunting-shirts, leggings and moccasins" (Lester 11). On Thursday, June 8, 1775, at Harrod's Landing, Nicholas Cresswell saw a canoe floating down the Kentucky with a crew of four hard-looking men. Three were dressed more Indian than white, in breechcloths, leggings and soiled, dirty linen hunting shirts that barely hid their nakedness (Cresswell 82-84).

Leggings were common wear for scouts. On a mission to Point Pleasant in October 1776, Robert Patterson, "for want of a better, had on a hunting shirt and britch clout and flannel leggings" (Bradford 92). In 1778 Lieutenant John Bowman asked Simon Kenton to spy on the Shawnee towns. Kenton, Sergeant George Clark of Logan's Station and Alexander Montgomery were to reconnoiter and recover horses. Kenton also asked Daniel Trabue to come and the men "made preparation to go, got some nice halters made with grained

Entitled *The Attack by Indians on the Boones and John Stewart*, this engraving by an unknown hand appeared in 1812 as the frontispiece in Humphrey Marshall's *The History of Kentucky*. Unlike other more "heroic" illustrations, this engraving accurately depicts Woodland Indians, canebrakes and white hunters.

49

raw buffalo hides...deer leather leggings, parched corn meal, and some jerk. With 2 pair moccasins to each man, our guns and ammunition in the best order, the next morning we was to start" (Trabue 54).[1]

In 1795 Trabue met Steven Ruddell when he was with General Anthony Wayne on the Miami at the negotiations for the Treaty of Fort Greenville. Captured in 1780 at Ruddell's Station and adopted, Ruddell had grown to manhood among the Indians and married a woman Trabue described as an "old, ugly, black looking dirty wretch of a creature...with an old smoked blanket over her shoulders and some dirty old cloth

tied about her waist" (140). When Ruddell, able only to speak English "in a very broken manner," and his native family met Wayne, Trabue recalled, "They all had the appearance of Indians" (140). He continued:

They were all painted and very dirty and shabby....some had silver trinkets hanging about their necks and breasts, and some brooches in their breechcloths, and beads in their leggings and moccasins, I suppose they thought themselves fine: yet they were all dirty looking creatures. (140-141)

Ruddell's father, who had not seen his son since 1780, got Steven to wash up and don white man's apparel but within two hours he was once again dressed as an Indian. By 1805

---

[1] The original transcript of Trabue's manuscript is part of Lyman C. Draper's manuscript collection (57J), which is held by the State Historical Society of Wisconsin in Madison.

William Augustus Bowles (1763-1805), Director General of the Creek Nation. Here Bowles, twenty-eight, is wearing a gastoweh set with a gem, wampum belt, matchcoat, ruffled shirt, silver arm bands and twilled bag. Fluent in three native tongues, Bowles had two wives—one a Chickamauga, the other a Lower Creek—and several children. In 1803 Upper Creeks conspiring against the Tory white warrior seized him at council and delivered him into Spanish hands. Kept alive on a diet of oranges in a Cuban dungeon for two years, he languished and died in a Havana military hospital. (Portrait from life, March 1791, by Thomas Hardy.)

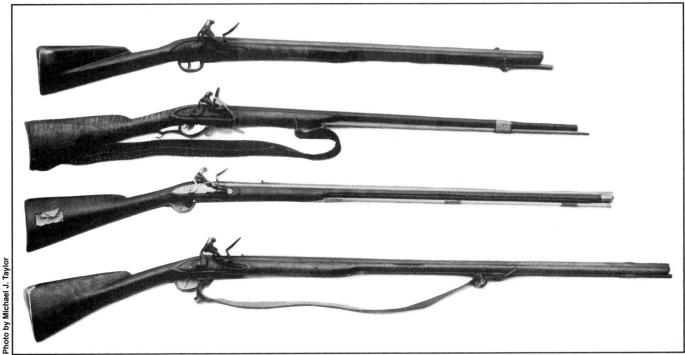

A fine quartet of guns, any one of which would serve an Indian-influenced woodsman well. From top to bottom: 1) cut down short land-pattern Brown Bess reworked into modified long land-pattern with brass forearm repair and other repairs; 2) transitional piece made of various gun parts, brass wire wrapped around muzzle to show field repair; 3) Rifle with fowler guard and thimbles, missing patch box lid and reworked Siler lock; 4) fowler made from long land Brown Bess parts and 1750s round-faced English lock. (Guns by Richard Meyers.)

Chippewa pack frame, made of ash or maple and bound with basswood bark. Tumpline was worn across the top of the head (as shown) or across chest.

Ruddell became a Baptist preacher. He "had a good deal that reminded you of the Indian in his manner," said one who heard him preach but who was taken aback by Steven's facial tattoos. "He wasn't a pretty speaker" (Draper 16CC: 307).

Woodsmen did not just wear hunting shirts, moccasins and leggings and resemble "dirty looking creatures." In 1780 John Redd saw Boone at Richmond serving in the Virginia legislature as a representative of Kentucky, and even then Boone's attire reflected his Shawnee/Long Knife image. "He was dressed in real backwoods style, he had on a common jeans suit, with buckskin leggings beaded very neatly...manufactured by the Indians" (Draper 10NN: 101). For the occasion Boone wore a scarlet weskit with sterling buttons engraved with his name. Boone's fancy buttons were a gift from his nephew, Daniel Bryan, who had made them for him (Draper 22C: 14 [14]).

On Christmas day, 1784, George Bedinger and John Stovall were hunting on the Green River. Bedinger toted a bearskin knapsack. Both wore long buckskin hunting shirts and leather breeches. Their leggings were crude, a hasty job. Whangs an inch or two apart and knotted at the ends were tied in holes

from thigh to knee; below that the leather was stitched with linen thread. Bedinger wore a faded camlet jacket of red wool and silk "that had seen its best days," a green baize shirt, a cocked hat from the Revolutionary War and deerskin moccasins stuffed with beech or white oak leaves. Stovall's hat was a wild affair made from a gray goose skin. Worn feather-side-out to shed water, Stovall tied the hat under his chin with a thong. Stovall's beard, goose cap and his "naturally ugly countenance" made him look, Bedinger said, "singularly ludicrous" (Draper 1A: 46). Bedinger later served in the United States House of Representatives. In his memoirs he speaks fondly of his days as a hunter yet he never expressed any longing to convert to native ways. But some white hunters did.

The *Louisville Courier*, on July 11, 1816, announced Boone's arrival at Fort Osage that April. He had "hired a man to accompany him—a noted woodsman by the name of Indian Phillips" (Draper 15C: 56). Boone's days with Charles "Indian" Phillips began in 1778 when Phillips, a "white Shawnee" captured Boone at the Lower Blue Licks, chased him to the Ohio when he escaped and fought against him at Boonesborough. He had once whipped Simon Kenton with a ramrod during Kenton's captivity. Charles Phillips, according

Not a sport for the timid, but killing buffalo by hand was a feat admired by many on the frontier. In 1791 Nathan Boone was treed by a buffalo he tried to stab to death. Such bravado nearly cost more than one man his life.

Watercolor by Fleury Generelly depicting a hunter's camp in the lower Mississippi Valley, circa 1820.
Items include: 1) half-face lean-to; 2) cradle of blue stroud; 3) log for pounding corn; 4) hide rack.
On the far right is a rack for making jerk; to its left near the shelter is a beaming
log to dehair hides. The hunter is wearing a blue cloth turban and a black breech cloth.

to Delinda Craig, Boone's granddaughter, "was tall and spare—wore Indian leggings and moccasins: walked and acted like an Indian. All were afraid of him" (Draper 30C: 72). Major John Gibson's remarks show the bias typical of most whites regarding their kinsmen who had "turned Indian," saying, Indian Phillips often went with Boone. He was a dirty fellow of no account...pretty much a savage; in feelings and appearance" (Draper 15C: 107ff). Another remarked Phillips "had such an Indiany appearance, that he was suspected and apprehended as a spy" (Draper 23S: 132). Frontier hothead Robert Frazier once threatened to shoot him and make a razor strop from his skin. But Boone knew his man and bore him no ill will. Charles "Indian" Phillips, hunter, blacksmith, trapper, was the ideal hunting companion for Sheltowee, his Shawnee brother.

Joab Barton was kidnaped by the Shawnee when a boy and grew up as a warrior. During Daniel Boone's captivity, Barton would lead him around "like a horse by a rope to drink and sometimes would jerk him around to annoy him" (Draper 22S: 170). In the early 1800s, Barton moved to what is now Florissant, Missouri, with the Shawnee band of Jimmy "Fish" Rodgers. There he left his native kinsmen, married a white woman, reared a number of children who were educated in white schools and did well. One who knew Joab said, "He was very sensible, smart, and good-looking. Had his ears rimmed...small-sized, dark complexion; and retained Indian habits to the end" (Draper 22S: 186).

Captured with Boone's salt boilers in 1778, Micajah Callaway was adopted by the Shawnee and spent over five years leading a "tribal nomadic existence." Ezekiel Lewis was a survivor of Colonel Archibald Lochry's flotilla that was ambushed on the Ohio by Joseph Brant and some Wyandot on August 24, 1781. During the attack Lewis spied Callaway. "'Cage Callaway was the worst savage amongst them!" he reported (Draper 30J: 80). At a prisoner exchange at Louisville in July 1783, Callaway was freed and his linguistic skill and knowledge of the Ohio Valley served Kentuckians well. In 1787 during a parley with the Shawnee at Maysville, Boone recorded, "Macagy Callaway served twenty days as interpreter" (Bishop 38). He died April 11, 1849.

Joseph Jackson was also captured with Boone's salt boilers and adopted. In 1844 Lyman Draper interviewed him, observing that he "chose to live with the Indians, becoming an Indian in every sense" (Draper 11CC: 35). Jackson fought the Americans at Blue Licks, then fought against the troops of Colonel Josiah Harmar, General Arthur St. Clair and General "Mad" Anthony Wayne at Fallen Timbers (Draper 11C: 62ff). In 1800 Jackson returned to Kentucky to "make a good citizen," but his life soured. Unhappily married and unable to resolve his past, at age eighty-eight he hanged himself.

Phillips, Barton, Callaway and Jackson were men of confused cultural and social identities, white captives whose mores were transformed while living in the tumultuous social, racial, political and culturally charged milieu brewing north of the Ohio in the land known as the *pays d'en haut,* the Middle Ground.

TRADERS, BARONETS & MAD DOGS OF THE MIDDLE GROUND

ordered on the south by the Ohio, and on the west by the Mississippi and in the north by the Great Lakes to the western tip of Lake Ontario, the Middle Ground was a true cultural melting pot. Fragile, shifting alliances roiled by waves of Indians fleeing from east of the Alleghenies and by the presence of French, British, American and Spanish intruders brought even greater tension. The *pays d'en haut* not only had its share of heroes and rogues, but its fertile, culturally diverse soil also spawned some of the most colorful, most controversial Indian-influenced men on the frontier (White x-xv).

Louis Lorimier was a cosmopolitan member of this unique fraternity. Born in 1748 in Canada, Lorimier spoke fluent Shawnee and other dialects. A veteran of the Seven Years War whose honesty had gained him respect among native people, he ran a trading post at Piqua. After 1763 he was allied with the British. Diplomat, advisor and mediator, a genteel man of Old World manners and polish, Lorimier enjoyed great prestige among the Indians, French, Spanish and British. He was with the British in February 1778 when his Shawnee kinsmen seized Boone and his salt boilers, and he may have helped besiege Boonesborough that September. His store at the headwaters of the Miami, at "Lorimier's Town," did a brisk business in fur and trade goods. But in November 1782, Colonel Benjamin Logan and his American army sacked the outpost and Louis barely escaped. "We took all that was there and burnt it up," recalled William Clinkenbeard, who was in on the raid (Beckner, "Interview with Clinkenbeard" 125). But some of the plunder was saved. Over $20,000 worth of calico, trade silver, wool and Irish linen was loaded on two hundred horses and taken back to Kentucky and sold.

In 1786 Lorimier moved to Illinois and married Charlotte Pemanpieh Bougainville, the Shawnee daughter of Louis Antoine de Bougainville. In 1793 he moved his family to Cape Girardeau, Missouri. With the permission of Baron de Carondelet, he persuaded many Delaware and Shawnee to join him. In 1797 Nicolas de Finiels met the Frenchman and his son, Louis Jr. Both men, he wrote, "adopt European and Indian customs, and appear...sometimes in European garb and sometimes in the dress of these children of Nature." Lorimier's storehouses were "stocked with Indian trade goods and he provides exclusive market for all their furs" (Finiels 35, 119).

In 1811 John James Audubon saw Lorimier at Cape Girardeau. Audubon's comical but precise description reflects Lorimier's dual status as a marginal man:

Imagine a man not more than four feet, six inches, thin in proportion, looking as if he had just been shot out of a popgun. His nose formed decidedly, the most prominent feature of his spare, meager countenance...and garnished with the eyes of an eagle. His hair was plastered down close to his head with a quantity of pomatum; it ended in a long queue rolled up in a dirty ribbon that hung down below his waist. The upper part of his dress was European, once rich but now woefully patched and dilapidated with shreds of gold and silver lace here and there. The fashion of his waistcoat, as antique as that of his nose, had immense pocket flaps that covered more than half

Fox warrior, circa early 1700s, the terror of the Middle Ground. Note tattoos, quill-wrapped roached hair, bow and arrows, and a European trade shirt wrapped around his waist. Translated from French, the caption reads: *Fox Indian warrior feared by all nations because of their valor and speed. Can go twenty-five to thirty leagues per day without provisions other than grasses and leaves from the woods. There are about four to five hundred men bearing arms. Divided into three or four villages since they have been at war with the French. Almost all the nations do their hair in the manner of the Fox Indian. They take off their shirt and put it around their waist when they fight.*

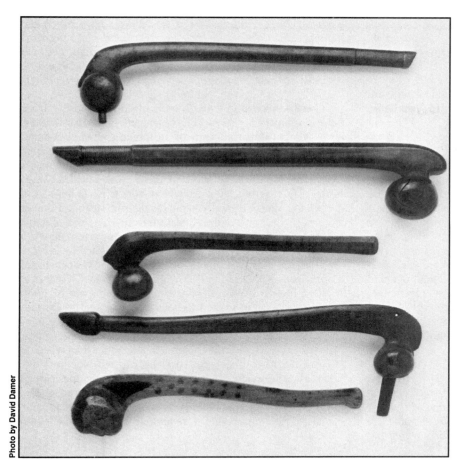

For close combat, maple ball-head war clubs, also called death mauls, death hammers or tomahawks, were the Woodland Indian's arm of choice. Long Knives prized them as trophies. These five originals are typical of those used east of the Mississippi. From top to bottom: a maple club, 22 inches long, collected in 1774 by frontiersman James Robertson near Kingsport, Tennessee, during Lord Dunmore's War; maple club, 24 inches long, dating to the 18th century; a ball-head club of curly maple, about 17 inches long; a 23-inch Kickapoo death maul; an Eastern Sioux war club with the ball end carved into the face of a man, circa 1820-1840. (From the collection of Jim and Carolyn Dresslar.)

Three Iroquois neck knife sheaths quilled in pre-1770 geometric design on smoked, brain-tanned moosehide. Quills dyed with cochineal, bloodroot, indigo, yellow root, poke berries and wild grape and sealed with beeswax and tallow. Embellished with naturally dyed horsehair wrapped in homemade brass cones and antique irregular beads. Straps of center and far right sheaths are quill-wrapped. (Made by Lally Bartman, Woodbury, Kentucky.)

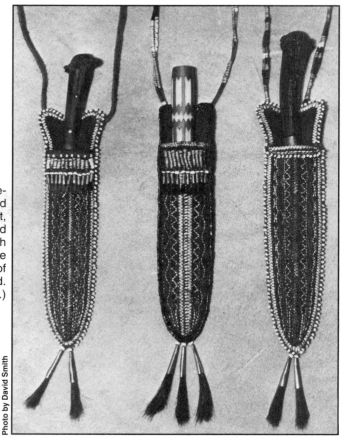

his tight buckskin trousers that were ornamented with big, iron knee-buckles to support Indian hunting gaiters long past their prime. His moccasins, to complete his costume, were...of the most beautiful workmanship. (Ford 49)

Louis Lorimier died on June 26, 1812. He and his wife are buried at the Old Lorimier Cemetery in Cape Girardeau, Missouri.

In 1774 Nicholas Cresswell, at 24 years of age, sailed from England to buy a farm in Virginia. By April 1775 he was at Fort Pitt with hopes of going down the Ohio. That month he, James Nourse and a band of men left for Kentucky and did not return until July. By fall Nicholas was near the forks of the Muskingum. Here he lived with the Delaware and took a Mohawk mistress. "Employed an Indian woman to make me a pair of moccasins and leggings," he wrote. "Got a calico shirt made in the Indian fashion, trimmed up with silver brooches and arm plates so that I scarcely know myself." At an Indian dance he was "painted in the most elegant manner. Divested of all my clothes, except my calico short breechcloth, leggings, and moccasins" (102-103). He received gifts of wampum, "an Indian tobacco pouch made of a mink skin adorned with porcupine quills," and wrote vividly of native attire:

The dress of the men is short, white linen or calico shirts which come a little below their hips without buttons at neck or wrist and in general ruffled and a great number of small brooches stuck in it. Silver plates about three inches broad round the wrists of their arms, silver wheels in their ears, which are stretched long enough for the tip of the ear to touch the shoulder, silver rings in their noses, breechcloth and moccasins with a matchcoat that serves them for a bed at night. They cut off their hair except a lock on the crown of the head and go bareheaded, and pluck out their beards. (120-121)

Cresswell's enlightened comments differ sharply from those of many of his peers. "I have...a great regard for Indians. If we take an impartial view of an Indian's general conduct with all the disadvantages they labor under, at the same time divest ourselves of prejudice, I believe every honest man's sentiments would be in favor of them" (Cresswell 117). In June 1777 Cresswell sailed from New York to his father's farm in England, married and lived out his days in Suffolk. Forever touched by the spirit of the American frontier, he willed to his kin after his death in 1804, among other things, a tomahawk, a gastoweh, snowshoes and a buffalo horn mounted in silver.

One of the most dramatic examples of native-influenced attire was that of Sir John Caldwell, Baronet. In 1776 at Fort Niagara Ensign Caldwell joined the 8th Regiment of Foot, and he was soon promoted to lieutenant and sent to Detroit. But young Caldwell, barely twenty, hated the "old crazy fort" and instead roamed the forests with his majesty's Indian allies. "I never enjoy myself more nor my health better than when on a voyage with a bear skin to sleep on and salt pork for breakfast," he wrote to his father. In the woods one learned "to be a hardy soldier [and] a voyage of a hundred or two miles is looked upon as nothing...a bear skin and blanket, gun, etc. and a little provision" were all that were needed (Boston 316-317).

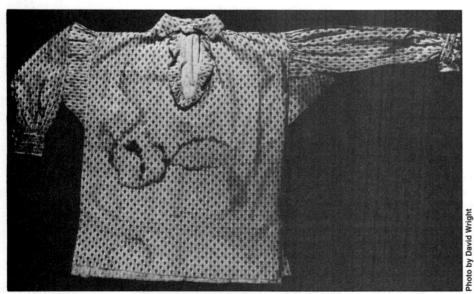

Photo by David Wright

Trade shirt from the Eastern Great Lakes. This is the shirt worn by Sir John Caldwell in his portrait painted from life, *Soldiering with the King's, 1780*. Shirt is cotton cloth decorated with a block print, ruffled sleeves and edges of neck opening, ties at neck and sleeve ends, down-turned collar, sewn with cotton thread. Fabric stained and in back are several small holes. **Length at middle is 92 cm.** (Speyer Collection, formerly in the collection of Sir John Caldwell.)
Courtesy of Canadian Museum of Civilization, Ottawa

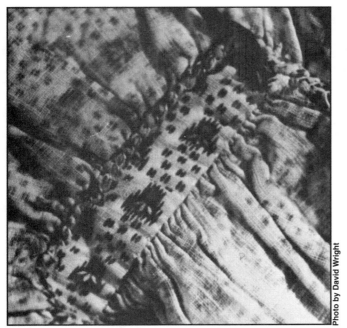

Close-up of sleeve opening and cuff of Caldwell shirt, showing tight hand-stitching. Typical of the day, there are no buttons on this shirt. (Speyer Collection, formerly in the collection of Sir John Caldwell.)
Courtesy of Canadian Museum of Civilization, Ottawa

country helped fend off raids on Allegheny cabins, but some of his men were men of blood, hunting Indians the way men hunted deer. Lewis "Death Wind" Wetzel was in Brady's employ and in spite of his ruthless shedding of Indian blood, he looked decidedly native. His cousin, Lewis Bonnett, Jr., said Wetzel was "as swarthy as an Indian—not a little resembling one....has his ears bored and wore silk tassels in them or some other ornament" and when he untied his long black hair it would reach to his calves (Lobdell 6, 9). In a letter to Lyman Draper in 1860, John Cuppy, ninety-nine, the last living scout of Sam Brady, described the "Dress and Customs of Spies," circa 1778-1790:

Spy dress—a handkerchief tied around the spy's head of any color, sometimes a capeau (shorter than a hunting shirt) of cloth or a hunting shirt, and moccasins; and thick, loose woolen leggings reaching above the knee, so thick that a rattlesnake

Caldwell lived with the Ojibway for two seasons. Trusted by both Indians and whites, fluent in Algonquin dialects, he was commended by his superior officers to General Frederick Haldimand, commander of Canada. Adopted by the Ojibway and named "Apetto," meaning "the Runner," Caldwell took a leading role at the councils at Wapatomica in 1780, appearing in his best native wear. By late 1782 Caldwell was in England with a dispatch from General Haldimand to Lord Sackville, then went home to Ireland with his chests heavy with relics and his head full of memories.

Apetto never forgot his days with his native kin. To recall those moments, he dressed in his Ojibway finest and posed for a full-length portrait. From the original two copies were made. The best-known Caldwell painting is a copy in the archives of the King's Regiment Collection in the National Museums and Galleries on Merseyside at Liverpool. The second is "held by the 1st Battalion, The King's Regiment" (Jones), and the original, as of June 1964, hung in Snitterton Hall, Derbyshire, in the home of the Bagshawe family. Many of Sir John's relics were acquired from Castle Caldwell, County Fermanagh, Ireland, by Arthur Speyer, Jr. and are now in the Canadian Museum of Civilization, Ottawa, and are pictured in *"Bo'jou Neejee!" Profiles in Canadian Indian Art* (Brasser 72).

Americans had their share of Indian-influenced woodsmen in the Middle Ground too. One of the most important yet least known was Captain Samuel Brady (1756-1795). He and his rangers dressed Indian, adorning themselves in feathers—one scout wore a coonskin cap topped off with a hawk feather—and war paint. His men "practiced before going on a scout, shooting at a mark, throwing their tomahawks and sticking them in a tree [at] two or three rods and jumping over fences" (Draper 9S: 37). Brady's forays from Fort Pitt into the Ohio

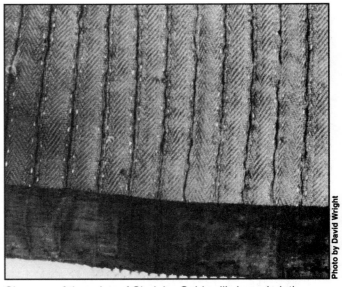

Close-up of the edge of Sir John Caldwell's breechcloth, most likely the same one he wore in his famous painting. Description by museum cataloger, J. Thompson, given on June 1975 states: "Made from blue blanket cloth, covered in middle portion with natural canvas, edged with silk ribbons (olive green, faded blue, and two-color brown and beige.) At one end, solidly appliqued faded red worsted tape in transverse strips. Edging of opaque white beads. Sewn with cotton thread." Length 125 cm. (Speyer Collection, formerly in the collection of Sir John Caldwell.)
Courtesy of Canadian Museum of Civilization, Ottawa

Photo by David Wright

The leggings of Sir John Caldwell, most likely the same pair worn in his portrait. Description by museum cataloger, J. Thompson, given on June 1975 states: "made from red wool cloth, edges bound with purple, green, and pale blue silk ribbons. Edging of opaque white glass beads. Curving seam down outer leg, with seam allowance to the outside. Unseamed at lower leg, with three sets of metal hook and eye closures. Single tie of red wool cloth attached at top of each legging, and remnants of foot loop at base. Sewing with cotton thread." Has extensive holes and damage to beading. Length 70 cm. (Speyer Collection, formerly in the collection of Sir John Caldwell.)
Courtesy of Canadian Museum of Civilization, Ottawa

could not penetrate through with their fangs. Sometimes we took along wheat bread, and bacon and flour to make ashcakes, and sometimes chocolate; and [we] could always get venison, turkeys, and sometimes bear meat, but never took any parched corn meal. (Draper 9S: 36-37)

Simon Girty (1741-1818) is one of the most controversial Indian-influenced white men. Maligned, misunderstood and hated, Girty emerged by the early 19th century as the prototypical "white savage renegade." Much of the real man is hidden behind myths, distortions and half-truths. At fourteen Simon and his brothers were captured by French-allied Delaware and Shawnee within the *pays d'en haut*, separated and adopted by different tribes. Thomas, the eldest, escaped and returned to American life. Simon was adopted by the Seneca. Brother George was taken by the Delaware but was later given his freedom. Like James, who was adopted by the Shawnee, George maintained his tribal identity till the end of his days. All three were active in the British Indian Department (Hoffman 661). Simon's role as a "white Indian" was more complex than that of his brothers. Deeply imprinted by native life, "Girty would dress up like an Indian when he was out on service with them," Samuel Murphy said (Calloway, "Simon Girty" 48). Yet, unable to cut his ties to Anglo society, Girty lived on the fringes of both, truly belonging to neither. Fluent in native dialects, influential, eloquent, he carved his own niche.

Girty's temper was mercurial, made worse by mood swings and bouts with the bottle. Reverend John Heckewelder found him "as brutal, depraved, and wicked a wretch as ever lived..." (152). Girty railed at Oliver Spencer while Spencer was held captive at Blue Jacket's Town in 1792. Spencer deemed him "the very picture of a villain," and said he wore "the Indian costume, but without any ornament; and his silk handkerchief, while it supplied the place of a hat, hid an unsightly wound in his forehead" (Quaife 92). In 1781 Joseph Brant had slashed him from his right ear to his temple with a sword—"the beating

A likeness on display at Fort Malden Historic Park, Canada, purporting to be that of Simon Girty. The photo was taken by Madeline Malott, descendant of Simon and Catherine Malott Girty. It is used with the consent of Dwight Girty of Windsor, Ontario, the great-great-great-grandson of Simon Girty.

of the brain was plainly discernible," recalled Girty's daughter, Sarah Munger (Draper 20S: 197). The wound gave him trouble till his dying day, perhaps causing his later blindness because of a damaged optic nerve and affecting his mind "more or less."

During his captivity Spencer met Blue Jacket at his town on the Auglaize. Purportedly captured by Shawnee and adopted when he was a white youth named Marmaduke Swearingen, Blue Jacket, now fully Shawnee with native wife and family, was attired in "a scarlet frock coat, richly laced with gold and confined around his waist with a party-colored sash, and in red leggings and moccasins ornamented in the highest style of Indian fashion" (Quaife 91). His outfit was garnished with gold epaulets, silver arm bands and a gorget. Spencer's own dress that winter consisted of "a white shirt, blanket capote, blue leggings, and waist cloth...so that I was dressed in full Indian costume" (Quaife 117).

But it is the "white savage renegade" Simon Girty, not Blue Jacket, who unnerved Oliver Spencer. Through 18th century American eyes, it is not hard to see why Girty—patriot turned Tory, defender of Indian rights, willing tool of the British Indian Department—had a price on his head. Yet Girty, haunted by his own dark side, helped those he could. He befriended Boone during his Shawnee days and was a sworn brother to Simon Kenton and saved Kenton's life. John Burkhart, Thomas Ridout, Samuel Murphy, William May, Margaret Handley Erksine, Henry Baker and at least a dozen more captives were saved by his efforts.

Simon Girty was in a social class of his own making. There were many other marginal men of shifting, sometimes ambivalent identity in the Middle Ground—Alexander McKee, Jimmy "Fish" Rogers and John Tanner are but three—but it is beyond the scope of this essay to try to cover them all.

This brief overview of European and American frontiersmen, traders and such folk marks the end of the first part of this chapter. Now, for the benefit of reenactors emulating the look of 18th century half-caste woodsmen, I will list representative goods that were available at the time, including trade items, cloth, dress, staples, delicacies, accoutrements and the like.

This Great Lakes gastoweh features a front panel of nine bands of porcupine quill wrapping (colors are red, yellow-orange, white and black) and line embroidery on brain-tanned deerskin that has been dyed with black walnut hulls. Feathers are red-dyed turkey and ostrich plumes.
Gastoweh and photo by Michael J. Taylor

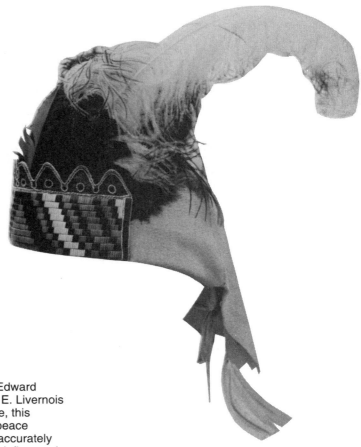

Fictitious image of Girty, c. mid to late 1800s, perhaps based on Edward Chatfield's Huron sketches or photographs of Hurons taken by J. E. Livernois in Quebec in 1880. Despite its late date and unknown provenance, this sketch—showing trade silver, wampum belt, finger-woven sash, peace medallions, leggings, embroidered quilled strips and gastoweh—accurately depicts the hybrid blend of European/native dress worn by Indian-influenced frontier whites from the mid-1700s to the early 1800s.

Randy Corse depicting an Indian-influenced Englishman, circa mid-1750s. His musket is a transitional Brown Bess made by Kit Ravenshear of both long and short land components, his center-seam moccasins (bound with red wool ties) and side-seam leggings are buckskin, and his finger-woven sash is beaded in a linear design. Underneath his reddish-brown, sleeved English coat is a sleeveless weskit of linen or wool, depending on the season. Often he wears a cartridge "belly box" and frog to hold his bayonet and tomahawk.

WARES FOR INDIAN-INFLUENCED WOODSMEN: SALE OR BARTER

By the mid-1700s, as traders George Croghan and John Findley were pushing down the Ohio, the Philadelphia firm of John Baynton, Samuel Wharton and George Morgan was making ready for an all-out thrust into Illinois. Their partnership was well-financed (by 1766 the firm had over £75,000 tied up in the venture) and their idea simple. By shipping goods to the West they hoped to supply French citizens and British troops and cash in on the Indian trade. The Peoria, Kaskaskia, Shawnee, Wea, Quapaw, Chippewa, Fox, Osage and Potawatomi traded at Fort de Chartres, bringing in tons of fur. It was George Morgan who took his partners' hopes and wares to Illinois. The main store was opened in Kaskaskia in 1766. Smaller stores were set up at Cahokia and Vincennes. Five boat convoys were needed to move goods from Fort Pitt to Kaskaskia. Sixty-five more vessels were ordered for the 1767 fall trip and Morgan employed over 300 boatmen.

Letters and inventories make clear the type of goods that could be had by woodsmen like Simon Girty, who was hired by Morgan as a hunter. Morgan wrote to Baynton and Wharton in February 1768:

Dear Partners:
....I have already sent you a general order for the goods which are in demand here and which will afford a great advance....As to Muscovado and Loaf Sugar, Coffee, Chocolate, Men's, women's and children's best and common Leather shoes, Tin

Ware, Pewter, Silver, Appalachian Handkerchiefs—beaver traps, and Soap, you cannot send too great a quantity....
(Alvord and Carter 163)

To take advantage of spring rains that raised the Ohio, making it safer for his flotilla, Morgan wrote on April 15 that "before the fall of the waters—we shall be in want of the following particular articles, viz":

loaf sugar	steel spurs	candle wicks
muscovado	salt peter	candle molds
hyson tea	worsted or cruels	sheep skins
bohea tea	short pipes	beaver traps
chocolate	blotting cloths	nails
pepper	Irish linen	scythes
shoes	chintz and calico	knives
tin ware	white & red flannel	forks
swanskin	pitch and cordage	spades
pewter basins	black cravats	axes
black bandanas	brass candle sticks	cheese
writing paper	small gilt trunks	beeswax
spike gimblets	bed ticking	buttons
tap bores	table cloths	castile soap

(Alvord and Carter 230-231)

Equally impressive are Morgan's transactions in 1768. Below is an abridged but typical account:

powder	vermilion	wrist bands
balls	flints	beads
tobacco	ruffled shirts	coats
knives	breech clouts	plain shirts
paint	rings	jews harps
handkerchiefs	rum	match coats
awls	shirts	cutteaus
leggings	gartering	wampum
brass kettles	ribbon	thread
silver crosses	fuzees	strouds
calico shirts	narrow stroud	petticoats
silver brooches	pipe tomahawks	pipes

(Alvord and Carter 391-405)

But profits to the firm were never as high as the Philadelphians thought they should have been. The cost of transporting goods was too steep, and the French did not care much for the English or their trade goods and moved deeper into French territory. Competition from the rival firm of Bernard and Gratz also cut into the firm's earnings, and within two years the western enterprise of Baynton, Wharton and Morgan would be no more.

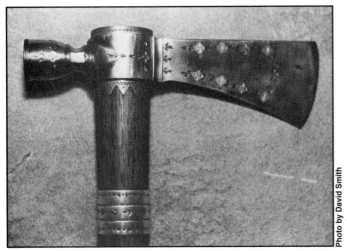

Photo by David Smith

Presentation pipe tomahawk, hand-forged from a gun barrel and a bit inserted in blade. The twenty-two sterling flowers accentuating the floral engraving were chiseled out and hammered into the blade, head and bowl.

In April 1779 General Daniel Brodhead wrote this "Estimate of Goods to be sent for the Delaware":

400 matchcoats	24 strouds, blue	20 rifles
600 wt. powder	2 strouds, scarlet	40 saddles
60 hoes	1600 wt. lead	100 axes
1,000 shirts assorted, white ruffled, calico ruffled, plain white and checked		
1250 yd. legging stuff, moulton, half-thick or stroud		
50 brass kettles	60 tin kettles or rolled iron	
100 white wampum	40 black wampum	2,000 flints
silver ware	50 lb. vermilion	100 lb. shot
40 doz. cutteaus	30 regimental coats	12 rasps
48 black silk handkerchiefs		36 files
36 black silk cravats		48 razors
80 pieces taffia ribbons: yellow, blue, green, purple		
30 regimental hats with silver lace		12 augers
1,000 lb. shingle nails		handsaws
30 mirrors	48 pewter buttons	72 flasks
48 pewter plates	12 tea kettles	door latches
12 frying pans	1 set Cooper's tools	bolts

1,000 fish hooks	120 stockings	40 spoons
60 pr. shoes and buckles [with] 10 pr. silver buckles		
blacksmith tools	masons trowels	
12 frying pans	12 pr. saddle bags, black and red	
10 small tents	1 bolt strong osnaburg for bags	
40 horse bells	set of carpenters tools	
60 tin pints	1 gr. pewter spoons	576 needles
40 beaver traps	thread—all colors	100 combs
100 coarse coats	200 lb. coffee	100 scissors
6 bushels salt	30 lb. bohea tea	sickles
50 worsted caps	50 pr. yarn mittens	100 tweezers
40 lb. smallest white beads		10 pr. boots
20 pr. white linen breeches		

(Draper 1H: 68-71)

Bartering and buying were traditional ways in which Indian-influenced woodsmen of the cane outfitted themselves. But in place long before trading firms or traders was a more lively form of exchange—raiding, theft and looting—that strongly affected cultural relations, shaky alliances and border warfare.

WARES FOR INDIAN-INFLUENCED WOODSMEN: PLUNDER & BOOTY

Thievery often resulted in a dramatic transfer of goods. Even extortion offered possibilities. In the 1730s a warring band of Natchez captured some French women, children and slaves, demanding for their ransom:

...200 guns, 200 barrels of powder, 200 barrels of balls, 2,000 flints, 200 knives, 200 hatchets, 200 pickaxes, 20 qts. brandy, 20 casks of wine, 20 barrels of vermilion, 200 sheets, 20 pieces of linen, 20 coats with lace, 20 hats bordered with plumes, and 100 coats of the plain kind.
(Thwaites 68: 191)

Horse stealing was a manly rite of passage for both races, a sport of high adventure spiced with deadly risk. But horses were not the only items stolen; before cabins were torched they were pilfered and the wares packed hundreds of miles to Indian towns north of the Ohio and south to the Florida Panhandle. And to the victors went the spoils of war. On March 3, 1778, John Fitch was captured by Indians near Fort Pitt. His knapsack and budget were taken and he was stripped of his "noble camlet cloak well-lined with green baize" and his "striped livery coat and jacket with silver buttons" (Draper 8CC: 103, 109). On August 19, 1782, as the smoke lifted from the killing field of

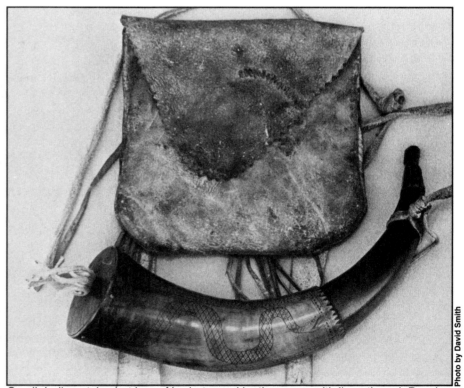

Small, Indian-style shot bag of brain-tanned leather sewn with linen thread. Powder horn scrimshawed in the native fashion with a snake motif. Horn and bag by David Wright. **Courtesy of Tony Gerard**

Photo by David Smith

Blue Licks, fleeing Kentuckians saw Indians fighting over booty, dashing from body to body, smashing skulls, grabbing knives, swords, powder horns, shot bags, rifles. One brave groping among the dead had three or four powder horns hung from his shoulder (Draper 13C: 114-115).

The ending of the Revolutionary War unleashed an armada of rafts, dugouts, canoes, bateaux, keelboats and flatboats down the Ohio, many supplied like floating general stores, making them tempting targets. Captive whites or Tories were used as decoys to call for help as the warriors hid along the banks. Those taking the bait and steering their vessels to shore were often killed. James Girty, "white Miami" William Wells and Ragin, a "half-Indian" of unknown lineage, were masters of such tactics.

Indians were not alone in such high-risk war games. Just the chance for loot was often enough to entice volunteers and selling stolen trade goods helped pay the militia. Booty was "sold at vendue on the spot" or taken to forts to auction (Draper 23CC: 44ff). Trade silver could be redeemed at face value. And slung from the shoulder of more than one Long Knife was a twilled bag of finger-woven scarlet or indigo wool or a bag of brain-tanned deerhide dyed black, trimmed with brooches and beads, garnished with deer hair wisps dyed red and crimped in metal cones and embroidered with orange, red, yellow, white and black quills woven into motifs of thunderbirds, sturgeon and malevolent underwater panthers. Maple ball-head war clubs made good trophies of war and Spencer Records' younger brother, Laban, tacked to his cabin garret Shawnee scalps plaited with quills, brooches and beads (Draper 3QQ: 73ff; 10BB: 26 [2]).

Daniel Trabue was seventeen years old when he and his brother and a few others came to Kentucky in spring 1778. Nine miles past the Cumberland Gap where the Warrior's Path merges with Boone's Wilderness Road, the men saw fresh moccasin tracks. On past a bend they saw two Shawnee crouched in the trace, eating. Daniel fired, spooking the pair into flight and causing them to leave behind a pile of loot from a Shawnee raid on a Cherokee town. Their loot consisted of:

...7 packets, 5 bows and arrows, 3 shot bags and powder horns, several blankets, several new shirts, new fine leggings full of silver broaches, breechcloths full of silver broaches, one brass kettle, and many other things. (Trabue 46)

A slave boy grabbed a raven fetish fletched with black feathers, said to be a "thing to conjure with" (Trabue 46). At Boonesborough the booty was sold and Trabue bought "some nice wampum and a shot bag and powderhorn" (Trabue 47).

Not all raids were a success. On August 30, 1778, Boone and eighteen men crossed the Ohio, "painted their faces assuming the disguise of savages" and, hoping for "a great speck," attacked some Shawnee camped on Paint Creek (Trabue 57). But they got little plunder and only one scalp. And sometimes dressing Indian had its tragic side. At Cassidy's Station (in Fleming County) Michael Cassidy shot and killed a white scout attired "in Indian dress." Peter Harper, "a half-Indian," was also killed in a case of mistaken identity, as was Joseph Rogers, a cousin of George Rogers Clark. Captured near the Lower Blue Licks on December 28, 1776, in 1782 Rogers ran to greet the Long Knife army as it marched on Piqua, but being "dressed fine in Indian dress" he was shot dead (Beckner, "Interview with Clinkenbeard" 110, 120, 125).

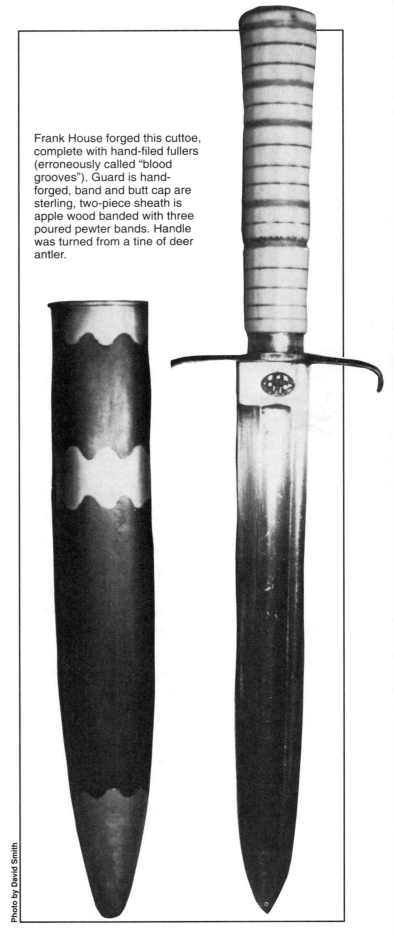

Frank House forged this cuttoe, complete with hand-filed fullers (erroneously called "blood grooves"). Guard is hand-forged, band and butt cap are sterling, two-piece sheath is apple wood banded with three poured pewter bands. Handle was turned from a tine of deer antler.

Photo by David Smith

After the siege of Boonesborough in spring 1779, Colonel John Bowman led an assault against the Shawnee towns at Old Chillicothe. Black Fish, the Chalahgawtha chief who was mortally wounded during the fray, "was dressed in a beautiful white shirt richly trimmed with brooches and other silver ornaments," said George Bedinger, who was there. "The articles of plunder consisted chiefly of silver ornaments, of which a large number were found together with a goodly quantity of very good clothing" (Draper 1A: 22). A fine scarlet vest was recognized as belonging to Simon Girty, as was his fancy double-barreled gun (Draper 1A: 27).

In August 1779 Lieutenant Colonel George Rogers Clark and his Long Knife army returned victorious to Louisville from Clark's rampage through the Old Northwest. Many of his men were clad in British regimentals and fancy shirts appropriated at Vincennes where they had commandeered seven keelboats loaded with six tons of supplies (worth $50,000) destined for the King's men and his Indian allies. Rum, wine, taffia and sugar made up a large part of the loot, and all of it, along with a cache of Brown Bess muskets and hundreds of pounds of

Typical plunder: sterling ear wheels, nose rings and brooches, copper gorget, shot bag, buffalo horn powder horn on fingerwoven strap with red deer hair tufts in metal cones, copper box, otter turban with beaded red wool panel bordered with silk ribbon, and trade beads. (Bag and knife by Jack Hubbard, gorget by Joseph Keeslar, silver by Chuck Leonard and turban by Michael J. Taylor.)

Contemporary copy of a quilled Shawnee bag, circa 1780s, by Mike Taylor. The original is currently in the Linden Museum, Stuttgart, Germany. Quills are used in the white and dyed red and yellow-orange. Embellished with dyed deer hair in metal cones, the bag measures 11-1/2 inches by 8 inches.
Photo by Michael J. Taylor

Presentation pipe tomahawk, hand-forged from a gun barrel and a bit inserted in blade. Eye socket and mouth piece is cast pewter. Engraved bands encircling hickory haft are sterling. The twenty-two sterling flowers accentuating the floral engraving were chiseled out and hammered into the blade, head and bowl. Inspired by three original pipe tomahawks dating from 1758 to 1761 (one of which belonged to Sir William Johnson), this exquisite piece was made by Frank House.

powder and ball, was stored at Fort Nelson (Derleth 72). Squire Boone also wore a British regimental (Draper 22C: 10 [9]).

In 1779 Alexander McConnell's life was spared by an Indian who gave him "his blue cappo" so he could slip away in the night and hide from the brave's approaching comrades. But the warriors killed his horse to "cut off the mane and tail to dye for moccasin purposes and etc. They could make it any color they pleased" (Draper 13CC: 142).

William Clinkenbeard was with George Rogers Clark in November 1782 when Clark stormed up the Miami with 1,050 men, launching a whirlwind counterattack on the Shawnee after the devastating Battle of Blue Licks on August 19. Michael Cassidy, a strutting "little chunk of an Irishman" was in one ambuscade that left five braves dead. Cassidy pounded off on a horse to get the scalps. Soon he was back "with his fingers all bloody" proudly displaying a cache of body parts flashy with silver. He "was showing me he had cut off their fingers and noses and ear bobs to get their trinkets....Had a whole handful of trinkets that he got," recalled William, who also saw "a splendid squaw...I believe she had 1,000 ornaments on her; was all covered over with them." Tom Pierce returned to Kentucky wearing "a very nice Indian shot pouch...all beaded off" (Beckner, "Interview with Clinkenbeard" 125-126). One Indian killed "had fifty-nine silver brooches plaited in his hair and a large silver plate on his breast and superior dress to common Indians" (Beckner, "William Suddeth" 49).

On April 11, 1791, near the falls of the Ohio, Hugh Dickey, Chris Strong, James Walker and one or two others chased seven Indians "committing depredations." After a blistering forty-mile ride, the whites closed in, killing several warriors, causing the rest to flee and leave behind "8 horses, 7 or 8 blankets, 2 or 3 bridles, 1 brass kettle, 1/2 bushel of jerk, a bear's gut 1-1/2 or 2 yards long full of bear's fat, and 7 or 8 deer skins." Dickey shot one Indian with "a coon-skin cap on his head with a long tail hanging down" (Draper 13CC: 240-242). In Ohio during a Shawnee raid that year, Oliver Spencer saw a warrior "wearing the dress coat of a field officer of the infantry, with silver epaulets on his shoulders and a watch suspended from each ear" (Quaife 28). Near Knoxville in April 1794, twenty-five Indians repulsed in a skirmish left in their wake "a rifle-gun, a scalping knife, 1 blanket, a French chapeau, 8 ramrods, and 8 gunlock covers" (Haywood 319).

Admittedly, such a wealth of trade goods, clothing, sundry staples and delicacies shows what could be had in some unique situations. Yet a perusal of such lists, diaries and firsthand narratives gives modern-day Indian-influenced woodsmen—depending on the nuances of their historical personae—more options than just eating parched corn and jerk and wearing moccasins and a breech cloth. But besides inventories, firsthand accounts of frontier skills and articles used west of the Appalachians always intrigue today's Indian-influenced men of the cane. I will discuss some of the lesser-known facets of Woodlands art and craft, focusing on some of the more important skills and items overlooked by reenactors.

Delaware pouch by Mike Taylor. Copied from an original in the Heye Foundation. Brain-tanned deerskin bag (approximately 12 in. by 7 in.) has been dyed in black walnut hulls, quilled in colors of black, natural and yellow-orange and garnished with deer hair tufts in metal cones.

Photo by Michael J. Taylor

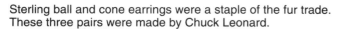

Sterling ball and cone earrings were a staple of the fur trade. These three pairs were made by Chuck Leonard.

Courtesy of Chuck Leonard

HIDES & BUCKSKIN

Those who emulate the dress of their native-influenced mentors know the advantages of brain-tanned buckskin for coats, moccasins and leggings. Smoked, brain-tanned leather warms the body, breathes well and has the "right look." If it gets wet it can be wrung out and rubbed back to its former self. Brain-tanned hides are not cheap. But there are authentic alternatives. To place these long-ignored tanning methods in context, it is helpful to know a few facts about the 18th century skin trade.

Besides being sewn into coats and breeches, deerskins were a common currency, but only those skins taken in the summer and fall. After the frosts, the deer's thick, hollow hair takes deep root and blood vessels in the dermis swell to feed the winter coat. In tanning methods of the day, leather made from winter hides was more prone to crack along vein lines. Hides tanned from summer-killed deer did not have this bent. "By Christmas," said one profiteer of the trade, "they are not worth hunting for" (Draper 31C: 50). Skins were readied for market by shaving off the hair and grain "with a knife, as a currier

dresses leather," then vigorously rubbed back and forth over a staking board until rendered soft and pliant to make them easier to pack. "Half-dressed skins," averaging 2-1/2 pounds each, were wrapped in bear hides in lots of 50, bound with buffalo tugs, "made by cutting hides round and round into long strips and twisting them," and the bundles loaded onto horses to take to market (Draper 2B: 181).

In the mid-1750s, Pennsylvania Indian trader James Logan sorted deerskins for sale in the white towns into three types: "Ordinary" skins sold for one shilling each; a "Fall" skin sold for one shilling and ninepence; and brain-tanned "Indian drest" deerskins cost three shillings and sixpence (Jennings 92). Since Anglo tanneries on the edge of white settlement used bark tanning or decoctions of salt, ashes and alum, I infer that the first long hunters across the Blue Ridge wore home-tanned leather, "Indian drest" leather or commercially tanned leather bought or traded for in the settlements.

Skins used for footwear might be tanned or half-dressed. Dr. Thomas Walker was hired by the Loyal Land Company of Albemarle County, Virginia, on December 12, 1749, "to go westward, in order to discover a proper place for settlement" (Johnson 6). By spring he and his men were fording the Rockcastle. On May 10, 1750, they "dressed an elk skin to

Close-up of modified short land-pattern Brown Bess showing Indian-influence. Note zigzag of red paint and inlay of irregular antique beads. This gun has been artificially aged. (Gun by John Bergmann.)

make Indian shoes." As the river swelled from rain the men stayed in a cave, he wrote, to "put our elk skin in order for shoes" (Johnson 59-60). On May 14 they used the shank of a fish hook and two horseshoe nails for awls and made their moccasins. For five woodsmen it would have been easy to flesh the hide, soak it till the hair slipped, half-dress it, then yank the damp skin over the end of a log or rock till it was soft enough to sew.

In April 1786 William Sudduth saw some Shawnee who had just "killed a buffalo and were busily engaged in cooking and making moccasins of the raw hide" (Beckner, "William Suddeth" 48). In the winter Kentuckians wore buffalo moccasins made of green hides. "We made socks to go over our shoes with buffalo skins, putting the wool inside," wrote Daniel Trabue (23-24). In snow and ice woodsmen wore two or three pairs of "buffalo socks" over their footwear. Hugh Bell said buffalo socks "would not easily saturate; at night they were taken off and thrown to one side away from the fire...for the buffalo moccasins were all the better for being frozen" (Draper 30S: 260-261).

"Shoe-packs were much in use," said Philip Bruner of Illinois, who described shoe-packs as "a kind of moccasin, made of undressed, unfinished leather...tanned with oak bark until the hair would rub off" (Draper 20S: 217). Such footwear was durable and cheap, being used when people could not afford leather. When the bottoms wore out, one sewed "on a sole of the same material with a whang" (Draper 20S: 217). But in wet weather, he said, shoe-packs did not keep the feet dry.

For chemical tanning water was warmed in thirty-gallon malt kettles, then alum, salt, ashes and deerskins were stirred in. When the hair slipped, hides were fleshed with a draw knife,

Belue's guns, both influenced by native culture. Top: "Aunt Bess," a short land-pattern Brown Bess, beaded with antique barley corn beads, 36-inch barrel, front and rear sights, leather sling, streaked with red paint and aged. Below: "Myra Janell," a transitional rifle of Reading, Pennsylvania, circa mid-1760s. It has a 46-inch swamped, .60 caliber Getz barrel with maple stock, Chambers round-faced English lock, Davis jaeger set triggers, jaeger sights, Edward Marshall 2-1/8 inch buttplate, Brown Bess wrist escutcheon, aged and inlaid with antique barley corn and cornaline d'allepo beads. (Guns by John Bergmann, Puryear, Tennessee.)

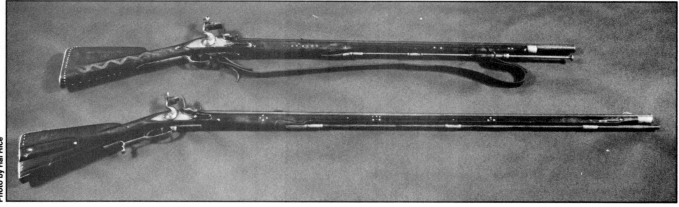

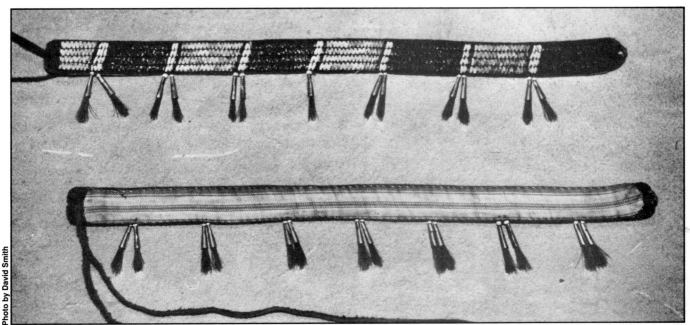

Front and back of Iroquois garters, circa 1760. Natural-dyed quills are embroidered on smoked, brain-tanned moosehide backed with pillow ticking dyed with black walnut hulls and sewn with linen thread. Garters embellished with human hair wrapped in homemade brass cones. (Made by Lally Bartman, Woodbury, Kentucky.)

then whipped over a beam until dry. This is how Peter Houston tanned hides at Boone's Station during the hard winter of 1779-1780 from which "trousers and jackets were made; principally for the men, but some of the women were under the necessity of wearing them" (Draper 20C: 84 [25]). To make heavyweight moccasin leather, Houston smeared a glop of alum, salt and ashes on buffalo robes to slip the wool, then tanned the skin. When robes were to be tanned with the wool on for quilts or saddle rugs, he only "covered the flesh side with the solution made the consistency of paste and after a few days, all of the flesh was removed and the hides pulled and rubbed until dry" (Draper 20C: 84 [26]). (For more on tanning, see the chapter, "Tools and Techniques of Bark Tanning," by Mark Odle in this book.)

At many forts pits were dug for white oak or sumac bark tanning. In 1790 John Evans Finlay cryptically recorded how settlers at one Kentucky station bark-tanned cowhides:

1) Take off the horns from the hides, then soak the blood out of them in ye water pool.

2) Then put ye hides into ye lime pit...carefully observe when the hair comes off, will be in a week or less—during this time draw them out twice a day letting them stay out 20 or 30 minutes to air.

3) Then unhair them, and put them into bast—bast them twice a week in cold weather and three times in warm. [word illegible] twice a day. Ye bast is a mixture of water and hen dung—You will know by the water when the lime is quite out of the hides then they are sufficiently basted, out of the bast rub hides with a rounding edge iron over a hollow tree out of ye bast.

4) Then handle them in a strong [word illegible] of bast in box or pit of bark—and 4 calf skins in a handler....leather is laid down in a clean pit—a layer of clean dry bark and a hide [and so on] and then pour on water and in four or five weeks raise and lay down as before. (Draper 12ZZ: 77)

Months later the skins were taken from the vats, beamed and oiled. Two men could tan 500 skins a year. But tanning was risky. By day tanners might get shot; at night Indians raided tanyards to take back what they saw as theirs. James Girty was shot while stealing hides "from the tan vats" at Bryan's Station in August 1782; the skin stopped the ball but the impact knocked Girty flat (Clark 53). At Boonesborough a hail of lead from the fort sent a band of Shawnee stealing hides from the tanyards scampering for cover (Draper 12CC: 199). Hide stealing was common. Thus not only did frontier whites wear commercial or home-tanned or Indian-tanned buckskin, but so did the warriors that raided their tanning vats.

For today's Indian-influenced woodsmen, then, there are well-documented alternatives to brain-tanned buckskin.

BELTS & SASHES

Spencer Records (1762-1849) lived in Kentucky near Washington and Limestone (Maysville) during the 1780s. Limestone was three miles north of Washington on the Ohio. Easy access to the river and to the web of buffalo traces emigrants took to the forts made the towns targets for raids stemming from as far away as the Great Lakes. Records helped defend the two towns. He scouted with Simon Kenton and knew Lewis Wetzel and Daniel Boone. Standing five feet eight, with long black hair and raven-hued eyes, Spencer often went bareheaded in the woods and wore a "dark, colored hunting shirt" belted around him (Draper 10BB: 27; 28 [43]). Lean and tanned, more than once he was taken for an Indian.

Spencer's dress is reminiscent of that of typical woodsmen as described by Joseph Doddridge in his *Notes on the*

Frank House is plainly dressed as a Bluegrass woodsman, circa 1770s, with plenty of Indian influence. Lally Bartman's attire is Woodland Indian, circa 1775, and some features are an overblouse, wrapped skirt and finger-woven sash by Dick Carney.

Settlement and Indian Wars of the Western Parts of Virginia and Pennsylvania, 1763-1783, published in 1824. "The hunting shirt was universally worn," he wrote. It "was a kind of loose frock, reaching half way down the thighs, with large sleeves, open before and so wide as to lap over a foot or more when belted." Commodious, caped, at times "handsomely fringed," hunting shirts were closed with a "belt, which was always tied behind." Elaborating on hunters who "became enamored of the Indian dress," he notes that "these belts were sometimes ornamented with some coarse kind of embroidery work" (qtd. in Kercheval 250-251).

Taken in context, Doddridge's description of such a "belt, which was always tied behind," was most likely a sash of woolen yarn. Sashes were tied off to the side (as seen in Peter Rindisbacher's early 19th century eyewitness sketches of voyageurs) or in back to keep the loose ends out of the way. Isaac Leffler's letter to Lyman Draper, dated June 6, 1862, makes this clear. In a close scrape years before Kentucky was settled, Leffler and Edmund Butts were fired on and an Indian rushed upon Butts, "caught the end of his belt, and it, being tied in a bow knot, it drew out" (Draper 6E: 85 [19]).

But Indian-influenced woodsmen wore leather belts too.

In 1820 Chester Harding traveled to Missouri to paint Daniel Boone "from the life," completing two half-lengths and one full-length portrait. In all three paintings, Boone is wearing a red weskit and a buckskin coat. In two the coat is trimmed with otter fur. That same year James O. Lewis engraved Harding's full-length painting. In the engraving Boone is dressed in a caped hunting coat belted with a leather belt buckled in front.

Similarly, in 1834 David Crockett hired John Gadsby Chapman to paint a likeness of him dressed in the garb of a Tennessee hunter. (The portrait appears on the dust jacket of *The Frontiersman: The Real Life and Many Legends of Davy Crockett* by Mark Derr.) Crockett went to some trouble—even rounding up three stray mongrels for props because Chapman's purebred hounds were not "authentic" enough—to make sure his gun, accoutrements and dress were that of a Cumberland Valley hunter (Derr 209). Chapman's oil was done years after the frontier had moved west, but it still reveals a lot about the dress of an Indian-influenced woodsman. Rifle, moccasins, side-seam leggings, tomahawk, shot bag and powderhorn are vividly shown, and Crockett's hunting shirt is cinched tight with a leather belt, buckle *forward*.

Early Woodland powder horn strap, circa 1760s. Natural dyed quills are embroidered on smoked, brain-tanned moosehide backed with pillow ticking dyed with black walnut hulls and sewn with linen thread. The horn, a whopping three-pounder, was made by virtuoso artisan of frontier Americana Frank House. (Strap by Lally Bartman, Woodbury, Kentucky.)

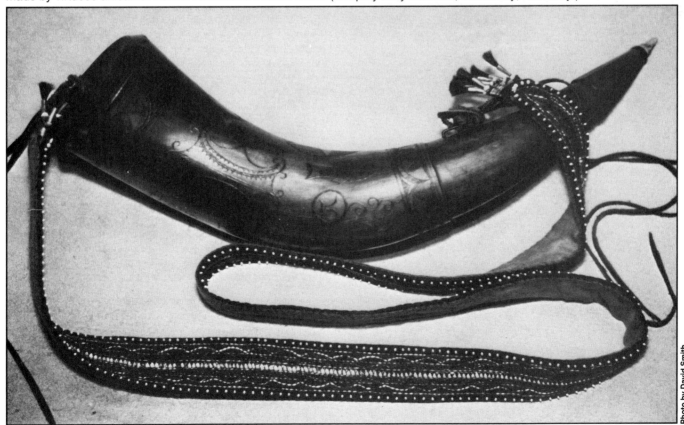

Photo by David Smith

HIDE BOATS, SHELTERS & HOPPUSSING BUNDLES

In the first far west, traveling by water was no problem for Indians and woodsmen able to make a buffalo hide boat. Such coracles were buoyant, had little draft and could be easily replaced. The inside was smoked and greased and the seams smeared with hot pitch to make them watertight. When pulled up on the bank, flipped over and propped up on sticks, hide boats became huts. Though unstable in high winds, such boats were versatile craft. In the 1770s Shawnee warriors crossing the Ohio at Maysville had a ferry made from four buffalo hides that held twenty men.

Trade silver was a stable commodity of the fur trade and worn by Indians and whites. One of today's masters of the art of silver craft is Chuck Leonard, shown here with his wife, Evie, at Fort Michilimackinac the summer of 1994.

White hunters used hide boats too. Daniel Boone's description of how he made a buffalo boat is not very detailed but does provide clues to how such boats were made. On one fall hunt in 1791 in the Kanawha Valley with his son, Nathan, Boone shot two or three bears and nine buffaloes. He "got a couple of long hickory poles, and made a hoop, and fastened the edges of a buffalo hide to it, making it bag down like the half of an egg, then ribbed it with poles, like a basket—longer than wide." One hide boat could carry 800 pounds, so Boone made several, placing "two and two alongside and one in the bow and stern," lashing them together with saplings (Draper 19S: 168). Using the meat for ballast, he floated his wild beef and bear bacon to market.

Nathan must have learned well. Years later, as captain of the United States Army dragoons, he elaborated on the construction of buffalo boats to his men patrolling the Missouri River:

Get poles a little larger than a man's wrist and split them and bend them over...for the ribs of a boat, making the boat 8 or 10 feet long according to the size of the skin, and four or five, or six feet wide....Lay the skin down with the hair next to the ribs and stretch it down to the whaling or rib which forms the gunwale of the boat, trim off the edges and cut loops through it and lash it along. (Branch 111-112)

Robes from buffalo killed in the spring were shaved clean of wool, tanned and sewn into bags. Bags for carrying were fitted with a burden strap up to fifteen feet long (called a "hoppus," a tumpline or a "Sapper's string") made of hemp or buffalo wool interwoven with nettle. The hoppus's center three-foot section was embroidered and 2-1/2 inches wide. From there it tapered to one inch at the ends. The wide part lay across the forehead or chest, so while lugging the burden, the budget sat high on the back. Hoppus's were used by woodsmen as a handy way to tote meat (Draper 4B: 142-43; Johnston 67).

If white hunters spotted buffalo, the men might wait until late afternoon before shooting to avoid alerting Indians. Then a few men stood guard as hide and gristle were severed by knives and tomahawks and the meat was boned and wrapped in buffalo hide bags—a hide usually made two—brought from the fort or made on the spot and laced with tugs. After the bags were each stuffed with 100 pounds of meat, they were tied off and swung across the saddle with tugs for the ride back to the fort. Solitary hunters on foot might tie tugs or a burden strap or a Sapper's string to the bundle and "hoppus the budget" upon their shoulders to lug the wild meat home (Draper 1A: 17-18, 95).

A hunter's shelter was often a half-faced camp—a three-sided lean-to with an open front. Half-faced shelters could be made any size, though most were no more than three or four feet tall in the back. Pegs driven into the ground against the side walls helped to stabilize them, while at the back the side logs were notched into the lower, rear wall. There was sometimes a large log at the back of most hunters' half-faced shanties; eight to ten feet from the back log two pairs of stakes were driven into the ground several inches apart to hold the

Parley in a canebrake. Cane (Arundinaria gigantea) once covered much of the Ohio and Cumberland Valley, rising to heights of forty feet, providing buffaloes with winter forage until spring when the grassy barrens turned green. Indians and whites sought cane thickets for cover, backing into them with ramrods in hand to flip up the cane to cover their trail as they plunged deeper into the brake.

Photo by David Smith

poles that made the shelter's sides. "The whole slope of the roof from the front to the back was [made of] slabs, skins, or...the bark of hickory or ash trees" (Jordan and Kaups 219-220). Moss was stuffed in the cracks to make the sides airtight. In 1747 Thomas Mitchell, an unlicensed Indian trader in western Pennsylvania, lived in "a rude shelter or shack, made of bark, branches, saplings, or logs" and the site appeared on local maps as a landmark called "Mitchell's Sleeping Place" (Hanna 1: 255).

Half-faced camps to be used for a season were tall enough in front for a man to stand in and were spacious enough to cache staples and peltry. Boone's family passed a fall and winter in a half-face. Benjamin Allen of Winchester, Kentucky, told John D. Shane that John Baker's half-face was built of red oak logs and big enough to keep "his family in one end and a barrel of whiskey in the other" (Beckner, "Interview with Allen" 68-69).[2] During the hard winter of 1779-1780 on his newly approved 400-acre tract on Boofman's Fork five or six miles from Boonesborough, Boone's party erected "half-faced camps made of boards and forked sticks" (O'Malley 173). William Sudduth's half-faced shed was "8 feet wide and 10 feet deep, covered over with puncheons and built up on three sides with logs." Once in a rainstorm he and John Wade "cut some poles and stretched a blanket" for a temporary shelter, then "cooked their supper and sat down to eat" (Beckner, "William Suddeth" 2: 53-54).

---

[2] The original transcript of Shane's interview with Allen is found in the Draper manuscripts (11CC: 67-69).

Like Indians, white hunters also made hide shelters. One used a "buffalo hide stretched across poles overhead for a covering from the damps and rains" (Draper 1A: 38). On the Green River in 1780, Daniel Trabue and his meat-getters lived in "a camp covered with buffalo hides" (Trabue 74). One old man living near Prestonsburg, Kentucky, "had a meat house that was made out of buffalo hides" (Draper 13CC: 244). In a storm in 1784, Spencer Records and Alexander McConnell camped under an elkhide on poles. Casper Mansker stayed in a "skin house," possibly a three-sided shelter made from buffalo hides or perhaps a half-faced camp used as a base camp to store peltry. Mansker made two buffalo boats and a hide hut in 1794 during the Nickojack War in Tennessee (Draper 6XX: 72).

Often, when the winter winds howled, white hunters built their fires as Indians did: narrow, many yards long, and knee-high or higher. Lieutenant-Governor Henry Hamilton of Detroit jotted in his journal on the night of November 16, 1778, that in Indian camps "large fires are kindled before which they lie in rows on each side with their feet towards the fire. At their heads are placed their arms leaning on a rock" (Barnhart 122). Blankets or skins were laid on beds of cane or boughs. Sleeping in such parallel lines made strategic sense too. "If any noise is made," said Hamilton, "or alarm is given, the first who hears it touches his neighbor and the whole are roused in silence and take to their arms without bustle or confusion" (Barnhart 122).

Though modern-day Indian-influenced woodsmen may not have the means to get buffalo hides for shelters, budgets, hoppusing bundles or boats, or to make bark and log half-faced huts for weekend "long hunts," perhaps these glimpses of their forebears of kindred spirit will inspire some to try. For the benefit of those hardy folk in fall and winter camps who find they must steadily fight their way to the fire pit, only to be sooner or later elbowed back out in the cold by their chilled, red-faced comrades, reenactors would do well to emulate the fire-building methods of their native kinsmen.

FOOD FOR THE TRAIL

The last topic to be discussed is food or, more precisely, food for the trail. What did our Indian-influenced forebears eat? Bluntly, they ate what they could carry with them, what they could forage and what they could kill along the way. Besides wild meat roasted over low flames, deer, elk and buffalo meat were "jerked" and toted by the haversack full.

For white woodsmen jerking meat was easy as long as Indians did not see the blue-gray plumes of smoke rising from the fire that cured and dried the meat. In a letter to Lyman Draper, George Michael Bedinger explained the process. Four forked saplings five or six feet tall were cut and pounded upright in the ground. Parallel poles were placed across the forks and transversing the poles a number of small, straight sticks were laid three or four inches apart. Slicing the beef with the grain into long strips a half inch thick and weighing up to a pound, Bedinger laid the fillets on top of the rack and kindled a small fire underneath. Blankets stretched overhead "as protection against the night dews" kept buzzards from flying off with the next day's dinner (Draper 1A: 35). It might take two days of smoking until the meat was deemed "jerked."

Some smoking racks were made lower to the ground. In Kentucky in 1775, Nicholas Cresswell described how he made buffalo jerk:

The meat is first cut from the bones in thin slices like beef steaks, then four forked sticks are stuck in the ground in a square form and small sticks laid on these forks in the form of a gridiron about three feet from the ground. The meat is laid on this and a slow fire put under it, and turned until it is done. (Cresswell 75-76)

Parched corn was a staple for Indians and their Long Knife counterparts. Pounded into meal, mixed with maple sugar, beans or peas and nuts, such a gruel was light, nutritious and sustaining. As Henry Hamilton observed, it was "a provision which they are seldom without" (Barnhart 123). In 1781 at Detroit, American captive Robert Orr wrote:

...when Indians go to war [they] prepare a mixture of parched corn pounded fine and mixed with sugar and sometimes chestnuts and beans. Each one will have a small bag of this mixture with a little dry venison—it is palatable and strengthening and is used very sparingly and lasts them a long time as they only use it when within our borders and [are] afraid to shoot [for fear of] alarming the whites, but in their coming and returning home they can kill enough by the way they need and roast it or boil it—they can make a small vessel of bark...and fill it with water and put their meat into it and have some stones heated hot and put them into the vessel and cook them. (Draper 6NN: 179)

Besides game and maize, other edibles could be had, depending on where one lived. While among the Cherokee near Chota, Tennessee, in 1761, Henry Timberlake feasted on buffalo and deer and on "potatoes, pumpkins, hominy, boiled corn and peas....not to mention a number of other vegetables imported from Europe...which flourish as much or more here" (Williams 57ff). At Harrod's Town, Kentucky, on June 14, 1775, James Nourse dined on "boiled beef and buffalo, bacon and young cabbage plants, fritters, hominy and wheat bread." Another day he feasted on buffalo stew, endive and lettuce. An excellent meal, he remarked, "as good as ever I would wish...but no bread." On the banks of Ohio River, Nourse swapped a traveler a hunk of bacon for two catfish and took "an iron pot with half a pint of water and between each layer, butter, pepper and salt, putting sticks to keep the fish from the bottom and then put the fire over and under the pot." Fish cooked in such a way was "a good dish for those that loved seasoned meat" (Nourse 29.2: 127). At a frolic at a Kentucky station, one chef with an odd sense of wit roasted a few whole shoats "with an Irish potato stuck in the one end of each and a sweet potato in the other" (Draper 12C: 56).

In 1776 at Detroit, Henry Hamilton noted that "wheat, Indian corn, barley, oats, peas, and buckwheat yield a great increase" (Barnhart 16-17). On August 23, 1778, Hamilton ordered for his Miami allies, "15 large pirouges of supplies...26,800 lbs. of flour in bags, 24 firkins of butter, 37 half-barrels of pork and 31 bales of dry goods" (Barnhart 16-17; 103-104).

With Hamilton's memorandum, I end this section on trail food and close my chronicle.

Besides what is presented here, whether in regard to food, clothing, shelters or accoutrements, there is so much more that could be written. Yet, perhaps I have opened a door for some by giving a true glimpse of Indian-influenced woodsmen and marginal men—unique, complex individuals, cast from dies of conflicting cultures and blurred alliances. They found their way and etched themselves into history. We can do no better but to find our own.

DEDICATION

A week before I began writing this chapter I was in Oklahoma visiting a few of the Bird Creek Shawnee and attending the Skiatook Powwow. In the course of things, I explained to Robert Sisk, a Shawnee, my caution in accepting this literary task. He encouraged me to go on with it but suggested I present marginal types not as "white Indians" or, even worse, as "white savages," but rather as men who were "Indian-influenced." So I have. My thanks to Robert for his insights and to his family, who took me in and treated me with kindness and put up with my awkward stomp dancing. It is to the Sisk family and to all Shawnee, past and present, of the Eastern Shawnee, Absentee Shawnee, Loyal Shawnee and the Shawnee Indian Nation United Remnant Band, that this essay is dedicated.

I would like to thank the following: Mark Ball, Lally Bartman, John Bergmann, Bibliotheque Nationale (Paris), Warren "Hawk" Boughton, Marcus Cope, Randy Corse, Sharon Cunningham, David Damer, Larry Doyle, Jim Dresslar, Filson Club, Tony Gerard, Dwight Girty, Gray Stone Press, Neal O. Hammon, Houston Harrison, Frank House, Jack Hubbard, Simon Jones and Ann O'Leary of Merseyside Museums (Liverpool), Kentucky Historical Society, Tom Lawrence and his 2nd Company boys, Chuck Leonard, Peter Matthiessen, Missouri Historical Society, Richard Meyers, Tom Nagel, Canadian Museum of Civilization (Ottawa), Tim Nichols, Pathfinder Press, Roger Ressel, William H. Scurlock, David Smith, State Historical Society of Wisconsin, Tennessee Valley Authority—Land Between the Lakes, Lee Teter, Bobby Thompson, Jack Turbeville, Chance Watson and George "Butch" Winter.

At Murray State University, in Murray, Kentucky, I wish to express my appreciation to the librarians at the Forrest C. Pogue Special Collections Library—Dr. Keith Heim, Dr. Ernie Bailey, Susie Adams and Dortha Bailey—and to interlibrary loan librarian Aleeah McGinnis at the Harry Lee Waterfield Library. Dr. Jerry A. Herndon, Department of English, and Dr. Ken Wolf, Department of History, helped proof the manuscript. Photographer Hal Rice, Faculty Resource Center, helped with illustrations.

Finally, I am especially humbled by my debt to Frank and Myra Belue, Lavina Belue, Michael J. Taylor and David Wright.

APPENDIX A: WORKS CITED

Alvord, Clarence Walworth, and Clarence Edwin Carter, eds. *Trade and Politics 1767-1769*. 20 vols. Springfield: Illinois State Historical Library, 1921. Vol. 3: 230-231; 391-405.

Baldwin, Carl R. *Captains of the Wilderness*. Belleville, IL: Tiger Rose, 1986.

Balesi, Charles J. *The Time of the French in the Heart of North America, 1673-1818*. Chicago: Alliance Francaise, 1992.

Barnhart, John D., ed. *Henry Hamilton and George Rogers Clark in the American Revolution; with the Unpublished Journal of Lieutenant Governor Henry Hamilton*. Crawfordsville, IN: Banta, 1961.

Beckner, Lucien. "A Sketch of the Early Adventures of William Suddeth in Kentucky." *Filson Club History Quarterly* 2 (1928): 44-70.

___. "John D. Shane's Interview with Pioneer William Clinkenbeard." *Filson Club History Quarterly* 2 (1928): 95-128.

___. "John D. Shane's Interview with Benjamin Allen, Clark County." *Filson Club History Quarterly* 5 (1931): 63-98.

Bishop, Julia Truitt. "Old Papers Give Lights as to How Daniel Boone Ran His Store." *The Kentucky Explorer* June 1993: 38ff.

Boston, David. "The Three Caldwells." *The White Horse and Fleur De Lys* June 1964: 316-317.

Branch, E. Douglas. *The Hunting of the Buffalo*. 2nd ed. Lincoln: University of Nebraska Press, 1962.

Brasser, Ted J. *"Bo'jou Neejee!" Profiles in Canadian Indian Art*. Ottawa: National Museum of Man; Apex P, 1970.

Butterfield, Consul Wilshire. *History of the Girtys*. 2nd. ed. Columbus, OH: Long's College Book, 1950.

Calloway, Colin C. "Neither White nor Red: White Renegades on the American Indian Frontier." *Western Historical Quarterly* 17.1 (1986): 43-66.

___. "Simon Girty: Interpreter and Intermediary." *Being and Becoming Indian: Biographical Studies of North American Frontiers*. Ed. James A. Clifton. Prospect Heights, IL: Waveland Press, 1989. 38-58.

Clark, Thomas D., ed. *The Voice of the Frontier: John Bradford's Notes on Kentucky*. Lexington: University Press of Kentucky, 1993.

Cresswell, Nicholas. *The Journal of Nicholas Cresswell 1774-1777*. 2nd ed. New York: Dial Press, 1928.

Derleth, August William. *Vincennes: Portal to the West*. Englewood Cliffs, NJ: Prentice-Hall, 1968.

Derr, Mark. *The Frontiersman: The Real Life and Many Legends of Davy Crockett*. New York: William Morrow, 1993.

Draper, Lyman C. Manuscript Collection. 486 vols. Microfilm ed. Madison: State Historical Society of Wisconsin, 1980.

Finiels, Nicolas de. *An Account of Upper Louisiana*. Eds. Carl J. Ekberg and William E. Foley. Trans. Carl J. Ekberg. Lincoln: University of Nebraska Press, 1980.

Ford, Alice, ed. *Audubon, By Himself*. New York: Natural History Press, 1969.

Guild, Jo. C. *Old Times in Tennessee*. 2nd ed. Knoxville: Tenase, 1971.

Hanna, Charles A. *The Wilderness Trail*. 2 vols. New York: Knickerbocker Press, 1911.

Haywood, John. *The Civil and Political History of the State of Tennessee*. 2nd ed. Knoxville: Tenase, 1969.

Heckewelder, John. *History, Manners, and Customs of Indian Nations*. Facsimile reprint. Bowie, MD: Heritage Books, 1990.

Hoffman, Phillip. "Simon Girty." *The American Revolution 1775-1783: An Encyclopedia*. 2 vols. Ed. Richard L. Blanco. New York: Garland Publishing, 1993. Vol. 1: 660-664.

Jennings, Francis. *The Invasion of America: Indians, Colonialism, and the Cant of Conquest*. New York: Norton, 1976.

Johnson, J. Stoddard. *First Explorations of Kentucky*. Filson Club Publications Number 13. Louisville: Morton, 1898.

Johnston, Charles. *A Narrative of the Incidents Attending the Capture, Detention, and Ransom of Charles Johnston*. 2nd ed. Cleveland: Burrows Brothers, 1905.

Jones, Simon. Archivist at Merseyside Museums, Liverpool. Personal correspondence. 19 August 1994.

Jordan, Terry G., and Mattie Kaups. *The American Backwoods Frontier: An Ethnic and Ecological Interpretation*. Baltimore: John Hopkins University Press, 1989.

Kercheval, Samuel. *A History of the Valley of Virginia*. 4th ed. Strasborg, VA: Shenandoah Publishing, 1925.

Lester, William Stewart. *The Transylvania Colony*. Spencer, IN: Samuel Guard, 1935.

Lobdell, Jared C., ed. *Recollections of Lewis Bonnett, Jr. (1775-1850) and the Bonnett and Wetzel Families*. Bowie, MD: Heritage, 1991.

Nourse, James. "Journey to Kentucky in 1775." *The Journal of American History* 29.2 (1925): 121-138; 29.3: 251-260; 29.4: 351-364.

O'Malley, Nancy. *"Stockading Up": A Study of Pioneer Stations in the Inner Bluegrass Region of Kentucky*. Archaeological Report 127. Frankfort: Kentucky Heritage Council, 1987.

Phillips, Ruth B. *Patterns of Power*. Klienburg, Canada: McMichael Canadian Collection, 1984.

Potter, Dorothy Williams. *Passports of Southeastern Pioneers: 1770-1823*. Baltimore: Gateway Press, 1982.

Putnam, A. W. *History of Middle Tennessee*. 2nd ed. Knoxville: University of Tennessee Press, 1971.

Quaife, Milo Milton, ed. *The Indian Captivity of O. M. Spencer*. New York: Citadel Press, 1968.

Smith, James. *An Account of the Remarkable Occurrences in the Life and Travels of Col. James Smith*. 2nd ed. Cincinnati: Robert Clarke, 1870.

Thwaites, Reuben Gold, ed. *The Jesuit Relations and Allied Documents*. 73 vols. New York: Pageant Books, 1959.

Trabue, Daniel. *Westward into Kentucky: The Narrative of Daniel Trabue*. Ed. Chester Raymond Young. Lexington: University Press of Kentucky, 1981.

White, Richard. *The Middle Ground: Indians, Empires, and Republics in the Great Lakes Region, 1650-1815*. New York: Cambridge University Press, 1991.

Williams, Samuel Cole, ed. *Lieut. Henry Timberlake's Memoirs, 1756-1765*. 2nd ed. Marrietta, GA: Continental Book, 1948.

APPENDIX B: FEATURED ARTISANS

Please enclose a SASE with all correspondence.

Lally Bartman
108 North Church Street
Woodbury, KY 42288
—*Quillwork*

The 18th Century Gentleman's Shoppe
Don and Marion Ekola
12167 S.R. 24
Grand Rapids, OH 43522
—*Trade silver, clothing, historic jewelry*

Frank House
4178 Woodbury Loop
Woodbury, KY 42288
—*Aged guns, knives, pipe tomahawks*

Jack Hubbard
Box 99
Dunbar, KY 42219
—*Aged knives and shot bags*

Chuck Leonard
2013 E. Kimmel
Jackson, MI 49201
—*Trade silver*

Richard Meyers
1559 Eight Mile Road
Cincinnati, OH 45255
—*Indian-style guns*

Michael J. Taylor
233 Rockaway Avenue, #4
Cincinnati, OH 45233
—*Quillwork, gastowehs, finger weaving*

Art & Writing on the Frontier

by Cathy Johnson

Cathy Johnson has been interested in living history for 30 years. Her first job was as an interpreter at the Old Jail Museum in Independence, Missouri. Beginning with an interest in Civil War reenacting, she has worked backwards to 1812 (and earlier). Most often she is to be found at Missouri's Historic Fort Osage drawing or painting on site or in the nearby woods collecting specimens. Johnson is corresponding secretary for the Friends of Fort Osage and a member of the Coalition of Historical Trekkers.

Johnson has written seventeen books on a variety of subjects and is a contributing editor for the living history journal *The Female Spectator Revived*, *The Artist's Magazine* and *Country Living,* for whom she is also staff naturalist. She has written for periodicals as diverse as *Early American Life*, *Science Digest*, *Harrowsmith*, *Sports Afield* and *MUZZLELOADER*. Much of this chapter is taken from Johnson's newest book, *Living History; Drawing on the Past*. Recently Johnson has started her own company, Graphics/Fine Arts Press, publishing works related to her interests in history and nature.

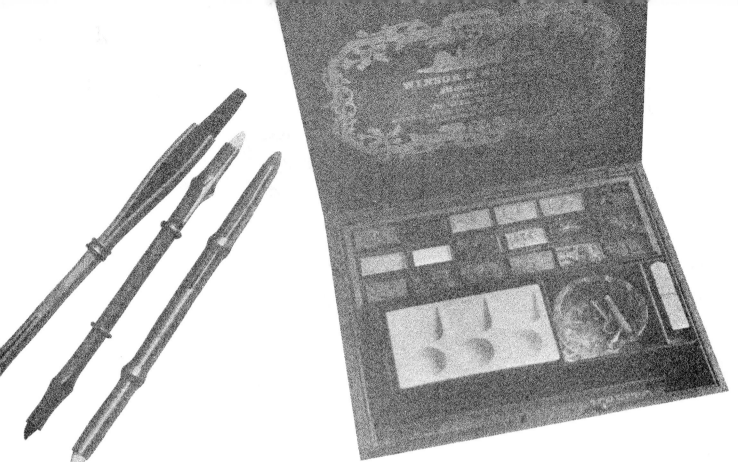

The names of George Catlin, Karl Bodmer, Albert Bierstadt and Alfred Jacob Miller may be first on our roll call when we think of artists on the frontier. Washington Irving, Zebulon Pike, John C. Fremont (and his chronicler/spouse Jessie), and the journal-keepers of the Lewis and Clark Corps of Discovery may come to mind when we think of the writers and journalists of this country's past. And, among other adventurous souls, these were all certainly important in recording their treks among the wildlife, the landscape and peoples of the American West. The records they left—visual and written—tell us all we know of westward expansion. But we should broaden our perspective, not think only of paintings of Indians and their living conditions or chronicles of exploration west of the Mississippi.

The Western frontier was not an indelible line on somebody's map to mark the eastern edge of the Rocky Mountains. The Western frontier began where the first explorer set foot on these shores, and it just kept moving, at least in the minds of the European settlers, each time they pressed westward, displacing native peoples and wildlife. It didn't become static until we had pushed it all the way to the Hawaiian Islands and settled virtually everything in between.

In the beginning the frontier was the New World itself; explorers from Sir Francis Drake to Captain Cook brought their artists with them to record their finds for posterity—or for king and country. The frontier was also 1585 Roanoke Island when John White, the first governor, painted the fish, birds and native peoples he found there, carefully recording what he learned. The frontier was coastal Carolina and Virginia where Mark Catesby explored the birds, animals and plants of this new territory and kept a written record of his finds and working methods. The frontier was northern Colonial New York where Jane Colden illustrated the first natural history of plants in that region with some 300 pen and ink drawings. Jane was the daughter of Cadwallader Colden, scientist and friend of naturalist John Bartram and the inimitable Benjamin Franklin.

As pioneers moved westward from the original Colonies, art and artists, as well as writers, moved with them. Liwwät Böke, an unfamiliar name to most of us, captured frontier Ohio in her pen and ink sketches. They stand as the record of the newly populated land. Böke was also a writer, poet, historian, linguist, immigrant, wife and mother who somehow found time to draw literally hundreds of things (Knapke).

Courtesy of Minster County Historical Society, Minster, Ohio

Liwwät Böke sketch of flatboat on the Ohio.

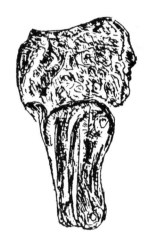

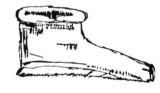

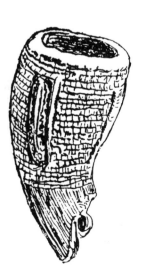

"Indian tobacco pipes from our woods at St. John."
Liwwät Böke Journal, 1844.

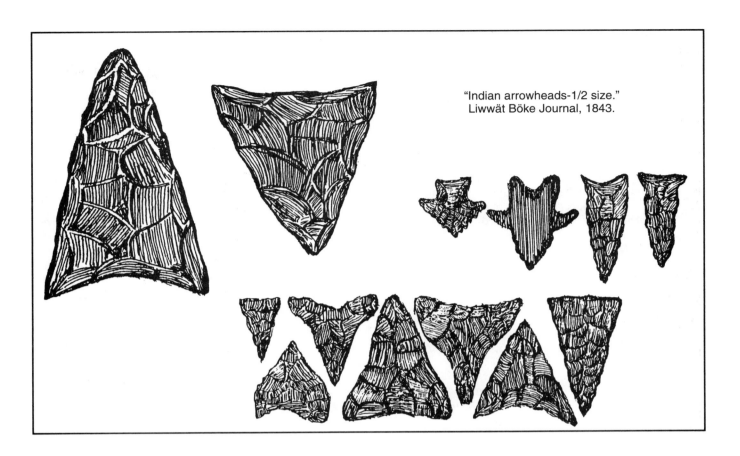

"Indian arrowheads-1/2 size."
Liwwät Böke Journal, 1843.

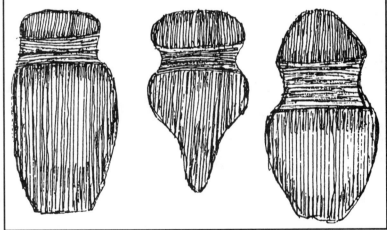

"Indian axes from our woods and fields-1/2 size."
Liwwät Böke Journal, 1843.

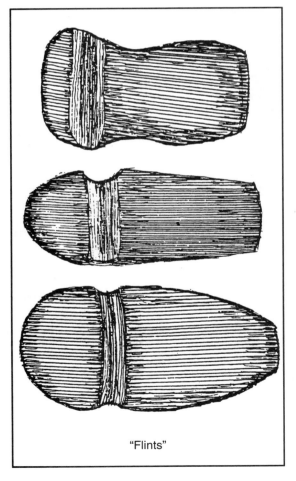

"Flints"

Margaret Van Horn Dwight experienced frontier travel in 1810 Ohio and kept a journal to chronicle the trip for a cousin back East.

Major Stephen Long's 1819 expedition also included "Thos. Say, Zoologist, &c., T.R. Peale, assistant Naturalist, and Saml. Seymour, Landscape Painter" (Edwin 425). Interestingly enough, Titian Peale was much better known as an artist than as a naturalist, and Say was described by Audubon as an entomologist. Say's wife, Lucy, illustrated several books of his findings.

In 1833 the young Swiss artist Karl Bodmer was hired by Prince Maximilian to accompany a journey that retraced much of Lewis and Clark's route. Although his paintings of native Americans are the most familiar images, *Karl Bodmer's America* includes many seascapes, landscapes, settlements, people and natural history illustrations, from the East Coast, Louisiana and the frontier settlement of New Harmony, Indiana (Hunt and Gallagher).

While at New Harmony, Bodmer painted the artist-naturalist Charles-Alexandre Leseuer at his work. Leseuer was a Frenchman who set out along the Mississippi and the Great Lakes area, making sketches along the way. One of his sketches of a tiny settlement appears in *American Canvas: The Art, Eye, and Spirit of Pioneer Artists*. Entitled *Tyawapatia Bottom or Commercetown on the Mississippi in Missouri* and painted on April 13, 1826, it consists of only a cabin and a cleared field (Erisman 122).

Alexis de Toqueville describes a similar cabin in *Journey to America* of 1831:

Like the field around it, this rustic dwelling shows every sign of new and hurried work. It is seldom more than 30 feet long. It is 20 feet wide and 15 high. Both its walls and its roof are made of unsquared tree-trunks between which moss and earth have been rammed to keep the cold and rain out....A resinous fire crackles on the hearth....Over this rustic fire one sees trophies of war or hunt: a long rifle, a deerskin, some eagle's feathers...by it on a single shelf of ill-squared planks are a few tattered books; there one finds a Bible with its cloth and boards already worn out by the piety of two generations, a prayerbook and, sometimes, a poem of Milton or a tragedy of Shakespeare.

(qtd. in Erisman 122)

It appears that even on the frontier, reading was important, for many inventories, wills and advertisements list books among the more mundane items.

Bodmer painted the twin of this cabin in *A Settler's Farm in Indiana* (Hunt and Gallagher pl. 73). In his journal Maximilian describes a more somber scene of children outside one cabin gnawing on the bones of wild turkey with the family dogs, a single bed visible through the door of "the dark hut." But Bodmer's painting looks more inviting. In the background a woman hangs clean clothes on a line and neat fences surround the log cabin and its door yard. Her husband rides away while a child watches—both indistinct penciled figures.

The business arrangements between Bodmer and the Prince

After Karl Bodmer: *The Travellers Meeting with Minatarre Indians,* engraving with aquatint, hand-colored. Completed after return of the 1832-1834 North American expedition led by Prince Maximilian of Wied-Neuwied, Germany.

ZUSAMMENKUNFT DER REISENDEN MIT MONNITARRI INDIANERN

RENCONTRE DES VOYAGEURS AVEC DES INDIENS MEUNITARRI

THE TRAVELLERS MEETING WITH MINATARRE INDIANS

were at first too restrictive for the artist. The Prince was to supply paper "and other needs." Although Bodmer was expected to bring his own equipment, all pictures would remain the property of the Prince. The artist would be permitted to make copies but could exhibit them only with his employer's permission. Irritated that these arrangements did not fully reflect earlier discussions, Bodmer complained that the proposed salary was inadequate and "that it would be unrealistic of his patron to claim all paintings, such as trees and foreground, which he would surely want to paint for himself during his spare time....But in the end he [the Prince] relented and...agreed to raise Bodmer's salary. Moreover, the artist could keep twelve studies of his own as well as copy landscapes on his return and even publish them," still, however, after a period determined by the Prince (Hunt and Gallagher 353).

In 1837 big game hunter and adventurer William Drummond Stewart brought Alfred Jacob Miller along to record his finds, to our unending benefit. Despite the romanticized and sometimes inaccurate nature of some of Miller's works, his images of native Americans and their camps are illuminating. Many of these can be seen in the Gilcrease Museum in Tulsa, Oklahoma.

Young George Caleb Bingham moved from Virginia with his family into the new state of Missouri. There he painted unforgettable images of the growing frontier settlements, the Missouri River and its trappers and traders and flat boatmen from his home in Arrow Rock, Missouri, a few miles down river from Fort Osage. (Bingham's home is now open to the public in this small river town.)

Other names, like John Mix Stanley, Alfred Tait, David Johnson, Gustav Sohon and the Kern brothers are less recognizable than Bingham, Bodmer and Catlin. Anna Maria Von Phul visited St. Louis in 1818 and painted the first known watercolors of its people, buildings and landscapes. The little-known Maria Martin helped Audubon in the 1830s, working on volumes two and four of his famous portfolios as well as illustrating John Edwards Holbrooks' *North American Herpetology*. Nicholas Point's small sketches are interesting and informative. From John White's 1585 paintings to the dawning of the age of the camera, the images made by artists— amateur and professional, accomplished works and doodles— tell us much of what we know of our natural history as well as our human history, the land and our day-to-day lives.

Writers and journalists (in the broad sense of the word, those who kept journals) were more common than artists, but the records they left may be less familiar. In fact library shelves are full of their accounts of the West. Here you'll find more formal accounts as well as diaries, journals and letters. Contemporary accounts in newspaper articles are also available, bound or on microfilm. The *Louisiana Gazette* in St. Louis carried a number of articles describing the lands to the west, as did many periodicals of the time. (Public libraries as well as university and research libraries are excellent places

Indian Squaw by Anna Maria Von Phul.

Creole Cart and Driver by Anna Maria Von Phul.

to find these, as are many museums.)

Among those who could write, keeping a record of their day-to-day lives was quite common. Some of these personal accounts, meant originally only for their own use, later became books published for a larger audience. These men and women left us a great deal to go on—what they did and what they saw, if not what tools they might have used to work with. Thanks to them, we have many fascinating sources we now use as primary documentation.

Explorers, scientists, travelers, missionaries and just plain folks kept written records. Whether sending reports to the government back East, writing novels or books of their travels and discoveries, recording their capture by Indians, crafting treatises to attract settlers, sending dispatches to newspapers worldwide or making notes in their own diaries or journals, writers of the period give us an enduring account of early America. Personal letters, such as the voluminous correspondence of John James Audubon, tell us a great deal of our history. Court records, wills and probates, indentures, minutes of Quaker meetings and other official documents round out the picture that begins with an individual with a pen in hand.

These are priceless records for an historian, though many were crafted simply for their author's own enjoyment. Abby May, 24 years old in 1800, wrote, "So long as a scrap of paper remains, I shall keep scribbling." Abigail Adams, wife of our

second president, noted "...when there is no writing there is less pleasure in working" (Sprigg frontmatter). Like the special and individual motives of these "scribblers," there were as many reasons for making art as there were artists.

Many scientists, especially naturalists (an early catchall term that covered disciplines from botany to geology) captured their subjects with pencil and paint as well as in the form of skins and pressed plant samples. Mark Catesby left wonderful paintings of the flora and fauna of the Tidewater. William Bartram (son of John), also a naturalist, was noted for his artistic talents.

Map-makers used ink, graphite and watercolor to chart this new world. These cartographers often embellished their maps with fine or fanciful illustrations of sea beasts, ships under full sail or the curious and beautiful things they actually saw in the New World. In *The Mapping of North America: Three Centuries of Map-Making 1500-1860*, many of the early maps are illuminated with real or imagined native Americans. Color was used to highlight land features, clarify details or to provide decoration. A wall chart-sized map of America by Henri-Abraham Chatelain (1719) may have been inaccurate, as many maps of the time were (California was shown as a large island off the coast), but it is wonderfully complex and decorated with details that betray careful observation as well as talent (Goss 116).

Many military academy students were trained in the use

Creole Woman by Anna Maria Von Phul.

From *Our Western Border 100 Years Ago* by
Charles McKnight, 1876.

Some of the military men who left us their paintings, drawings and journal sketches were Lieutenant Richard Bryon, who painted *View of a Long Wharf and Part of the Harbor of Boston, 1764* (Davidson pl. 36) and Captain Ashley Brown, whose diary is in the collection of the Marblehead Historical Society, Marblehead, Massachusetts.

Many pieces were made for religious purposes. Not only the native Americans appreciated the symbolic nature of art. Early Shakers created "theorem paintings" that expressed their beliefs in color and ink. Father Nicholas Point, a Jesuit missionary who was also an artist, architect and college educator, set out for the Bitterroot Valley with Father Pierre-Jean De Smet in 1841. Fr. Point used his drawings to teach and convert the Salish Indians to Christianity saying, "I made great effort to speak to them through pictures....Some scenes showed the mysteries; others, the sacraments. This method of instruction had two noticeable advantages. While the truths entered their souls through the eyes, the great virtues were infused into their hearts" (qtd. in Peterson and Peers 108). His many intricate paintings and drawings tell us a great deal about the native peoples, traveling conditions and clothing of 1841.

From *Our Western Border 100 Years Ago*. Published in 1876.

of watercolor for map-making and landscape painting, not as a pleasant pastime but to aid their possible work as spies and military tacticians in the days before the surveillance camera:

...artists traveled on voyages of discovery, and it is hardly surprising that the British navy, then a great power in the world [circa 1750], should be fully cognizant of the value of having artists make topographic studies and charts of both friendly and potentially hostile harbors and havens. Artists, often working in watercolor, therefore performed the tasks that today are carried out by reconnaissance aircraft and spy satellites. Similarly, the British army recognized the value of having artists who could provide gunners with a knowledge of any given terrain that might be of strategic importance; as part of their training, artillery officers at the Royal Military Academy at Woolrich acquired a rudimentary expertise in draftsmanship and watercolor painting. (Finch 15)

Sometimes the purpose of art was to entice settlers to this new land, whether Ohio, Kentucky or the Far West. It performed the same function as many of the books penned by travelers. Some of our most magnificent landscape paintings were of this school. Other times art was simply decorative. When he visited New York in 1750, Peter Kalm described the houses of the town, which was then smaller than Boston or Philadelphia. They were "whitewashed within, and I did not anywhere see wall paper....The walls were covered with all sorts of drawings and pictures in small frames" (Kalm 132).

The flamboyant Audubon is today a household name, a name he earned with paintbrush, gun and a certain flair for self-promotion. He paid his dues through years of hard work, hardship and poverty, as did his family. His wife, Lucy, supported the family for many years, believing in his work as he did himself. Audubon's confidence in his work was shaken on only one occasion, when three years' worth of bird paintings were lost to Norway rats. After a few bleak days of self-questioning, Audubon was again in the field, working to replace them with the thought, "Now I can do them better."

Audubon's journals and letters are as interesting as his paintings. Here we read of the American frontier from the early to the mid-19th century, when he took his last trip to the West. We read of his meeting with Daniel Boone, the painter Alexander Wilson, "the eccentric naturalist" Rafinesque, and others. We get a surprisingly complete narrative of an Independence Day celebration in Kentucky and a step-by-step account of how to load a flintlock rifle; you could do it from his description alone. In addition we get a feeling for the hardships he endured in order to reach his goal of painting all the birds of North America—and later, the mammals—from life.

Less trained or talented artists sketched for their own information and entertainment. William Clark sketched in his diary of the 1803-1805 expedition to supplement the hundreds of samples collected, drawing birds, fish and sketches of the Flathead Indians' custom of forming their infants' heads into the desired shape using pressure applied by means of a board tied to tender young skulls. Prince Maximilian's first two volumes were published before his more celebrated trip to the American West with Bodmer. He illustrated them himself with accurate if not particularly inspired drawings.

If it weren't for these records in words, drawings and paintings, we would know much less about the country as it was in the early days of America. The dodo bird and the passenger pigeon (the Pigeon of Passage, as Mark Catesby called it) would be not only extinct but forgotten.

Many annotated personal diaries of the period give us intimate glimpses of private lives. Travelers who crossed the Appalachians and on to Santa Fe and California filled thousands of pages with their observations and sketches. In the National Frontier Trails Museum in Independence, Missouri, there are many examples. Among others, James Wilkins, William Henry Jackson, J. Goldsborough Bruff and Paul Kane drew or painted the landscape as well as their fellow travelers.

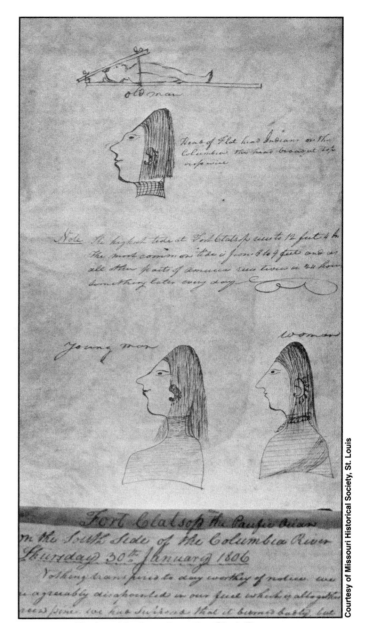

Flathead Indians from the Clark Papers.

Wilkins was both journalist and artist, noting on June 19, 1849:

Camped tonight in the vicinity of Courthouse Rock. This is an immense rock in the shape of a building standing alone in the prairie....Took a sketch of it.

July 10:

Passed that noted rock called Independence Rock....Five miles further on we came to the Devil's Gate. This is a great curiosity, being a gap in the mountains, for the passage of the Sweetwater River, through which it leaps and boils with fury. The sides of the gap are so perpendicular as to leave no room even for a foot passenger to pass...I regret I could not pass two or three hours here to finish the sketch of it more highly.[1]

[1] Quoted from display at National Frontier Trails Museum, Independence, Missouri.

Views of oxen being yoked, fording the Platte River, tents and wagons, mountains and deserts, give us an indelible picture of early-day travel and its hardships. Kane's *Willamette Valley at Champoeg* is an ink and watercolor wash drawing of a broad landscape near the end of the trail. Bruff's *Preparing to Feed* shows cooking on buffalo-chip fuel; if you ever doubted, here's primary documentation.

Some writers of the period were influenced by and aware of art, even if they didn't make it themselves. Author/attorney Henry Marie Brackenridge, who kept a journal of his 1809 trek up the Missouri River, which included the naturalists John Bradbury and Thomas Nuttall as well as Manuel Lisa and Wilson P. Hunt, remarked, "...The Council bluffs are not abrupt elevations, but a rising ground, covered with grass as perfectly smooth as if the work of art" (Brackenridge 78). And again, "The sky is as clear as that represented in Chinese painting" (91). Brackenridge was apparently well-educated and somewhat cosmopolitan, aware of the artwork of other cultures.

Prince Maximilian had Karl Bodmer for the more formal illustrations, but he still continued to draw. His personal journals of their trek, kept over a two-year period, contain over 500,000 words and many sketches; one of the Prince's more famous drawings was of a painted buffalo hide of the Blackfoot tribe (Thomas and Ronnefeldt 17).

Lewis Miller, who filled hundreds of pages with watercolor sketches of his neighbors and their activities in early Pennsylvania, was also interested in the study of botany. On page 148 of *American Folk Paintings* is a botanical study of the cucumber magnolia and the Jerusalem oak. In the margin Miller notes: "To learn the Science of Botany, and names of plants without personal assistance, we ought to direct....attention whenever we go into the forest and field" (Rumford). He annotated and measured his subjects, noting their function for carpentry, mechanics, medicine and other uses.

Whatever the motivation of these writers and artists, the end product retains its importance. They make the past alive for us, and whether we are dedicated reenactors or simply interested in American history, we owe them a debt of gratitude.

THE ARTIST & HIS TOOLS

There is, in fact, a tangible treasury left us by these early artists and writers. Many, many paintings and drawings still in existence show us what they did, from Nicholas Point's tiny graphite drawings and equally small watercolors (most the size of a large postcard) to magnificent oil landscapes by Bierstadt, Peale and Asher Durand. What is lacking, in most cases, is information about *how* they worked and what equipment they used. We can tell something about their tools and chosen medium by the works themselves, of course, but what of specifics?

If you want to reenact this aspect of the past, you will come up against practical questions almost immediately. What kind of brushes were available? What form did watercolors take? Were supplies made here or were they imported from Europe or the population centers of the East Coast? (The answer is both.) What would a traveling artists' kit look like?

When were metal pens first commonly used? How was ink made, and was it available commercially? Would a writer have loose sheets of paper or a hard-bound journal to work in and what might that book look like? How do you cut a quill pen? How should I dress, and what other accoutrements should I have? For those of us interested in accurate historical reenactment, there's been a real void here. When I first became interested in interpreting the persona of an artist/writer/naturalist, finding the answers to these questions became paramount. Gradually I found a number of sources. Some I was led to by my friends in living history; others I ferreted out by contacting university libraries, art galleries, museums and books. I picked George Woodbridge's brain till it must have hurt. (George is the artist who illustrated *The Collector's Illustrated Encyclopedia of the American Revolution* by Neumann and Kravic.) I also called art supply companies and spoke to their company historians.

Winsor & Newton, one of the finest manufacturers of artists' supplies today, boasts a wonderful museum in London. Customer service representatives can answer questions on early supplies from their company's beginnings in 1832 and before. *The Artist's Colourmen's Story*, a Winsor & Newton publication, shows many early supplies, from steel engravings (many of which turned out to have been from the Diderot encyclopedia) to photos of original watercolor boxes, which contained everything from cake colors to water containers (Staples).

If you are fortunate, you may be able to come by a copy of the first catalogs from Winsor & Newton. I have photocopies of those from 1832, 1845, 1851, 1857 and 1861. They were not illustrated, unfortunately, until mid-century, but from the written descriptions (and from the assurances of the company itself) many of these items did not change.

We can use Diderot's *Encyclopédie* from the late 1700s as a source for much information, but unfortunately, it's necessary to go to the original, in French. The editions currently published by Dover Publications

Top: Original crayon holder from the antique Winsor & Newton box. Middle: Peter Goebel's reproduction. Bottom: Art supply store model, still available. Ask for a charcoal holder.

are abridged and don't include art or writing supplies. There are some seventeen large-format volumes in the original set. Try a university library or similar data bank. Here we find ink in stick form very much like the Chinese ink available today; clam shells used as palettes or mixing bowls; mullers or grinding tools for grinding pigments for paint and/or crayons; brushes (often called hair pencils—other drawing instruments were called lead or dry pencils); dividers; mahl stick; palette knives; and portfolios tied with string or narrow tape for carrying paper or finished paintings. This flat surface also doubles as a portable work table.

Portfolios were a basic item of equipment. The French painter Chardin shows at least two in use in the 18th century. An 1817 painting of Anna Maria Von Phul by Matthew Harris Jouett shows her holding a large black portfolio with red spine and fine gold striping. The Missouri Historical Society in St. Louis owns a very small portfolio that belonged to Miss Von Puhl. It is made of green, cream and purple marbled paper covering the traditional cardboard (solid stuff, not corrugated) with dark green leather spine and corners—a much more colorful item than I expected.

It was not only artists who used portfolios, however. Naturalist and writer John Bradbury noted: "Our equipments were, a blanket, a rifle, eighty bullets, a full powder horn, a knife, and a tomahawk, for each. Besides these, I had a large inflexible port-folio, containing several quires of paper, for the purpose of laying down specimens of plants..." (76.)

Portfolios similar to those shown in Diderot are still available at art supply stores. They are heavy, cardboard covered with textured black paper and tied with narrow black tape. They come in a variety of sizes, but I prefer a small size for field work, about fourteen inches by eighteen inches. The Kings' Arms Press makes a more elegant (though still smaller) model.

With some digging, we can let the artists and writers of the period talk to us across the centuries about how they worked and what supplies they used. From 1731-1743, Mark Catesby described his manner of working as direct observation, although some of his plates are obviously plagiarized from the earlier works of John White. He states:

As I was not bred a painter I hope some faults in perspective, and other niceties, may be more readily excused; for I humbly conceive that plants, and other things done in a flat, though exact manner may serve the purpose of natural history, better in some measure, than in a more bold and painter-like way. In

designing the plants, I always did them while fresh and just gathered; and the animals, particularly the birds, I painted while alive (except a very few) and gave them their gestures peculiar to every kind of birds. (Feduccia 138)

Catesby also commented on the quality and durability of the paints he used. "Of the paints, particularly greens, used in the illumination of figures, I had principally a regard to those most resembling nature, that were durable and would retain their luster, rejecting others very specious and shining, but of an unnatural color and fading quality" (Feduccia 139).

Bodmer found watercolors initially frustrating, complaining to Maximilian that "he found watercolor painting 'too intricate' because of the need to leave open spaces, and that with an easier method he would have produced twice as many sketches" (Hunt and Gallgher 354).

Anyone who has ever worked with watercolor can sympathize with this complaint. With this medium the untouched white page acts as your lightest light. It's necessary to protect this white paper from the beginning or paint around these lights, because they are very difficult to reclaim once they're lost. In other techniques, such as gouache, oil or pastel, small light highlights are added last.

There are other suggestions to be found. Audubon drew a rough self-portrait in his woodsman's gear—fringed buckskins, leggings, fur hat, tomahawk, long rifle, portfolio and other accoutrements (Ford, *Audubon, by Himself* pl. 6). Bodmer included himself in his painting of the expedition's meeting with the Minataree, and Lewis Miller, whose work is included in the York County (Pennsylvania) Historical Society's collections as well as that of Colonial Williamsburg's Abby Aldrich Rockefeller Folk Art Collection, also depicted artists at work. He depicts an artist—himself—sketching under a tree in an illustration reproduced in *American Folk Paintings* (Rumford 135). William Ricarby Miller painted *Self Portrait at Weehawken*, a watercolor, in 1848. Catlin painted himself at work. It is through these paintings that we begin to get an idea of how the artists looked and worked and their tools.

BASIC EQUIPMENT

Pencils in a form very similar to those we know today were more or less commonly available from the 18th century onward and were used for both writing and sketching. Many early diaries are written in spidery pencil lines. The earliest known illustration of a wood-encased graphite lead is from *De Omni Rerum Fossilium Genere* by Conrad Gesner, but small drawing sets like that owned by Thomas Jefferson included dividers, rulers, ruling pens—and small graphite pencils.

Graphite is the crystalline form of carbon. "Black lead" or "plumbago" was available in London by 1610. Sir John Pettus described graphite set into deal (fir or pine wood) or cedar cases and called "dry pencils." Faber brand wood pencils were first made in 1760. Various hardnesses in lead were possible after 1795, when French chemist N.J. Conté patented the process of mixing graphite and clay and firing it in a kiln. The more clay in the ratio the harder the lead. (Other sources date this process to 1586.) Faber and Conté are still in business and art supply stores carry their products.

This graphite mixture was fired flat, sliced into long squared rods and glued into wood that had been routed to receive them. Another piece of wood was glued on top, then the pencils were cut and finished. Flat sketcher's pencils were also available, as they are today. Look at an art supply store or hardware supply (ask for a carpenter's pencil). For a discussion of all you ever wanted to know about the subject, see *The Pencil* by Henry Petroski.

Pencils did not originally have erasers, but India rubber or "gum elastic" was used by draftsmen as early as 1788. In a letter written circa 1790, Thomas Jefferson wrote to his friend David Rittenhouse, "Using a black lead pencil the lines are very visible and easily erased with India rubber" (Stein 373). Before that time emery powder and scraper knives, or "gratoires," were used to remove dried ink and moist rolled bread crumbs to remove graphite marks. (A bagel is about the right consistency—think in terms of catfish bait dough balls.)

I buy regular pencils, usually round black or unfinished ones, and saw off the eraser for reenactment use. Try a kneaded eraser or a wad of dried rubber cement for a period look to replace the handy pencil-mounted eraser. A good sharp knife keeps your pencil sharp in lieu of an electric sharpener. A pen knife is handy for this and gives the proper look to the pencil. Real *lead* pencils, which were also used, can be made by hammering that metal—bullets, or what have you—into shape, and though the marks they make are rather light, they are serviceable for note-taking and some drawing.

"Mechanical pencils" or lead holders (*porte-crayons*) are shown in the Diderot encyclopedia along with one of the "crayons," as well as on the cover of *The Universal Penman* by George Bickham from 1743.

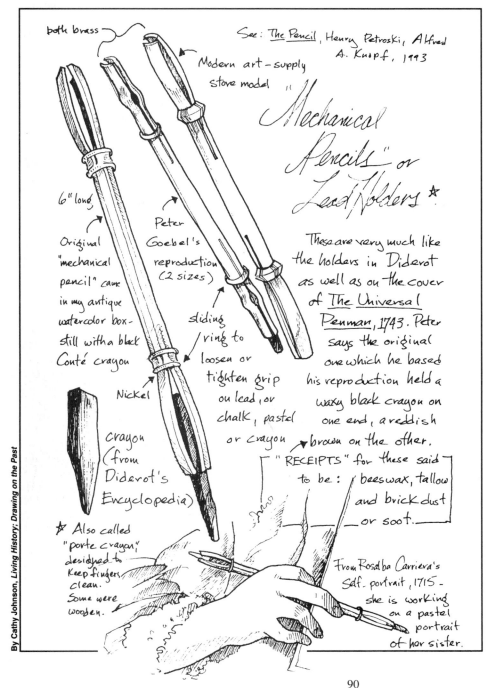

both brass

See: *The Pencil*, Henry Petroski, Alfred A. Knopf, 1993

Modern art-supply store model

"Mechanical Pencils" or Lead Holders ★

6" long

Original "mechanical pencil" came in my antique watercolor box - still with a black Conté crayon

Peter Goebel's reproduction (2 sizes)

Nickel

sliding ring to loosen or tighten grip on lead, or chalk, pastel or crayon

crayon (from Diderot's Encyclopedia)

★ Also called "porte crayon" designed to keep fingers clean. Some were wooden.

These are very much like the holders in Diderot as well as on the cover of *The Universal Penman*, 1743. Peter says the original one which he based his reproduction held a waxy black crayon on one end, a reddish brown on the other.

"RECEIPTS" for these said to be: beeswax, tallow and brick dust or soot.

From Rosalba Carriera's Self-portrait, 1715 - she is working on a pastel portrait of her sister.

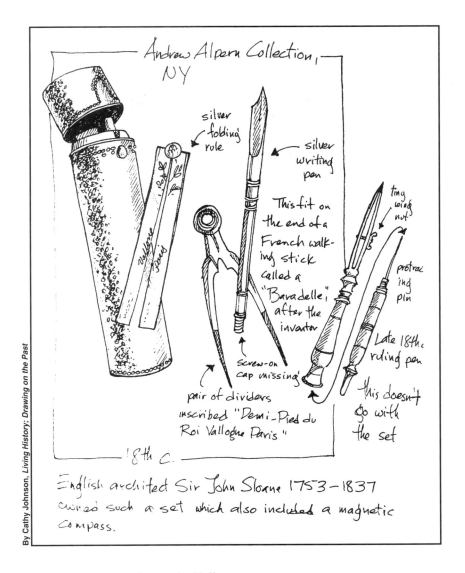

Andrew Alpern Collection, NY

silver folding rule

silver writing pen

This fit on the end of a French walking stick called a "Baradelle," after the inventor

tiny wing nut

protracting pin

Late 18th c. ruling pen

this doesn't go with the set

screw-on cap missing

pair of dividers inscribed "Demi-Pied du Roi Valloghe Paris"

18th C.

English architect Sir John Sloane 1753-1837 owned such a set which also included a magnetic compass.

Rosalba Carriera holds one in her 1715 self-portrait (Heller 54), and the Nelson Gallery in Kansas City owns paintings that show the porte-crayon in use, including two in one work, *The Arts—Drawing*, by Gaspare Traversi, 1760.

Some of the "leads" or crayons that fit these brass or German silver holders were made from beeswax, tallow and brick dust or soot (lampblack); others were what we think of as pastels or chalk. Conté still manufactures these, though in a slightly different shape (early Conté crayons bulged in the middle and tapered at the ends.) Koh-i-noor makes a very similar wax-based product that fits a lead holder, and Peter Goebel makes a good reproduction porte-crayon.

Vine charcoal was also used for sketching; ideally it was of a size to fit the porte-crayon. It can be bought in any art supply store—or picked up from your hearth. It was blended with a finger or a "tortillon" or "stump" made of rolled buckskin or heavy gray paper. The stump was sometimes bound with a colored paper to hold it in place. Mine is maroon. Charcoal, of course, is easily available from the remains of last night's campfire.

Quills for drawing or writing were easily available from the primary wing feathers of domestic and wild turkeys, geese and other birds. There were numerous methods of hardening quills to make them better and longer-lasting writing tools,

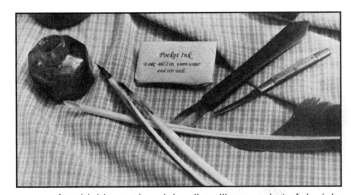

An old, blown-glass inkwell, quills, a packet of dry ink, a scraper (gvatoire) used to erase in lines or (possibly) to cut quills and a small pen knife. The well-cut quills and pocket ink are available from Tim Greene.

91

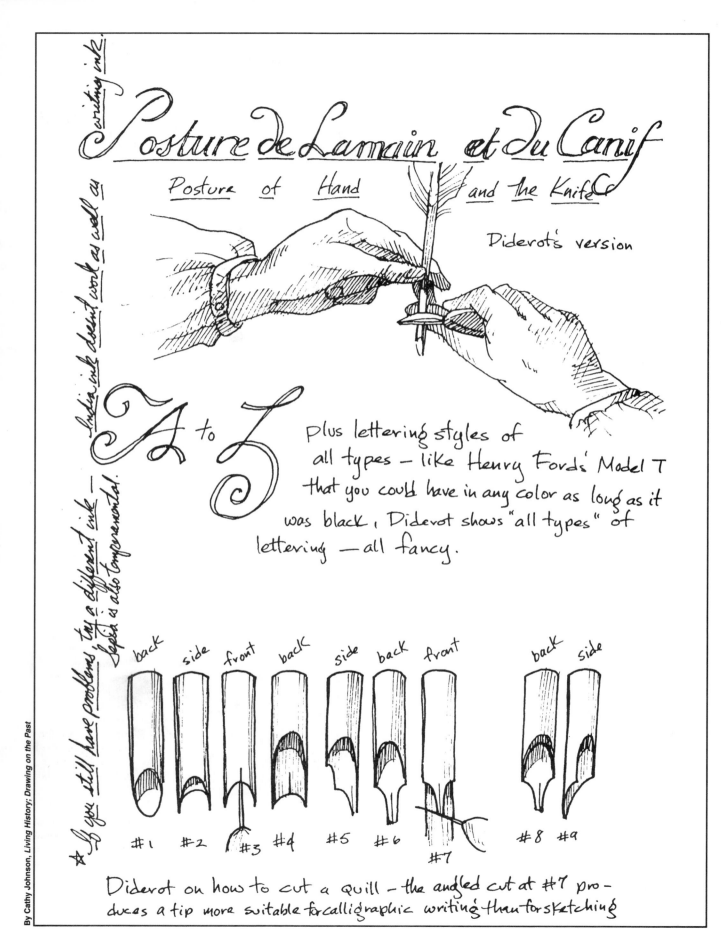

writing ink. India ink doesn't work as well as

If you still have problems, try a different ink — Sepia is also temperamental.

Posture de La main et du Canif

Posture of Hand and the Knife

Diderot's version

𝒜 to 𝒵 Plus lettering styles of all types — like Henry Ford's Model T that you could have in any color as long as it was black, Diderot shows "all types" of lettering — all fancy.

back   side   front   back   side   back   front   back   side

#1   #2   #3   #4   #5   #6   #7   #8   #9

Diderot on how to cut a quill — the angled cut at #7 produces a tip more suitable for calligraphic writing than for sketching from plunging the nib into hot sand to simply aging them in a sunny window. In his 1826 journal, Audubon made frequent mention of pen knives, which indicates that he used a quill to write with. On the frontier most people made their own. Liwwät Böke did all her voluminous drawing and writing with quills of her own manufacture and lists them among her possessions brought to America.

Diderot shows a clear method for cutting quills, which were tailor-made for various purposes. For example, a calligrapher or court clerk might prefer a broader tip, while an artist might use a very fine point. Experiment with various nib shapes to suit your needs.

A quill pen *will* wear out, but it may simply need some maintenance. If yours seems to need re-sharpening, try simply scraping off old ink and any residue remaining on the nib with the edge of a sharp blade. If that doesn't get it, you can soak the pen for a while to soften it, then re-shape the point. Always re-harden before using or sharpen an unsoftened nib *a bit at a time* using a very sharp knife. When your pen becomes flabby with age or humidity, clean it, soak it in hot water (or tea) for a while, then put it the sun for a week or two.

The fully-feathered pens displayed at many historic sites are impractical, by the way. It would be uncomfortable trying to write for very long with a handful of feathers. Instead, the vanes were stripped from the central rib, either completely, the length of the pen or with a small flag left at the end. Sometimes most of the vanes were left on but only stripped off for a comfortable distance of a hand-span.

Steel nibs were invented circa 1780 by Samuel Harrison of Birmingham, England. Silver and gold

The traveling artist or writer might have a small tin, copper, leather or papier-maché inkwell (the ones pictured are from Peter Goebel), a stick of sealing wax (from Tim Greene) and an assortment of seals. The large one in front is an original.

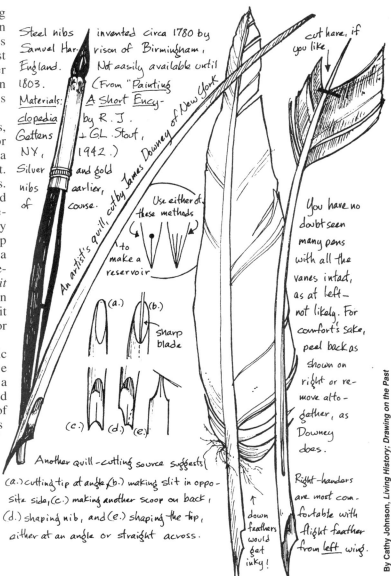

Steel nibs invented circa 1780 by Samuel Harrison of Birmingham, England. Not easily available until 1803. (From "Painting Materials: A Short Encyclopedia" by R. J. Gettens + G.L. Stout, NY, 1942.) Silver and gold nibs of course earlier, of course.

An artist's quill, cut by James Downey of New York

Use either of these methods to make a reservoir

(a.) (b.) sharp blade

(c.) (d.) (e.)

Another quill-cutting source suggests (a.) cutting tip at angle (b.) making slit in opposite side, (c.) making another scoop on back, (d.) shaping nib, and (e.) shaping the tip, either at an angle or straight across.

cut here, if you like

You have no doubt seen many pens with all the vanes intact, as at left — not likely. For comfort's sake, peel back as shown on right or re-move altogether, as Downey does.

Right-handers are most comfortable with flight feather from *left* wing.

↑ down feathers would get inky!

By Cathy Johnson, *Living History: Drawing on the Past*

nibs were available earlier, however, and iron nibs were in limited use. Samuel Johnson used at least one silver pen point, circa 1750-1780, and many of the early 18th century sets of drawing tools include a silver "quill" pen. A German quill-style metal pen made circa 1580-1600 was shown in *Mathematisch-Physikalicher Salon* (illus. in Hambly 59).

The steamboat *Arabia*, a boat that sank in 1856, is a time capsule for reenactors. At the new Arabia Steamboat Museum in Kansas City, Missouri, there are metal nibs in 68 different styles, many manufactured in the United States.

By 1872 metal nibs were everywhere. According to *Great Industries of the United States,: Being an Historical Summary of the Origin, Growth and Perfection of the Chief Industrial Arts of This Country*, "The invention and general introduction of metallic pens has nearly driven quills out of common use—the new pens save the time consumed by the writer in making, *and they are infinitely cheaper*....In 1810 a patent was granted in the United States to Peregrine Williamson, of Baltimore, for metallic writing pens—the first of the kind manufactured in this country" (456).

Lewis and Clark had metal nibs, as well, though they could hardly be considered ordinary citizens. For common usage, quills were most easily available. An artist accompanying a government expedition (or one underwritten by someone with nearly unlimited funds, like Maximilian or Stewart) or stationed at a fort might be expected to have the latest technology.

Weskit inkwells were available that held a tiny bottle of

elderberry juice, a tincture of black walnuts, water and vinegar, and similar recipes that substituted wild berries (strawberries, blackberries, etc.) for the walnuts (for more information see Cathy Johnson 25).

Chambers Information for the Million, an undated book that appears to be from the mid to late 19th century, says:

...in most fluid writing inks galls *and* sulphate of iron *are the chief* [ingredients], *with the addition of gum-arabic to render the ink a little adhesive and make it flow properly from the pen. Some very black ink is made with oxide of manganese....the ink with which ancient manuscripts were mostly written was not, like ours, a chemical compound, but was made simply of charcoal dust suspended in water with a little gum; the color of this compound must have been much more enduring than that of our inks, but it would be both disagreeable and tedious to use. Red ink derives its color from Brazil-wood, a well-known dye, and blue is colored with Prussian Blue.* (229-230)

The book also describes the making of Chinese or Indian ink from "the finest lamp-black, carefully prepared, and animal

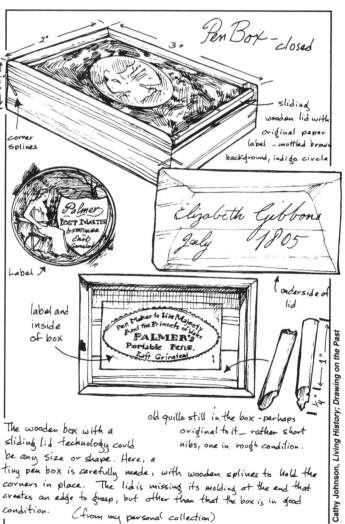

ink plus one or two quills. Peter Goebel makes a similar well in two styles, one round and one a smaller oval. "Originals were tin, copper, silver, brass (like the one in the *Collector's Illustrated Encyclopedia of the American Revolution*, 275), leather, horn and even papier-mâché. The tiny glass bottles were generally blown in place," says Goebel.

Sepia (brown) ink was commonly available and popular with artists and writers, in spite of the idea that the brown tone we see in old documents and art was simply black ink that had faded—some was, some was not. Several period tradesmen's cards mention ink in various colors. Dorothy Mercier, who advertised in London in the 18th century, offered "Fine Black, Brown, and Blue India Ink" in addition to papers, watercolors, hair pencils (brushes) and chalks (Heal). Red was also available commercially.

Inks were also manufactured at home and recipes abound. Kalm refers to a black ink-like tincture made by boiling sumac berries and branches together (42). I have been told that a common Colonial recipe consisted of rusty iron steeped in fermented cow's urine, a recipe I have not personally tested, having limited access to cows. Other recipes consist of

94

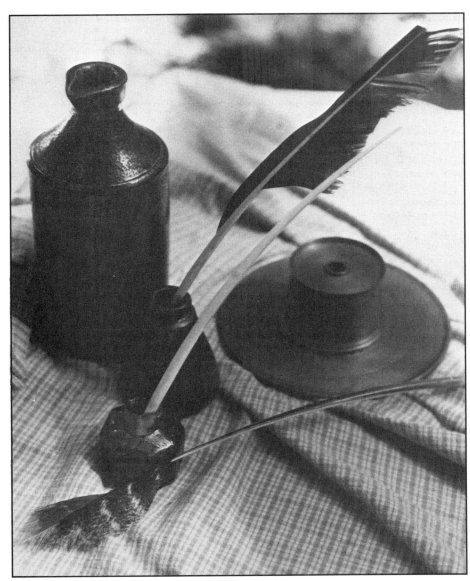

Clockwise from upper left: large pottery ink bottle, ship's pewter inkwell (large, flat bottom kept it from turning over), quill pen (from Tim Greene) showing typical trimming of feather, blown glass inkwell, and pottery inkwell. All are originals except quill pens. (The pen in the glass well has been completely stripped, typical of pens for artists' use.)

On the left is a sander, a reproduction from Butch Baker (japanned). Sand was sprinkled on wet ink to dry it. The inside label reads "Palmer's Portable Pens" and the additional note reads "Pen maker to His Majesty and the Princess of Wales, East Grimstead." The cover label on the outside reads "Palmer—Post Master & Stationeer, East Grimstead." The most interesting part is the handwritten inscription inside: "Elizabeth Gibbon, July 1805."

MAKING PRIMITIVE PIGMENTS

Recently, as I was preparing for Children's Day at Fort Osage, I decided to make my contribution as period correct as I could, while still giving the kids something fun to do. As an artist I often share what it was like for those of my profession in early America, including what materials were available, how artists worked and what they did, especially their work as spies, which always gets the kids' attention! This time I decided to let the youngsters make their own pigments, using some of the materials that would have been available on the frontier. Earth pigments, made as the name suggests from dirt or rock, and charcoal were the obvious answer. (If there had been white chalk outcroppings near my home, I would have used those, too.) I thought it would be fun, and more instructive, to let the kids help grind their own pigments and then paint with them.

Before I could show the youngsters, though, I had to do a trial run myself. I've made my own paints from powdered pigments, but I'd never dug the wherewithal from a creek bed. This was a learning experienced for me, too, and one that anyone interested in depicting early artists or native Americans might find interesting.

First, I visited the creek to find the raw materials. A soft, yellow rock that occurs close to limestone outcroppings, limonite is an iron oxide that contains a great deal of water and is sometimes call hydroxide. According to Richard Gentile, professor of geology at the University of Missouri at Kansas City, this rock can be hard or soft. A similar rock, which has more iron in it but without the water molecule attached like limonite, is hematite (Fe_2O_3), a redder-colored rock you find in many of the Southern states as well as in the Ozarks of Missouri and Arkansas. Around here, these rocks are called Indian paint rock. In their softest form, they are almost like clay and can be used like chalk to draw with. A sufficient quantity can be rubbed loose with a finger to allow you to paint your face if you're so inclined. These same pigments were used to decorate pottery or buffalo skins before the traders made brighter, more refined colors like vermillion available to the native Americans.

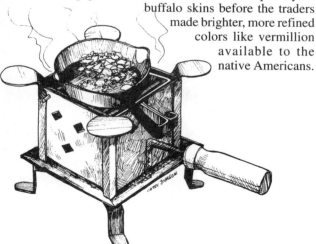

Drawn with a piece of raw limonite rock.

I gathered a good double handful of the softest stones, then broke them into small pieces against a flat granite rock with the back of my hatchet (keeping some whole to show the kids where our paint came from, of course). These chunks ranged in size from a grain of corn to a lima bean. Some of these I ground to a powder in a mortar and pestle. I'd recommend a mortar and pestle made of stone or brass, because the bits of rock are hard enough that they must be banged on pretty enthusiastically. You could break a china mortar, and what I tried to break up on a wood surface simply imbedded itself in the wood fibers.

Many basic pigments are changed in color by heat. For example, yellow ochre becomes red ochre; raw sienna (yellowish brown) becomes burnt sienna (red-brown); and raw umber becomes burnt umber. So, I decided to add to our color

This engraving was colored using the Velasquez palette. To see the colors, turn to page II of the color section.

repertoire by roasting some rock.

I quickly got a fire going in my little officer's brazier and put an indestructible iron skillet on it, then added a handful of the broken bean-sized rocks. I stirred them constantly with a wooden spoon, watching them turn from a light brownish yellow to a light red-brown. When they were cool, I ground some of them, too.

To complete the range of paints, I ground some charcoal from my firepit. For a finer product to make my black, I'd use lamp-black or soot, which I experimented with at the cabin—the bottom of my skillet was coated with the stuff since I hadn't waited for my fire to die to red coals before heating the rocks! The smoke deposited a nice, thick veneer I could paint with by dampening it with a brush and clear water.

These three colors—yellow ochre, red-brown and black—make up what is known as the Velasquez palette, a subtle variation on the primaries. If you remember your grade school art classes, you'll remember that the primaries are red, yellow and blue, and from these three colors you can mix almost anything else. Well, in the Velasquez version, the primaries are much more subdued than in a box of crayons and the color takes a bit of imagination—the black stands in for blue, and the other two are almost as subtle—but you can do a creditable painting by mixing the three or using them as is.

Normally, paints are made by mixing powdered pigment, water and honey (gum arabic is used today in place of honey). The honey acts as a humectant to keep the paint softer and more easily mixed and also to bind it to the paper. For the purposes of demonstration and to keep from attracting bees to the kids, I decided to use powdered pigment and water alone, and it worked surprisingly well.

A classical method of learning to paint in the 18th century involved coloring in prints of classical scenes, much like the coloring books of today. For my purposes I had prints made of the engravings in an old book, *Our Western Frontier: 100 Years Ago*, of things I thought would interest the kids. To test out my new paints, I got out one of these prints (which I had had simply blown up and Xeroxed onto a heavier-than-normal paper), dipped my brush into clear water and then powdered pigment to make a pool of paint, then proceeded to color in the print as usual. The effects were amazingly satisfying, as shown in the above illustration.

The kids loved it, too. Although some did choose to paint with the more colorful "imported" stuff we provided, many of them ground rock and charcoal to dust and made a good beginning toward understanding how the first art might have been made—by hand and without benefit of imported supplies.

Another typical early technique was to do your own ink under-drawing to color in with watercolor. You can see this technique in use as early as the Middle Ages, but a more familiar example might be found in Karl Bodmer's work. Although he generally worked in pencil and watercolor, occasionally Bodmer made sketchier products, such as *Bison Grazing on the Upper Missouri* from the book *Karl Bodmer's America* (Hunt and Gallagher 270). We made ink sticks for Children's Day by cutting pencil-length maple twigs, then sharpening one end. The kids dipped these in ink to draw with, a technique as old as drawing itself. With homemade ink of rust and vinegar, walnut hulls and water or berry juice to provide the preliminary drawing and a wash of color made of rock and soot pigments, the primitive artist could produce some credible work.

glue...made into solid cakes or sticks...ornamented with letters or figures, in colors or in gilding" (229-230). Very similar stick inks can be bought today.

Artists' brushes were very similar to those still available. However, many had actual bird quills in place of the metal ferrule of today and were sized according to the type of bird; a "crow quill" was not the metal writing or drawing pen we know today, but a small brush. (Ferrules cover the joining of

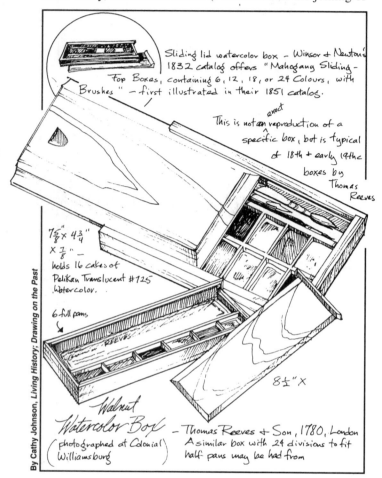

Sliding lid watercolor box - Winsor & Newton's 1832 catalog offers "Mahogany Sliding - Top Boxes, containing 6, 12, 18, or 24 Colours, with Brushes" - first illustrated in their 1851 catalog.

This is not an exact reproduction of a specific box, but is typical of 18th & early 19thc boxes by Thomas Reeves

7⅝" × 4¾" × ⅞" - holds 16 cakes of Pelikan Translucent #125 Watercolor.

6 full pans

REEVES

8½" ×

Walnut Watercolor Box (photographed at Colonial Williamsburg) - Thomas Reeves & Son, 1780, London. A similar box with 24 divisions to fit half pans may be had from

handle and hairs, protecting and holding them in place.) Duck, goose and swan quill brushes were also available commercially. You bought the brush with hairs already inserted into the quill, then added your own stick for a handle. It wouldn't have been uncommon to visit an artists' colorman's shop and see a jar of these quills of various sizes. My antique watercolor box still contains the remains of three of these brushes.

The business end was made of mink or weasel, fitch (otherwise known as polecat), "miniver" (a mixture of ermine and weasel mentioned by Richard Symonds, 1617-1672), or sable, as many brushes are today, though sable was not apparently mentioned until the end of the 18th century (Fairbairn 35, 70). The stiffer boar bristle, goat or horsehair were used for oil painting.

According to an article in *Great Industries of the United States*, "The delicate brushes made for artists are made by taking the delicate hairs from the furs of animals which are sufficiently soft, and arranging them into a bundle of the proper shape; they are then fastened and run through the larger end of a quill until they project sufficiently beyond the other end. The quill having been soaked beforehand, in order to enlarge

it, shrinks sufficiently on drying to hold the brush securely. *Brushes of this kind are also often made by being mounted in metallic caps*" (emphasis added; 277-284). The author was not big on writing skills, but you get the idea. I recently constructed brushes from three different sizes of quills for a variety of painting tools. It's advisable to soak or boil the quills to soften them after cutting them to the length you want, then insert the bundle of hairs. If the quill splits, you can wrap the ferrule with linen thread and secure it with hide glue. Then insert sticks of a comfortable length.

Until very recently, brushes called "fashion quills" were available from Winsor & Newton. These were very similar to the early brushes, with different sizes of brushes tied with various colors of silk, then fixed in quills. They have been discontinued since today's artists didn't know how to care for them. (Occasionally the quill ferrules come loose from the handle. They simply need to be soaked in warm water and the handle gently re-inserted with a twisting motion.) You may still be able to find a few of these brushes in one of the larger art supply stores. There are several squirrel-hair brushes from Isabey made with the hairs held to the unfinished wooden handle with quill wrapped with a fine brass wire. Squirrel-hair brushes are a bit flabby for modern tastes used to sable or synthetics, but they will suffice for casual sketching.

Besides lead or graphite pencil and pen and ink, watercolor was the most common choice of frontier artists. However, it is difficult to find mention of the medium by that name in the

These held about everything. Under the tray of cakes of color are rolled buckskin stumps for blending and a crayon holder for lead or chalk. Beneath the small porcelain mixing tray or palette are a selection of charcoal sticks and Conté crayons.

earliest records—and there is a reason.

"Watercolor painting is not defined in any dictionary or technical guide of 18th century France due to a simple linguistic circumstance—the late appearance of the word 'aquarelle' [another term for watercolor]. The technique did exist, but is described in several works under the heading of gouache or wash. Of course a gouache...does not look like a watercolor [gouache is opaque while watercolors are transparent]; and a wash really ought to be classified with drawings. Nevertheless, no distinction was made between color-drawing, wash, watercolor and pure gouache; this quadruple modern distinction was at once a reality and an anachronism in the eighteenth century" (Huisman 115). The book from which this quote was taken, *French Watercolors on the 18th Century*, also has a section on "The Technique of Watercolor," which includes period steel engravings of equipment and artists at work.

French materials and those available to Americans of the period would have been virtually interchangeable, since there were few (or no) American manufacturers until the early 19th century. Fine art supplies imported from Europe included paper, paints, brushes, pastels, paint boxes and so forth.

From the earliest times, artists generally made their own paints (or had their apprentice do it) by grinding pigments with water, oil, tallow, honey or other mediums, depending on their use. By the 18th century, most European cities and many towns and villages boasted an artists' colorman's shop, where everything from paints to papers and frames were available. America was not far behind, even if supplies were imported.

Winsor & Newton was aggressive in sales; it was comprised of a company of sailors who traveled up the Congo and to the New World to sell their wares. Within ten to fifteen years, they branched out beyond the United Kingdom and opened a lot of early markets, going up and down the coasts of America to supply artists. The agent would call, but business was mainly mail order.

If a colorman's shop was not handy, you might have bought the raw materials from the local apothecary shop, such as the 1792 Stabler-Leadbeater Apothecary Shop in Alexandria, Virginia, the oldest continuously run retail, wholesale and manufacturing drug business in the United States. This company sold goods to George Washington, Daniel Webster, John Jacob Astor and J. E. B. Stuart. The Clay County Museum in Liberty, Missouri, was once such an emporium, and the bottles lining the walls offer a variety of artists' pigments. (These same compounds were used as dyes, house paints and medicinals.) The apothecary also sold the oils, gums and resins needed to make artists' paints.

William Reeves (1739-1803) produced a moist ready-to-use paint cake, with ingredients similar to those prepared for illuminated manuscripts but never

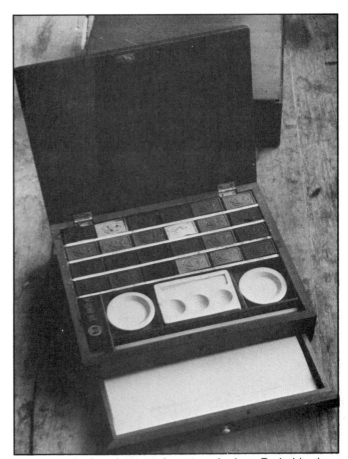

An American-made watercolor box. Probably close to mid-19th century but very much like boxes from Thomas Reeves Company in the 1780s.

Powdered pigments were kept in apothecary jars

Vermillion

This color is made from mercury (red sulphide)— no wonder it's so heavy.

before compounded together in such a way as to make a salable paint for a popular market serving artist and amateur alike" (Staples 1). Thomas Reeves and Sons, a branch of the same family, made art supplies that included large wooden watercolor boxes and small, sliding-lid paint boxes. A Reeves box at Colonial Williamsburg that holds six cakes of paint is from the 1780s (*Williamsburg Collection* 44-45.) The larger "caddy-lid" boxes held everything the traveling artist would need. These boxes could be quite elaborate, with crystal water containers, charcoal, stumps, brushes, Chinese stick ink and china mixing palettes. Some of these boxes had drawers for extra storage.

Metal paint boxes haven't changed much. They were available in japanned tin very early on. (Japanning was a resin/oil with dryers for a hard, enamel finish.) Small, portable sterling silver watercolor boxes were sold in India in the early 19th century for the growing British trade, and in form if not in substance, they are indistinguishable from today's metal boxes.

Winsor & Newton was credited with adding glycerin to their watercolor mixtures around 1841, making them much easier to use. Honey was used before glycerin and after the hard pigment sticks, which were available for much of the 18th century. These hard sticks were still available in the 1950s! The sticks, made of powdered pigment mixed with gum arabic or gum senegal, but without a humectant like glycerin or honey, had to be abraded with a pumice stone to scour the surface to

99

break loose the color for washes. The advent of semi-soft cakes made with glycerin and gum arabic made watercolor much more convenient to use.

Watercolor cakes, both hard and semi-soft, were molded in decorative designs. If you find a paint box from that period, you are likely to see what looks like untouched cakes of paint. If you are able to remove them, you'll usually find that the backs have seen use. It was considered proper to remove the paint cakes, use them on the edge of your palette, allow them to dry when you were finished and then replace them. (Messy or spontaneous folk like myself just use them where they are.)

Before tubes of paint were available, semi-moist glycerin and pigment mixture was sold in pig bladders. A stick-pin opened the bladder and paint was squeezed out, then the pin was re-inserted to seal. It didn't do a very good job, because these leaked under pressure and dried out easily. Oils were also available in pig bladders. Metal syringes became available after 1822, and tubes similar to those we see today came in 1845. They won prizes all over the world. Winsor & Newton exhibited their new tubes in the Chicago World's Fair. Period engravings of their booth gives the picture of the variety available.

All paints are a mixture of binders and other mediums like glycerin, gum arabic, gum senegal, honey or oil, and pigments, which give them their color. Prehistoric artists used those most easily available: the red and yellow earth colors, chalk, and charcoal (carbon black). Later, other colors were discovered. Those listed here were all used pre-1850—by no means an all-inclusive list but simply some of those I've been able to personally document. Most information included here is from *The Artists' Colourmen's Story* (Staples) and *Paint and Painting* (Fairbairn). Other sources such as *Webster's New Unabridged Dictionary* were used as well for some chemical compositions of pigments.

Some of these colors are no longer available. Others are called by the same name but have different compositions. Many are still in use in their original form, however.

Colors from Winsor & Newton's 1832 catalog that are still available include Prussian Blue, Antwerp Blue, Ultramarine, Cobalt, Cobalt Green, Chrome Yellow, Lemon Yellow, Blue-Black, Purple Madder, Purple Lake, Carmine, Rose Madder, Scarlet Lake, Crimson Lake, Brown Madder, Indian Red, Venetian Red, Light Red, Vermillion, Terre Verte, Raw Sienna, Burnt Sienna, Yellow Ochre, Naples Yellow, Ivory

Pre-1850 Color Key

C—Used by cave artists   E—Egyptian
G—Greek   I—Italian
(?)—Unable to pin down to an exact period of time, but still pre-1850

Reds, roses:

Dragon's Blood—(?)	Resin of Calamus Draco tree
Vermillion—G, I	Red sulphide of mercury
Carmine—(?)	Cochineal beetles
Madder—E, G, I	Madder root
Cinnabar—E, G, I	Mineral
Red lead—G, I	Lead

Blues, greens:

Azurite—E, G, I	Blue ore of copper
Malachite—E, G, I	Mineral
Ultramarine—I	Lapis lazuli (gemstone)
Smalt—(?)	A cool blue-violet similar to "Egyptian blue frit," according to Winsor & Newton—much like Manganese blue)--made by powdering glass made from silica, potash and oxide of cobalt
Blue verditer—(?)	Basic copper carbonate; replaced by ultramarine
Indigo—E, G, I	From indigo root (today's "indigo" is made from a mixture of lamp black, Alizarin crimson and Winsor blue; not as reddish as original color)
Verdigris—G, I	Copper treated with acetic acid
Terre verte—I	A greenish earth
Cobalt—18th, 19th C.	Metallic oxide

Yellows:

Gamboge—18th, 19th C.	Gum from a bamboo mold
Indian yellow—18th, 19th C.	Earth mixed with urine of a cow fed on mango leaves
Naples yellow—I	Lead antimoniate (from Vesuvius)
Orpiment—E, G, I	Sulphide of arsenic
Massicot—G, I	Yellow oxide of lead
Chrome yellow—18th, 19th C.	Chromium

Browns, blacks, whites:

Raw umber—C onward	Earth containing iron hydroxide and manganese oxide
Burnt umber—C onward	Roasted earth
Carbon black—C onward	Soot
Sepia—(?)	Cuttlefish ink
Cologne earth—(?)	Now called Vandyke brown
White lead—G, I	Lead
Burnt Sienna, Raw Sienna—I	Earths
Mummy—18th, 19th C.	Pretty much what you'd expect, the ground bodies of mummies

(The winding sheets were used to make paper, thus releasing diseases from ages past—hence, "the mummy's curse.")

oil paint
in pig bladder
(after Diderot)

Black, Lamp Black, Vandyke Brown, Burnt Umber and Raw Umber.

"List of Ackermann's Superfine Water Colours" from 1801, which appears in *Paint and Painting*, adds more exotic hues, including Bister, Bone Black, Carmined Lake, Calcined Vitrol, Gall Stone, Peach Black and Smalt. Ackermann was an artists' colorman.

The 1809 *Missouri Gazette* lists "White and Red Lead, Venetian Red, Vermillion, Dutch pink, Spanish Brown, Kings Yellow, Patent Yellow, Yellow Ochre, Umber, Prussian Blue, India Ink, 'Verdigrease' [green made from corroded copper] and Ivory black" along with blank books, fine papers, Dutch quills, "durable ink for writing on linnen" and copal varnish.

Oil paints were made from these same pigments; the difference was that they had an oil binder (usually linseed oil) that kept them workable much longer than the water-soluble watercolors. When dry, oil paints are impermeable to water, unlike watercolors, which will dissolve or lift to some degree even years after they have dried.

Paper, being rather expensive, was not wasted, particularly if you were on the frontier where supplies were limited. Alfred Jacob Miller painted on the back of one drawing, a watercolor of one of the heads on the reverse side. Then, not satisfied with the likeness of the "Shoshone or Snake Indian," he pasted another sheet of paper over the subject's face and neck and completed the portrait, apparently more to his liking.

Liwwät Böke made her drawings on a good quality paper that has stood the test of time. "Paper was a scarce and valuable commodity so she wasted very little space on her early drawings, one sheet often containing several sketches" (Knapke 11). Later sketches allowed for wider margins and room for notes. Lewis Miller may have gone back to his journal pages many times, adding new work till the pages were full. Bodmer's watercolors were painted on a heavyweight sketching paper. Most range in size between 9 by 11 inches and 12 X 15 inches—small by today's standards with a few pieces smaller still.

The best-known artists' paper supplier is the French manufacturer D'Arches. They have been in business since 1492, so a living history interpreter could use this brand without concern. However, until the late 18th century, papers were not made exclusively for watercolorists, who generally look for a bit of "tooth" or texture. They would have had to search through a supply of ordinary drawing paper to find random sheets of a texture they preferred. With the growing interest in watercolor as more than just a sketching medium, papers began to be made in several textures especially suited to the medium, with rough, cold pressed and hot pressed surfaces. As you might surmise, paper pressed with a hot iron is very smooth to the touch.

Canvas for oil paintings was generally woven from linen, but wood panels were a common painting support as well.

FIELD SUPPLIES

For the most part, traveling artists tended to use watercolors or pastels (dry pigment in stick form); "crayons," which were in fact black, red-brown or white "leads" that fit into metal holders (or porte-crayons); inks; or pencils for ease of transport. In writing about Alfred Jacob Miller, Joan Carpenter Troccoli said, "We can easily imagine Miller sketching in watercolor under the kinds of wilderness conditions that would render the painter's easel, palette, and maulstick ridiculous or impossible" (2). (The maulstick or mahlstick is a long rod that rests on the edge of a painting. You then lay your wrist or hand on the stick at the desired spot in the painting to steady your hand to avoid smearing wet paint. It also aids control when rendering small details.) Considering the difficulty of carrying large, wet canvases, it's no wonder watercolor was the more popular medium for field work.

Even here on the frontier of the Louisiana Territory, art and writing materials were available from Louisville, New Orleans and St. Louis. Expeditions of exploration or trade—and more casual travelers—often outfitted themselves at St. Louis, the largest European settlement west of the Mississippi. The *Missouri Gazette,* published in that city between 1809 and 1811 (also called the *Louisiana Gazette*), contains a number

of advertisements that list artists' and journalists' necessities. Not listed are brushes or pens. Presumably these were either imported directly, homemade, or included in the ubiquitous "&c" of these ads.

Among the items offered by Richard Ferguson of Louisville, Kentucky, who advertised in the *Gazette* in June of 1809, were "Patent Yellow, Prussian Blue, Verdigrise, Lampblack, Yellow Ocre, &c., &c. just received from Philadelphia...a general assortment of Medicines, Paints, Dye-stuffs, &c. &c., all of which he is determined to sell upon a very small advance."

Hunt and Hankinson's ad for February 20, 1809, includes under the headline of "Cheap Bargains" an assortment of fabrics, women's boots and shoes, saddlebags, bridles and men's and women's saddles as well as "Blank Books and Writing Paper, &c. &c. &c."

Zebulon Pike's 1806-1807 supply list includes small books used to take notes (Quaife 188). Long's 1819 expedition lists "Several blank books, port folios, &c," (James 426).

Other journals that have survived in museums and collections appear to be of rougher manufacture than the commercially available blank books and may have been homemade. William Clark's field journal, bound in elkskin and tied with strips of leather, is in the Missouri Historical Society in St. Louis. Alfred Jacob Miller apparently constructed his own book to contain his "Rough Draughts for Notes to Indian Sketches." These were "written on loose sheets of ruled paper of the sort used for school compositions; he used at least two different kinds of paper. After they were written, some of the Rough Draughts were taped and glued into a brown paper cover; later, more were added, and the pages were loosely stitched together" (Troccoli 2).

An antique lap desk may be outfitted with everything you need. Under the writing surface is room for loose paper, a small journal and a small pocket pistol if needed for protection. The small box with the oval label contains two original quills; date on the box's inscription on the underside of sliding wooden lid is 1805. The quills were short and would have fit a handle of some sort.

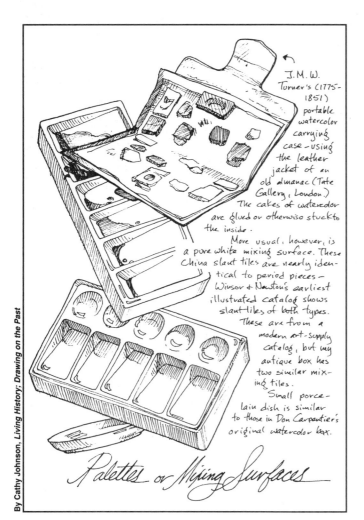

J.M.W. Turner's (1775-1851) portable watercolor carrying case — using the leather jacket of an old almanac (Tate Gallery, London.) The cakes of watercolor are glued or otherwise stuck to the inside.

More usual, however, is a pure white mixing surface. These China slant tiles are nearly identical to period pieces — Winsor & Newton's earliest illustrated catalog shows slant tiles of both types. These are from a modern art-supply catalog, but my antique box has two similar mixing tiles.

Small porcelain dish is similar to those in Don Carpentier's original watercolor box.

Palettes or Mixing Surfaces

By Cathy Johnson, *Living History; Drawing on the Past*

Audubon's 1826 manuscript journal, which contains the notes of his trip to England and Edinburgh, is 428 pages long. It has fly leaves of coarse laid paper, bound in "worn brown covers that have the outward appearance of a ledger, measuring 12-1/8 inches by 7-3/4 inches" (Ford, *1826 Journal* v).

Other items that could have been home manufactured with some ease included earth pigments (browns, ochres, red-browns, grays and a kind of earth green), lamp or carbon black, and dyes such as indigo and cochineal, as well as quill or reed pens, brushes, journals, even paper. Oil painters would have known how to stretch canvas using hide glue, which they would prepare themselves. The painting surface was then primed with white lead, a common ingredient in artists' materials.

102

Botanist's tin (vasculum) by Peter Goebel is big enough to hold entire kit—wooden Winsor & Newton box, porcelain palette, shell palette, blown glass flask for water, small journal, brushes, etc. Artists often used leather cases for carriers and large rigid portfolios as well.

PERIOD TECHNIQUES

Bodmer used a combination of pencil, pen and ink and watercolor wash in many of his works. This was a very common technique (and a good demonstration to reproduce). His use of brown ink is particularly noticeable in the painting/sketch of Fort McKenzie on pages 122-123 of *People of the First Man* (Thomas and Ronnefeldt). In this work some details remain un-inked and faint pencil marks are visible. It's possible that the artist painted in watercolor over the pencil drawing, allowed it to dry, then added the sepia ink, as some inks will lift or smear when painted over. The painting of the herd of buffalo on pages 170-172 of *People of the First Man* shows a more finished work with a similar technique.

It is very typical for an artist to sketch first in pencil, with varying degrees of detail, then to add watercolor washes (broad areas of color). However, it's interesting to note that a close examination of John White's 1585 watercolors shows that, in addition, he sometimes drew directly in watercolor, using a small brush and admirable control.

It's obvious that Bodmer also used opaque paints for lighter highlights in some works, as did many of his contemporaries, Alfred Jacob Miller included. Today, watercolorists generally choose pure transparent watercolor instead of mixed media, reserving white paper for highlights instead of using opaque, but 18th and 19th century artists often felt free to use any combination they chose to make their point.

George Catlin usually (but not always) worked in oils. Unlike the heavy impasto (a thick application of oil paint) or the many-layered studio approach common today, Catlin used what is called an *alla prima* technique. That is, he applied oils quickly, thinly and on the spot, a practical approach for painting outdoors and on the go. He worked on canvas for his North

American Indian studies in the 1830s, rolling the paintings for transport. Obviously, thick applications of paint would be disastrous. For his South American studies, where humidity was a factor, he switched to Bristol board, which is still available today (Ross vi).

Other typical period techniques include the use of toned or colored paper, often tan, gray and blue-gray, as a painting or drawing surface. Sometimes the paper was colored integrally in the manufacturing process, other times by putting over all a smooth watercolor wash of the desired color and shade, which could be variegated, then allowing it to dry before over-painting or drawing. Several of Anna Maria Von

Phul's works show the latter technique. Dark lines are added with charcoal, ink or watercolor, then highlights are picked out with opaque white crayon, chalk or paint. It makes a very three-dimensional effect and has been popular since the Renaissance.

Colored chalks were used alone, as well. Audubon describes drawing a portrait of an Osage Indian on his way to St. Genevieve, Missouri, in 1812: "...they were delighted to see me draw, and when I made a tolerable likeness of one of them with red chalk, they cried out with astonishment, and laughed excessively..." (Audubon 41).

ADDITIONAL EQUIPAGE

Compasses, rulers and dividers would have been part of most artists' and all cartographers' and draftsmen's equipment. They often were included in the small drawing sets that fit in one's pocket. Thomas Jefferson apparently had a holder made for a set of tools he had bought separately that included the pencil mentioned earlier. An artists' triangular, canvas-topped stool and a painting tent were shown in Winsor & Newton's illustrated catalog from the mid-19th century, though the stools were mentioned much earlier in other sources from the 18th century. The tent was simply a small canvas wedge of the type familiar to anyone at a French and Indian encampment onward. The inventory for Lewis and Clark's Corps of Discovery also included a field desk, which their journals mention as being damaged on their journey. Lap tables or desks were common and affordable, as were the elaborate watercolor "caddy boxes" (now, Winsor & Newton's Jubilee box, a similar product, costs approximately $800.00). The small wooden watercolor boxes with sliding lids were portable and inexpensive. Portfolios protected stores of unused paper and finished work, and a leather or canvas bag or knapsack would carry additional materials. Audubon mentions that Rafinesque carried his notebook in a waterproof bag.

But additional equipage would have included, in most cases, a gun of some sort, a shooting bag, a powder horn and other shooting paraphernalia. These were necessary not only for protection in the wilderness, but also because artists and naturalists, having no access to binoculars or cameras with telephoto lenses, often shot their subjects to enable them to see details up close. Not, one assumes, their human subjects.

Clothing ran the gamut from Audubon's buckskin-fringed outfit, Catlin's Indian-style clothing and Bradbury's buckskin moccasins and leather coats, all of which typify our idea of frontier attire, to Rafinesque's outlandish attire as described by Audubon:

The naturalist pulled off his shoes, and while engaged in drawing his stockings down to hide the holes in his heels, he explained that his apparel had suffered from his journey....A long, loose coat of yellow nankeen, much the worse for the many rubs it had got in its time, and stained all over with the juice of plants, hung loosely about him like a sack. (Audubon 67-68)

By contrast, Bodmer looks natty in his striped trousers, frock coat and top hat. Some paintings that depict artists at work or people engaged in writing show them in full regalia— breeches and flowing banyans for the men and ornate satin dresses on the women. Other times we know that people snatched a few minutes at the end of a long and tiring day to jot a few notes or sketches; they might have been dressed as anyone on the frontier. Depending on where you are and what your persona is, dress to suit locale, station, ethnic background and personality.

For the reenactor, half the fun (and half the challenge) is in recreating the materials and techniques of our forebears. This is no less true for those of us who portray artists or writers. Make your own brushes, grind your own pigments, cut a quill pen, concoct your own ink, snatch up your flintlock, and you are that much closer to those who held the past intact.

APPENDIX A: REFERENCES

Audubon, Lucy, ed. *The Life of John James Audubon, the Naturalist.* 1868. New York: Putnam, 1894.

Berkeley, Edmund, and Dorothy Smith Berkeley. *The Life and Travels of John Bartram from Lake Ontario to the River St. John.* Tallahassee: University Presses of Florida, 1982.

Bickham, George, engr. *The Universal Penman.* 1743. New York: Dover, 1954.

Bigelow, John. *Bigelow's Life of Colonel Fremont including His Explorations and Discoveries.* Cincinnati: Derby and Jackson, 1856.

Brackenridge, Henry Marie. *Early Western Travels.* Vol. 6. Ed. Reuben Gold Thwaites. Cleveland, OH: Arthur H. Clark, 1904.

Bradbury, John. *Travels in the Interior of America in the Years 1809, 1810, and 1811.* Lincoln: University of Nebraska Press, 1986.

Bruff, J. Goldsborough. *Preparing to Feed.* National Frontier Trails Museum, Independence, Missouri.

Chambers Information for the Million. New York: Hurst, n.d.

Clarke, Michael. *Watercolor.* Eyewitness Art Series. London: Dorling Kindersley, 1993.

Constant, Alberta Wilson. *Paintbox on the Frontier: The Life and Times of George Caleb Bingham.* New York: Thomas Y. Crowell, 1974.

Davidson, Marshall B. *500 Years of Life in America: An Illustrated History.* New York: Abrams, 1983.

de Bray, Lys. *The Art of Botanical Illustration: The Classical Illustrators and Their Achievements from 1550 to 1900.* Secaucus, NJ: Wellfleet Press, 1989.

Diderot, Denis. *Encyclopédie, ou Dictionnaire Raisonné des Sciences, des Arts, et des*

Métiers. Paris, 1763.

Dwight, Margaret Van Horn. *A Journey to Ohio in 1810*. 1912. Lincoln: Bison Books—University of Nebraska Press, 1991.

Erisman, Fred, comp. *American Canvas: The Art, Eye, and Spirit of Pioneer Artists*. London: Thames and Hudson, 1983.

Fairbairn, Lynda, comp. *Paint and Painting*. London: Tate Gallery—Winsor & Newton, 1982.

Feduccia, Alan, ed. *Catesby's Birds of Colonial America*. Chapel Hill: University of North Carolina Press, 1985.

Finch, Christopher. *19th Century Watercolors*. New York: Abbeville Press, 1991.

Ford, Alice, trans. *The 1826 Journal of John James Audubon*. Norman: University of Oklahoma Press, 1967.

—, ed. *Audubon, by Himself: A Profile of John James Audubon*. Garden City, NY: Natural History Press, 1969.

Fordham, Elias Pym. *Fordham's Personal Narrative, 1817-1818*. Bowie, MD: Heritage Books, 1989.

Gesner, Conrad. *De Omni Rerum Fossilium Genere*. Zurich, Switzerland, 1565.

Goss, John. *The Mapping of North America: Three Centuries of Map-Making 1500-1860*. Secaucus, NJ: Wellfleet Press, 1990.

Great Industries of the United States; Being an Historical Summary of the Origin, Growth and Perfection of the Chief Industrial Arts of This Country. Chicago: Burr—Hyde, 1872.

Hambly, Maya. *Drawing Instruments, 1580-1980*. New York: Harper, 1988.

The Handmaid to the Arts, Volume the First. London: J. Nourse, 1764.

Heal, Ambrose. *London Tradesmen's Cards of the 18th Century*. n.p.: Smith, Peter, Publishers, n.d.

Heller, Nancy G. *Women Artists*. New York: Abbeville Press, 1987.

Huisman, Phillipe. *French Watercolors of the 18th Century*. New York: Viking Press, 1969.

Hulton, Paul. *America 1585: The Complete Drawings of John White*. Chapel Hill: University of North Carolina Press—British Museum Publications, 1984.

Hunt, David C., and Marsha V. Gallagher. *Karl Bodmer's America*. Omaha, NE: Joslyn Art Museum—University of Nebraska Press, 1984.

James, Edwin, comp. *Account of an Expedition from Pittsburgh to the Rocky Mountains*. Barre, MA: Readex Microprint, 1966.

Johnson, Cathy. *Living History; Drawing on the Past*. Excelsior Springs, MO: Graphics/Fine Arts Press, 1994.

Johnson, Susanna. *A Narrative of the Captivity of Mrs. Johnson, Together with a Narrative of James Johnson, Indian Captive of Charlestown, NH 1757*. Facsimile ed. Bowie, MD: Heritage Books, 1990.

Jouett, Matthew Harris. Anna Maria Von Phul. Illus. in "Anna Maria Von Phul." By Charles Van Ranenswaay. *Missouri Historical Society Bulletin* 10: 369.

Kalm, Peter. *Peter Kalm's Travels in North America: The English Version of 1770*. New York: Dover, 1987.

Kane, Paul. *Willamette Valley at Champoeg*. National Frontier Trails Museum, Independence, Missouri.

Knapke, Luke B., ed. *Liwwät Böke, 1807-1882 Pioneer*. Minster, OH: Minster Historical Society, 1987.

Lipman, Jean, and Tom Armstrong, eds. *American Folk Painters of Three Centuries*. New York: Arch Cape Press, 1988.

Louisiana Gazette. See *Missouri Gazette*.

Mell, George. *Writing Antiques*. Princes Risborough, Aylesbury, Bucks, Great Britain: Shire, 1980.

Missouri Gazette (aka *Louisiana Gazette*). Advertisements. Microfilm. 1809-1811.

Neumann, George C., and Frank J. Kravic. *The Collector's Encyclopedia of the American Revolution*. 1975. Texarkana, TX: Rebel Publishing, 1989.

Nuttall, Thomas. *A Journal of Travels into the Arkansas Territory, during the Year 1819*. Readex Microprint, 1966.

Peterson, Jacqueline, and Laura Peers. *Sacred Encounters: Father De Smet and the Indians of the Rocky Mountain West*. Norman: University of Oklahoma Press, 1993.

Petroski, Henry. *The Pencil*. New York: Knopf, 1993.

Quaife, Milo Milton. *The Southwestern Expedition of Zebulon M. Pike*. Freeport, NY: Books For Libraries Press, 1925.

Ross, Marvin, ed. *George Catlin: Episodes from "Life Among the Indians" and "Last Rambles."* Norman: University of Oklahoma Press, 1959.

Rumford, Beatrix, ed. *American Folk Paintings*. Boston: Little, Brown, 1988.

Rumford, Beatrix, and Carolyn Weekley. *Treasures of American Folk Art from the Abby Aldrich Rockefeller Folk Art Center*. Boston: Colonial Williamsburg Foundation—Bulfinch Press, 1989.

Scott-Scott, Michael. *Drawing Instruments*. Princes Risborough, Aylesbury, Bucks, Great Britain: Shire, 1986.

Shelley, Donald A. Introduction. *Lewis Miller Sketches and Chronicles*. Ed. Robert P. Turner. York, PA: Historical Society of York County, 1966.

Sprigg, June. *Domestick Beings*. New York: Knopf, 1984.

Staples, Peter J., ed. *The Artist's Colourman's Story*. Middlesex, England: Reckitt and Colman Leisure, 1984.

Stein, Susan. *The Worlds of Thomas Jefferson at Monticello*. New York: Abrams, 1993.

Studley, Vance. *Make Your Own Artist's Tools and Materials*. New York: Dover, 1979.

Thomas, Davis, and Karin Ronnefeldt, eds. *People of the First Man: Life among the Plains Indians in Their Final Days of Glory*. New York: Dutton, 1976.

Troccoli, Joan Carpenter. *Alfred Jacob Miller: Watercolors of the American West*. Tulsa, OK: Thomas Gilcrease Museum Association, 1990.

Williamsburg Collection of Antique Furnishings. Williamsburg, VA: Colonial Williamsburg Foundation, 1973.

APPENDIX B: RESOURCES

Please include a SASE with all correspondence.

Goose Bay Workshops
Peter Goebel
Rt 1 Box 297C
Crozet, VA 22932
—*Tin and copper inkwells, quills, journals, documents cases*

The Kings' Arms Press & Bindery
Oldwick, NJ 08858
—*Portfolios, paper goods*

Kannik's Korner
PO Box 1654
Springfield, OH 45501
—*Re-prints of* The Handmaid to the Arts

Tim Greene and Carol Neville
PO Box 277
Greenbush, MA 02040
—*Pens, ink and other writing supplies*

Smoke & Fire Co.
PO Box 166
Grand Rapids, OH 43522
—*Pottery inkwells*

Historic Pottery Series
Sprinkle Pottery
218 S. Main
Irving, TX 57060
—*Pottery inkwells*

After Karl Bodmer: *The Travellers Meeting with Minatarre Indians* engraving with aquatint, hand-colored. Completed after return of the 1832-1834 North American expedition led by Prince Maximilian of Wied-Neuwied, Germany.

Some of the equipment an artist/naturalist would carry into the field includes a small water flask, a shell palette and a porcelain mixing palette with a wooden watercolor box.

RECOVERY OF CAPTIVE CHILD ON BOUQUET'S EXPEDITION.

Above: An example of the natural pigments used by Cathy Johnson in her painting demonstration on Children's Day at Fort Osage.

Facing page: *The Color of Terror* by Lee Teter, Bedford, Pennsylvania. Armed, shirted and accoutred with plunder from a slain Long Knife, this inspired rendering of a Shawnee warrior, circa 1770s, shows the true face of border warfare.

Below: Journals, a lap desk and Peter Goebel's traveling inkwell.

Photo by Cathy Johnson

Sir John Caldwell. On a brass plate at the base of the frame, the inscription reads: "Portrait of Sir John Caldwell, Bart.—8th The King's Regiment—who Colonel de Peyster sent from Detroit to Sandusky to requise of the Shawnee, Delaware, Mingoes and other to bury the hatchett at the Preliminaries of Peace, which was signed between Great Britain and the United States 1782." Caldwell, dressed in his Ojibway finest, is holding a wampum belt in his left hand and a pipe tomahawk in his right.

Photo by Hal Rice, Murray, Kentucky

Tenskwatawa ("He-Opens-the-Door"), the brother of Tecumseh, was a leading figure in the early 1800s during the Indian resistance in the Middle Ground. James Otto Lewis first painted his portrait in 1824. Lewis' watercolor was used by Charles Bird King in 1829 to produce this likeness. Though he is wearing a turban, ear wheels, gorget and arm bands, his dress is Anglo. In 1832, when George Catlin painted Tenskwatawa, the aging holy man posed in traditional clothing.

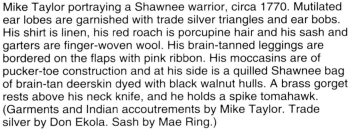

Mike Taylor portraying a Shawnee warrior, circa 1770. Mutilated ear lobes are garnished with trade silver triangles and ear bobs. His shirt is linen, his red roach is porcupine hair and his sash and garters are finger-woven wool. His brain-tanned leggings are bordered on the flaps with pink ribbon. His moccasins are of pucker-toe construction and at his side is a quilled Shawnee bag of brain-tan deerskin dyed with black walnut hulls. A brass gorget rests above his neck knife, and he holds a spike tomahawk. (Garments and Indian accoutrements by Mike Taylor. Trade silver by Don Ekola. Sash by Mae Ring.)

Right: Original slat-style quilled knife sheath and knife with quill-wrapped handle. From the John Painter Collection.

Above: Left to right: a slat-style case, a sheath with zig-zag technique, and a loom-quilled case.

Original knife with quilled sheath from the John Painter Collection.

Original quilled knife sheath from the John Painter Collection.

Facing page: Steven Lalioff's collection of original 18th and 19th century trunks from which he has created exact reproductions.

These leathers were all tanned using bark by Mark Odle. They were finished by several methods. Included from the bottom, counter-clockwise, are bear, hog, buffalo, calf, goat and the black hide is deer. The small shiny, dark hide in the center is kidskin.

The largest leather-bound trunk Lalioff has found. It's English-made, circa 1779, 48" long, 25" wide and 20-1/2" tall.

Officer's uniform trunk on display at the Old Barracks Museum, Trenton, New Jersey. The reproduction campaign trunk's lid is open to reveal its period contents.

Writing or drawing implements (left to right): pen knife, quills, steel nib, reed pen, Venetian glass pen, stick, pencil, crayon holder, and Peter Goebel's traveling inkwell.

Great Lakes & Eastern Woodlands Knife Sheaths

by Jan Zender and Rochelle Dale

Jan and Rochelle went sledding on their first date. They must have liked each other, for a few months later Rochelle sold everything except her car and moved to Pine Ridge, South Dakota, with him. But after several years of being scorched by the sun and broken by horses, they decided to settle in Michigan's Upper Peninsula where they could pursue sledding again, along with traditional snowshoeing for Jan, skiing for Rochelle and dog-sledding for the whole family. They get plenty of practice in these pursuits since their automobile is three miles away from the house during winter.

Jan and Rochelle built their octagonal log home from logs which they cut and peeled themselves. During the building process, they lived in their wigwam. They still live without modern conveniences and the children do not complain about it!

Jan first went to Friendship in 1965 or 1966. He later went to college at the University of Montana where he received a degree in religious studies and native American studies. He met Rochelle in 1982 right after she finished her philosophy and German degree from Indiana University at Indianapolis.

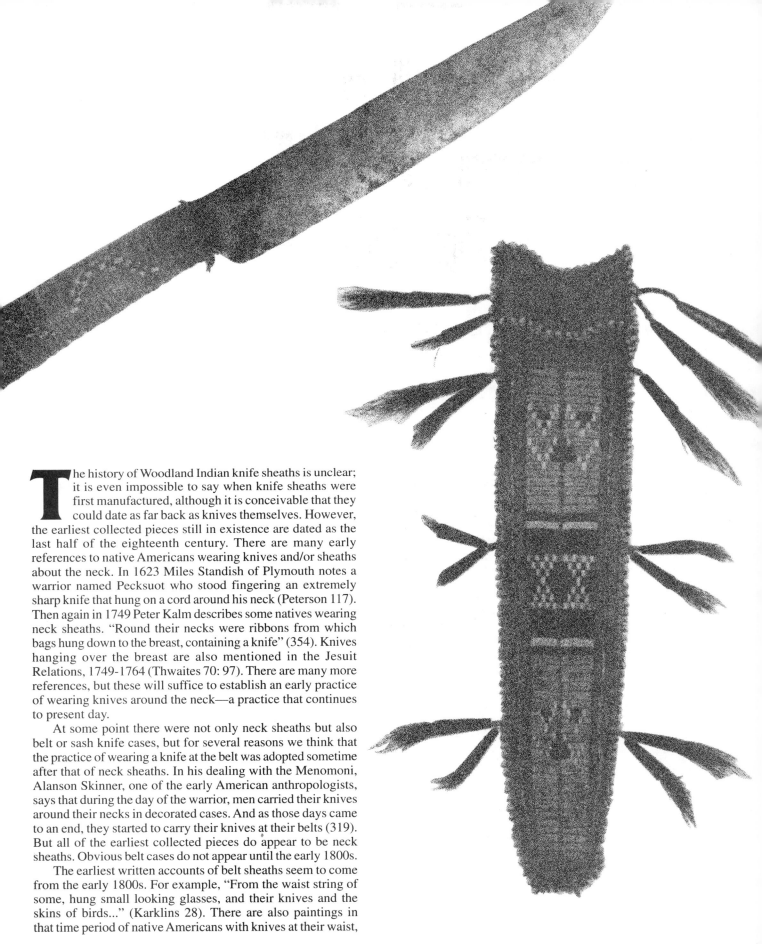

The history of Woodland Indian knife sheaths is unclear; it is even impossible to say when knife sheaths were first manufactured, although it is conceivable that they could date as far back as knives themselves. However, the earliest collected pieces still in existence are dated as the last half of the eighteenth century. There are many early references to native Americans wearing knives and/or sheaths about the neck. In 1623 Miles Standish of Plymouth notes a warrior named Pecksuot who stood fingering an extremely sharp knife that hung on a cord around his neck (Peterson 117). Then again in 1749 Peter Kalm describes some natives wearing neck sheaths. "Round their necks were ribbons from which bags hung down to the breast, containing a knife" (354). Knives hanging over the breast are also mentioned in the Jesuit Relations, 1749-1764 (Thwaites 70: 97). There are many more references, but these will suffice to establish an early practice of wearing knives around the neck—a practice that continues to present day.

At some point there were not only neck sheaths but also belt or sash knife cases, but for several reasons we think that the practice of wearing a knife at the belt was adopted sometime after that of neck sheaths. In his dealing with the Menomoni, Alanson Skinner, one of the early American anthropologists, says that during the day of the warrior, men carried their knives around their necks in decorated cases. And as those days came to an end, they started to carry their knives at their belts (319). But all of the earliest collected pieces do appear to be neck sheaths. Obvious belt cases do not appear until the early 1800s.

The earliest written accounts of belt sheaths seem to come from the early 1800s. For example, "From the waist string of some, hung small looking glasses, and their knives and the skins of birds..." (Karklins 28). There are also paintings in that time period of native Americans with knives at their waist,

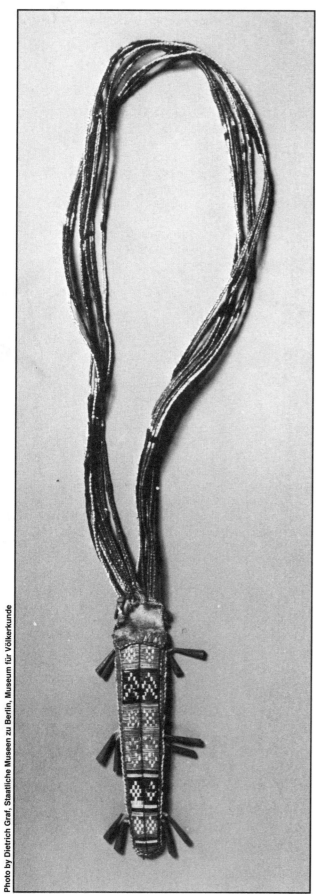

Mohawk/Iroquois type, dated late 18th century, sheath is made of smoked leather with two quilled slats down the front. It has an unusual edging using a combination of quills and opague white beads. Metal cones with red hair. Knife has a wooden handle wrapped with leather and then wrapped with porcupine quills. Length of case 22.5 cm. Length of knife 28 cm.

and those cases look just like what we generally consider a neck sheath. Therefore the sheaths with extravagantly decorated straps, that is, loom-quilled or plaited strings, must truly have been neck sheaths. But those cases with only a leather thong or ribbon strap may possibly have been worn at either the neck or waist. Also, there is a mid-eighteenth century account of Indians wearing several knives simultaneously. "When savages go to war they are armed with guns, tomahawks and knives. They usually have three knives; one hung around the neck, one in the belt, and one fastened in the garter on the

Slat-style knife sheath with quill-plaited strap. The length of the sheath is 20 cm; length with the strap is 65 cm. As with several other sheaths and straps, the strap involves considerably more work than the sheath. Compare this sheath with the Mohawk/Iroquois type above.

108

outside of the leg" (J. C. B. 147).
While trying to determine when knife sheaths were first used, we must also take into consideration tribal or individual preferences. It is possible that some may have preferred to carry their knives at the waist and so never adopted the practice of wearing neck sheaths. Although the use of neck sheaths was widespread (even Southeastern Indian men are pictured with neck sheaths), it was probably not a universal practice.

So perhaps we cannot really know which type of sheath—belt or neck—came first or even if they came about at the same time. Much information is still lacking, including information about the sheaths carried in garters.

For those of us who are trying to depict a certain tribe in Indian history, it would be nice to know which knife case styles belong to whom. But, unfortunately, most of the collected pieces have no tribal designation, only perhaps to say Great Lakes for instance, while those that have had an origin attributed to them may be disputed by modern authorities. One current example of this concerns the neck sheaths decorated with quill-wrapped slats with checked geometrical designs. These cases are generally given an Iroquois and more specifically a Mohawk attribution. In 1954 W. Krickeberg attached Iroquois provenance to a piece in the Berlin Museum für Völkerkunde. In 1968 another similar case was given the same attribution based on the Berlin case. Then in 1976 T. Brasser named a sheath from the former Speyer collection "Mohawk-Iroquois type," and so on down the line (Feest 296). But Dr. Christian F. Feest suggests that there is no concrete foundation on which to assume that these cases are in fact Mohawk, but rather finds evidence to the contrary and believes instead that they may be Great Lakes. One of his arguments against the Mohawk attribution is that these quilled slats are made from birch bark. Perhaps it was assumed that the Iroquois did not have a ready supply of birch bark.

As Frances Parkman in *The Parkman Reader* states, "The Iroquois in the absence of birch bark were forced to use the bark of elm" (32). The Iroquois did make dugout or elm bark canoes instead of birch bark and they covered their long houses with elm bark. However, the Adirondack Mountains do contain birch trees, although during the eighteenth century the main body of Iroquois was probably to the south of those mountains. So it is difficult to say whether or not birch bark was easily available.

But even if it was not, this would not be a sufficient reason for assuming that the Iroquois did not

Reproductions showing three distinctive styles: (left) loom quilled; (middle) zigzag, line and saw-tooth techniques; and (right) slat style with bead and quill edge.

use birch bark for quill wrapping. Iroquois warriors were known to have traveled hundreds of miles in all directions. Possibly they could have deemed birch bark valuable enough to carry home small pieces (especially if they had ever seen writing or any work done on it). Also we must take into account the extensive Indian trade amongst the tribes that was already well established before white contact. Raw materials were certainly a part of this trade.

Still another point where modern authorities may disagree is in the current categorization of certain museum pieces. Many collected pieces came with little or no information with them. Some of these were classified in the early twentieth century by museum personnel who may not have been experts in that particular area. Yet these classifications may be difficult to disprove and even more difficult to change.

Correctly classifying existing knife sheaths is made even more uncertain by the historic Indian trade already mentioned. For example, the Hurons prized the painted coats of the Algonkians and traded for them whenever possible. And the Hurons were not alone in their admiration of the Algonkian's painting skills. The Ottawas then were known for the outstanding quality of their reed mats. It is said that they were so finely woven that they were likened unto Turkish carpets (Phillips 57). So the Ottawas had no trouble trading these mats for other goods. Also the Illinois and Miami were being supplied with porcupine quills by the Potawatomi and Ottawa (Kinietz 176).

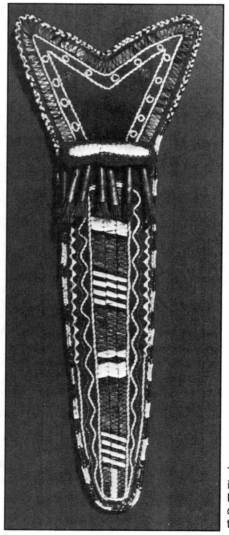

So, with all this trading, unless we are very astute, we may assume that a mat collected from the Hurons is a Huron mat, when actually it was Ottawa-made. We can imagine then that knife sheaths may also have been traded from time to time. A talented woman could easily trade her handiwork for necessary or unusual items from other tribes. Also, then as well as now, many items were simply given as gifts.

Not only does the trade and gift-giving between tribes make classifications difficult, but other factors do as well. As Lawrence M. Hauptman points out, "By the late 18th and early 19th centuries when many of the works of Woodland Indian art in our museums were collected, wars, epidemics, the fur trade and white settlement had created multi-ethnic Indian communities throughout" (128-139).

Because of these wars and epidemics, the Indian populations at this time were severely declining. To help deal with this problem, adoption of captives and prisoners became more and more frequent. These adopted ones must obviously have brought some of their own cultural styles, techniques and beliefs with them. And with encroaching white settlement, the tribes were forced to live closer and closer together, permitting more

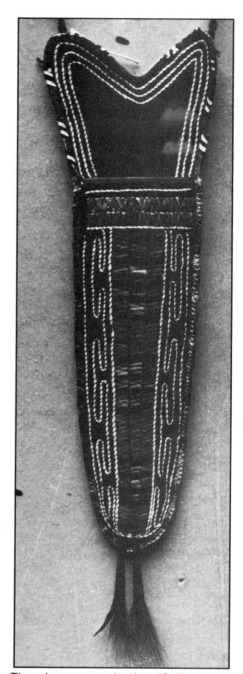

The above reproduction (S-2) shows similarities with Ottawa case on the facing page. One exception is the different style edging technique.

The original of this reproduction (S-1) is on display in the Peabody Museum. Note the similarities with the Ottawa case on the facing page, particularly the quill edge and the cut of the top.

frequent contact (Phillips 57).

Indeed, correctly identifying a particular knife sheath may seem impossible, but perhaps after much study, some reasonably sound judgments can be made. For instance some collected knife sheaths do have reputable documentation concerning their history and origin. One example is the large, quilled Ottawa case, shown at right, with the three zigzag-style lines down one side and V-shaped line work on the other side. The original case is housed in the Museum für Völkerkunde in Vienna and its origin seems unquestioned. With close observation, similarities between this case and at least one or two others will be noticeable. The first similar case is on display in the Peabody Museum in Massachusetts. A reproduction of the Peabody's sheath, which we will call S-1, is shown at far left on the facing page. The basic colors of the Ottawa case and the Peabody case are the same: red is the background and main color, with black and white V-shaped and slanted stripes. Both have extensive, intricate line work and both have the same style quill edging with alternating black and white quills. The color of the leather seems much the same as well as the cut and shape of the knife case top. Overall, the two cases have a strikingly similar style or appearance about them, which could lead one to believe that the sheath at the Peabody Museum may also be an Ottawa or Ojibwa case.

Another point of interest about S-1 is the saw-tooth line work down the side. It may be that this technique is also an indicator of a Great Lakes origin, since it shows up predominantly in the Western Great Lakes (Ottawa, Ojibwa, Potawatami, etc.) and with the Eastern Sioux and the Cree. At this time though, this theory is only a conjecture and not to be taken as fact.

One other case, which we will call S-2 (near left on the facing page), is also much like the original Ottawa sheath in the Museum für Völkerkunde. It has most of the same similarities as S-1 except for a different style edging technique. Perhaps this original is also an Ottawa or Ojibwa case. These two tribes were and still are close neighbors, and as with other tribes who live in close proximity to one another, their art becomes difficult to distinguish.

Now to return to the knife cases with quill-wrapped slats. If we assume that the Iroquois/Mohawk designation is the correct one, then we may be safe in thinking that all like knife cases are also Iroquois. Taken as a group (there are at least twelve) these cases exhibit several distinct characteristics. The tops are all cut very much the same. They are relatively small and not at all like the top of the Ottawa case. Down the sides

Two styles of knife case tops found on slat knife cases. The style on the left is the most common, while the one on the right is very unusual.

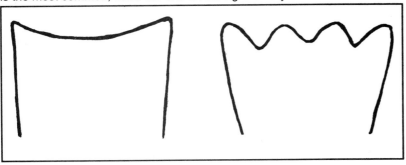

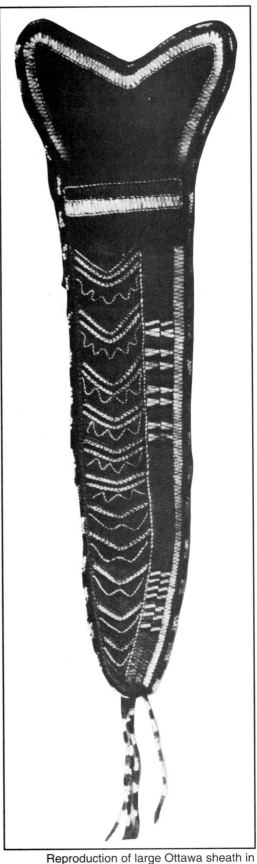

Reproduction of large Ottawa sheath in Museum für Völkerkunde, Vienna. Length 15-1/2 inches.

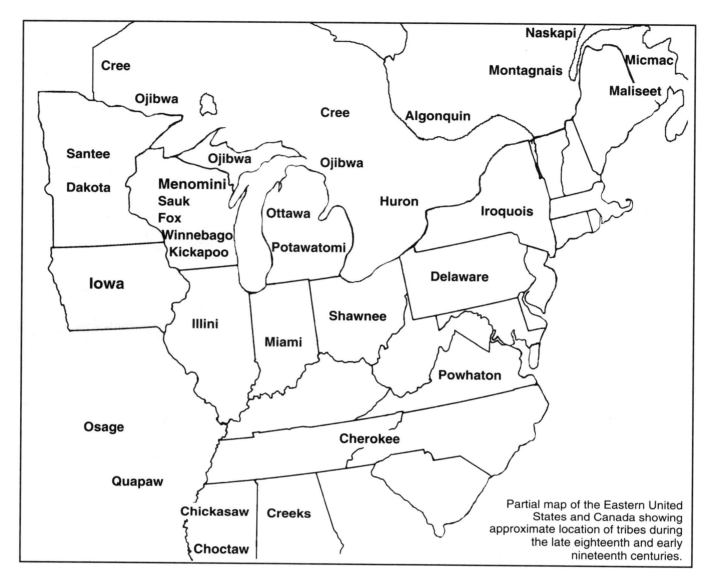

Partial map of the Eastern United States and Canada showing approximate location of tribes during the late eighteenth and early nineteenth centuries.

Map labels: Cree, Ojibwa, Santee, Dakota, Menomini, Sauk, Fox, Winnebago, Kickapoo, Iowa, Illini, Miami, Osage, Quapaw, Chickasaw, Choctaw, Creeks, Cree, Ojibwa, Ojibwa, Ottawa, Potawatomi, Shawnee, Huron, Algonquin, Naskapi, Montagnais, Micmac, Maliseet, Iroquois, Delaware, Powhaton, Cherokee

are pairs of cones with hair or their remains, and down the front is a pair of quill-wrapped, birch bark slats. This wrapping technique is done with a stitch of sinew down the middle between the slats to which the quills are attached. Thus both slats are done at the same time.

Stylistically these cases are all very similar, except for one whose top is cut in an irregular fashion. The quill style on this particular case is also a bit different. So could this one then be from a different people? There is one other case, collected from the Eastern Sioux, that has its top cut in the same way. Perhaps that may have some bearing, since these are the only two sheaths known at this time to have tops cut in that fashion.

By studying styles, techniques, cut and shape of cases and their tops, colors and so on, we do find striking similarities. So much so that sometimes we may want to think that some pieces had the same maker. For example the Berlin case with five zigzag rows of vertical quillwork with truncated designs in red-orange and white has its twin in Ottawa at the Canadian Museum of Civilization. (See David Wright's article in the 1988 issue of the *Dixie Gun Works Blackpowder Annual*.) The only difference is that the colors are reversed.

Even so, we must be very careful. Since many of the art styles within tribes living in the same geographical area do overlap, perhaps the best we can safely do is assign pieces to an area. For this reason, as we stated earlier, many collection pieces are titled "Western Great Lakes" or "Eastern Woodlands." This is by far the safest route to follow.

So far all of the cases we have discussed have been quilled cases. But what about beaded cases? At one time the general opinion seemed to be that beadwork was a later style, say 1800 or later, but historically speaking, beads, even the tiniest of beads, have been found in pre-eighteenth century sites. Le Clercq describes beadwork among the Micmac as early as 1680 (17). In the collection of Benjamin West, shown in *American Indian Art*, Winter 1991, we find woven beaded garters dated pre-1770, not to mention the finely bead-worked finger weaving pre-1776 (34-47). (For more early beadwork see the article by J.C.H. King in *American Indian Art*, Spring 1993.)

However, the earliest collected beaded knife sheaths are dated around 1835. These cases are usually belt sheaths with a

112

Common style of early beaded belt sheath. This type of case was also made with a loom-quilled panel rather than a beaded panel. Neville Public Museum of Brown County, Wisconsin. Ojibwa, c. 1830. Length including strap 40 cm.

Body done in zigzag-style quillwork, quilled wrapped fringes at top and filler-style quill edge. An almost identical case (the colors are reversed) exists in the collection of the Canadian Museum of Civilization. Length 22.5 cm.

Top row: quilled Great Lakes sheaths, lengths without straps are 23 cm, 23 cm and 22 cm. None of these cases are made of black leather. Middle sheath has a turquoise-colored ribbon strap. Bottom row: (left) knife with bone or antler handle, sheath possibly Bungi Ojibwa or Cree, length 43 cm; (middle) knife with a horn handle inlaid with bone and cartridge butts, sheath probably Cree with loom-woven quillwork, length 38 cm; (right) knife with bone or antler handle, length 36 cm.

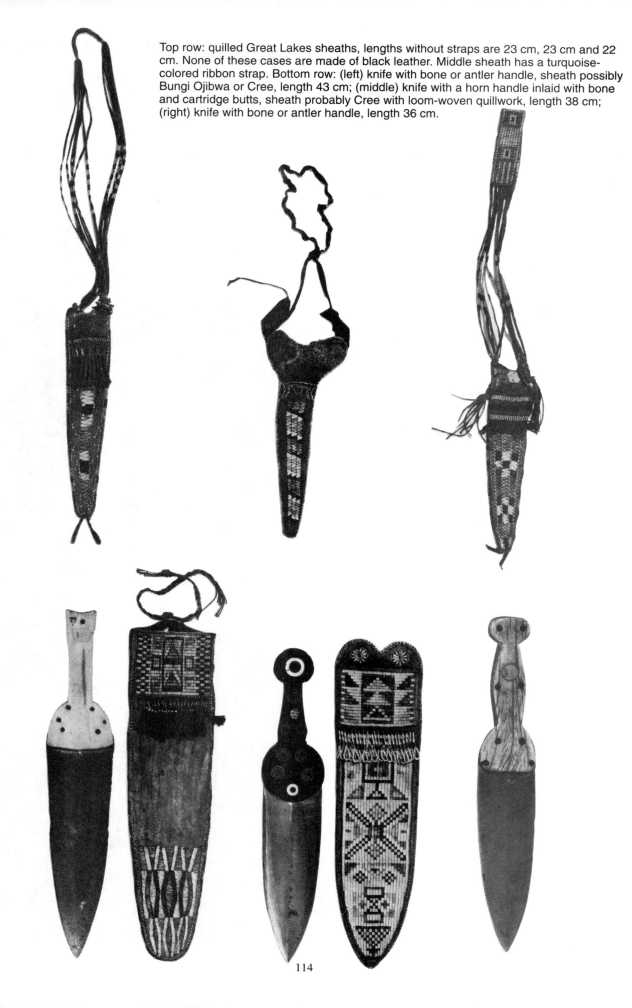

114

115

beaded square at the top with long fringes hanging from below the beadwork. There are also cases made in the same style, only with loom-quilled squares and quilled fringes.

It seems quite possible, owing to the collected pre-1780 beadwork, that beaded knife cases could also have been in existence at that time. It may be that they simply were not sought-after and collected by the early collectors. They would have been familiar with beads already, but quilled items would have been a novelty and purely native American. So, although we may find good reasons to believe that certain styles of beaded cases were pre-1800, still the fully beaded, intricately designed cases seem to be late 1800s' pieces.

Most of the collected knife sheaths still in existence were highly ornamented, either quilled or beaded. Some plain ones do still exist, although they seem rare. Obviously many collectors simply would not have been interested in undecorated cases, but there may have been other reasons to explain why so much time and effort were used to decorate a simple item.

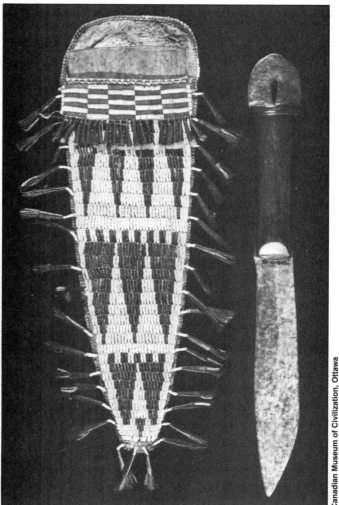

Early beaded belt sheaths follow the style illustrated by this reproduction. These kinds of sheaths are depicted in many early 19th century paintings. Possibly Cree or Ojibwa. Loom-quilled with quill-wrapped fringes. Length 15 inches without fringe.

Canadian Museum of Civilization, Ottawa

Northern Ojibwa-type case, c. 1800. Front covered with porcupine quills in netted technique with a rectangle of loom-woven quillwork at the top that ends and begins with white glass beads. Brass cones with red hair. The case is quill-edged and has a birch bark liner. The knife is a single-edged iron blade with a horn handle. Length of knife 31 cm. Length of case without fringe 30 cm.

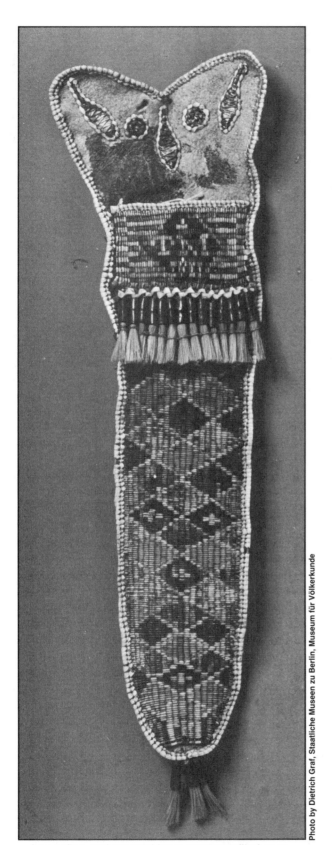

A very fine and unusual loom-woven quilled case with the initials "TM" on the top panel. The hair inside cones is white. Length 23 cm.

It may not have been respectful for an important hunter or warrior to keep the knife used for such serious matters in a plain, uncared-for case. Most tribes considered killing a very serious matter and so the preparations for hunting or war were carefully executed. The implements used in these activities, such as knives for skinning or scalping, tumplines for carrying meat, and even the person's clothing, were important and regarded with due respect.

An Ojibwa hunter's song shows the importance of the hunter's appearance:

> *Like a star*
> *I shine*
> *The animal, gazing, is fascinated by my sight.*
> (Densmore 86)

A fine loom-quilled case in green, blue, yellow and white zigzag technique on flap and netted and plaited quilled strap. Strap colors are red, orange, blue and yellow. Metal cones with red hair. The iron blade on the knife is marked "A. Hatfield." Length of knife 24.5 cm. Brass and probably tortoise shell handle. Great Lakes, before 1800. Length of case 22.5 cm.

117

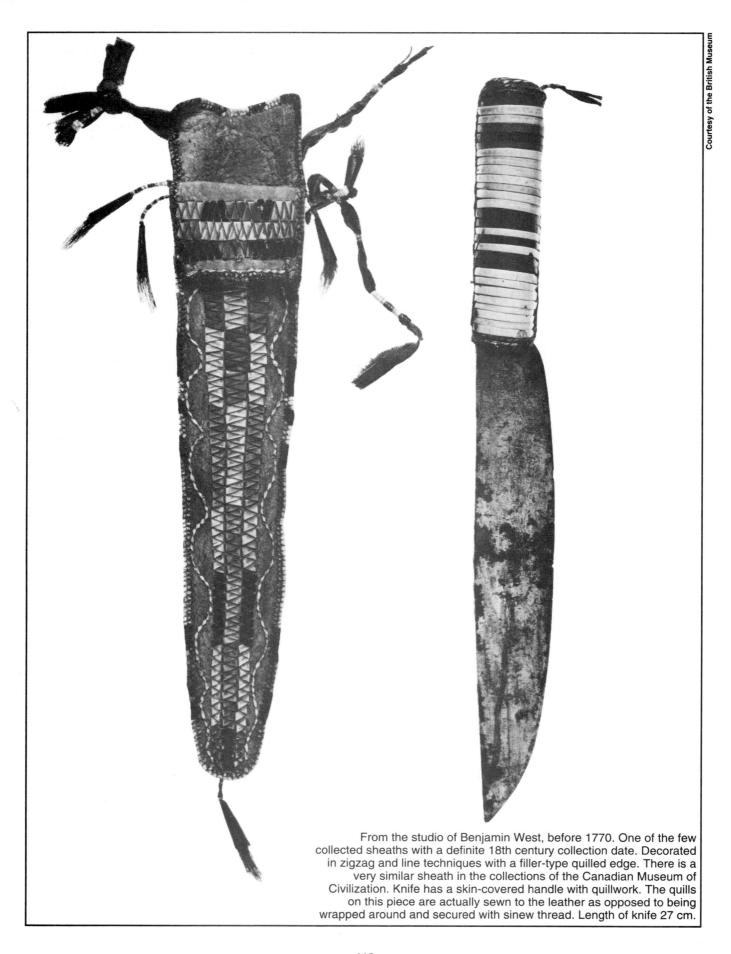

From the studio of Benjamin West, before 1770. One of the few collected sheaths with a definite 18th century collection date. Decorated in zigzag and line techniques with a filler-type quilled edge. There is a very similar sheath in the collections of the Canadian Museum of Civilization. Knife has a skin-covered handle with quillwork. The quills on this piece are actually sewn to the leather as opposed to being wrapped around and secured with sinew thread. Length of knife 27 cm.

Left: Huron belt sheath decorated with a panel of black dyed skin with moosehair and possibly porcupine quills, edged with red cloth. Length 30 cm. Middle: Possibly Huron, this sheath is made of black dyed leather. The front is decorated with a loom-quilled strip. This same loomed design appears on many pieces attributed to the Huron. Loomed strip surrounded on both sides by zigzag technique. Top decorated with zigzag and line techniques. Right: Another knife with brass and probably tortoise shell handle.

Courtesy of the British Museum

Original "push" type knife with carved horse-head handle and sheath made from buffalo calf (or unborn) with tiny hoof at end. Winnebago. Collected from Black River Falls, Wisconsin, in the Loren Herrington Collection. This knife and sheath come from a "horse stealing" bundle. To prove his manhood, a fifteen-year-old boy walked from Wisconsin to South Dakota, killed a Sioux horse herder of the same age, took his complete scalp and rode back with the horses. This bundle was made as his reminder of that episode.

It was imperative to show the proper respect to the animal being hunted. This was particularly so concerning the hunting of bears.

Of all the animals that exist in their forests, the Indians respect the bear most. They regard it almost in the light of a human being. Indeed they will often say that the bear is a 'Anijinabe' (Indian). They will converse with it, thinking all the while the animal must understand them. (Kohl 408)

This respect must have been because of the bear's uncanny cleverness and also its resemblance to humans.

What follows is a lengthy description of a Cree bear hunter's preparations, given by David Rockwell. It shows the importance of the hunter's preparation and the importance placed on the articles for the hunt:

On the morning of the hunt, the hunter unwrapped his very best hunting clothes: his special skin coat, his leggings, garters and moccasins, his mittens and cap. Like his body, his clothes had to be clean. All but the skin coat were heavily embroidered and beaded by his wife, with designs that he had dreamed. The designs, like his songs, gave him power and pleased the animal. He carefully unfolded his tapiskakan, a richly beaded kerchief, and strung it across his chest. The image on the cloth, which had come in a dream, was of a bear, either symbolically or realistically depicted. When he killed the bear, he would put the cloth on its chest and the bear would wear it as it was carried into camp.

Next, he took out his knife sheath, the bear's carrying line,

and the club, ax, or spear that he would use to kill the bear. Each had been decorated according to bear hunt dreams, for it was known to the Cree that "everything a man uses in hunting, he has to dream it first." The carrying line recreated the hunted animal's spirit. His wife made it from woven strips of caribou or bear hide. She made a head and tail, and she decorated it with quills, beads, ribbons, and feathers. Unlike a carrying line for caribou, beaver or geese, the bear's was not actually used to carry the bear home—its function was purely ceremonial. As with the tapiskakan, the hunter placed it upon the dead bear to please its spirit. (34)

So we see that the bear was a very respected animal and certainly the deer, beaver and even fish were given their proper due.

The preparations for war were not any less complicated than those for hunting. Through the media, clichés and prejudices, and many ungrounded generalizations, we sometimes may be persuaded to believe that the Indians in general were always at war with someone, that there were always war parties out there and someone looking for scalps. But in fact this was probably just not the case. A war party's expedition took many months of preparation. These preparations were done in a serious and respectful manner, usually commencing during the winter when the leaders would

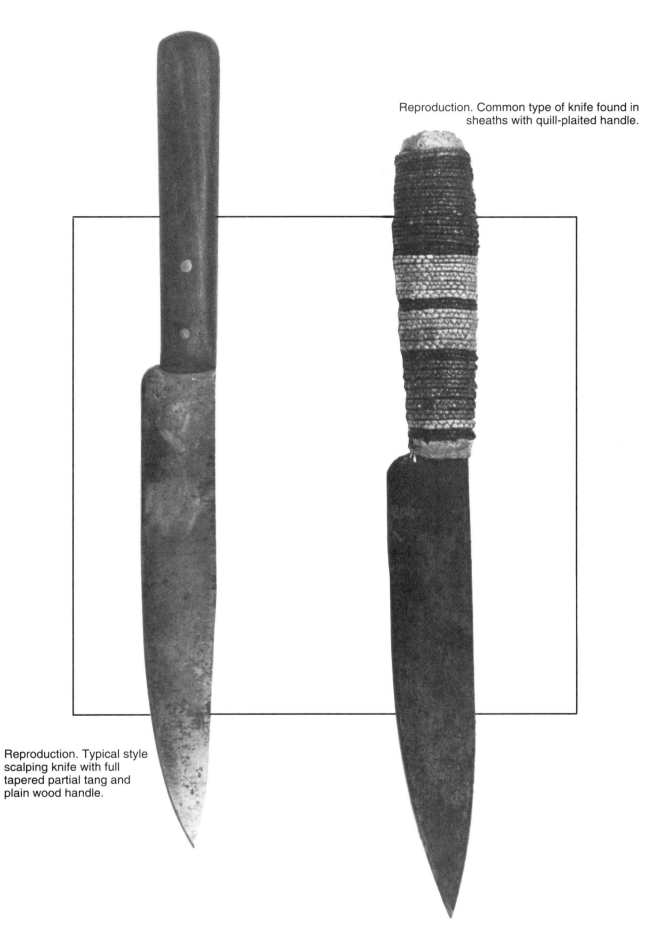

Reproduction. Common type of knife found in sheaths with quill-plaited handle.

Reproduction. Typical style scalping knife with full tapered partial tang and plain wood handle.

fast, drum and sing, and smoke seeking spiritual guidance and recruits to carry out their plans. A time would be set for the foray: spring or summer. When it approached, war dances would be performed. All would be painted black, including the women. All sorts of taboos and customs were observed along the road, such as fasting, not because they had to through circumstances, but because it was a kind of "religious war custom" (Kohl 342-344). If the foray were a successful one, the warriors would hang up after the engagement deerskins or other items in the trees on the battlefield. These were a sort of expiatory offering to appease the dead men's spirits and the spirits in heaven (Kohl 342-345). It has also been noted that the Indian's holy men were "absolutely forbidden to slay" (Adair 159).

So we may gather then that war was no simple undertaking. Thus, as great the care taken concerning the articles for the hunt, so would it be for the instruments of war, including the sheaths that carried the scalping knives.

They "speedily draw their long sharp-pointed scalping knife out of a sheath from their breast..." (Adair 415-416). Scalping was a custom of many Indians, though not all. The scalp itself was more than just a trophy. First, it may be seen as a symbol of bravery. There was no honor in killing a man from a distance with a gun or arrow without even seeing his face, but only in actually touching the enemy was there honor. The scalp then becomes a symbolic reminder. These were often decorated or painted and brought out at special occasions. Many Indians braided, greased or manured a small section of hair or shaved their head leaving only a small portion at the top and back, a scalp lock, as a way to tease the enemy, as if to say, "try and take this!" Also, some say that this section at the top back of the head is where the soul resides. If this is the belief, then the taking of a scalp may have more significance than we can even guess. So then, it must follow that the sheaths which carried such an important weapon would also have to be very important and most likely elaborately decorated.

The knives used in these sheaths were varied. The earliest collected knife that was known to have been used by an Indian came from a raid an Deerfield, Massachusetts, in 1675. It is a type of French plug bayonet with helmeted male heads on the pommel and quillon terminals.

In an incident involving Miles Standish in 1623, another type of knife, perhaps a French quillon dagger, which immediately proceeded the plug bayonet, is described. As Wituwamat taunted Miles Standish with a knife with a woman's head on the pommel, he said, "But I have another at home wherewith I have killed both French and English. And that hath a man's face on it and by and by these two must marry..." (qtd. in Peterson 117).

Likely there were specific knives for specific purposes. In some of the old trade lists, certain kinds of knives are listed. For instance David McCrea at Michilimackinac in 1777 presents a list, followed by John Johnston's listing for the years 1802-1811.

6 dozen Buck Cutteaux (knives)
2 dozen red handled scalping knives
1/2 Grohorn handled folding knives
2 dozen wood handled folding
    knives
6 fine ivory handled knives
7 tranches (cutting knife)
                        (qtd. in Armour and Widder 199)

5 dozen Scalping knives-4 sizes
1 dozen pen knives
1 dozen Barlow knives
2 9/12 dozen Jack knives
6 dozen butcher knives
2 dozen 4-bladed pen knives
                        (qtd. in Peterson 119)

Although any type of knife could have been used as a scalping knife, we see from the trade lists that the traders at least had a certain style knife that they considered scalping knives. This kind of knife followed very specific patterns, and many of them were identical. They commonly had plain wooden handles, sometimes painted red or black. The tangs did not go all the way to the end of the handle. They had what is known as a full, tapered, partial tang. The handles were then secured with three pins. The thickest part of the blade (80-90 thousandths of an inch) was at the choil where the blade ends and the handle begins. The average blade length was six to seven inches with the widest section measuring 1-1/4 inches. After all this precision, many of these knives had the handles covered with brain-tanned leather to which quills were then applied in a decorative manner. The two most common quill techniques for these handles were plaiting and a style of wrapping. These "scalping" knives, either plain-handled or quilled, are commonly found in existing collected knife sheaths and also in archaeological sites.

Another type of knife commonly found is one with a brass filigree handle with tortoise shell. The brass was cast and then pressed on over the shell. Then there are some knives with carved handles. They may have a human head carved at the end or an animal representation.

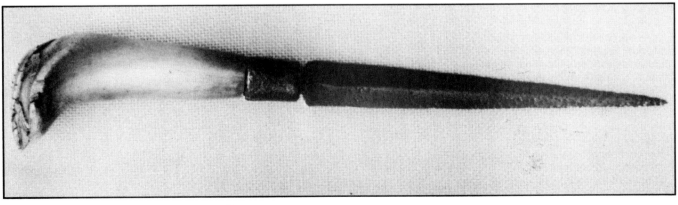

Illustration of turtle carved on butt end of original knife, shown below.

So there are a variety of knives found in cases. We have discussed only some of the most common ones. But in most of the sheaths, the knives had thin enough handles to allow them to slide into the case so that about half the handle would be covered. The knife thus sheathed is easy to remove yet safely secured.

We have discussed the use of knives and their sheaths for hunting and war, both generally men's fields, but did women wear knife cases too? This is a question not easily answered since there does not seem to be much information on this subject. There is one painting showing an Athabascan woman wearing a sheath around her neck. But the Athabascans live in Canada's far northwest. Can we logically conclude from this painting that Great Lakes and Eastern Woodland women also wore neck sheaths? It seems a big stretch. But then in an archaeological site in Michigan, the remains of two women with metal knives on their chests have been found (Mainfort 329-330, 334-335). This may indicate that they were worn, though some may argue that the knives were simply placed on their chests at burial. The chest would be the most natural place to lay anything at burial, since that would be the largest flat surface.

So, while there is not much evidence of Eastern and Great Lakes women wearing knife cases of any kind, there is also no evidence that shows they did not. We know that Plains women wore them at their belt along with their awl cases. Surely the Eastern women also carried a knife somewhere. With all the various activities that the women performed, a knife would at times be indispensable, not to mention its function as a possible means of self-defense. Perhaps more information on this subject will surface in the future. At this point, there seems to be no hard evidence to say whether women did or did not wear knife cases.

Original knife with turtle carved on butt of handle. In the collection of John Painter.

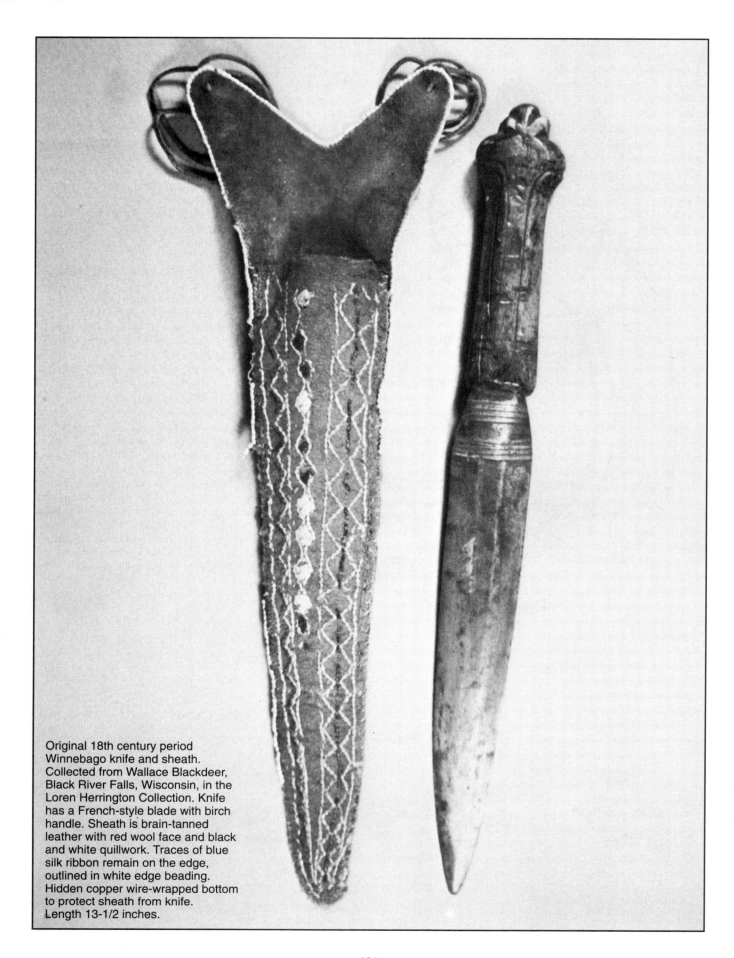

Original 18th century period
Winnebago knife and sheath.
Collected from Wallace Blackdeer,
Black River Falls, Wisconsin, in the
Loren Herrington Collection. Knife
has a French-style blade with birch
handle. Sheath is brain-tanned
leather with red wool face and black
and white quillwork. Traces of blue
silk ribbon remain on the edge,
outlined in white edge beading.
Hidden copper wire-wrapped bottom
to protect sheath from knife.
Length 13-1/2 inches.

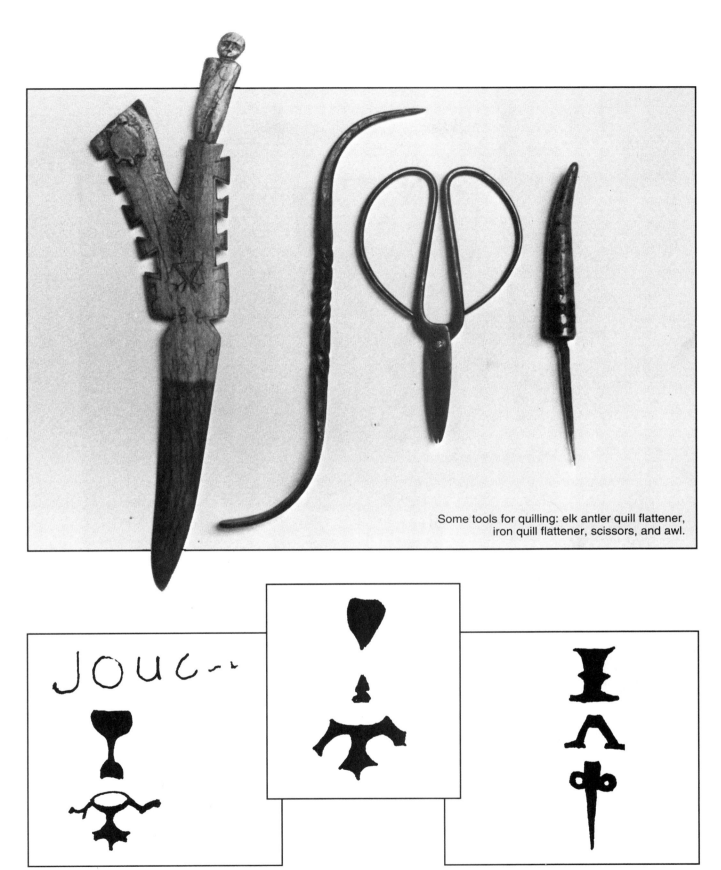

Some tools for quilling: elk antler quill flattener, iron quill flattener, scissors, and awl.

A group of unknown touch marks found on Indian knives all with quilled handles. Those at left and center are in the John Painter Collection. The touch mark at right is on a knife pictured in *Bo'jou, Neejee!* (Brasser 124). To identify these marks would be a valuable means of placing these knives and their cases in history.

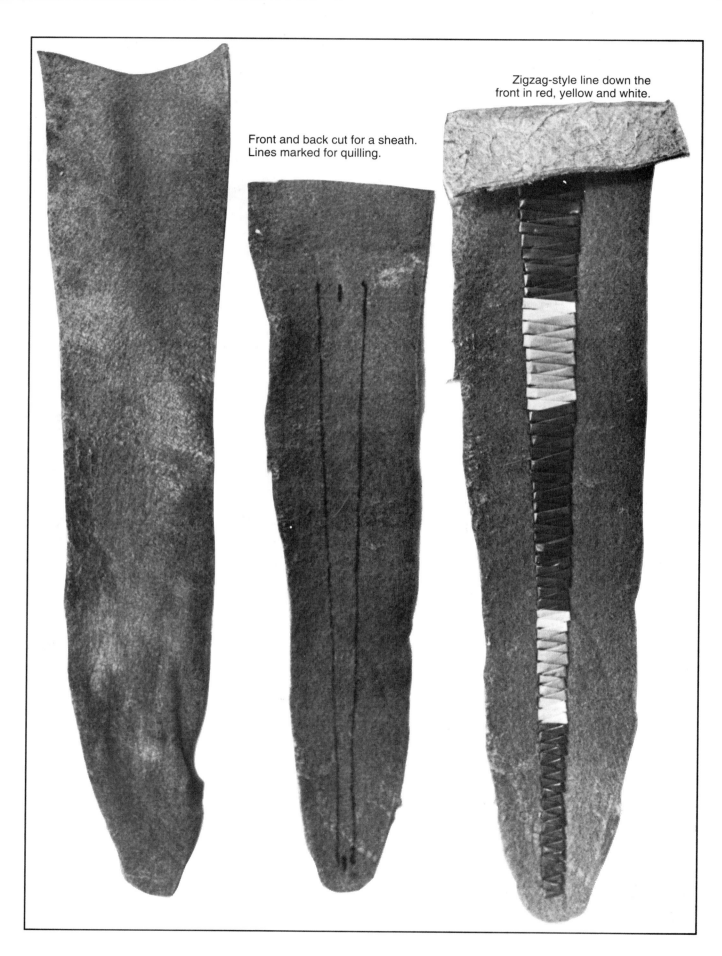

Front and back cut for a sheath.
Lines marked for quilling.

Zigzag-style line down the
front in red, yellow and white.

126

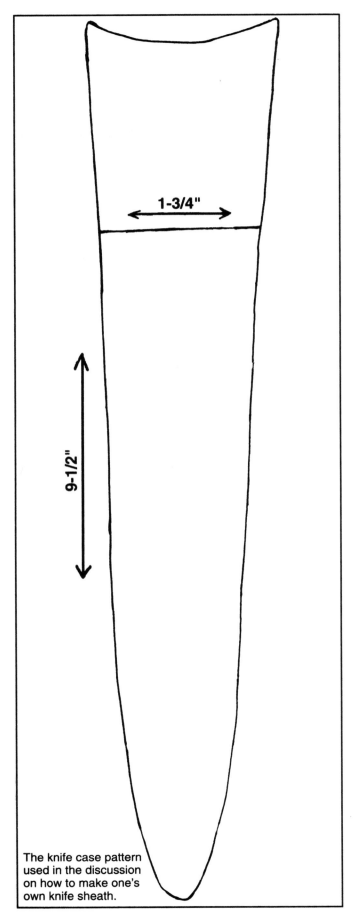

1-3/4"

9-1/2"

The knife case pattern
used in the discussion
on how to make one's
own knife sheath.

Finally, we should say a few words on making one's own knife sheath. First of all, almost all cases were made from brain-tanned leather, either smoked or dyed black. A few cases were made from wool, but either this was very rare or very few survived. To make one's first sheath, leather would be the best choice as wool can be difficult to quill or bead. Be sure to use brain tan! It holds those little stitches so much better and looks better too.

Then pick a pattern style and size. Cut a back and a front. The front piece will come up to where the ears of the back start to flair out. Set the back aside, and you are ready to begin.

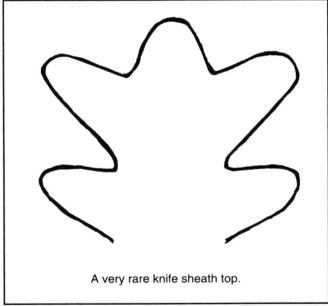

A very rare knife sheath top.

SOME COMMON SHAPES FOR KNIFE SHEATH TOPS

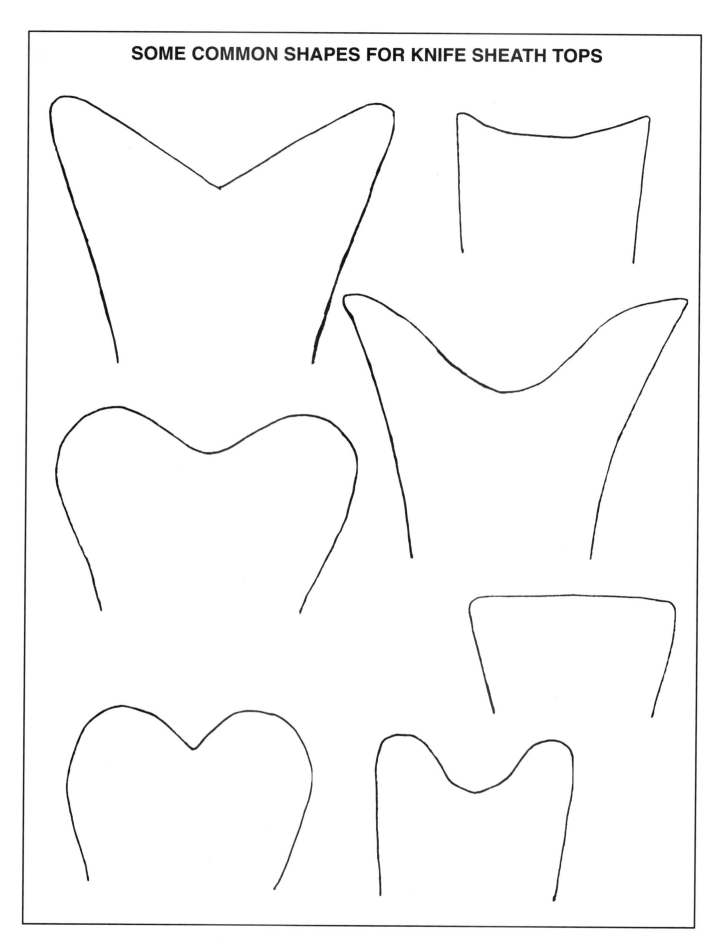

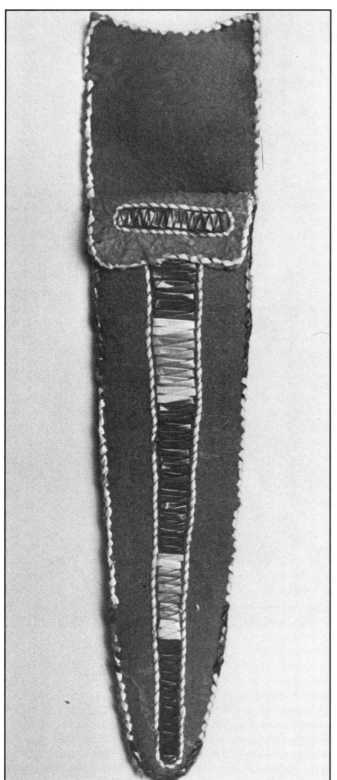

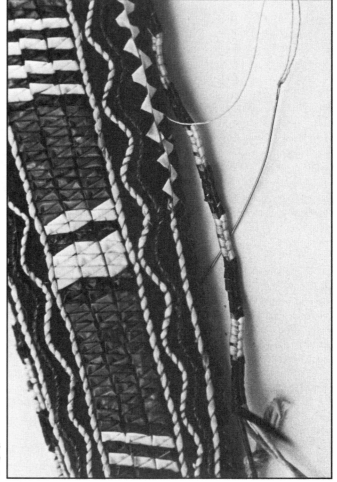

Finished reproduction case with quill edging using a single thread. Cones with deer hair could have been added although the original had none.

Close-up of a plaited quill edge. Plaiting is completed, then applied to sheath. Next to the edging, note the saw-tooth line work.

Rochelle quilling outside the wigwam.

For a simple but correct quilled case, going from side to side, find the center of the front piece. Lightly mark it at the top and bottom. This is a reference point. Now make two lines, one on either side of the center line. This will be the place for the quilled strip. Make the two lines about two inches apart at the top, narrowing to about 1/8 inch at the bottom. For a first quill project, stick with the zigzag technique. You will find good explanations of this and other techniques in the chapter "Quillworking" by Cathy Smith in *The Book of Buckskinning III*, in William Orchard's *The Technique of Porcupine Quill Decoration among the Indians of North America* or in *A Quillwork Companion* by Jean Heinbuch, to name a few. Good quill colors are red, white, black-brown, yellow-orange and indigo blue. After the vertical zigzag strip is complete, it would be common practice to go around it, usually with white quills,

in the simple line technique.

Now you are ready to assemble the case. Most edging techniques can be done as you are sewing the pieces together. There are several styles of quill edging as well as bead edgings. If you use beads, choose good old colors: white, greasy yellow, pony trader blue and some reds for instance. But before you start the edging, it is good to tack the front and back pieces together at two or three places so that they do not move.

Next, you will probably want a liner for your case so that the knife tip does not push through the bottom of the case. These are usually made from birch bark in the Eastern regions, although rawhide could also be used. Cut two pieces for the liner the same size as the front piece of the outer case. Attach them together and slide them into your case.

Finally, you will need a strap. A simple leather thong or

130

Rochelle flattening a porcupine quill with an elk antler quill flattener. Nearby is an iron quill flattener. Small quilled birch bark boxes are used for storage.

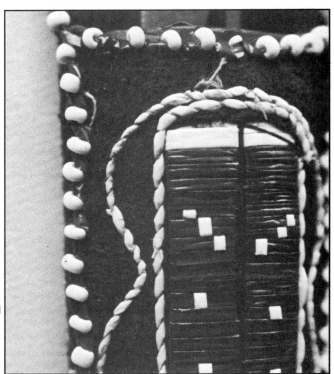

Another edging using beads and quills. Although it is difficult to see, there is a quill between every bead.

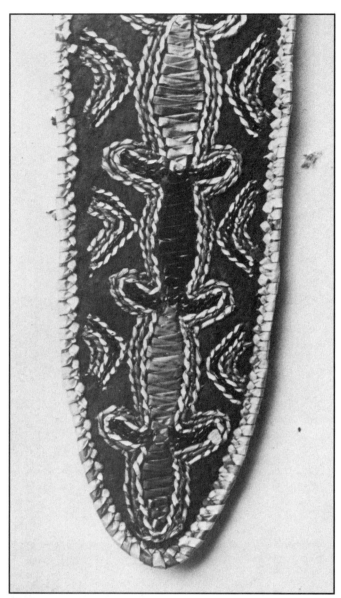

Close-up of quill edging done with a sinew filler. Note the alternating quill colors at the bottom, done by using two quills at the same time.

ribbon strap may be attached by poking one hole in each of the corners of the case top (you will need an awl). Insert the ribbon or thong from back to front. Make a knot at the ends and pull tight. A strap could also be stitched on the back, but the knotting method is easiest.

Good luck and have fun!

Writing this chapter has been an educational and fun experience for us. We would like to thank Bill and Linda Scurlock for allowing us the opportunity. We would also like to thank Dirk Ahler, Tom and Tim Connin, Laura Herrington and Scott Meachum for all their help.

Close-up of loom quillwork. The strap on this case is attached right above the quillwork rather than at the top of the sheath.

APPENDIX A: WORKS CITED

Adair, James. *History of the American Indians*. Ed. Samuel Cole Williams. London, 1775.

Armour, David, and Keith R. Widder. *At the Crossroads: Michilimackinac during the American Revolution*. Mackinac Island, MI: Mackinac Island State Park Commission, 1978.

Brasser, Ted J. *Bo'jou, Neejee! Profiles of Canadian Indian Art*. Ottawa: National Museum of Man, National Museums of Canada, 1976.

Densmore, Frances. *Chippewa Music*. 1910. Minneapolis: Ross and Haines, 1973.

Feest, Christian F. "Some 18th Century Specimens from Eastern North America in Collections in the German Democratic Republic." *Jahrbuch des Museums für Völkerkunde zu Leipzig*. Berlin: Akademie Verlag, 1987.

Hauptman, Lawrence M. "The Iroquois Villages of the 18th Century." *American Indian Environments: Ecological Issues in Native American History*. Eds. Christopher Vecsey and Robert W. Venables. Syracuse, NY: Syracuse University Press, 1980.

J.C.B. *Travels in New France*. Eds. Sylvester K. Stevens, Donald H. Kent, and Emma Edith Woods. Harrisburg: Pennsylvania Historical Commission, 1941.

Kalm, Peter. *Travels in North America: The English Version*. 1770. New York: Dover, 1987.

Karklins, Karlis. *Trade Ornament Usage among the Native Peoples of Canada*. Ottawa: Minister of Environment, Canada Parks Service, 1992.

King, J.C.H. "Woodlands Artifacts from the Studio of Benjamin West, 1738-1820." *American Indian Art Magazine* 17.1: 34-47.

Kinietz, Vernon. *The Indians of the Western Great Lakes 1615-1760*. Ann Arbor: University of Michigan Press, 1940.

Kohl, Johann. *Kitch Gami: Life among the Lake Superior Ojibway*. 1860. St. Paul: Minnesota Historical Society Press, 1985.

LeClercq, Christien. *New Relations of Gaspesia*. 1691. Toronto: Champlain Society, 1910.

Mainfort, Robert Jr. *Indian Social Dynamics in the Period of European Contact: Fletcher Site Cemetery, Bay County, Michigan*. East Lansing: Publications of the Museum— Michigan State University, 1979.

Parkman, Frances. *The Parkman Reader*. Boston: Little and Brown, 1955.

Peterson, Harold. *American Knives*. New York: Scribner's, 1958.

Phillips, Ruth B. "Northern Woodlands Artistic Traditions." *The Spirit Sings*. Toronto: Glenbow Museum—McClelland and Stewart, 1987.

Rockwell, David. *Giving Voice to Bear*. Niwot, CO: Roberts Rinehart, 1991.

Skinner, Alanson B. "Material Culture of the Menomini." Indian Notes and Monographs, Misc. Ser. 20 (1). New York: Museum of the American Indian—Heye Foundation, 1921.

Thwaites, Reuben G., ed., *Jesuit Relations and Allied Documents: Travels and Explorations of the Jesuit Missionaries in New France, 1610-1791*. 73 vols. Cleveland: Burrows, 1896-1901.

APPENDIX B: WORKS CONSULTED

Art of the Great Lakes Indians. Exhibit. Flint Institute of Arts, Flint, Michigan, 1973.

Beadwork and Textiles of the Ottawa. Harbor Springs, MI: Harbor Springs Historical Commission, 1984.

Heinbuch, Jean. *A Quillwork Companion*. Liberty, UT: Eagle's View Publishing, 1990.

King, J.C.H., "Art as Depicted by Sarah Stone in the Collection of Sir Ashton Lever." *American Indian Art Magazine* 18:2: 32-45.

Krickeberg, Walter. *Altere Ethnographica aus Nordamerika im Berliner Museum für Völkerkunde*. Berlin: Verlag von Dietrich Reimer, 1954.

Orchard, William. *The Technique of Porcupine Quill Decoration among the Indians of North America*. New York: Museum of the American Indian—Heye Foundation, 1971.

Papers of the Peabody Museum of American Archeology and Ethnology. Vol. VIII. Cambridge, MA: Harvard University, 1920.

Smith, Cathy. "Quillworking." *The Book of Buckskinning III*. Texarkana, TX: Rebel, 1986.

Wright, David. "Pouches and Knife Sheaths of the Great Lakes Indians." *Dixie Gun Works Blackpowder Annual* (1988): 17-20.

A Wardrobe for the Frontier Woman 1780–1840

by Beth Gilgun

Beth Gilgun is a researcher of 18th and 19th century clothing and lifestyles as well as a seamstress of reproduction 18th century clothing. She received her degree from Cornell University where, among other courses, she studied pattern making, fashion, writing for publication and various other types of communication.

Gilgun is a member of the Costume Society of America and the Brigade of the American Revolution. She lectures on 18th and 19th century clothing and textiles and has also worked with museums as a consultant on costume and textiles. Gilgun worked with the props department of the film *Summersby* and the television movie *Heart of Darkness* supplying clothing accessories and props related to the needle arts.

She has been a regular contributor to *MUZZLELOADER* magazine since 1984 and is the author of the book *Tidings from the 18th Century*, which is based on her long-running and popular column. Gilgun and her husband, Chris, owned and restored two 18th century houses before moving to Warwick, Massachusetts, where they currently reside in a reproduction 1750s gambrel Cape.

People are generally...not half so heathenish as many imagine...people expect taste and tidiness in dress, at least in ladies, just as much as in the East.
—Letter from Harriet Carr in Kansas
(qtd. in Myres 151)

In the early years of the United States, the frontier wasn't very far west. In 1787 Congress opened the Territory of the United States North West of the River Ohio to settlement and in 1788 pioneers established Marietta, Columbia, North Bend and Cincinnati. Middle Tennessee was being settled by 1780. The lands west of the Mississippi River that were the Louisiana Purchase were not annexed by the United States until late 1803, although it must be mentioned that there were thriving French settlements such as Ste. Genevieve and St. Louis along the west bank of the Mississippi River. It wasn't until 1841 that emigrants started traveling over the Oregon Trail, leaving from the bustling town of Independence, Missouri, a town that had only been in existence for thirteen or fourteen years at that time.

Settling the frontier was not exclusively a male activity, although some men traveled to new lands to build houses and then they sent for their wives and children several months later. One such man was Jonathan Hale who left Glastonbury, Connecticut, on June 12, 1810, and headed for the Cuyahoga Valley of Ohio. He made the 646 mile trip in 28 days (this averages 23 miles per day) with a team of horses and a canvas-topped wagon holding two chests and at least two boxes of tools and personal belongings (Halverson 20-21). When he arrived at his land, Jonathan found a squatter had built a cabin and planted wheat. The two agreed to trade the cabin and the wheat for Jonathan's wagon and horses so that the squatter could move. Jonathan's nephew, Theodore Hammond, who left the day before Jonathan, found similar circumstances upon arrival at his father's land. Apparently finding an already built cabin and cleared fields was not an uncommon experience for the pioneer. Friedrich Gerstacker, writing of his travels in the western lands from 1837 to 1843, also mentions that settlers would offer newcomers from the East their own farms for fifty dollars and within two weeks would be moving wife and family from a farm settled barely two years before ("Backwoodsman" 64). Jonathan's wife, Mercy, and their three children arrived at the farm about three months later on November 5. Along with Mercy came Theodore's parents, Jason and Rachel, and their four other children, as well as Sarah and Elijah Hale and their two children.

While discussing the clothing of frontier women during the first fifty years that the United States was a country, there are three preconceptions that have been overdramatized. The first is the definition of the word "frontier." For many the word conjures up isolation, a harsh existence and the total lack of goods for purchase or barter. However, while this may have been true during the earliest stage of settlement, this stage in general only lasted two to three years.

The second preconception that must be reconsidered is that families on the frontier were very poor, had few possessions and no resources. Emigrants (as these people were called in the 19th century) carefully planned what goods to bring to establish their new home. A move westward had to be financed, so the very poor were unlikely to be able to afford such a move. Most families were able to bring clothing and household goods to their new homes. Jonathan Hale wrote to Mercy telling her to bring "no more heavy articles than you are obliged to, get two pair of shoes apiece, a side sole of leather (which is very scarce here I've given 25 cents for a pair of soles for my Boot) & get a set of Tea cups and stow in a tight box among your clothes and a few plates." He also advised her to "purchase such articles as you want for yourself in wareing apparel" (qtd. in Halverson 24). Also, most families did *not* settle miles away from the nearest neighbor, so that within two to three years it was likely that a community had developed and goods from the East were available.

The third thing to keep in mind is the way we think about fashion. "The typical assumption is that following fashion is a frivolous activity, and that the change in lifestyle created by the frontier shocked women into a more 'common sense' attitude about their clothing. This assumption inevitably leads to the conclusion that fashionable dress played an insignificant role on the frontier because it was not physically functional. However, this overlooks the social function of fashion" (Helvenston 141). Homesteads on the frontier were usually close enough so women could visit each other and take the measure of each other's affluence and standing in the community. Unfortunately clothes and possessions have always been a measure of self-esteem and self-worth. They had the opportunity to discuss fashion and share patterns and knowledge of sewing and clothing construction. Certainly the latest urban fashions may not have been suited to the demands of frontier life, but women wanted to know what the fashions were and could adjust them to frontier life.

In *Seedtime on the Cumberland*, Harriette Simpson Arnow states, "there is nothing to indicate that the colonial and pioneer women in America dressed differently from English women of comparable economic and social conditions" (359-360). Some women planned clothing specifically for their trip west, while others would have brought whatever clothing they had. Narcissa Whitman made a black bombazine dress for her wedding in 1836 knowing that she would be able to use it on her trip to and once she arrived in Oregon. She also made some print calico[1] dresses. At the time dark calico prints were

recommended for use for dresses worn by servants or for chores, as the cloth would hide spots and dirt well. There is no reason to think that the dresses Narcissa made were of anything other than the current fashionable style although not perhaps of the highest style. In the 18th century, the women on the Spanish expeditions to California received "three chemises, three white Puebla cotton petticoats, a serge skirt, and a baize skirt as well as underskirts, jackets, shoes and a hat. In addition each was provided with two pairs of 'fine Brussels stockings...and six yards of ribbon'" (Myres 124). This list evokes the picture of well-dressed women, not women wearing sensible, unfashionable clothes, men's clothes or native dress.

An indication of what women had for clothing can be found in various sources, including inventories, store invoices, paintings, travelers' accounts and even court records. In 1784 (about five years after settlement) Catherine Lefever of Davidson County, Tennessee (Nashville area), was found guilty of slander against another woman. She was fined 200 pounds hard money. She couldn't pay so the court sold her possessions. Clothing that was sold included a scarlet cloak, five calico petticoats, six cotton jackets—chiefly calico, two calico gowns, two robes, a black silk shade, a black silk handkerchief, four yards of black silk, two papered caps, some gauze aprons—one corded, two calico shifts, four of cotton gauze, a striped riding habit, leather gloves, silk mitts, a dressed chip hat, a fan, four pairs of cuffs, a stomacher, silk stockings, silk handkerchiefs, cotton stockings, a basket with sewing silk, scissors, many short lengths of calico and other cotton cloth, some lace—both silk and cotton, bows, tape, pieces of ribbon

Lisle stockings were popular in this period. They are cotton knit with a seam up the back and patterns on the front to look pretty when showing the ankle.

and five yards of silk lace (Arnow 361-362). This woman certainly did not change the type of clothing she wore for her move to the frontier!

There is evidence that even when a woman did not arrive with much finery it would not be many years before goods

[1]The definition of calico in the 1804-1807 *Encyclopedia* by Thomas Sheridan is: "In commerce a sort of cloth resembling linens made of cotton. The name is taken from that of Calicut, the first place at which the Portuguese landed when they discovered the Indian Trade.... Calicoes are of different kinds, plain, printed, stained, dyed, chintz, muslins, and the like, all included under the general denomination of *calicoes*" (qtd. in Montgomery 184). Please note that this definition clearly states that all calicoes were **not** printed fabrics. A mid-18th century dictionary states, "Callicoe—one of the general names for cotton-cloths of India;...both **white** and colored;..." (qtd. in Montgomery 184; emphasis mine).

from the East were readily available. Cincinnati was settled in 1788 and by 1790 there was at least one tailor, shoemaker and store already established. Goods were brought from Baltimore or Philadelphia to Redstone in an average of 23 days. Redstone was on the Monongahela River and was a starting point for goods going down the Ohio River. The goods were then put on flatboats to go to Cincinnati and other points. By November 1790, store invoices list "fourteen and a quarter yards of Drab Cloth No. 189 at thirteen shillings twopence a yard; narrow black ribbon; two scarlet cloaks at one pound sixpence each; six Hatts [sic] No. 5 at four shillings tenpence each; sad irons" (Shine 44). For reference, pay for a woman for a day's cleaning or washing was one shilling sixpence. By 1791 the list of clothing-related items invoiced had grown to include, "Indian calico, striped chintz, purple calico, cotton check, linen check, large cotton shawls, ten and a half dozen coat buttons, horn combs, beaver fustian, blue strouding, superfine cloth, brown cloth, worsted hose, cotton hose, olive sattinet and printed linen" (Shine 44). All of this was available only three years after the first settlers arrived.

There is other evidence that the early frontier settlers were not always preoccupied with subsistence. The officers at nearby Fort Washington gave balls in both 1791 and 1792. These would be occasions for wearing "best" or fancy clothing as fashionable as one could get.

Some years later, in 1838, at least one ball was held in Welasco, Texas. A woman named Mary Austin Holley wrote in a letter, "The gentlemen dress remarkably well—The clothes being all brought from N York ready made & of the newest fashions. I expect it will be a great occasion" (Kidwell and Christman 55-57). It is probable that the women attending the ball would also be in the newest fashions, since they would be able to get fashion plates from New York if the men were getting clothing from there. The women would have been wearing clothing of local make. Although the men could have clothing brought in from New York ready-made, the women could not. Men's clothing was available on a ready-made basis many years before women's clothing could be purchased "off

the rack." Most towns had a dressmaker who could competently cut and sew dresses of a new style, and most women were capable of producing the other garments necessary. Mercy Hale was a tailoress before her marriage to Jonathan. She brought her cutting and sewing skills to Ohio and cut the fabric for many of the women in Bath, Ohio. By the 1820s her work was a cash rather than barter product (Halverson 71). Some women who could sew well bartered that skill in return for skills such as weaving or spinning that they may not have had or perhaps did not have time to do.

In his travels during 1837 to 1843, Friedrich Gerstacker visited Arkansas. He noted that women "even of the lowest classes...were simply but tastefully dressed" (Riley 46). He also attended a Fourth of July celebration and commented:

American maidens are seldom offered the opportunity to let other people admire their ornaments and finery. So they make the most careful use of every such opportunity to show what they own of adornments and better clothes. At such a ball a girl would have to be very poor who could not change clothes twice, and the more prosperous do this five, even six times, without once changing their hairdos, which are always quite simple.

By the way, in no wise do they demand costly materials for their frocks; pretty calicos are much in evidence. Only the cut of their dresses has to be tasteful, and in this respect they yield nothing to 'city women,' from whom they also differ very little in behavior. (Gerstacker "Women" 16)

Gerstacker's comments suggest that these country women were dressed in the same styles as those worn by their city cousins. This is most likely the case. Women took their clothing with them when they emigrated and it was most likely fashionable at the time. If Mercy Hale purchased clothing for her move in 1810, the garments would have been of the current style. When new women came to a settlement, they would bring news of the latest fashions. Letters from home often contained tidbits about the latest style. Sarah Everett would ask her sister in New York for news of the latest fashions. One time when she was too sick to write she had her husband include a fashion question in his letter: "Sarah says if Jane has this Spring's basque pattern she would be glad if she would send it to her. She would like to know what kind of trimmings are worn and all about the latest fashions" (Helvenston 144). After its beginnings in 1830, *Godey's Lady's Book* became the source of the latest fashion information, especially in the rural areas. Godey's even offered a mail order service for the braids and laces that the rural woman may not have been able to get otherwise. Newspapers (many of which were established within five years of a town's settlement) often carried fashion columns, some of which were copied from papers published in the East. In the September 7, 1803, issue of the *Tennessee Gazette* (Nashville), the editor was "against the fashion of overly long earrings, and advised the young girls to wear strings of pearls in their ears as a substitute, 'but a few white ostrich feathers rising on the head before and a train of silk sweeping on the ground below, add so much grace to a moving female figure as to attract all eyes with unceasing admiration" (Arnow 363).

Current fashion was even important in the wilds of Canada at the outposts of the Hudson's Bay Company and the North West Company. According to journal entries from the 1770s to the 1790s, at the North West Company posts the Indian women who became wives of the traders were dressed in "Canadian fashion," which was made up of a shift, short-gown, petticoat and leggings. No doubt they had moccasins on their feet, as shoes—even flat ones—never gained favor with the Indian women or their mixed-blood offspring. The men traders must have felt that dressing in the European fashion was more civilized and they went to great lengths to achieve the current fashion for their wives. In the Book of Servant's Private Commissions (Hudson's Bay Company), which lists imports from England on private account for 1790 through 1810, Robert Godwin requested "issues of 'Ladys Magazines', specifically with pictures of fashionable dresses" (Van Kirk 99). By 1840 the mixed-blood wives and daughters of the officers were attempting to keep up with English fashion. Harriett Gladman, the mixed-blood wife of a chief trader of the Hudson's Bay Company dressed in her best for a social occasion at York Factory in 1840. She was "dressed to death in a Waterloo blue Merino [gown], moccasins, a straw bonnet lined with lilac satin with a profusion of lilac blue & white ribbon & a cap border of very broad blonde [silk lace], the same depth all around no gloves & a silk shawl, the old fashion white around and green pattern" (Van Kirk 101).

So the frontier woman is wearing clothing of the fashionable style, or a close approximation, but what does it look like? The silhouette of fashion changed drastically around 1800. During much of the 18th century, the general silhouette was that of narrow shoulders, narrow waist and full skirts worn over some kind of hooping. Gradually toward the end of the century, the fullness of the skirts moved toward the back and the petticoats were worn over a false rump or bustle pad. The bodice remained fitted with a pronounced waist. The Empire fashion, which was influenced by the new government after the French Revolution and by the interest in ancient Greece and Rome that was aroused by the archaeological finds at Pompeii and Herculaneum, changed the silhouette of women's dress dramatically around 1800. After years of very constructed shapes and heavy boning, softness and draping came into vogue. This fashion was inspired by the dress of the ancient Greeks and the intent was for the wearer to look like the classical statues of Rome and Greece. Thus, the muslins used were quite sheer and often white, to mimic the white marble of the statues. It sometimes worked, for *The Lady's Monthly Museum* in March 1803 wrote that if "a party of high-bred young ladies...could either their limbs or their tongues have been kept quiet, and had they been placed on pedestals or niched in recesses, they might have passed for so many statues very lightly shaded with drapery..." (Bradfield 86).

A gown, 1800 to 1810 style, made from a sturdy cotton cloth in a dark ground print. Notice how the back has quite a bit of fullness. This gown ties at the neckline and closes with a button at the high waist.

The Empire fashion was characterized by very high waistlines, low-cut necklines, short sleeves and slim skirts. Arms and necks were exposed, stockings were of thin silk and shoes were no longer substantial but of thin kid or satin with flat soles and pointed or round toes. It was also about this time that dresses began to close at the back rather than at the front. The gowns of this period were floor length and often had trains in the back. The sleeves were puffed on the upper arm and often ended there. If they were long, the puff of the upper arm was retained and the rest of the sleeve was closely fitted. The fullness of the skirts was either pleated or gathered in the back, often worn over a bustle pad, although not a large one. The bodices often had fullness gathered over the bust. This fullness was controlled by drawstrings. These sheer gowns were often worn over only a shift, although some women retained the use of at least one under-petticoat. The heavily boned stays of the 18th century were no longer needed, so corsets, if they were worn at all, were shorter and only lightly boned. Some gowns were made with linen flaps inside the bodice to support the bust so that no corset was worn. The shifts were either linen or cotton and had short, straight sleeves and a square neckline. It is said that some women actually wet their skirts to make them cling to their legs, thus really imitating the clinging gowns of the classical statues. Whether it is from this practice of wetting down or just because the thin fabrics gave no protection from the cold, the gowns came to be nicknamed "influenza gowns." Of course "influenza" gowns would not be common on the frontier but modifications of them could be.

The fabrics favored for the Empire gowns were imported Indian cottons, although silks and fine woolens were still used by many. Shawls were a new item of women's clothing. In the listing of inventories made in Chester County, Pennsylvania, the first decade in which shawls are mentioned is 1800-1809 (Schiffer 68). Cashmere shawls were the most desirable and expensive. It is said that they became popular after Napoleon brought some back to Josephine after the Egyptian campaign in 1798. Cashmere shawls were rectangular and fairly long. Measurements were usually 20 to 30 inches wide by 100 to 115 inches long. Another new item to women's clothing was the reticule or purse. Up to this period, women wore large hanging pockets underneath their petticoats. These pockets carried everything a woman needed, from keys to sewing supplies. Now that gowns were form-fitting and rather transparent, pockets would cause unsightly lumps and bumps so women adopted the small drawstring reticule for carrying their necessities. Although the dresses were often plain colored, accessories, shawls and Spencer jackets were often quite bright.

This fashionable dress was lovely and may have been suited for going calling in the afternoon but certainly was not suited for doing any kind of physical work. After all, white muslin and flimsy shoes would be rather ridiculous attire for milking the cow! So fashion was adapted for life in the country and for doing chores. Not all Empire gowns were made from flimsy white muslin. Cotton prints with dark backgrounds or in the "Drab-style" of paler browns, olives and yellow were also in style. These prints could be of heavier weight cotton than muslin and would stand up to wear and washings. Wool, linen and silk were also used at this time, but cotton became quite common.

After the invention of the cotton gin, cotton became an inexpensive fabric to produce and the mills of northeastern Massachusetts were busy. By 1800 the United States was exporting $5 million worth and by 1810 it was $15 million.

1809 DAY WEAR

Courtesy of Patterns for Period Impressions

139

This is also the time when the factories at Jouy, France, were producing the printed cottons that have come to be called toiles de Jouy. America was not far behind in printing cotton cloth. In 1810 cotton cloth printed with engraved rollers by Thorp, Siddall and Company was available for sale in Philadelphia. By 1822 large-scale printworks were established in "Taunton, Fall River and Lowell, Massachusetts, Dover, New Hampshire, Baltimore, and Columbiaville, N.Y. and elsewhere" (Pettit 187).

Besides adapting the cloth used, the style needed a little change. The skirt lost the train and was made ankle length. The sleeves could still be short and puffy, long and narrow or elbow length and slightly gathered at the cap. The neckline might be raised slightly or covered with a kerchief. These kerchiefs were often strong colors and could be plain, checked or printed. They were also quite fashionable if they were fringed around the edge. A working woman would also need an apron.

For the first time in many years, aprons were not a part of high fashion dress but were still worn by those who needed to keep their clothes clean while they worked. A plain apron on a waistband could be used. It would be tied around the high waist of the gown and made long enough to cover the dress. Another style of apron covered the front and back of the dress. It has a wide neckline, armholes and narrow shoulder straps. This apron is straight and has ties in the back at the neckline and at the point of the high waistline. The neckline ties are short and the waistline ties are quite long so that they can cross in back and tie in front, creating a high waistline for the apron. This type of apron can also be worn straight, that is without the lower strings brought around to the front. Pockets can be added to this apron. While sometimes white, these aprons would be easier to keep looking clean if made from unbleached gray or blue. Small checks or even dark prints would also be appropriate. Shoes needed to be sturdier and could be made of

SPENCER JACKETS

the fashionable style but of heavier leather. Short laced boots also came into fashion and when made in a heavier leather were quite suited to a working woman.

White linen caps were still worn to cover the hair and keep it clean. Some of these were made with a ribbon-trimmed band going around the head and a circle gathered to it. This differed from some of the 18th century caps because there was no ruffle around the face. This type of cap looks somewhat like a turban. Wrapped turbans were quite fashionable at this time and could be worn by all classes of women. The hair or turban of the fashionable woman was often decorated with large ostrich plums. This is what the editor of the *Tennessee Gazette* was referring to in the earlier quote, "but a few white ostrich feathers rising on the head before...add so much grace...." (Arnow 363).

High-waisted short-gown. Work clothing of the 1800s to 1820s.

Hats were no longer the wide-brimmed, flat hats of the 18th century but rather bonnets with brims close around the face. These bonnets could be of straw or cloth. Cloth bonnets with corded, starched or quilted brims, full backs and a ruffle at the back neck became the popular sunbonnet worn throughout the 19th century.

While it was fashionable to wear shawls, it was during this period that women began to wear jackets and coats for outerwear. Short high-waisted jackets were called Spencers. The Spencer jacket became a style for men as the result of a hunting accident involving the Earl of Spencer. In the accident most of the tails and sleeves of his coat were torn off. The earl bet that he could make his seemingly ridiculous state into a fashion. For men it became little more than extra chest protection, but by 1805 it had become an important part of women's dress. The woman's Spencer had very short tails in the back, was straight across the front and had long, narrow sleeves. Some women were wearing coats called redingotes that followed the lines of the dress. But coats and jackets did not replace the warm and practical hooded cloak. This would be especially true on the frontier. The hooded cloak was worn in Canada until the mid-19th century. An 1805 watercolor by Sempronius Stretton is titled *A Canadian Man and Woman in Their Winter Dress*" (Beaudoin-Ross 72). The woman is wearing a gray cloak with a huge hood and is carrying a large fur muff.

Many rural women were still wearing short-gowns and skirts. Short-gowns are simply made garments cut rather like a kimono in shape. They are shaped to the body by the use of drawstrings or pleats and darts. Short-gowns had been worn throughout the 18th century. During the 19th century, the sleeves of the short-gowns were lengthened and narrowed so that they followed the fashionable line. A drawstring could be added to the neckline and a tuck made under the bust for a drawstring there. This mimicked the bodices of fashionable gowns. If the short-gown came down over the hips, the petticoat would still be on a waistband and worn at the waist.

There is an interesting short-gown and petticoat from this period at the Smithsonian Institution, Division of Costume, National Museum of History and Technology. They are made from an indigo-dyed cotton fabric. The short-gown is very short, coming only to the natural waist or a little below, and the waist area of the garment is up under the bust. The sleeves are long and narrow. The pleating of the back of the short-gown is sewn down to the waist area and then left unsewn below, which makes a little puff at the back. Although this short-gown was made in the classic shape, when worn it ends up looking like a Spencer jacket, which was the fashionable high-waisted jacket worn over Empire dresses.

It also is like one shown in a colored engraving, *Habitants in Their Summer Dress*, by John Lambert in *Travels through Canada and United States of North America in the Years 1806, 1807 and 1808* (London 1814) showing a Canadian man and woman (illus. in Beaudoin-Ross 74). The woman is wearing a gray short-gown that comes just below the waist. It has long, narrow, cuffed sleeves. She is pictured from the side and the back of her short-gown is puffed out over her skirt from the waist area. The rest of her outfit consists of a high-crowned straw hat worn over a ruffled white linen cap, a printed neckerchief and a vertically striped skirt that comes to just above the ankles. Her shoes are described by Lambert as being *"liste"* shoes, that is made of strips of fabric sewn together.

They look like a house slipper more than a shoe.

Another picture of Canadians is a pencil sketch by Peter Rindisbacher done around 1825 (illus. in Van Kirk 100). It shows a mixed-blood man and his two Indian or mixed-blood wives. One of the women is wearing either a Spencer jacket or a short-gown made like the two just discussed. Her neckline is quite low and is filled in with a neckerchief. The back has the same flare out over the back of the skirt. Her skirt comes to just above the ankles and she has leggings and moccasins.

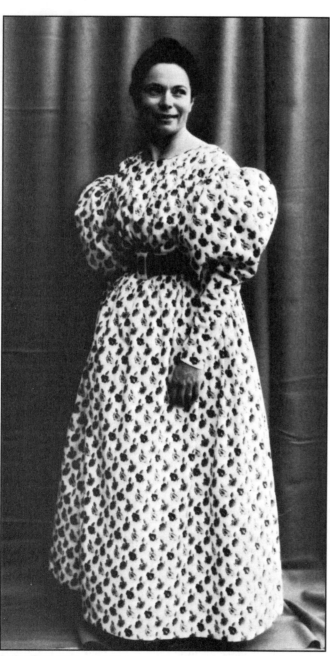

Left : This style could be worn by a woman employed at home or as a shopkeeper. It would be worn with a chemisette, collar or pellerine. Right: Undergarments of the 1830s: chemise, pocket, corded petticoat.

The outfit is completed with a blanket worn over one shoulder, brought around the back of the body and the two ends held together with her hand.

The short-gown in the Smithsonian has a matching skirt. This skirt has a smooth front and has pleating that starts just in front of each hip and continues around the back. This distribution of fullness is also found on fashionable gowns of the time. This skirt is pleated to a strip of the same fabric, which forms a band. It is also attached to a white sleeveless bodice that would hold the skirt above the natural waistline. A riding habit shown on page 46 of *Patterns of Fashion 1* by Janet Arnold has the same type of arrangement to hold up the skirt, and the basque of the jacket puffs out over the back of the skirt, giving much the same silhouette as the three short-gowns discussed above. So it was both possible and probable that rural or working women could copy the fashionable silhouette by adapting the short-gown and petticoat that had been worn by rural and working women for the last century.

The continued wearing of short-gowns during the first 20 years of the 19th century can also be documented by their appearance in inventories. Inventories of Chester County, Pennsylvania, were compiled and analyzed by Margaret Schiffer. In her book, articles of clothing are listed with their descriptions and the decade they appeared in an inventory. From 1790 to 1819 there are thirty short gowns listed. Thirteen are listed as linen, one linsey, fourteen calico, one red flannel

(flannel was wool at this time) and one is listed just as striped (Schiffer 56-57). The names of items in inventories are subject to the person taking the inventory, so there may be other short-gowns that are described as just gowns and by no means is all clothing listed separately in every inventory. It usually is lumped together as simply "clothes."

By the 1820s fashionable women were again wearing more petticoats under their gowns. This filled out the skirts and a wider, more flared shape was seen. Gores were put into the sides of the skirts to give the hems more fullness. As this happened the gathers of the skirts, which had been concentrated in the back, spread around the waistband, although the center front of the skirts was still flat. Skirts were raised from shoe to ankle length. The waistline gradually returned to a more natural level and waistbands were one to two inches wide. The shoulders widened until the leg o' mutton sleeves came into style. Bodices of these dresses were often gathered across the bust and the back, but they were cut in a more fitted manner than were the Empire dresses. Necklines were being filled in with neck ruffles. These frills were usually on a garment called a chemisette. It was like a modern dickey, filling in the neckline but separate from the garment. Chemisettes were of equal length front and back and tied under the bust line. The backs of the bodices were often seamed in either a diamond or "V" shape. The seams of the bodice and armholes were corded. The narrow cording was made from the dress fabric and served to reinforce the seams. The necklines were no longer low but were often wide. There was an increasing amount of decoration on both bodices and hemlines. Cotton printing as an industry was in full gear, and printed cottons were the fabrics of choice for dresses at this time. Many of the prints were based on stripes, and new, bright colors were beginning to be available— yellows, green, Prussian blue and Turkey red.

Women were once again wearing corsets, but they now had gussets for the bust and hips. They also were not heavily boned—often using cording or quilting for the stiffening. Most corsets did retain a wooden busk in a pocket down the front. The undermost garment was still the shift, now called the chemise. It had a wide, low neckline and could have puffy or straight sleeves. It did not show once the woman had her dress

1830 DAY DRESS & PELERINE

Courtesy of Patterns for Period Impressions

on. Under the chemise the woman may have worn drawers. Drawers began to be worn around 1810 and by 1830 were worn fairly universally. Also worn was at least one petticoat and probably more. With the return of wide skirts, women began wearing separate pockets once again although I suspect that less fashionable women wearing short-gowns and skirts had kept wearing hanging pockets. Pockets were so much more practical than the small reticules of the Empire period.

By 1830 the fashionable woman's shape was very wide at the top, narrow at the waist and wide at the bottom. Sleeves were at their most extravagant. Gigot sleeves were cut on the bias and were very full at the top and came down to tight forearms and wrists. To give you an idea of the amount of fabric in these sleeves, the top part was often as much as 35 inches wide—gathered into the armhole, of course. These sleeves required a puff of stiffened fabric or a puff filled with down or wadding attached at the inside top to keep them standing out.

Along with these extremely wide sleeves, dresses now had wide collars and skirts. In fact, the style needed wide skirts and collars to balance the huge sleeves. Many of the huge collars were actually separate garments called "pelerines." They were often embroidered muslin and double layered. A large round cape-like separate collar that matched the dress was also used. Pelerines often came down the front to be held under a sash or buckled belt. The width of the shoulders of these dresses (including the gigot sleeves) was around 28 to 31 inches.

The waist was now at a natural level and once again narrowed by a corset. Corsets were laced up the back and were made of heavy white cloth. Tight lacing was becoming the fashion. A letter written by a middle class tradesman in 1828 deplores the new fashion. "My daughters are living instances of the baleful consequences of the dreadful fashion of squeezing the waist until the body resembles that of an ant. Their stays are bound with iron in the holes through which the laces are drawn so as to bear the tremendous tugging which is intended to reduce so important a part of the human frame to a

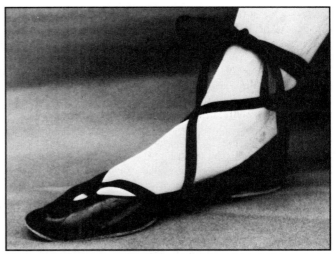

One type of shoe popular for much of the 1800-1830 period.

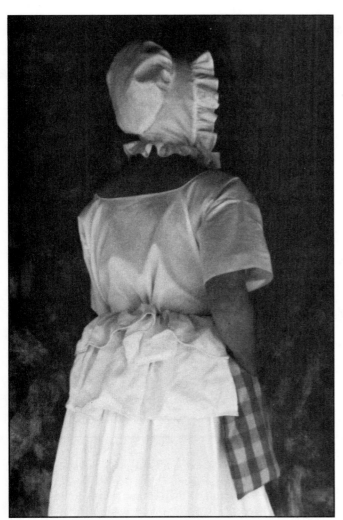

A flounce with several rows of stiffened material used at the back waist to hold a skirt out.

third of its natural proportion. They are unable to stand, sit or walk, as women used to do. To expect one of them to stoop would be absurd" (Cunnington and Cunnington 132). Women wore corded petticoats to hold out the hems of their skirts. These petticoats had rows of cording placed into tucks going around the hem and up to about the knee. Two corded petticoats will do a nice job of holding the skirt out in a bell shape. Women also wore a bustle pad stuffed with down or flounce of several rows of stiffened material at the back waist to hold the skirt out. The flounce is a simple thing to make, being a piece of cloth with cording set into the edges and folded over and gathered on a drawstring. The gathers at the waist of the gown now extended across the front of the skirt, but the front of the skirt was less heavily gathered than the rest.

Shoes were still flat but now had square toes. They were dainty and slip on, although they often had ties that crossed over the foot and tied around the ankle. Black kid leather was probably the most common material. Caps were also still worn. They were ruffled around the face and had big pouffes at the crown to accommodate the hair, which was pulled up into a bun or knot at the crown. Hats also had large crowns and wide brims that framed the face. The hats were often straw and were trimmed with many yards of ribbon made into bows and furbelows.

Toward the late 1830s, sleeves were being brought under control. The wide leg o'mutton sleeves were now gathered or smocked into a narrow sleeve cap. The sleeves were still cut from the same pattern, but with the smocked gathers the look was beginning to moderate. However, with the sleeves being gathered in and set low on the arm, arm movement was greatly reduced. In fact the woman could not have raised her arms over her head without ripping her dress. Uncomfortable as this sounds, fashion usually restricts movement in some way, and it only seems strange if you are not used to the particular restriction. Of course working women needed to stoop and to raise their arms so their dress was modified to look similar but be less drastic.

The waist was still at a natural level, with about a two-inch waistband. The bodice decoration was still often in a "V" shape—wide at the shoulders and coming to an open point at the waist. The "V" decoration often consisted of fine tucks or gathers of the dress fabric. This "V" would soon extend below the natural waist and the waistband would be eliminated.

During the 1820s and 1830s, skirts continued to widen or get fuller. In the early 1820s, skirts were about 72 inches around. By the end of the 1830s, they were from 120 to 140 inches around. With larger skirts, more under-petticoats were worn, and gradually the bustle, which in some form had been worn throughout the 1800s supporting the back of the skirt, increased in size. (Note that these bustles were not the exaggerated bustles seen at the end of the 19th century.) By 1840 a stiff petticoat made of horsehair was being worn under the skirts, and by the late 1850s, this was replaced by a hooped petticoat.

A valuable resource when trying to create clothing for the decade of the 1830s is *The Workwoman's Guide*. This book was published in 1838 by "a Lady." (It was fashionable at the time not to use your name for this sort of thing.) This book is available in a facsimile version today and it contains diagrams and text along with pattern-making instructions for most if

not all items of women's and children's clothing—including hats—and the clothing a woman might make for men. It also covers household linens, upholstery and other things. The pattern instructions are clear, and once you get the hang of using her measurement system, you can make patterns for almost anything you might want to wear for recreating this period. In this discussion of clothing for the frontier woman of the 1830s, I relied upon this book heavily.

In the 1830s, once again the fashionable silhouette may not have been very practical for the frontier woman milking her cows or gardening, so some changes were likely made. Obviously, a woman doing any kind of physical labor could not lace herself as tightly as the tradesman's daughters referenced before, for she would not be able to perform her tasks. A corset of cotton jean either corded or quilted without heavy boning does not restrict movement a great deal. In *The Workwoman's Guide* the author states, "It is well to observe that unless particularly feeble, or otherwise an invalid, it is most desirable to wear as few bones as possible; and that for healthy persons, the two back bones, with steel in front, are quite sufficient" (81).

Calico dresses in dark prints were fairly practical. Gowns had full skirts but the width varied according to both the material and the level of fashion. The fitted bodices did not restrict necessary movement and sleeve type could be adjusted. *The Workwoman's Guide* says, "[Gowns] commonly worn by servants, and the working classes, are of print, linen, stuff,

This short-gown has an economical type sleeve with half the fullness of the wide gigot sleeve. It was worn a lot by the working classes.

147

and for best, light ginghams, merino, or bombazine" and that high-necked gowns open in front "are particularly suitable for house-maids, dairy or kitchen-maids, chair and washerwomen; they should be made in the strongest print....[T]hey should be of dark and good washing colours, deep blue and lilac are the best for wear" (106; 110). Narcissa Whitman's calico and bombazine gowns that she made for her marriage in 1836 could have been made in this fashion. Her choice of fabrics certainly fits this description. Although not specifically stated, it is probable that the gowns "A Lady" describes would have what she titles "An Old Woman's Sleeve" but immediately goes on to say that it is an economical type of sleeve worn a lot by the working classes. This sleeve has half the fullness of the wide gigot sleeves for fashionable clothing and can be pushed up over the elbow or somewhat rolled up to get them out of the way of the wash water or whatever.

Aprons could be tied around the waist, made with a sleeveless bodice attached or even have a bodice and sleeves for a complete coverall. They were generally made a yard wide (the normal width of cotton cloth at the time) and could be made of any number of fabrics. The author of *The Workwoman's Guide* suggests white, brown, blue, black or checked linen, black stuff, calico, Holland, nankeen or print. Aprons with straight bibs attached to the band and pinned to the front of the gown were still in use, a holdover from the 18th century. All types generally had enough length to cover the skirt to within several inches of the hem.

Some women in rural areas, which includes the frontier, were still wearing short-gowns and skirts in the 1830s and even later. This was considered old-fashioned but was probably appropriate for their station in society. Hawthorne includes a "woman in a white short gown and green petticoat" in the *House of the Seven Gables* although he describes her as "very ancient." Old Sturbridge Village has a 19th century short-gown in its collections. It is of blue and white striped linen, with a high neckline, straight collar and a sleeve with a gathered cap that is very similar to the one that *The Workwoman's Guide* described as much used by the working classes. This short-gown has a drawstring at waist level in the back and has no front closures, so it would have been held together with the apron strings or with straight pins.

What appear to be short-gowns are also seen in the paintings of Cornelius Krieghoff, who worked in Canada in the mid-19th century. In *French Canadians at Cards,* two women are shown wearing mantelets (illus. in Beaudoin-Ross

Working clothes for an 1830s woman: linen cap, neckerchief, short-gown, petticoat and checked apron with stout shoes.

76). (By the early 19th century short-gowns were being called "mantelets" in Quebec.) These mantelets have a dropped shoulder line with a separate sleeve attached to this seam. The skirts are long and come to the knee when sitting. The waist is probably gathered in with a drawstring. The necklines of these mantelets are slightly scooped and wide like those seen in earlier pictures. One woman wears a neckerchief draped around her shoulders and knotted at the front.

Similar mantelets are seen in the 1838-1840 engraving by Benjamin Beaufoy called *View of Quebec* that is at the McCord Museum (M19891). "As was usual, rural costume conservatively followed certain selected non-complicated elements of fashion, such as this sleeve which allows for easy movement" (Beaudoin-Ross 77). Even in England short- or bed gowns were being worn by women in rural areas. An 1850s engraving shows a woman ore-dressing on a barge (illus. in Tozer and Levitt 121). She is wearing a bonnet in the style of the 1840s, a neckerchief, short- or bed gown, skirt and probably bare feet. She is shown from the back so we cannot see her apron, but there are ties around her waist to indicate an apron. Her hat is a sunbonnet. It has a wide brim and a short curtain at the back to cover the neck.

The frontier woman would need sturdier shoes than those worn by her urban sister. Stout leather flat shoes that tied across the instep were most likely used. Narcissa Whitman bought a pair of "smallish gentlemen's boots to wear while riding" (Horn 55). During the summer it is quite likely that many people went barefoot most of the time to save their shoes. Shoes were being manufactured for the ready-made market as early as 1788, so even in rural frontier areas one did not have to rely on having a shoemaker in the settlement for the family to have shoes.

Caps of white linen or cotton were worn by rural women, but they were often replaced by the sunbonnet when working outdoors. Sunbonnets could be white, but they were also made from solid colors, checks or calico. They rarely matched the dress or other clothing. Fashionable hats of the time had high crowns and face-framing brims called "pokes." *The Workwoman's Guide* contains patterns for many caps and for several bonnets. To keep their heads warm in cold weather many women wore quilted bonnets. These bonnets were usually silk both outside and inside with a lining of wool batting. They would prevent wind from penetrating and in the poorly heated house or cabin would even be serviceable worn indoors.

Shawls were popular for outerwear. By the 1830s it had become fashionable for them to be either square or triangular. A good size is 65 inches square. Shawls could be made from various materials and could be of one layer or two. A fringed square of woolen cloth made a serviceable shawl. Cloaks were still worn although attached hoods were less common. Red wool was no longer the fashion for cloaks; indeed it was thought old-fashioned. Plaids were fashionable for much of this time period.

For a feel of the clothing of any era before the use of the camera, paintings are usually the best source. Anyone wanting to portray the upper classes or a well-dressed middle class person will not have trouble finding examples in paintings of their period. It is always harder to find illustrations of the working and lower classes and one must often extrapolate from written sources and a few illustrations what was everyday clothing for the commoner. It is important to keep your garments true to your station whatever it is.

Sunbonnet with quilted brim.

PATTERNS

Following are patterns for many of the garments mentioned above. All of the directions assume the use of a sewing machine and fabrics of modern width. Cotton in the 19th century was generally woven 36 inches wide so if you are trying to be totally correct, cut the cloth to that width before using. Most cottons today are woven at least 45 inches wide. By the 19th century, cotton was an inexpensive fabric and was commonly used. Fine woolens are also a good choice, and some linen was still in use. When using printed cottons, it is necessary to familiarize yourself with prints common to the period. Modern small-print calicoes so popular for quilting are generally not suitable for period clothing. Several books have been recommended in the bibliography for the study of fabrics.

Graphs for the following patterns are to the scale of one square equals one inch. Pads of one-inch-square graph paper that is 27 inches by 34 inches are available at most office stationery stores. You may use this pre-drawn graph paper to enlarge the patterns or draw your own.

19TH CENTURY CHEMISE

The chemise is the undermost garment worn by all women. It is always white and should be made out of fine linen or cotton or for lower classes a heavier linen or cotton. It is cut simply in rectangles and triangles and is not meant to be seen once other garments are put on. The measurements given are a starting point; you may want to adjust them to suit you better. If your cloth is 45 inches wide, you will need three yards. Wash it first so that the finished garment will not shrink. Refer to the diagram for cutting measurements. Note that four triangular pieces are cut off the top of the sides to be sewn onto the bottom of the sides to give extra width.

Chemise should be sewn using flat-felled seams, although you might find it easier just to overcast the raw edges. The first step in sewing the chemise is to sew on the triangular pieces cut from the side tops of the main piece onto the side bottoms. Make sure to match the straight grain of the fabric. Next assemble the sleeves. The five-inch-square gussets will be under your arm in a diamond shape when the chemise is put together. Fold the sleeve pieces in half and sew the seam, leaving a five-inch opening at one end. The gusset is inserted into this opening and sewn. After the sleeves are sewn, fold the main body of the chemise in half and mark the shoulder lines either by pressing or with a pin. Mark the center of the top of the sleeve and match the center of the sleeve to the shoulder. Be sure to put the right sides of the fabric together. Pin the sleeve and gusset to the body. These sleeves do not have any tucks or

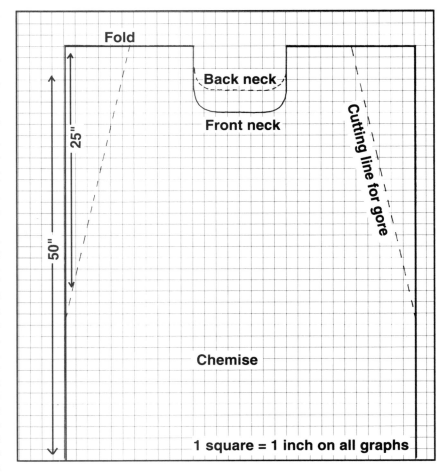

gathers in them. Sew the sleeves to the chemise and then sew the side seams. The bottoms of the sleeves and of the chemise as well as the neckline are finished with a narrow rolled hem.

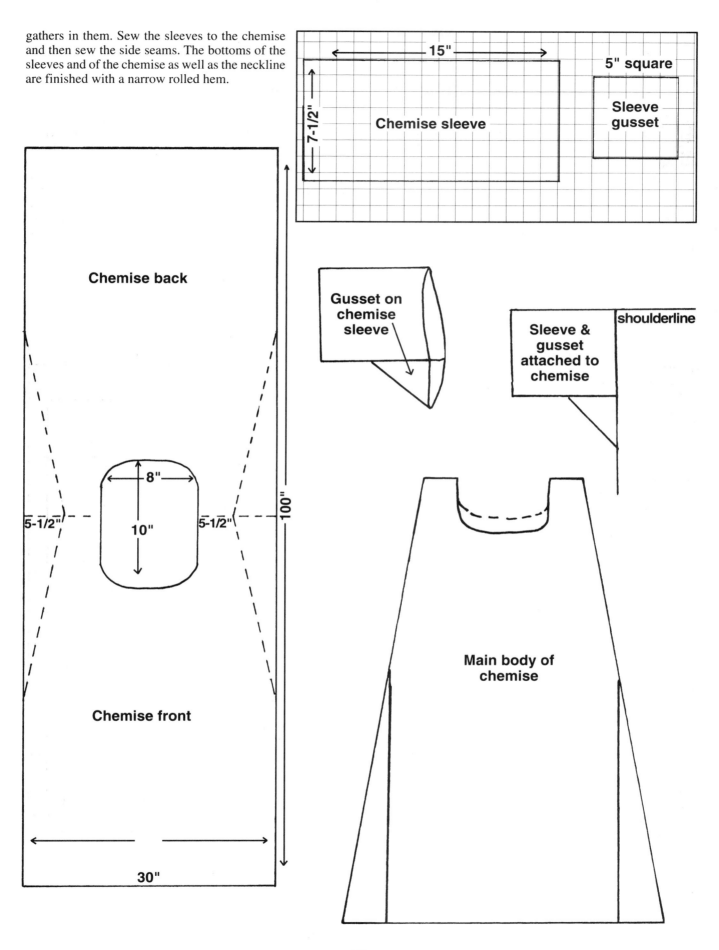

15"

7-1/2"

Chemise sleeve

5" square

Sleeve gusset

Chemise back

Gusset on chemise sleeve

shoulderline

Sleeve & gusset attached to chemise

8"

5-1/2"   5-1/2"

10"

100"

Main body of chemise

Chemise front

30"

PETTICOATS

By the 1820s all women were once again wearing petticoats under their gowns. By the 1830s women were using petticoats with rows of cording at the bottom to hold out their skirts. Quilted petticoats were worn under other clothing for warmth in the winter and also served to give shape to the outer skirt. Petticoats can be made with a waistband or with a drawstring waist and can be made from lightweight wool, cotton or linen.

For a corded petticoat you need white cotton. The amount depends upon your height and the width of the finished petticoat. If your petticoat is to be 100 inches around and you need a finished length of 36 inches, you need three yards of 45-inch-wide cloth or two yards if your cloth is 54 or 60 inches wide. To allow for the cording, add 18 inches to *each* length, which means you need an extra yard and a half of 45-inch cloth and an extra yard of 60-inch cloth. This will actually be more than enough, but it is easier to cut some off once the cording is in than to take a row of cording out because the petticoat is too short. Sew the lengths of cloth together leaving a 10-inch opening at the top of one seam. This will be the center back opening. For a corded petticoat, mark every 1-1/2 inches from the bottom of the petticoat up to knee level (this will be 14 to 18 inches on most people) and draw lines around the cloth. The cording should be 1/4- to 3/8-inch-thick cotton cording, although it is possible that the only cording available will be polyester. If your petticoat is 100 inches wide and you have 14 lines of cording, you will need 39 yards of cording. Start at the top line of cording and place cording along the line drawn on the cloth. Fold the cloth over the cording and sew as close to the cording as possible by hand or using a zipper foot on the sewing machine. This is much easier than trying to sew casings for the cording and then trying to draw the cording through. Once you are finished with the cording, hem the petticoat or arrange for a line of cording to be the bottom of the petticoat. Check the length of the petticoat—it should be at least one inch shorter than the skirt of the gown—and cut off any extra at the top edge.

The waistband can be fashioned in two ways. One is fitted and the other a drawstring. For a drawstring you can either cut a band or use the excess length of the petticoat fabric. There is no need for a slit in the back seam of the petticoat if you are using a drawstring waistband, so the slit can be sewn up. To add a band, cut a piece three inches wide and the width of the petticoat. Sew one side of the band to the petticoat using a 1/2-inch seam. Before sewing the other side of the band to the petticoat, work two buttonholes opposite each other at what will be the two sides of the petticoat. Now sew the other side of the band to the petticoat after you turn under the 1/2-inch seam allowance. For the drawstrings you need two pieces of twill tape long enough to go all around the band. Take one of these tapes and fasten it to the edge of one buttonhole. Make sure that you do not sew all the way through the waistband because you will lose the casing if you do. Thread the free end of this tape through the casing all around and out through the same buttonhole as where you started. Do the same with the

other tape and buttonhole. Gather up the waist to fit and tie the string in front.

To make a fitted band, cut a piece of cloth four inches wide and your waist measurement plus one inch long. This allows for 1/2-inch seam allowances. Place the right side of the band against the wrong side of the petticoat and pleat or gather the petticoat to it. You can leave the center front hardly gathered if you wish. The opening in the seam is at the back of the petticoat. Make sure to allow 1/2 inch on each short edge of the waistband to turn under as a seam allowance. Sew the waistband to the petticoat. Turn under the remaining seam allowances on the waistband and sew to the garment. To close sew two ties to the ends of the band. You could also make the band two inches longer than the waist measurement so that you have a tab for a buttonhole and can use a button as the closure.

A HANGING POCKET

Women were once more wearing hanging pockets tied around their waists under their skirts by the 1830s. These commodious pockets carried everything from pocketbooks to sewing or knitting projects. They could be worn singly or in pairs. Pockets were generally made from stout cloth and were attached to a wide tape long enough to tie around the waist. While most pockets were made from plain cloth, there are many extant examples of 19th century pockets made up of patchwork.

To make a pocket, follow the diagram for cutting. The front and back of the pocket do not have to be made from the same fabric, so this is a good opportunity to use scraps. It is recommended that new cloth be used, however, as the pocket receives a lot of wear. After cutting the two sides of the pocket, cut the slit. This slit can either be bound with cloth or tape or cut in the shape of an "I", with the two sides of the slit being turned to the inside and hemmed. Once the slit is finished, place the two sides of the pocket wrong sides together and sew all around about 1/4 inch from the edge. Turn the pocket inside out, press the seam and sew around the edges again, making sure to enclose the first seam in the second. Turn the pocket right side out and attach to a tape to form the strings. The tape may be sewn either all the way across the top or two pieces may be attached separately, one at either corner of the

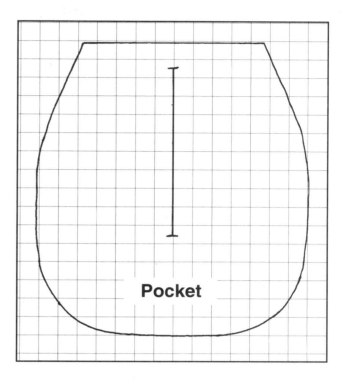

Pocket

pocket. If you are making a pair of pockets, it is best to attach them both to the same tape, so as to lessen the number of ties around your waist.

BUSTLE

This bustle is made from a heavy cotton like jean or heavy osnaburg. Cut a rectangle 36 inches by 18 inches. Most cotton in the early 19th century was woven 36 inches wide, so this is a common width to use when the width is somewhat arbitrary. Hem both short sides and then hem the two long sides, enclosing a thick cord in them. This gives the bustle more body. Then fold along the fold line, which forms two uneven flounces. Sew the casing for the drawstring two inches down from the fold and through all layers. Run a piece of tape through the casing and draw up the bustle into a flounce. This bustle is worn with the two-inch flounce created by the drawstring casing in between the other two flounces, or what seems like inside out. Bustles provide fullness at the back of a gown skirt, but are not the exaggerated bustles seen at the end of the century.

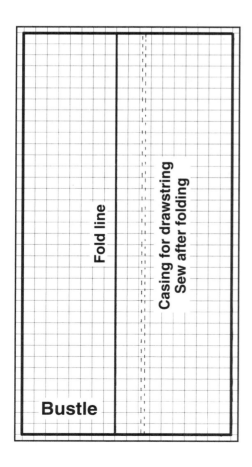

Fold line

Casing for drawstring
Sew after folding

Bustle

A SHORT-GOWN

This short-gown is cut in the common manner of the 18th and early 19th centuries. It can have many modifications to make it look more or less "fashionable." Common fabrics for the early part of the 19th century would be cotton calico of an appropriate pattern, plain colored or striped cotton or linen, heavier cotton or linen "homespun" type cloth and light woolens for colder weather. This short-gown can be lined for extra warmth.

To make this garment, first enlarge the pattern and check to see if it fits the way you want. Note that the front and back are cut the same except for the neckline. The length of this short-gown can be anywhere from just below the waist to hip length. To give a look like the fashionable gowns of the early 19th century, two drawstrings have been used, one at the neck and the other directly under the bust. Another way to shape this garment is through the use of darts and pleats.

Cut the center back and front on the fold of the fabric. Cut the fold for the center front and open up the fabric. You will need to piece the sleeves to obtain the length. Many original garments also have pieced skirts. This is because of the narrow widths of cloth available. To be most correct, piece the skirt and sleeve along the same vertical line. Sew the sleeve pieces to the garment and then sew the side seams. It is nice to sew these seams with a french seam so that all the raw edges are enclosed. Make a narrow rolled hem on the two front edges and around the bottom edge. The neck edge is folded over to form a narrow, 1/4-inch casing for a drawstring. Sew this down securely, as it will receive wear when gathered up by the drawstring. Try the short-gown on and check for the placement of the under-bust drawstring. If the line appears right, take an outside tuck to form a 1/4-inch casing for a fine piece of tape. This garment closes by tying the two drawstrings. Once the rest of the short-gown is finished, check the sleeve length and hem the sleeves to wrist length.

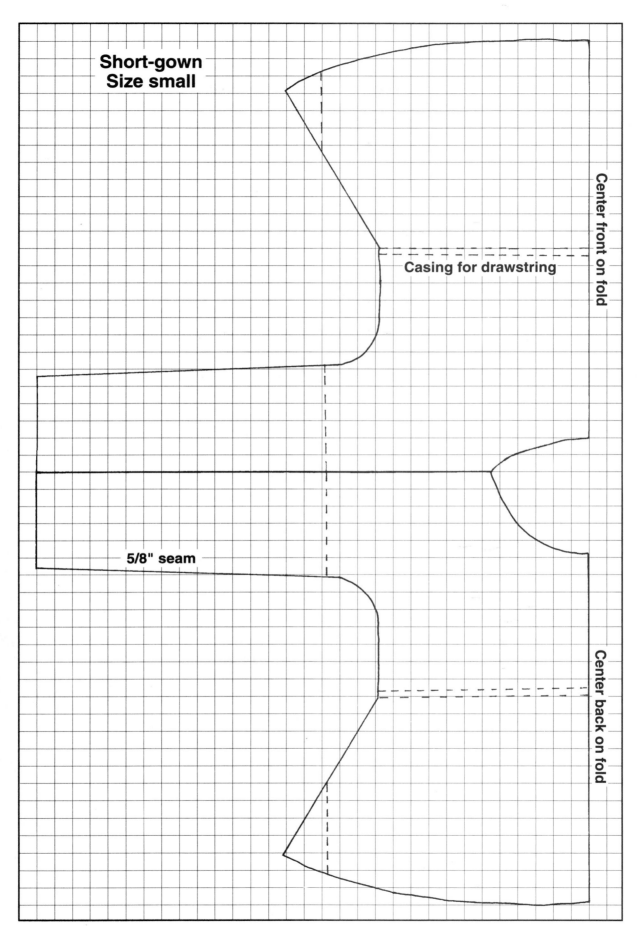

**Short-gown
Size small**

Center front on fold

Casing for drawstring

5/8" seam

Center back on fold

155

A SHORT-GOWN OR MANTELET

This short-gown is not cut in the classic shape used in the 18th and early 19th century but rather has a set-in sleeve that makes it look more like a shortened gown. Suitable fabrics for this garment are cotton calicoes of appropriate design, plain or checked cottons, fine woolens and homespun linen. The pattern includes shoulder seams, but you can place the shoulder seam line on a fold and eliminate those two seams. Before cutting into your good cloth, you should cut the body out of scrap fabric to check the fit of the neck and dropped sleeve seam. The sleeve seam should be off the shoulder 1-1/2 to two inches, but no more. If the garment is too big in this area, take a tuck in the pattern along the vertical dotted line. Also check the length. This garment has no "right" or "wrong" length. Its length should suit your proportions. The construction of this garment is very simple. Sew the shoulder seams and the center back seam, if you didn't cut it on the

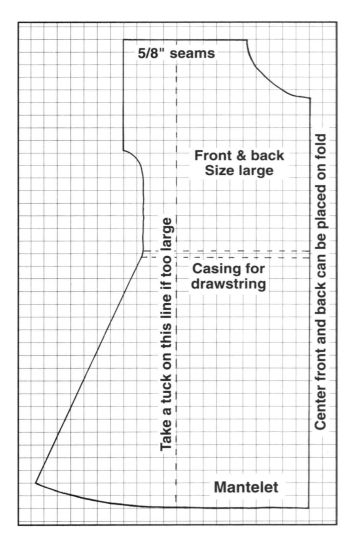

5/8" seams

Front & back
Size large

Take a tuck on this line if too large

Casing for
drawstring

Center front and back can be placed on fold

Mantelet

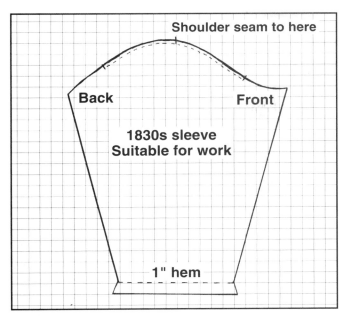

Shoulder seam to here

Back **Front**

1830s sleeve
Suitable for work

1" hem

fold. Then sew the side seams. Sew the seam in the sleeve and press. Run two rows of gathering stitches within the seam allowance at the sleeve head as indicated on the diagram. Match the sleeve seam with the side seams of the gown. The center of the sleeve head (see mark) matches the shoulder seam of the garment. Pull the gathers up so that the sleeve fits the opening and sew with a 5/8-inch seam. Try on the garment and check where the waistline casing should be. If everything fits the way you like, narrow hem the neck, front and bottom edges. Then take a tuck on the outside of the gown to carry the drawstring for the waist. The waistline closes by tying the drawstring and the neck can be closed by a straight pin or you could sew two short ties at the neck edge. The sleeve is hemmed with a one-inch hem.

Modifications can be made to this pattern. If you desire sleeves that can be rolled up, widen the sleeve by making the seams straighter. As is, this sleeve can be pushed part way up the forearm. The short-gowns worn at Old Sturbridge Village are hip length rather than below and they have a drawstring in the back only. They also have a higher neck with a simple straight band collar. The fronts are closed with pins.

APRONS

A plain apron can be made from a piece of cloth 36 inches wide. The length should be about 3/4 the length of your skirt. According to *The Workwoman's Guide*, the best fabrics are "blue, check, and brown linen" for dirty work and "white linen, Holland, and print for less dirty employments" (78). A simple band is made by sewing four-inch-wide strips of cloth to the desired length of the tie. This is then folded in half so that the band and tie will be about two inches wide when finished. Either pleat or gather the apron piece onto the band, fold up the raw edge of the other side of the band and sew it down to the apron, thus encasing the raw edges. Fold under the long edges of the tie and sew them to each other. Most aprons of this type cover only the front of the skirt.

A long apron covers the bodice and the back of the gown. It should be made in a stout cotton of a dark color or check since this will hide dirt the best. This is a very practical apron. Cut according to the adjacent pattern, adjusting the length to suit. If the length desired is 40 inches, the apron requires 2-1/2 yards of 45-inch cloth or 1-1/4 yards of 60-inch cloth plus three to four yards of narrow tape. Also needed and not included in the cloth yardage are three pieces of one-inch-wide bias strip. These pieces of bias will be used to face the top of the front and back pieces of the apron and they measure 22 inches for the front and 11 inches for each of two back

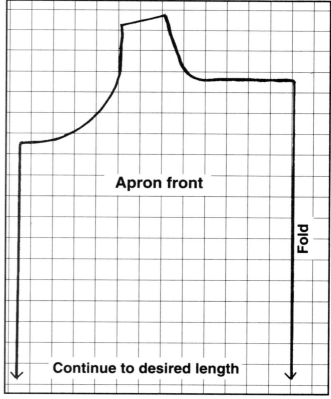

Apron front

Fold

Continue to desired length

pieces. Using the same cloth as the apron is probably the neatest look, but there is no reason not to use a piece of scrap cloth that coordinates with the apron cloth. To cut a bias strip, mark the lengthwise and crosswise grain of the cloth and draw a line at a 45 degree angle to them. This will give you a true bias. Then mark a parallel line one inch away from the first line and you will be able to cut a one-inch bias strip. The bias strips can be pieced, but if you choose not to piece them, you need a piece of cloth 18 inches square.

First narrow hem one long edge of each shoulder piece. This hem faces the neckline, not the shoulder. Pin one short edge of the shoulder pieces to the apron backs, right sides together. Next pin the bias strips along the top of the apron backs, also right sides together, and sew all layers together with a 1/4-inch seam. Press the bias facing to the inside of the apron. Next sew the bias facing to the apron front, also right sides together and with a 1/4-inch seam, and press to the inside. Narrow hem the center backs of the apron, making sure to hem the edges of the bias facing separately from the apron itself. Now fold under 1/4 inch of the long edge of the facings and sew them to the apron. You have formed a casing and should have an opening at both the center back and the armhole.

Turn under 1/4 inch on the long edge of the front facing and sew it to the apron, leaving a 1/2-inch opening at the center front. This will form a casing with openings at the top of the neck edge and at the center front. Run tape through all of the casings. On the front of the apron, you need enough tape to tie a bow at the center front after you have pulled the tape up slightly to gather the front. On the apron backs, you need enough tape to tie a bow to close the apron. Firmly attach the tape at the armhole and neck edges by sewing through all layers.

With *wrong* sides together, sew the shoulder pieces to the apron front with a 1/4-inch seam. Fold the pieces right sides together and sew another seam encasing the first. Next sew the side seams, making sure to finish the raw edges either with a flat-felled seam or by overcasting the raw edges. Narrow hem around the armholes and around the bottom of the apron. Ties are also added six to nine inches below the top edge of the back. These ties should be about a yard long and will cross over each other at the back and come around the front under the bust to tie there and form a high waist. An alternate treatment would be to make a casing anywhere from the waistline up on the back and to put ties in that gather only the back and tie there.

Shoulder piece

↖**Shoulder piece to here**

Apron back

Center back

Continue to desired length

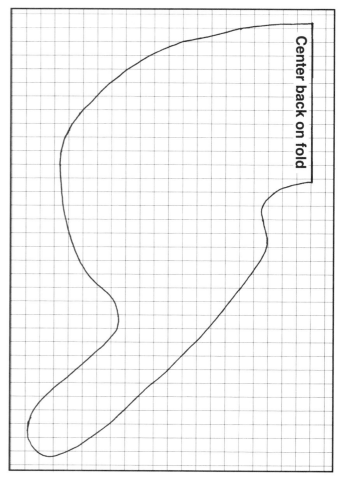

Center back on fold

A PELERINE

The pelerine is a collar or cape that goes over an 1830s gown. This pelerine is made from fine cotton. It is edged with either appropriate lace or a self-fabric ruffle that is hemmed with a narrow roll. This pelerine takes one yard of 45-inch or wider fabric, more if you choose to make a self-fabric ruffle. Cut out according to the pattern and finish all edges as you choose with either lace or ruffles. The pelerine is worn over a gown with very full sleeves with the belt or sash of the gown going over the long ends of the pelerine to keep them in place.

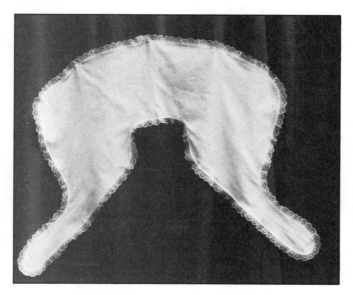

1830s CAP

This cap is made from fine white linen or fine white cotton. Sheer white cottons woven with white-on-white sprigs or checks are especially suitable but very hard to find. This cap is based upon caps seen in paintings and several extant garments. You will need one yard of 45-inch-wide fabric to make this cap. It is always wise to make a trial garment and this is true with caps, too. With this cap it is unnecessary to put the ruffles on the trial, but you should check to see if the band fits your head before you use your good cloth. The pattern for this cap includes 1/4-inch seam allowances.

After cutting all the pieces, sew the back seam and flat fell it or whip over the raw edges. Next run a gathering stitch around the circular crown and pull it up to fit the band. The gathers should be even around the band. Sew the crown to the band with right sides together. Whip over the raw edges. The ruffle most likely needs to be pieced. Sew the pieces together with narrow flat-felled seams until you have the 124 inches in length that you need. This ruffle overlaps itself at the top of the head so you can have a longer ruffle if you want it to overlap more.

Finish one long edge of the ruffle and the two short edges with a narrow rolled hem. Run a gathering stitch along the unfinished long edge and pull up the gathers to fit the edge of the cap band, remembering to allow for the overlap at the top. Pin the ruffle onto the band, make sure that it is even and sew to the band with a 1/4-inch seam. A good 19th century seamstress would be able to flat fell this seam, but if you aren't up to that, finish the raw edge by sewing a narrow piece of tape over the seam and then catching the tape to the cap band so that the raw edges of the band and ruffle are covered.

Make a narrow rolled hem on the two long edges and one short edge of the ties. Turn the short raw edge to the right side

of the ties and tuck the tie once or twice to fit onto the point of the cap band. Stitch the ties to the cap making sure they are on securely. Iron the cap to remove any wrinkles you created while sewing and it is ready to wear. If desired this cap can be further embellished with ribbon trim around the seam where the crown meets the band. This ribbon can be gathered, made into bows or wrapped around this seam and crossed at the top of the head and brought down the band to the points where the ribbon serves as the cap ties. The ribbon can be of a strong color and should coordinate with the gown.

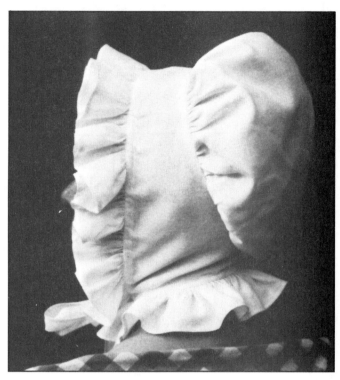

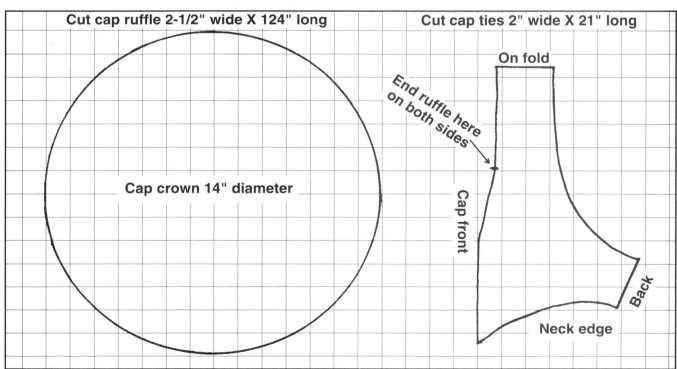

Cut cap ruffle 2-1/2" wide X 124" long

Cut cap ties 2" wide X 21" long

Cap crown 14" diameter

On fold

End ruffle here on both sides

Cap front

Back

Neck edge

SUNBONNET

ats that were the forerunners of sunbonnets appeared in the late 18th century. These hats of the 1780s were black with full crowns and stiff brims that shaded the face. A practical hat, its successor was adopted enthusiastically by rural American women throughout the 19th century and became the sunbonnet. This pattern is but one of many ways to construct a sunbonnet. This bonnet has a quilted brim, a full back and a long curtain over the shoulders. (The ruffle at the back of 19th century bonnets is called a curtain.) Sunbonnets do not usually match an outfit and can be made from leftover cloth. They can be white, solid colored or a print or check that is appropriate to the time period. Brims can be quilted (as this one is), corded, not stiffened at all, or stiffened over a piece of buckram or cardboard. This bonnet was

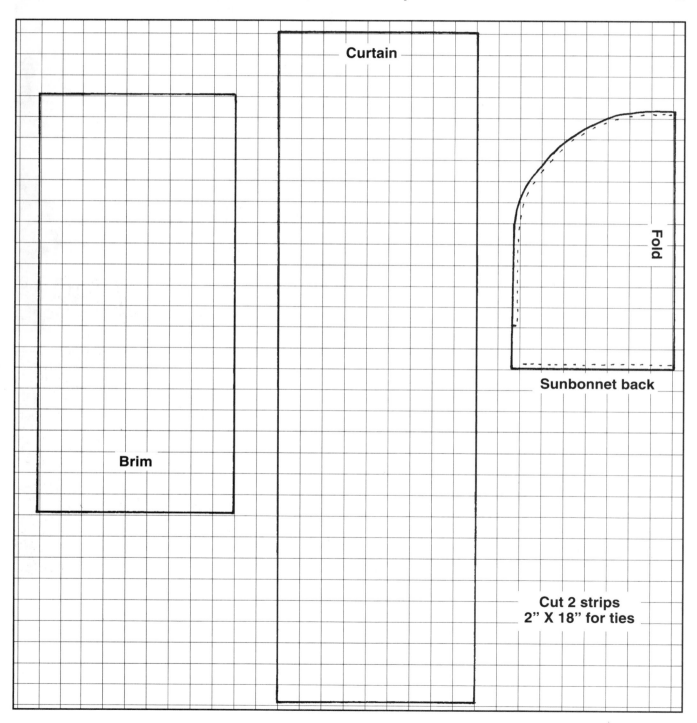

Curtain

Fold

Sunbonnet back

Brim

**Cut 2 strips
2" X 18" for ties**

or straight out to provide the wearer's face with the most shade.

Modifications to this pattern are many and all are fairly easy. The first would be to make the brim without batting. If a small amount of stiffening is needed, cords can be stitched in between the two layers of the brim. This cording need not be solid from the front to the back of the brim. Two or three lines then a space, then two or three more lines of cording create a nice effect. The brim can also be made narrower. Another modification is the size of the curtain. The curtain in this pattern is quite long and could be shortened to any length desired. Of course, a longer curtain helps keep the sun off the shoulders better. One last modification would be to add a narrow self-fabric ruffle along the front and bottom edges of the brim.

constructed with a large brim that can be folded back or can really shield the face from the sun. Because it is quilted, it is warm in the cold weather. For warm weather wear, you might prefer to have a corded or stiffened brim that would be less warm.

To make this bonnet as shown, you will need 30 inches of 45-inch fabric and a piece of batting nine by 20 inches. After cutting out all the pieces, place the brim pieces right sides together and sew the two short ends and one long end together using 1/4 inch for a seam allowance. Turn right side out and press. Put the batting inside this envelope and make sure there are no bulges. Pin through all layers and sew channels the long way every inch or so from the finished edge.

Next run a gathering stitch along the curved edge of the back piece and gather to fit the brim leaving 1/2 inch of the back below the edge of the brim. Sew the back to the brim using a 1/2-inch seam. Finish the raw edges, then run a gathering stitch along the bottom edge of the back and pull up to seven inches. Narrow hem the two short sides and one long side of the curtain and run a gathering stitch along the unhemmed long side. Gather the curtain so that it is long enough to go along the bottom of the back and overlap the sides of the brim by 2-3/4 inches. Sew the curtain to the bonnet back wrong sides together using a 1/2-inch seam. The part that overlaps the brim is sewn flat to the inside of the brim. If desired, a narrow band of cloth can be used to cover the raw edge.

The ties are folded the long way, wrong sides together, and sewn across the bottom and up the side using a 1/4-inch seam. Turn the ties right side out using a pencil or dowel to help push the end through the tube. Sew the ties at an angle where the brim and curtain meet. Turn under the raw edge and sew the ties securely to the brim and edge of the curtain. This sunbonnet can be worn with the brim folded back upon itself

163

CARTRIDGE PLEATING OR GAUGING

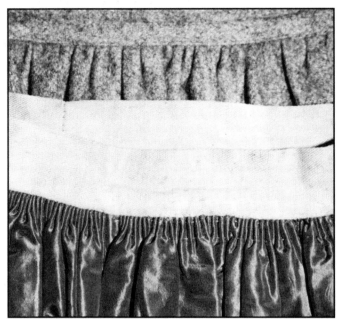

The skirt at top is gathered. The one at bottom is cartridge pleated or gauged.

In the 19th century a common way of taking in fullness is cartridge pleating, also called gauging. This was especially used to gather the skirts of gowns onto waistbands. Cartridge pleating is done by making two parallel rows of running stitches about 1/4 inch apart at the top of the skirt or whatever else you are pleating. It is best to use strong thread to do this. The stitches should be about 1/8-inch long. To gather the fabric, pull up the gathering threads to form tiny pleats. Cartridge pleats at the top of the skirt are attached to a finished waistband by whip stitching the outside of each pleat to the band with right sides together.

Unless otherwise credited, all photographs are by Raymond Poudrier.

The author wishes to thank Lynne Manring and Kate Reynolds for their valuable assistance with bibliographical information and consultation on pattern making.

APPENDIX A: WORKS CITED

Arnold, Janet. *Patterns of Fashion 1.* New York: Drama Books, 1972.

Arnow, Harriette Simpson. *Seedtime on the Cumberland.* New York: Macmillan, 1960.

Beaudoin-Ross, Jacqueline. "'A la Canadienne' Once More: Some Insights into Quebec Rural Female Dress." *Dress: Journal of the Costume Society of America* 7 (1981) 69-81.

Bradfield, Nancy. *Costume in Detail: Women's Dress 1730-1930.* Boston: Plays, 1975.

Boucher, Francois. *20,000 Years of Fashion: The History of Costume and Personal Adornment.* New York: Abrams, 1987.

Cunnington, C. Willett, and Phyllis Cunnington. *The History of Underclothes.* New York: Dover, 1992.

Davenport, Millia. *The Book of Costume.* New York: Crown, 1948.

Davidson, Caroline. *Women's Worlds: The Art and Life of Mary Ellen Best 1809-1891.* New York: Crown, 1985.

Fennelly, Catherine. *The Garb of Country New Englanders 1790-1840.* Sturbridge, MA: Old Sturbridge Village, 1966.

Frankenstein, Alfred. *William Sidney Mount.* New York: Abrams, 1975.

Gerstacker, Friedrich. "The Backwoodsman." Trans. Ralph Walker. *Early American Life* 12.1 (1981): 38+.

—. "Women in the Backwoods." Trans. Ralph Walker. *Early American Life* 13.6 (1982): 14-23.

Gilgun, Beth. *Tidings from the 18th Century.* Texarkana, TX: Rebel Publishing, 1993.

Halverson, Deborah. "The Journey of Johnathan Hale." *Early American Life* 11.3 (1980): 20+.

Helvenston, Sally. "Fashion on the Frontier." *Dress: Journal of the Costume Society of America* 17 (1990): 141-155.

Horn, Huston. *The Pioneers.* New York: Time-Life, 1974.

Johnson, Judy M., ed. *French Fashion Plates of the Romantic Era in Full Color: 120 Plates from the "Petit Courrier des Dames," 1830-34.* New York: Dover, 1991.

Kidwell, Claudia B. "Short Gowns." *Dress: Journal of the Costume Society of America* 4 (1978): 30-65.

Kidwell, Claudia B., and Margaret C. Christman. *Suiting Everyone: The Democratization of Clothing in America.* Washington, DC: Smithsonian Institution Press, 1974.

Myres, Sandra L. *Westering Women and the Frontier Experience 1800-1915.* Albuquerque, NM: University of New Mexico Press, 1982.

Nylander, Jane C. "Clothing a New England Family, 1800-1840." *Early American Life* 11.6 (1980): 48-52.

—. "Dressing for Role and for Winter." *Old Sturbridge Visitor* 24.4 (1984-5): 18-19.

Pettit, Florence H. *America's Printed and Painted Fabrics 1600-1900.* New York: Hastings House, 1970.

Riley, Glenda. *Women and Indians on the Frontier, 1825-1915.* Albuquerque, NM: University of New Mexico Press, 1984.

Rothstein, Natalie, ed. *A Lady of Fashion: Barbara Johnson's Album of Styles and Fabrics.* London: Thames and Hudson, 1987.

Schiffer, Margaret B. *Chester County, Pennsylvania Inventories 1684-1850.* Exton, PA: Schiffer Publishing, 1974.

Shine, Carolyn R. "Scalping Knives and Silk Stockings: Clothing the Frontier, 1780-1795." *Dress: Journal of the Costume Society of America* 14 (1988): 39-47.

Snyder, Gerald S. *In the Footsteps of Lewis and Clark.* Washington, D.C.: National Geographic Society, 1970.

Starobinski, Jean, et. al. *Revolution in Fashion: European Clothing, 1715-1815.* New York: Abbeville Press; Kyoto Costume Institute, 1989.

Tozer, Jane, and Sarah Levitt. *Fabric of Society: A Century of People and Their Clothes, 1770-1870.* Carno, Powys, Wales: Laura Ashley, 1983.

Van Kirk, Sylvia. *Many Tender Ties.* Norman, OK: University of Oklahoma Press, 1980.

Waugh, Norah. *Corsets and Crinolines.* New York: Routledge/Theatre Arts Books, 1954.

—. *The Cut of Women's Clothes 1600-1930.* New York: Routledge/Theatre Arts Books, 1968.

The Workwoman's Guide by a Lady. 1838. Facsimile reprint. Guilford, CT: Opus Publications, 1986.

Worrell, Estelle Ansley. *Early American Costume.* Harrisburg, PA: Stackpole Books, 1975.

APPENDIX B: USEFUL FABRIC INFORMATION

Brackman, Barbara. *Clues in the Calico: A Guide to Identifying and Dating Antique Quilts*. McLean, VA: EPM Publications, 1989.

Bredif, Joseph. *Printed French Fabrics: Toiles de Jouy*. New York: Rizzoli, 1989.

Hefford, Wendy. *The Victoria and Albert Museum's Textile Collection: Design for Printed Textiles in England from 1750-1850*. New York: Canopy Books—Abbeville Press, 1992.

Montgomery, Florence M. *Textiles in America 1650-1870*. New York: Winterthur/Barra—Norton, 1984.

Nylander, Jane C. *Fabrics for Historic Buildings: A Guide to Selecting Reproduction Fabrics*. Washington, D.C.: Preservation Press, 1983.

Tozer, Jane, and Sarah Levitt. *Fabric of Society: A Century of People and Their Clothes, 1770-1870*. Carno, Powys, Wales: Laura Ashley, 1983.

APPENDIX C: SOURCES OF PATTERNS

Please enclose a SASE with all correspondence.

Amazon Drygoods
2218 East 11th Street
Davenport, IA 52803-3760
319-322-6800

Jas. Townsend & Son, Inc.
133 North First Street
PO Box 415
Pierceton, IN 46562
800-338-1665

Period Impressions
1320 Dale Drive
Lexington, Ky 40517
606-273-5942

A Typical Day's Journey in Winter

by Fred Gowen

Just like seemingly everyone else who's now interested in living history of the 18th and 19th centuries, Fred Gowen was fascinated by the Davy Crockett series in the mid-1950s and lived much of his childhood with a homemade wooden flintlock gun in hand and a bag full of marble bullets hung over his shoulder.

A resident of Massachusetts himself, Gowen's ancestors have resided in Maine since the middle 1600s. His father and grandfather took an interest in passing on to him their skills at handling shotgun and rifle. Thanks to them, by the time Gowen was six or seven he could shoot fairly well and was familiar with what a flushing partridge sounded like.

One of Gowen's aunts had a casual acquaintance with Kenneth Roberts, the author of *Northwest Passage* and *Arundel*, and early on he became familiar with these books. During the two years Gowen spent as a Marine in Vietnam, he retained at least a part of his sanity by escaping to these wonderful books whenever he had the time and energy.

Gowen has done a lot of things since then for work— working at the post office, welding, teaching high school history and English, social work—but his consuming interest has always been the woods and history. After participating briefly in Revolutionary War and French and Indian War reenacting, Gowen now prefers to share adventures with a few close and good friends. As he puts it, "How can you beat a way of life that manages to combine interests in American history, antique guns, backpacking, canoeing, hunting and nature all in one?"

I n the Adirondack Mountains, February 1984. We stood stiff with cold near the ruins of Fort William Henry and looked out on the south end of 32-mile-long Lake George. To the north as far as we could see, snow-covered mountains rose steeply from the frozen lake surface that would be the road for our journey. We knew the temperature to be ten degrees, but a gusting wind penetrated our wool clothes and stole the warmth from our motionless bodies. The lake ice was covered with hard packed, windblown snow and we were pleased; this would provide our moccasins good traction for hauling, and we would be able to leave our snowshoes lashed to the toboggans.

I turned my head slightly to study my longtime partners, Mark Daiute and Chris Gilgun. They stood beside their heavily laden toboggans, looking as if they could have fallen into line with any of the winter parties of Robert Rogers, John Montressor or Alexander Henry and not have caused a head to turn. This would be our first 18th century winter trip of any considerable length, and I was very proud of my two friends and the work and research we'd done to get here.

My thoughts were interrupted when I realized Mark was grinning at me. He gave his toboggan's tow rope a pull and slid down the bank onto the surface of the lake, his sled slithering after him, twisting and flexing to conform to the contours of the snow. With the echo of Mark's exuberant war whoop ringing in the hills, Chris and I followed and we began our winter adventures.

On the Height of Land, Ten Years Later
February 1994

A Typical Day's Journey in the Winter

Six a.m. My dog Samantha's cold nose found the breathing hole in my blanket folds and she nudged her way in to make sure I was awake. It was finally dawn. Sammy had gotten up with me several long hours ago when I'd been frozen out by my snoring companions and had risen to stir up the fire and warm myself. Afterward I'd crawled back into my blanket, but Sammy had stayed up to guard the camp and do whatever else it is that dogs like to do in the pre-dawn. An hour ago the below-zero cold had begun to infiltrate my blanket again, and I'd been lying awake, trying to convince myself I was still warm.

Reluctantly, I began to work my way out of the blanket. Friction between my wool clothes and the wool of the blanket made it slow going. Even before I stood up, all three dogs were gathered around me, excited at the prospect of having someone else to play with and anticipating food. In the dim light, I slid the crumpled knit wool hat back from my eyes so I could see, drew up my sagging leggings, adjusted my coat and belt and then groped into my haversack for the fire kit.

My body was not yet functioning well and I was clumsy, both from sleep and the shock of the bitter cold. Finding the fire kit, I worked quickly to get out char and tinder before my fingers stiffened from the cold. Moving around was difficult, as the rectangular hole we'd dug into the snow the night before was cramped when filled with a fire pit, spruce boughs, three men and as many dogs. I crawled not too gently over the still dormant bodies of Dan and Mark and sat stiffly down by the fire pit. Last night Dan had tucked away birch bark and squaw wood in a near corner of the pit. I got them and made a nest of those combustibles. Beneath a charred piece of wood, deep in the ashes, live coals still glowed from last night's fire. I hurriedly lit my char from these and blew it and the tinder into flames. Soon after this the fire came wonderfully alive and began to drive the brutal cold from our small pit in the snow.

Once the fire was burning well, I shuffled over to the rear of our snow pit, stepped unsteadily up onto the snow pile and spent a full minute reveling in the pleasure of at long last emptying my bladder after having held it through eternally long hours. Every day begins and ends with this commonplace ritual. No sane person, once settled warmly into his blanket, leaves it without good reason. Heat is precious and the nights are very, very long.

Back down by the fire again, I enjoyed the quiet of the pre-dawn in the friendly warmth of the flame for a while before calling the dogs and encouraging them to play on the still recumbent forms of Dan and Mark. I decided that if I was up then they ought to be up and shivering right along with me. The dogs soon delivered the desired effect and both my human friends began to stir. I reached up and retrieved a copper kettle from the fire tripod and stretched over to fill it with clean snow from the edge of our pit. I then re-hung the kettle over the fire and pulled in a couple of sticks from our woodpile to liven up the flames.

Mark, having relieved himself and been greeted enthusiastically by his spaniel dog, Ginger, joined me in front of the fire, his blanket thrown over his shoulders. We exchanged no words but leaned close to the flame, soaking in the heat whilst waiting for the snow in the kettle to melt.

Behind us, Dan was struggling out of his blanket all the while being mauled by his young pup, Chloe, who was beside herself with excitement at seeing him awake. Soon three men and three dogs were together by the fire, slowly coming alive and relatively pleased to be up and active again after lying dormant through the fourteen-hour night.

I added a few cups of fresh snow to our kettle as the snow in it began to melt. Several minutes later the pot was half full of warm water. We needed a meal before traveling, so I got a food sack from my haversack and threw a fistful each of dried peas and corn into the pot. Mark added a few pieces of dried beef and a little salt.

Dan, by now showing some outward appearances of being awake and to whom morning coffee is considerably more than a mere luxury, impatiently snatched up the other kettle. He crawled over us to get his snowshoes, which, with the muskets, had been placed at the rear of the pit last night to keep from thawing and getting damp. He stepped up out of the hole, bent over stiffly to tie on his snowshoes and shuffled off down the trail that led to the pond. Minutes later he returned, swearing to himself under his breath. He snatched one of the axes out of a log where it had been stuck last night and headed for the pond again, this time equipped to open up the frozen water hole.

All the dogs followed Dan, leaving us room to move around more easily. Mark got up and spread our blankets over the tripod and woodpile to air out and we began to get ready to move. We both stripped off the spare shirts we'd worn last night, packed them away, then drew half-blankets up over our shoulders and belted them at the waist. Last, we collected the few stray belongings that were underfoot and packed them away.

Bivouac site in early morning, preparing to break camp and begin the day's march.

By the time Dan was back with water, the contents of the kettle were just beginning to smell like stew. He hung the kettle he'd filled low over the fire and then began to collect his gear. As we waited for the coffee water to heat, we each took turns rolling our packs, having to shoo the dogs out of our way every few seconds.

The water in the coffee kettle began to boil. I gingerly maneuvered it away from the flame to add several spoons of coffee, paying close attention now as this was very serious business. I repositioned the kettle over the flame and let it boil and simmer down several times in succession before being satisfied that it was strong enough. At last I pulled it completely off the fire and set it down securely on the boughs between my moccasins.

Mark and Dan were watching me anxiously, but I needed no reminders to move very carefully. A kettle full of stew might be accidentally spilled, a snowshoe could be stepped on and snapped, you might even break a man's musket stock by mistake, but to spill the morning coffee out here in the below zero cold would be disaster, pure and simple.

We each got out a cup, and I pulled a copper flask from my haversack. Setting the cups in front of me, I spooned a good amount of sugar into each and then added a stiff shot of rum and cream from the flask. To this mixture Dan added

Matt Bandella, Samantha and Fred Gowen ready
to begin a day on snowshoes.

donning powder horns, haversacks, blanket rolls, mittens, hats and finally picking up our muskets. We then moved around a bit to judge whether everything was hung correctly and adjusted comfortably.

Our fifth day on the trail began as Mark headed out over three-foot-deep snow, following our old tracks down to the pond several hundred yards from camp. When we came to the ice, we followed the contours of the shoreline, staying on a narrow apron of windblown snow that covered the ice's edge. Even though this was a longer route, it enabled us to leave our snowshoes on; if we'd headed straight across on bare ice, we'd have had to stop to don ice creepers and strap our snowshoes to our packs. We moved along the shore for a half hour, moving at a quick pace to warm ourselves up and enjoying the openness and light after having spent hours in camp in the shadowy forest of fir and spruce.

On yesterday's march we'd crossed this pond in the face of a cold, cutting wind, but this morning was typically windless, an advantage of an early start. We came to the end of the pond and turned up the inlet stream. Here we were slowed by deep, soft, drifted snow as soon as we left the ice. Mark soon stepped aside and Dan and I moved past him. We would repeat this maneuver every ten to twenty minutes all day long, usually without a word, understanding that breaking trail on snowshoes is tremendously difficult work. The lead man must be spelled regularly to avoid his getting too tired and overheated. Once relieved he falls in at the rear and recuperates while following the trodden-down path of the rest of the party.

Dan was now in the lead, and he slowly picked his way up the stream, skirting fallen timber, dense aspen stands and an occasional place where the stream was open. The dogs, bursting with energy, left our tracks now and then to plow through the deep snow. Their enthusiasm was dampened quickly on these occasions as each time the lead dog would swiftly lose momentum and then wallow in white, waist deep powder, going nowhere, soon to be overtaken and nearly trampled by the two that followed. The dogs would then lose their wanderlust and come trooping back to us, crowding close up on our heels, absolutely knowing that they were missing important goings on up ahead and stepping on the tails of our snowshoes trying to get past us to see what was happening.

We were climbing now, and I noticed that Dan was carrying his round felt hat in his hand to avoid overheating. A few minutes later in our climb, I took over the lead and soon appreciated how hard Dan had been working. The snow was deep and soft and I sunk in a half foot even with snowshoes. Whoever broke trail had to lift each snowshoe that half foot with every step and lift not only the weight of the shoe but also whatever snow lay on top of it. Luckily with the intense cold, the snow was dry and tended not to accumulate or ball up too badly on the snowshoes.

I soon felt myself heating up, so I slipped off my mittens and tucked them under my powder horn strap. Even though they're attached by a neck cord, they dangle awkwardly and will snag if not tucked away.

In fifteen minutes more, I crested a rise and came to another pond. The morning sun was a small orange disk low over the mountains to the east and shone through a haze that seemed to foretell weather. Dan and Mark caught up and we stood together, catching our breath, admiring the beauty of this pond and the chain of frozen hills beyond. A mile away, just behind

steaming coffee from the kettle. We reverently passed the cups around and all sat back, enjoying the heat the cups imparted to our hands and the warmth and well-being the coffee itself restored to our insides. What a miracle is morning coffee.

A while later our stew was edible, so we refilled our cups and spooned away. We were not really hungry but ate anyway, knowing that later on we'd need the energy and fluids. As we ate, we each fed our dogs bits of dried beef and finally let the dogs finish the contents of the kettle and cups. After the dogs were done, Dan added snow to each kettle and replaced them over the fire to warm again.

It had been light for almost an hour and we needed to be on our way. Days are short in the winter and every minute of light is precious. As soon as the snow in the kettles melted and warmed, we cleaned them up and packed them into our haversacks. This done, we gathered all our truck, then huddled by the dying fire to get some final warmth. According to my thermometer, the temperature away from the fire was now minus five, up from the fifteen below that I'd observed in the pre-dawn.

The fire soon died down to mere embers, and we reluctantly began to strap on our packs, first tying on our snowshoes, then

The dogs look on as Mark takes his bearings. Montressor's party traveled the area shown in the background.

those hills, was where Lt. John Montressor's party of rangers had begun to run out of food in the winter of 1760. They had left Quebec in early February, fourteen men in all, traveling on snowshoes, carrying memorized dispatches for Amherst in New York. Twenty-six days later they straggled into Brunswick Fort on the Maine coast, gaunt from starvation and exposure. They had lived on leather breeches, shot pouches, snowshoe strings, small animals and birds since crossing the Height of Land along the Maine/Canadian border. Montressor's journal of that trip was one of the things that had inspired us to come here.

The dogs, Sammy in the lead, raced out over the frozen pond, playfully chasing each other and slipping on the slick ice. "If only," Dan thought out loud, "we could train them to break trail for us." As we watched them, Ginger caught a scent trail and veered off from the others, her nose in the snow following the scent. The other dogs followed, and we were able to whistle two of them back from across the pond before they got out of sight. Ginger, however, was out of earshot, or at least pretended to be. When she finally joined us again ten minutes later, she was panting heavily, tongue hanging out and looked about ready to die from exhaustion. She'd obviously had a good time.

Mark led out once again, heading for the end of this upper pond. We cut the trail the dogs had been on and saw they'd

been tracking a small moose. It had been here not too long ago and had been in a hurry, undoubtedly having scented us as we approached. Coming to the end of the ice, we began working our way north following the course of the pond's outlet stream. Our route took us through deep snow and thick alders that choked the ravine the stream had cut. It was terribly slow going and not the first time we felt thankful that we'd left the toboggans home and packed light. This would have been very difficult ground for the sleds. Not only would dragging them have been torture, but also we might not have been able to reach this beautiful, solitary, frozen country.

After a time we broke through onto a trail that led north along the side of the main ridge. We followed this trail and each of us took several turns in front. At length we came to a stream and crossed it on a snow bridge. Once we were on the other side we ducked into the shelter of a stand of fir and began to make preparations for a "boil-up."

We dropped our packs in one pile and went to work quickly. Mark slipped the ax out from beneath the straps of his bedroll and went to collecting deadwood. Dan got the kettle from his haversack and snowshoed to the stream to get water. I tramped down a ten-foot circle in the snow, snapped off a few nearby fir boughs to sit on and then got out my fire makings. By the time Dan and Mark were back with water and wood, I had a small birch-bark fire kindled, to which I added some sticks. Dan had brought back a pole that we used to hang the kettle over the fire. We brushed the snow off of our clothes, untied our snowshoes and stuck them into the snow behind us, then settled down on our thin mattress of boughs. For the first time, I became aware of a gentle wind coming out of the north and saw that overhead the clouds were thickening. Out of curiosity I pulled the thermometer from my haversack and read a temperature of twelve degrees. These signs indicated we had weather coming.

As we sat enjoying the warmth from the fire, the kettle began to boil. Dan added a handful of raspberry tea to the water, and we let this boil for awhile as we chewed on dried beef and the remains of some fried bread I'd made yesterday. We were thirsty from the morning's march and anxiously got our cups out when the tea was ready. I spooned sugar into each of them and then added the hot, aromatic tea.

In spite of the fire, I was getting chilled. I untied the half-blanket from my haversack and drew it over my shoulders. We had a second cup and enjoyed the good effects of the tea, which warmed our innards and gave us relief from the penetrating cold.

The dogs, having used up considerable energy this morning, crowded around us to receive a little dried beef and

lay down on the boughs to rest. We were almost too content to leave but finally let the fire burn down. When it ceased giving warmth, we covered it with snow, scattered the spruce boughs, donned our gear and moved out again.

After we'd been fifteen minutes on the trail, the snow commenced, slowly at first, consisting of very fine flakes. Dan, who had led off after the boil-up, stopped under an overhanging fir tree. He dropped his pack and untied the half-blanket from his haversack. Mark and I followed his lead and after brushing the snow from each others' clothes, we fixed the half-blankets as capes, belting them around the waist and pulling them up over our heads. We shouldered our packs once again and continued along the ridge.

Over the next half hour, the wind grew rapidly in intensity and the snow accumulated with surprising speed. This would be a big storm. The trail finally turned abruptly and began to descend into the great valley to the east. We followed the path down, enjoying the novel ease of snowshoeing downhill and catching an occasional glimpse of clouds of windblown snow gusting through the valley below.

Perhaps halfway down the ridge, Dan stopped and hurriedly shed his pack. He ambled swiftly off the trail, calling over his shoulder as he went that we could either go on or wait but nature had called. The fried bread we'd eaten yesterday apparently had finally made its way through his digestive tract. We decided to wait. As we slipped off our packs, Mark good-naturedly called out to Dan reminding him to use his left hand and avoid snow containing sharp spruce needles.

Dan and Fred finishing quick repairs to a snowshoe—an everyday occurrence on winter trips.

This brought to my mind a debate over toilet paper I'd read about some time back. I remembered reading with amusement and growing puzzlement about what these folks speculated might have been used for toilet paper by woodsmen of the mid-18th century and what might best be used by their modern counterparts. Just about every substance was proposed, from tow to rags to vegetable matter. I might be mistaken but seem to remember someone even speculating that a linen rag might be used, presumably to be washed out and (shudder) carried in one's pack. (How disappointing it would be if this rag got mixed up with the coffee bag!)

My imagination got to work and my mind's eye conjured up a picture of one of George Croghan's pack trains heading across the Allegheny Mountains, loaded down with goods for the Ohio Valley trade and the last horse on the trail laden with packs bulging with multi-colored toilet paper that the traders knew the Delaware Indians coveted.

Sanity and logic finally reigned when some enlightened soul wrote in to suggest the use of any vegetable matter that might be available or, ultimately, the hand. To be fair to all the debaters, this subject has been one that few diarists mention, even though we all obviously are curious and need information.

As most winter campers are aware, snow is a perfect toilet paper. It's abundant, clean, does a terrific job and you don't have to carry it in your haversack. In summer plain water and, if you prefer, leaves, work very well. Water is cleaner and allows you to wash your hands afterward—if you use a kettle or cup you just have to remember to pour, never dip.

This high-minded, intellectual daydreaming was interrupted when Dan returned with a smile on his face. He contentedly picked up his pack and we moved off again. Just

fifty yards later Sammy wheeled suddenly and darted off the trail. I began slipping the lock cover off my musket, thinking she might be into snowshoe hares again as she had been up on the high ponds. Just then we were startled when a partridge exploded from under a spruce almost at our feet. The bird frantically wove its way through the trees, struggling for speed and altitude. It was a skinny bird, a living barometer of how hard the winter had been in these mountains.

In another hour we reached the valley floor and cut across our trail from the week before. We found that our old tracks were still evident although filling up fast with snow. We followed the tracks and soon came to the long, narrow pond we'd camped on earlier in our trip. We remembered having seen dense stands of spruce and fir on the east side of the pond when we'd passed here before and agreed that those stands should provide the shelter from the wind that we'd need for camp tonight.

We were about to head that way when Mark called to stop us. Dan and I turned to look and found him pulling from the crotch of a big cedar an old, rusted fry pan of a size and style that must have been used in an early 1900s lumber camp. We knew what Mark was thinking. Leaving his pack on, he snowshoed down the bank and across to the opposite shore of the pond, perhaps eighty yards away, and tied the fry pan to the limb of a tree with a piece of twine. By the time he was back, Dan and I had removed our lock covers and taken the tompions out of the barrels of our muskets. We whistled in the dogs as we loaded with cartridges from our belt pouches. Once loaded we took care to keep our primed locks tucked under our armpits and protected from the blowing snow while Mark loaded his gun. Peering across the pond, we could barely see the target through the white of the driving snow. Dan raised his musket and just before he pulled the trigger, intoned, "The last man to hit the gong digs the snow pit when we make camp."

A few minutes later we were on our way again, our musket balls having rung the metal pan often enough to satisfy our urge for play. Mark was already planning the size and shape of the hole he was going to dig, and Dan and I were feeling lucky, knowing that we'd also be doing our share of digging on the trips to come.

We trudged north over the hard, windblown snow that covered the pond's surface. The storm was funneled between the surrounding mountains, and the wind raced at us down the pond's three-mile length, driving the snow into our faces and slowing our progress. The freezing wind cut sharply through our clothes, and we pulled our hats down lower and our blankets closer. After a half mile, I pulled the silk scarf from around my neck and tucked it into the crotch of my breeches. The wind had found a vulnerable spot.

We finally came to the area where we wanted to make camp and turned toward shore. I found a small game trail, and we followed it a few yards through the dense growth of snow-covered spruce that crowded the pond's edge. Here we got lucky. About fifty yards in, the spruce gave way to fir and we stopped at what looked to be an almost perfect campsite. The thickness

of the forest had reduced the storm to windless, falling snow that filtered vertically, almost gently, through the trees overhead. Plenty of standing dead wood, a dense growth of spruce for boughs, and water all lay close at hand. We were greatly pleased with this site. One of the ironies of winter trips is that the most difficult part of the day is at the end. Making camp is extremely tough work and comes when your body is at its lowest ebb. Having all the materials close at hand would render our job much easier.

We tiredly let our packs drop from our shoulders and piled them with the muskets under a thickly branched spruce, covering everything with a piece of canvas. We then set to work, not knowing what time of day it was but guessing we had perhaps as much as two hours of light remaining.

Each of us went doggedly to our task without much conversation, as we'd done a hundred times before. Mark, having won the honor of digging the camp pit, found an open place about fifteen feet square next to the trunk of a downed tree and cleared it of brush. He then untied his snowshoes and began to use one of them as a scoop to remove snow from what would be our sleeping hole. Before long we could hear him cussing about how he was going to make a wooden snow shovel for our next trip.

Dan took his light ax and went to dropping dead spruce and stacking them next to what would be our fire pit. Spruce is never the wood of choice for an all night fire, but here it was

Fred Gowen and Dan Broderick are busy constructing a brush shelter.

174

Drying wet coats at camp in front of a six-foot fire. Note tripod, wooden pot hook and typical bough bed.

handy and abundant; we wouldn't be too picky this afternoon.

While Dan and Mark were occupied, I moved a few yards away from camp and began to gather spruce boughs, taking a few from one tree and a few from another. Snow from the storm had accumulated on all the trees and made this wet, hard work. Each time I brushed against a tree, more snow fell on me, and eventually I was soaked from sweat and melted snow. My felt hat was invaluable under these circumstances but it couldn't protect my whole body. I was further hampered by my snowshoes, which made maneuvering in the deep snow and heavy growth very clumsy. Often as I worked, my mitten straps or other clothing would become snagged in the boughs and I'd swear as I impatiently fought free.

I made small piles of boughs and then wearily carried each pile back to camp, stumbling over nearly every obstacle on the way. Mark had finished shoveling out the hole and was on snowshoes again, helping Dan gather and cut firewood. With exasperation I commented that doing this work while wearing mittens and snowshoes was no different than working in clown shoes and handcuffs. They chuckled and agreed with me.

By the time I'd brought in my last load, Mark was lashing together a fire tripod with twine and was nearly ready to kindle a fire. Dan, our brush shelter specialist, was busy at work making our lean-to with the boughs I'd collected. The snow that had been removed in excavating our sleeping hole would make the sides of the shelter. Dan had lashed together a frame of dead poles and began layering boughs into a roof. This would be the first lean-to we'd had to build on this trip. All of the previous nights we had needed shelter only from the cold, and the bother of putting a roof over our heads hadn't seemed necessary.

Though we'd stopped to boil-up at noon and had also stopped for water at several stream crossings, we were dehydrated and needed water. I snowshoed over to the snow-covered canvas that protected our packs, pulled it back and got the kettles from stiff, frozen haversacks. With ax and kettles in hand, I headed down the game trail toward the pond with the dogs following close behind.

When I broke out onto the pond's surface, I was surprised to find the storm still at full force. Back inside the tree line we'd been sheltered from its continuing intensity. Nearly a foot of new snow was on the ground.

About twenty yards from shore I stopped, used the ax to clear the snow down to the ice's surface and began chopping to get down to water. This is usually a strenuous but relatively quick task, but nothing is easy when a person is tired, cold and thirsty. The hole was nearly two feet deep when I came to frozen mud and realized that I'd made a mistake. I'd chosen a spot in the shallows where water had frozen all the way down to the bottom.

I glanced around in frustration, angry at myself for having wasted time and energy that could not be spared. Across the pond, a quarter of a mile away and just visible through the storm, I spotted a place where a ravine came down to the shore. I picked up my kettles and trudged doggedly across. Luck was with me. A small stream entered the pond here and the current had kept the ice thin. Open water showed in several places. I approached this area carefully, testing the thickness of the ice with the ax handle and at length reached a place where I could fill the kettles. After drinking my fill I headed slowly back to camp with kettles overflowing. For the first time I noticed it was beginning to get dark.

Dan and Mark had the shelter completed and fire built by the time I returned, and they were mighty glad to see I had water. They'd brought all the packs under cover and had begun to dry them out in front of the fire. The roof of the lean-to was already heavy with fallen snow and the camp looked cozy, lit by yellow and orange flame in the failing light.

Setting the kettles down by the fire, I untied my snowshoes, stuck them into a snow pile and joined the others under cover. Mark had built a good fire, making it almost six feet long and constructing it on top of two solid logs to keep it from sinking into the snow. Our camps and fires are shoveled as close to the frozen ground as we can get them but fires placed directly on the frozen surface have a tendency to burn below the level of the sleeping pit, wasting a lot of radiant heat and making smoke. The downed tree trunk had been used as a fire-back so that the fire's heat and light played into the lean-to all across the front. An all-night supply of wood lay close by to one side, all logs left long so that they could simply be fed in a little at a time as the ends burned down. Mark and Dan shared an entire kettle of water, then we sat for a time, exhausted but enjoying the relief from our labors and absorbing the fire's welcome heat. The dogs had settled down and curled up together in the rear of the shelter, a warm, wet pile of fur and snores. Dan had thrown his blanket over them.

We talked quietly, discussing the day's journey as we grew steadily warmer. Eventually our energy began to return. Each of us stripped off our damp moccasins and liners, stuffed them with handfuls of spruce twigs, and propped them up to dry on sticks placed well back from the fire. After putting on spare moccasins we removed some of our wet clothing, drying coats and shirts as best we could under the overhang of the shelter, out of the falling snow. Soon we were beginning to feel pretty good again, having dry feet and warm, though still somewhat damp, bodies.

Mark hung a kettle over the fire and leisurely made some raspberry tea as we relaxed. We had no desire for food yet; dehydration and fatigue had killed our appetites. The tea, loaded with sugar, restored some of our energy and afterward we began to think about eating. Dan put on the other kettle. Tonight, as usual, supper would be a stew of peas, corn, onions and beef—all dried. We never tired of this fare, as it was all we had left. An hour later when the stew was ready, our appetites had fully returned and we ate ravenously.

After supper we melted snow for water and made coffee. Coffee, after a long day on the winter trail, dulls the pain of aching muscles, lifts sagging spirits and warms the chilled internal fires. We settled back

with our steaming cups to enjoy the fire, the snowstorm and the quiet. One of the real joys of being out in the winter is that camps are a rich reward for the toil of the day, and the length of the night allows a good rest. Dan rummaged through his haversack to

get out a pouch of tobacco and his clay pipe. The sight of his stumpy pipe never fails to lift my spirits. Although it has grown shorter, the stem having been broken several times, it has survived through some good trips, and I associate the fragrance of its tobacco smoke with many pleasant times. As Dan primed and lit the pipe, Mark wrote in his journal by firelight, making notes and drawing a map of the day's journey that he later showed us. With his pipe clenched in his mouth, Dan propped a snowshoe up in front of him and began making repairs using brass wire and a splint he'd cut from maple. He'd stepped on a snow-covered stump while making camp and had cracked the frame near the tail. While the others were busy, I wrote in my journal and later sewed up yet another rip in my coat. The thermometer had been hung on a sapling away from the fire and a mid-evening reading showed the temperature to be a balmy twenty degrees Fahrenheit, the warmest weather we'd yet encountered on this trip.

Somewhat later Sammy painfully extracted herself from the pile of dogs and came up to see me about her supper. I gave her a cup of stew and slowly fed her a handful of dried beef. Her success at getting food interested the other pups and both Chloe and Ginger crowded up to us to be fed. Not long after their meal, the dogs were back in their nest, the shared wet heat of their bodies keeping them warm under the blanket we'd placed back over them.

We fought off sleep as long as we could, as the dark would last fourteen hours, but soon we could stall it no longer—we were exhausted. Each of us stepped outside the shelter to relieve himself, then we rousted the dogs out of the lean-to. They moved very reluctantly but knew the routine well by now. We unrolled our bedrolls and then took turns settling in.

I went first. I'd already put on my dry shirt and pulled the shirt I'd worn during the day over it, followed by my coat. That done, I put on my wool hat, pulled my hood on over that, made sure my mittens were tucked in the front of my waistcoat, and finally worked my way into the blanket and canvas sack. Once I'd gotten arranged, I called Sammy over and she crawled into place under the blanket next to my upper body. I then pulled my half-blanket up to get a second layer of wool over us. By the time I was settled in I'd worked up considerable heat and realized how tired I was. Even getting into bed was a chore after a day like we'd had.

While waiting for me to get arranged the others had built the fire up to give us heat and light for as long as possible. Afterward, each took his turn getting settled in. Mark, the last man in, pulled our canvas tarp up to cover us all. This would both retain the heat we generated and fend off any blowing snow. We all squirmed toward the center, knowing we'd be warmer if we shared heat. The dogs, we find, not only add to the fun of a trip with their playfulness, enthusiasm and ability to find game but also make it much easier to get through the cold winter nights. I've often warmed up a cold hand or nose by burying it in Sammy's warm fur; two bodies generate heat much more efficiently than one.

Before long we lay quietly in our blankets, bone tired from the labor of a difficult day but finally warm and comfortable with a good shelter over our heads and our bellies full with a good meal and coffee. The snow continued to fall beyond the fire and that made our lean-to seem all the more cozy. Tomorrow morning the forest would be beautiful in the aftermath of the storm. We looked forward to traveling in woods blanketed with fresh, clean snow, making new tracks in this Arctic paradise that we had all to ourselves.

THE LURE OF THE WINTER WOODS

In January, February and March, the woods and mountains of the Northeast offer isolation, an exhilarating freshness and traveling opportunities that are not available in the other seasons. There are none of the summer's plague of black flies, mosquitoes, ticks and deer flies. Few people are encountered. Journeying is often easier and more direct as frozen ponds, streams and swamps provide routes not available in other seasons and heavy snow covers obstacles that would stop a traveler in summer. Tracking conditions are wonderful and each trail tells an interesting story. Camps seem snugger, appetites sharper and simple trail rations tastier. The winter journeys my friends and I have made as 18th century New Englanders over the years, while never being easy, have been the trips we remember most fondly.

Each year in late fall, I find myself eagerly anticipating the first snows and begin looking over my winter gear, making small repairs to snowshoes, winter moccasins and other equipment. I study my patched and threadbare coat and wonder if it will make it through another season.

Our predecessors in the 18th century did not cease their outdoor activities in winter. In New England and upstate New York as well as Canada, people cut and transported lumber, trapped, visited neighbors, surveyed, scouted and cut more wood. During Queen Anne's War in the first decade of the 1700s, volunteers from the Massachusetts militia were equipped as "snowshoe men" to patrol the northern frontier and provide warning of incoming raiding parties from New France and also to hunt down Indians to collect the £20 bounty offered by the Massachusetts General Court for each scalp (Drake 167).

Military activity slowed down, but all armies needed scouting done and messages carried. Although large winter troop movements were unusual in the English Colonies, spring came so late in Canada that invading armies from the south could be on the move while there was still snow on the ground in Quebec or Montreal. Therefore, reinforcements and supplies from lower Canada to the outlying forts had to start for their destinations in mid-winter to arrive in time to be of use.

Journals and letters have left evidence of this activity, and from these it is possible to piece together how people adapted their equipment and clothing in order to continue to function in winter. My friend Mark Daiute recently emphasized his approach to winter trips. "The point is not just to go out in winter and survive. That's generally not much of an accomplishment by itself. The whole idea is to adapt ourselves to the winter, learn to function well in spite of the difficulties and then do the things we like to do." We've finally learned to do just that. This is what we use....

SNOWSHOES

Winter in the Northeast means a variety of snow—almost always deep but alternating from loose powder to ice-crusted hard pack with dozens of variations in between. Temperatures regularly fluctuate from thirty degrees below zero to thirty-five above. Untimely thaws are followed by long spells below zero. Our forests are thick and difficult to move through, especially as one goes farther north, where spruce, fir, hemlock and pine dominate. Flat ground is difficult to find and a traveler spends most of his day either climbing or descending hills and ridges. Water is everywhere, with ponds, streams and bogs tucked into every piece of low ground. Given these conditions it is not surprising that the first Europeans arriving on these shores quickly noticed and adopted the use of two wonderful pieces of technology—snowshoes and toboggans—that the Indians of the Northeast had developed to make their lives easier in winter. In the general order for the garrison of Quebec, dated November 4, 1759, we read:

...the regiments will have a number of creepers, snowshoes or rackets, and mogosans delivered to them, they will take care to keep them properly fitted, that they may be come at for use on the shortest notice; the snowshoes to be kept hung up, to prevent the rats and mice from eating them. (Knox 2: 259)

Snowshoes are familiar to just about everyone and have changed little in form over the years. Modern materials have made possible a number of ugly variations on the classic design but the principle is the same—spread your body weight over a large enough area, and you can indeed walk on top of any kind of snow. Given the differences in climate and lifestyle, Canadians of the 18th century were much more expert in the manufacture and use of snowshoes, but the knowledge was also common amongst the rural people of Massachusetts and Maine. Winter provided the need and contact with Indians made the knowledge available. Europeans visiting the area for war or sightseeing nearly always commented on snowshoes because they were unfamiliar to them. Lt. John Knox, serving with the 43rd Regiment of Foot in Nova Scotia in 1756, commented:

Our soldiers make great progress in walking on snow-shoes, but men, not accustomed to them, find them very fatiguing. These inventions are made of hoops of hickery, or other tough wood, bended to a particular form, round before, and the two extremities of the hoop terminate in a point behind, secured well together with strong twine; the inward space is worked, like close netting, with cat-gut, or dried entrails of other animals. The racket is from three quarters to one yard in length. At the broadest part, which is about the center, where it is fastened by thongs and straps to the person's foot, it is about fourteen, fifteen, or sixteen inches; a light lively man does not *require them so large as he who is more corpulent and less active; the hard-soled shoe is not at all suitable to them; they must be used under mogosans, as well, for the sake of the wearer's feet, to keep them warm and preserve them from the snow, as that they will not bind on so well or be so soon worn out.* (314-315)

Knox, although he was not an experienced woodsman nor intimately familiar with the use of snowshoes under all conditions, nevertheless touches on several important points from which we can learn. First, moccasins are an essential partner to the use of snowshoes. In looking at modern snowshoes, it is apparent that this lesson has been forgotten. Virtually every outdoor store has stocks of commercially made snowshoes. Construction material aside, nearly every pair is made with a huge toe hole and a very thick toe cord for use with heavy modern winter boots. The difference between an Indian-style pair of snowshoes used with moccasins and a modern pair used with boots quickly becomes apparent if you try out both styles. The Indian-style shoes are lighter, more flexible and therefore much less tiring. In addition, moccasins, being less confining and lighter, add greatly to ease of

Dan tying snowshoes using a squaw hitch.

movement and keep your feet warmer in the bargain, if properly made and worn with good liners. The components of modern snowshoes are made heavier to accommodate the weight and abrasion of boots. You lift this extra weight with each step you take and as a result end up considerably more fatigued at the end of a day's march.

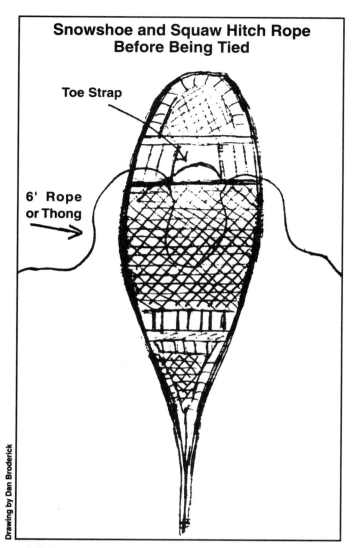

Snowshoe and Squaw Hitch Rope Before Being Tied

Toe Strap

6' Rope or Thong

Drawing by Dan Broderick

Another important point Knox makes is that the size of snowshoes must vary depending on the size of the man using them and, following that reasoning, the weight of his pack. Snowshoes that are too small are maddeningly inefficient and nearly as bad as none at all; those that are too large are very tiring to use. However, finding the perfect snowshoe is impossible. Snow conditions constantly change and terrain varies. One particular style of snowshoe might be perfect in the morning but tortuous to use by midday. The snowshoe that Knox described turns out to be just about right for our use. This shouldn't be surprising, since most of the snowshoes made for the French and Indian War armies were copies, however roughly or hurriedly made, of those used by the Indians of the Northeast who had arrived at the design through the experience of thousands of winters.

The snowshoes we've come to favor are round or square toed with a slight upturn. They are usually about 42 inches long and 14 inches wide and are made of ash, white birch or hickory with fine rawhide filling. The rawhide is cut to about 1/8-inch thickness and is woven to leave spaces from 1/4 inch to 1/2 inch in diameter between the fill, depending on the maker of the shoe. These shoes work very handily in most of the snow conditions we find in the Northeast. Up here, being able to climb hills and turn in brush is important. The generous width of these shoes allows for easier climbing than narrower

ones, and the relatively short length makes for easy turning. In making snowshoes larger for a heavier person, we extend the width, not the length, and make them fifteen or sixteen inches wide. These shoes are still a compromise in some respects, however. Longer, narrower snowshoes with upturned toes work much better in breaking trail. Shorter snowshoes, wider and with no tails, are superior for climbing and turning. Ours, however, do all these things pretty well and are at least adequate in all conditions, which can't be said of the others.

People from other regions often ask us what kind of a binding we use to strap on our snowshoes. The solution is simple, yet elegant. As far as I've been able to determine, fancy snowshoe bindings are an entirely modern invention. In the 18th century, woodsmen made do quite nicely with a toe strap and a six to seven foot length of leather thong or rope. They then simply tied the shoes to their feet using what came to be referred to as a squaw hitch.

To set up this binding, you cut yourself a leather strap about twenty inches long, tapering from about two inches wide at the center to 1/4-inch wide at each end. You then lace the narrow ends into the filling of the snowshoe, leaving the thick middle portion centered over the toe cord just behind the toe hole and just slack enough to slip the toe of your moccasin under. Since the strap is not permanently attached to the snowshoe, it may be adjusted to fit. You then use the long length of rope or thong to tie the snowshoe securely to your foot as shown in the accompanying sketch.

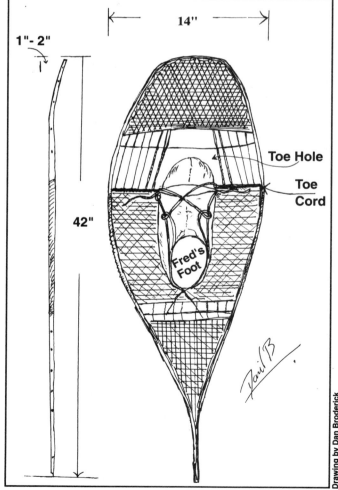

14"

1"- 2"

42"

Toe Hole

Toe Cord

Fred's Foot

Drawing by Dan Broderick

As with snowshoe styles, people have designed specialized bindings that give good stability in climbing or descending or some other specific activity but do nothing else well. The beauty of the squaw hitch is that it does all things adequately and is bare bones simple. It gives you good control of the snowshoe in most situations and can readily be tied on, removed or adjusted under the worst conditions without having to claw at frozen buckles. Quarter-inch hemp rope works very

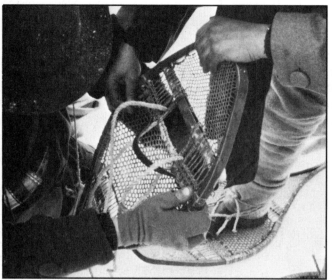

A snowshoe ready for tying on. Note the leather toe strap and the rope that will be tied into a squaw knot.

well for a squaw hitch as it is not susceptible to freezing to the point where it can't be flexed. It is easily untied even with stiff, frosted fingers. Leather thongs will work and were commonly used but don't work as well as rope. In the nineteenth century, lengths of cotton lamp wicking were commonly popular but wouldn't have been available in the 1700s.

Getting proper 18th century snowshoes is a problem. Most commercially manufactured wooden snowshoes available in outdoor stores are modern styles, plain and simple. As mentioned before, the frames are much heavier and the filling is much coarser than those designed for use with moccasins. The toe cord is very thick and the toe hole is made large to accommodate a boot toe. Try using any of these with moccasins for a day or two, and you'll find that the ball of your foot eventually becomes sore from constantly stepping on the thick toe cord. When you dig in for traction, your moccasin tends to slip forward through the large toe hole. If a modern-made pair is your only available option, try to find a pair with the thinnest toe cord and smallest toe hole that you can find. If this is possible, you'll do all right with them and they'll do the job.

Alternatives to store-bought snowshoes? Head for Canada, go antiquing or make them. Handmade snowshoes are still being made in Quebec Province (and perhaps other locations), and it is possible to buy a pair and have them shipped.

In the Northeast many antique stores have pairs of old handmade snowshoes hanging on the walls. In acquiring a pair this way, it's very important to gauge the strength remaining in the old, dried-out frames and rawhide filling. No snowshoe ever made is without potential flaws, that being the nature of wood and leather, so be sure to look for cracks and evidence

of rough wear. Avoid buying snowshoes with problems in strategic areas, especially at mortises and the rawhide in and around the toe cord. The good news is that, as with old tools, if they've survived this long, most of what was breakable is already broken. My friend Chris Gilgun, who has an especially good eye for judging old snowshoes with more winters left in them, has acquired several pair of fine old snowshoes in this way that we've nursed through several seasons of hard use. It's enjoyable to use shoes made by a late nineteenth or early twentieth-century craftsman and wonder how that person would feel if he knew that his skill and knowledge had produced shoes capable of being used again so many years later.

Constructing your own snowshoes is the best solution to equipping yourself. Their construction is a topic too long and involved to cover here, but there are some reference sources available (see *Camp and Trail Methods* by E. Kreps).

Remember that snowshoes are not permanent. By that I mean that a good pair of shoes will last one or two seasons of hard, continued use before they become risky to take on a long trip. On the trail we always carry twine, wire and a small pair of pliers for repairs to the frames and extra sinew or rawhide for mending rips in the filling. Snowshoe mending is a daily ritual on our trips. Quite often we're forced to make an unplanned stop, kindle a fire to warm our hands, boil up a pot of tea and set to fixing what broke. Never feel too badly when you've ripped a jagged hole in what moments before was an intricately and beautifully filled snowshoe. They're not made to be hung on a wall but to be used hard and used well.

Dan Broderick and Mark Daiute tying on snowshoes and getting ready to hit the trail.

TOBOGGANS

The toboggan, a word borrowed from the Micmacs of Eastern Maine, was variously called a sled or sledge by the English and a *traine* by the French. In English journals you'll usually see the word "sledge" or "sled" used instead of toboggan, with no distinction being made between those fixed with runners and those without. Although writers usually meant the version without runners, only when the words "toboggan" or *"traine"* are used can you be positive. You'll notice that I tend to use these names interchangeably also, however for the purposes of this text, the toboggan without runners is what I'm referring to when I say sledge or sled.

> *Our provisions were drawn by the men, upon sledges, made of thin boards, a foot in breadth, and curved upward in front, after the indian fashion"* (Henry 265).

The classic toboggan is another invention for which we can thank native Americans. It is a simple yet elegant work of functional art. They can be made of a variety of woods, availability being the key. Commonly preferred woods were white ash, cedar or white birch.

Bush toboggans generally range from six to ten feet in overall length and are usually not wide, generally being sixteen inches or less. The reason for this is obvious, as a narrow sled will fit in your snowshoe tracks, offers less resistance in hauling and fits between and around obstacles more easily. Two six- to eight-inch wide boards about ten feet in length and 3/8 inch thick are used in its construction. The two boards are attached to each other by means of four cross pieces and then are bent back almost 180 degrees in a severe curve. All pieces are drilled and lashed together where they join to give the toboggan a flexibility that enables it to bend, not break, when stressed. Where the lashing protrudes on the bottom, grooves are cut to keep the lashing below the bottom's surface, thus avoiding wear and cutting down on friction. Along each topside edge, from just behind the curve to the tail, either a cord or a stick 3/4 inch in diameter is attached to the crosspieces to provide lashing points for loads.

Toboggans are loaded by spreading a canvas wrapper or tarp over the sled and then placing whatever gear is to be carried on top of the tarp. Once everything is arranged, the front and back of the tarp are folded up over the gear, then each of the sides. Rope is then used to lash this package to the sled. Some people prefer to use one long rope, others cut and splice short lengths of rope to the lashing points and leave them there permanently. I prefer the second method, as long ropes tend to tangle and become difficult to cinch up when both the rope and hands are frosted. A tarp or canvas wrapper keeps snow and moisture off your equipment, keeps equipment securely on the sled and can also be used for a shelter.

Toboggans are hauled by means of a rope, the ends of which are tied off to the first crossbar behind the curve. Positioning the rope here provides

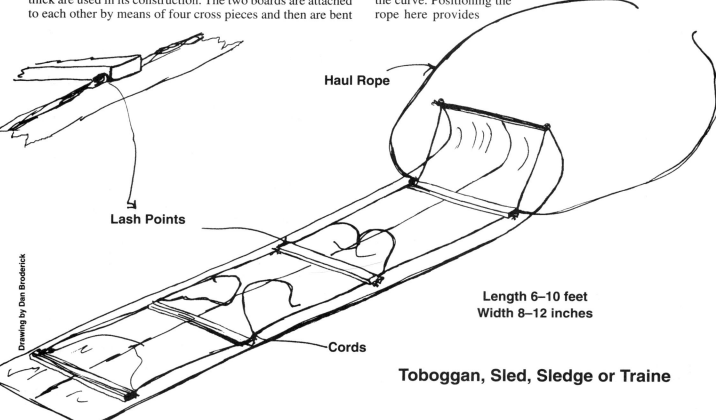

Haul Rope

Lash Points

Drawing by Dan Broderick

Cords

Length 6–10 feet
Width 8–12 inches

Toboggan, Sled, Sledge or Traine

both a pulling and lifting force when the toboggan is being hauled and helps it ride more easily over the snow and ice. The haul rope will vary in length depending on personal preference and the type of terrain over which you're hauling, however, it must be at least long enough to prevent the front of the sled from interfering with the tails of your snowshoes. Several methods are used in harnessing the toboggan to the hauler. In New France it was common for troops to be issued collars or harnesses that were attached to the hauling rope. This collar was either worn tumpline style across the forehead or was slipped across the chest, thereby leaving the hands free when hauling (Bonin 70).

Another alternative is to cut the haul rope, then tie off each end to a one-inch-thick stick about a foot long. The hauler can then pull the sled using the stick by slipping it over his head and keeping it on his chest or, in rough terrain, can simply pull the toboggan along behind using one or two hands on the stick, just like a child's sled. Dogs were also commonly used to haul toboggans, especially in Canada where winter journeys were most common. The dogs were not always the most willing of participants, but journals refer regularly to their use and cite dogs as being in high demand for this purpose when expeditions were being mounted (Bougainville 87). This is embarrassing to admit, but although we always bring our dogs on the trips, we haul our own sleds. My dog, Sammy, being spoiled beyond help, would never allow a collar to be attached to her body. Dan's pup, Chloe, would probably accept the collar with enthusiasm, but the ultimate destination of the load would be quite uncertain.

Toboggans are wonderful tools for winter traveling. When presented with a flat terrain or frozen water course to travel on, a toboggan will convey all of your equipment and pulls very easily on hard packed snow or slick ice. Occasionally on our journeys, we've encountered ice conditions that have allowed us to string several toboggans end to end to be hauled with ease by one man. (There can be amusing hazards to slick ice conditions. Once we were hauling sleds over bare ice on Lake George when a gale blew up behind us. I recall Chris Gilgun almost being run down by a heavy sled he was dragging when the wind caught it and pushed it ahead of him. That day we could have rigged for sail if the wind had stayed behind us.)

As good as a toboggan is on a frozen water course, hauling one in other types of country often exacts terrible punishment. In hilly country, close grown forest, thick brush, areas of downed timber and slash, and in many types of snow, a toboggan holds a traveler back like an anchor does a ship. As often as a toboggan has made a journey easy for me, I also have burning memories of struggling at the hauling rope for hours, dragging a reluctant sled through deep snows, being spilled head over snowshoes down a hillside while trying to stop a runaway sled on a downhill pitch, and having a sled overturn again and again while traversing an uneven slope, each time having to be manhandled upright.

Fortunately a traveler has choices. If you're going to travel over tough ground and the trip will be of ten days' duration or less, you should be able to pack all you need on your back and leave the sled at home. A toboggan is a good tool for conveying loads but drastically limits mobility, just as a canoe does in warmer weather. Even the strongest traveler eventually is worn down by a toboggan and will gradually begin to choose trails over-cautiously, avoiding much terrain that one in snowshoes traveling with only a pack wouldn't find very challenging at all.

ICE CREEPERS & SKATES

Ice creepers are handy tools for use in traversing ice and especially when fresh fallen snow lays on the surface. Creepers are simply strap-on spikes of iron or steel that fit under the instep of the shoe or moccasin. January 1758 at Annapolis Royal, Knox writes:

Most severe weather with an intense frost; and the snow flies in thick drifts; the ground is become so slippery that it is dangerous to stir out of doors: the troops, throughout this province, are obliged to have recourse to various expedients to prevent meeting with accident by falling; some by wearing coarse stockings over their shoes, with an additional sole or two, of thick frize or other woolen cloth; some wear moggosans; and others use what are by us termed creepers, which are an invention calculated for the hollow of the foot, that buckles on like a spur, it is a small plate of iron an inch broad, with two ears that come up on both sides of the shoe between the ankle and instep, with a stud on each of them, for the leathers: from the two extremities are four stout points turned downward, to the length of two thirds of an inch, which, *by the weight of the person who wears them, are indented in the ice; this contrivance is actually necessary, and prevents many fatal accidents.* (1: 133-134)

As a rule we carry creepers on all of our trips although we probably use them only one day out of three. When you need creepers, however, you tend to need them in a big way. As with snowshoes, most of us use rope to fasten the creepers to the moccasins. Knox mentions leather straps as an option but these tend to wear through quickly, resulting in lost creepers.

In order to tie on creepers, thread a rope through both eyes of the creepers. Then slip the toe of the moccasin between the rope and the creeper, cross the ropes over the top of the instep, snug things up and tie an overhand knot. Then loop the rope ends around the back of the moccasins and tie them off in front, just like a shoe lace. With moccasins you'll want shorter spikes on the creepers than you would when using them with shoes. This is noticeable when walking over bare ice. Overlong spikes force the creeper up painfully against the instep and can lame you over a day's walk. Experimentation is necessary

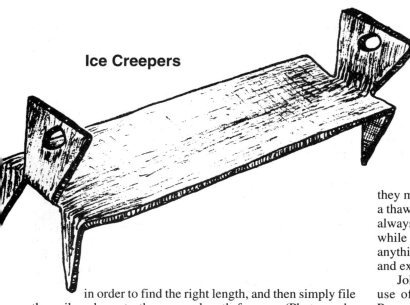

Ice Creepers

in order to find the right length, and then simply file the spikes down to the proper length for you. (Photographs and illustrations of many original pieces of equipment, including creepers and ice skates, can be found in the book *Collector's Illustrated Encyclopedia of the American Revolution* by George C. Neumann and Frank J. Kravic.)

An 18th century ice skate is made of a single blade of iron, usually with a dramatic upward curve at the front, and is secured to the groove in the bottom by a block of wood that is shaped roughly like the sole of a shoe. Skates are usually made for use with shoes; a nail sticking out of the wood block engages the heel of the shoe and straps secure the forepart. They are also easily adapted for use with moccasins by omitting the nail and making the straps more secure. We've done this, as shoes are of no use in the woods in winter.

Most of us winter trekkers own 18th century ice skates, but they are of very limited use on extended trips. Having skate-worthy ice for any length of time is unusual in these parts, and the weight and bulk of skates in one's pack is better taken up by food. Once in a great while, when the ice conditions permit and if your route lies over a long stretch of river or lake, they might be of use. However, as insurance in the event that a thaw softens the ice or a blizzard covers it, snowshoes must always be carried. Another thing to consider is that skating while wearing a pack is a very difficult thing to do. With anything other than a very light pack the skater is top-heavy and extremely prone to taking bad falls.

John Knox and other diarists refer to the recreational use of skates during the French and Indian War. Robert Rogers journals are the only place I've found mention of military use of skates. "January 14, 1756. I this day marched with a party of seventeen men, to reconnoitre the French forts; we proceeded down the lake, upon skaits, and halted near the fall of lake George into Lake Champlain. —at night we renewed our march..." (Rogers 10-11). Those of you familiar with Lake George will recognize that Rogers is saying he made a 32-mile march in a single day. Skates obviously had their uses, although only those few times when bare ice made it possible.

CLOTHING FOR WINTER TRIPS

We portray mid-18th century New Englanders, therefore our winter clothing is limited to what was then commonly available in New England. What did our predecessors use in the winter? Wool, of course. Clothing remained similar in type and style to that used during the rest of the year, but whenever possible it was made from wool. Near Cumberland House, on the headwaters of the Saskatchewan River, in January 1776, Alexander Henry writes, "...our clothing for night and day was nearly the same; and the cold was so intense, that exclusively of warm woolen clothes, we were obliged to wrap ourselves continually in beaver blankets..." (265).

Without wool we would not go out in winter hereabouts. It's that simple. Wool is the only cloth commonly available in the 18th century that, at low temperatures, allows moisture to pass through and still retains its insulating qualities. The other common choices, linen or cotton, insulate poorly when they get wet and dry out only with great difficulty.

Years ago, on one of my first 18th century winter trips, I made the mistake of wearing a linen shirt under an outer shirt of wool. Our first day out was glorious—twenty degrees, sunny, good snowshoeing. We were on the move all day, and in the late afternoon we stopped to make camp. We worked hard as the sun fell and temperatures dipped. I began to get chilled and realized that my linen shirt had been soaked from sweat. I stopped to take off the linen shirt and continued to work in the shirt of wool, all I had left. With only the wool shirt on, I was comfortable, even though it also was damp.

I hung up my linen shirt to dry in the front of our lean-to, and it froze solid that night as the temperature dipped to zero. By morning it looked like the corpse of a dead, crucified ranger (it was green, in those days everything "had" to be). During our three days out, the shirt metamorphosed almost like a living thing, from a stiff, frozen corpse to a sodden, limp, heavy rag and then back again but never, ever dried out. I almost threw it away but decided carrying it with me was good penance for my ignorance. A mistake can be a good teacher and I learned well from that one. Using linen or cotton in winter is a mistake I never made again.

The difference, experience taught, is that wool has loft and retains its insulating qualities when wet. It also lets moisture wick out and will readily dry out while being worn. Conversely, wet linen will actually draw heat from your body much like an air conditioner and will stay wet. Two or three layers of linen will be hardly any warmer, and if they get wet will weigh you down that much more while you freeze. Experienced winterers feel as fondly of their wool clothing as a knight must have felt of his armor. With wool clothing on, winter is much less threatening and the woods are a better place to be. Most of those people who recommend linen or cotton probably do their traveling in country where winter is less severe than in the mountains of the Northeast and, I suspect, have gotten their winter experience on short trips of two to four days. On a short trip, you may not be out long enough to run into really sustained severe weather, or when you do, you're out of the woods soon after, not being there long enough to experience the repercussions of poorly chosen clothing or equipment. If you plan a trip of any considerable length, you eventually will run into weather that will convince you of wool's overwhelming superiority. Wool—don't leave home without it!

Here is what we typically bring for clothing on winter trips: waistcoat of wool, with sleeves and fully lined; breeches of leather or wool; two light- to medium-weight wool shirts (one worn, one packed); wool leggings; two pair lightweight greased moccasins with wool liners; one pair stockings or footless hose (made of blanketing); felt round hat or tricorn—with wool sweatband; silk handkerchief; wool scarf; knit wool hat, Canadian hat, Scot's bonnet or hood; wool mittens with leather outer mitts and strap; and finally a half-blanket.

A look at this list will quickly reveal that we tend not to bring much in the way of extra clothing. There are several reasons for this. We generally go out to travel, not just to camp. We seldom spend more than one night at any campsite and extra weight makes sustained traveling difficult. On a long trip, weight needs to be carried in the form of food, not clothing that you can do without. Finally, you seldom need more than this in order to get along adequately under almost any weather conditions. Here are a few comments on each article of clothing:

WAISTCOAT—Our waistcoats are typical early to mid-18th century styles without collars and usually fully lined with wool. They have two large, working pockets positioned well below the belt line (and therefore accessible when equipment is being worn). I prefer my coat without cuffs, as these tend to gather falling snow and make the coat too heavy. I like horn or wooden buttons over those of metal because they are lighter and warmer to the touch. The roomier the coat the better.

SHIRTS—Always wool and always long, down to your knees if you have the material. Long shirts double as underwear and the tails can be torn off to patch things. Light or medium weight is best, as heavyweight shirts take longer to dry and tend to be too warm when on the move. If it gets very cold, we wear both shirts; if it's warmer we wear only one and roll the other in our pack. Shirts with high collars are preferable to those without, as collars help retain heat, keep snow from getting down your neck and keep pack straps from pinching.

BREECHES—Here is the only exception to the rule of always using wool. In the 18th century, leather breeches were by far the most common type of workingman's or soldier's breeches. We've experimented with both wool and leather and found distinct advantages for both. Wool is warmer, lighter and dries more quickly. Leather is nearly windproof, much tougher and is historically more likely to have been used by the people we're emulating. Many original journals refer to widespread use of leather breeches. On his 1760 snowshoe march through Quebec and Maine, John Montressor mentions the rangers who

accompanied him resorting to eating their leather breeches (Feb. 15). We tend to use leather breeches in combination with the long-tailed wool shirts mentioned above, and so far we haven't had to resort to breeches stew.

STOCKINGS—My friends and I belong to two schools of thought on wearing stockings. Some swear by the use of several pairs of thick, knit stockings that reach to mid-thigh. Stockings made of blanketing were also common. "[T]he commanding officers of corps are now permitted to cut up the blankets that were found in the French magazines, and delivered to them, to be applied to such uses as they shall think proper; these are a great acquisition to the soldiers, as they serve them for socks and gloves, etc." (Knox 2: 270).

Stockings, either knit or sewn of blanketing, work well. There is also another variation. Some of us take old, worn-out stockings and cut off the worn lower part at the ankle, then put them on underneath our leggings. An effective variation on this is to make a close-fitting tube of soft blanketing to fit from mid-thigh to ankle, like a second, more tightly fitted legging. Either method provides an extra layer of insulation under the outer legging and remains dry even if your feet get wet, thus you can change liners and moccasins without having to strip off leggings to get at socks that are wet only from the ankle down. In severe weather when every calorie of heat is

vital and frost-stiffened fingers balk at working, this is a great advantage.

LEGGINGS—Again, we are indebted to Mr. Knox:

Leggers, Leggins, or Indian spatterdashes, are usually made of frize, or other coarse woollen cloth; they should be at least three quarters of a yard in length; each Leggin about three quarters wide, then double it, and sew it together from end to end, within four, five, or six inches from the outside selvages, fitting this long, narrow bag to the shape of the leg. the flaps to be on the outside, which serve to wrap over the skin, or fore-part of the leg, tied round under the knee, and above the ankle, with garters of the same color. (1: 285-286)

Notice that Knox doesn't mention the use of woven or decorated gaiters, or garters, as they are also known, amongst the English he served with. He describes only simple strips of wool identical to the material the legging was made from. Given the beating our lower leg coverings take on any trip,

185

fancy gaiters hardly make sense. To further keep leggings up, two twelve-inch leather thongs are sewn to the legging's outside upper edge where the seam is joined and are tied off either to a belt or to a button or loop sewn to the breeches. The bottoms of the leggings are flared slightly to allow them to fall outside the tops of the moccasins thus keeping snow from entering the moccasin tops.

MOCCASINS AND LINERS—In the Northeast the predominant style of moccasin was the center-seam. Winter moccasins need to be larger to provide more room for insulation and freedom of movement, but there the difference between those used in other seasons ends. Even British regular troops quickly caught on to the fact that not only were moccasins the superior footwear for winter, but shoes were downright dangerous:

...these slippers are generally made of the skin of beaver, elk, calf, or other pliant leather, half dressed: each Moggasin is one entire piece, joined or sewed up in the middle of the vamp, and closed behind like the quarters of a shoe; they have no additional sole or heelpiece, and must be used with three or four frize socks, or folds of thick flannel wrapt around the foot; they are tied on the instep with thongs of the same

leather....they are exceedingly warm, and much fitter for the winters of this country than our European shoe, as a person may walk over sheets of ice without the least danger of falling;... (Knox 1: 111)

"...mogosans are to be issued to the men immediately...not only to prevent the soldiers being frost-bitten, but to save their shoes; it is therefore expected that no soldier parade for the future without them, for any duty whatsoever" (General Orders, British garrison of Quebec, winter 1760; Knox 2: 316)

The moccasins we use are identical to those described by Knox. Instead of the heavy, multi-soled moccasins and shoe-pacs that people seem to favor in other locales, our winter moccasins are constructed of one piece of light leather. Aside from historical accuracy, there are other good reasons for this. Traveling on snow does not tend to abrade footwear. It's not uncommon for a pair of our winter moccasins to last for several months' worth of trekking as long as proper care is taken. Heavy leather or additional layers of leather provide very little in the way of extra insulation, take much longer to dry and are not necessary for padding—snow is soft. My moccasins are usually of dressed deerskin or pigskin and are cut with a generous upper flap, which I wrap around my ankle and tie

This photo shows good detail of Mark and his outfit. He prefers a tricorn rather than a cut-down hat like Fred is wearing.

with a long thong that wraps around the ankle several times. In combination with the legging, this effectively keeps snow out of the footwear, even in deep powder snow. Our moccasins are greased with a combination of beeswax and tallow in equal proportions. This inhibits, but never stops, the moccasins from getting wet.

In winter, regardless of the footwear you choose, your feet will always get at least a little damp. This moisture can come from the outside (punching through thin ice or snow melted by the heat of your feet) or from within in the form of sweat. The purpose of greasing moccasins is twofold; it keeps the leather itself from absorbing water and inhibits water from penetrating too easily into the liners. But whatever you do, your feet will eventually become damp. That's where the liners come into action. The wool of the liners, not the leather of the moccasin, keeps the feet warm. Our liners are of two types, the simplest being a woolen copy of a center-seam moccasin, often with an extra wool sole added. The beauty of these liners is that they are light and not bulky and that several can be used in layers according to the snow conditions. They're also easy to dry over a fire and can even be used as mittens in a pinch. In the past we've used thicker, three-piece liners, similar in construction to a flat-soled moccasin. These work well as insulators but are harder to dry than the simpler liners.

HATS—After much experimenting most of us have gone back to wearing the round, cut-down felt hat that we use the rest of the year. This may sound like a cold proposition but it isn't. The felt hat is an inferior insulator when compared to most hats but does several other things they don't do. A felt hat doesn't get snagged and torn off by brush and protects your

Fred Gowen tying a squaw hitch. Notice the half-blanket tied to the haversack straps.

face and head from whipping branches when bulling your way through thick brush. In rain, sleet or snow, a felt hat provides you with a small roof through which no moisture penetrates. At the end of a day's march in bad weather, a felt hat is still relatively dry on the underside, while a wool or fur hat is usually sodden.

Wool and fur hats are usually too warm to wear comfortably for long on the march. After a short time on the trail, they usually end up stuffed into your coat or under your belt. The felt hat's inferiority in insulating is an advantage here. You can keep it on your head as shelter from snow or rain, but aren't bothered by being overly warm. If you require additional heat, it's a simple matter to pass a scarf over your head, tie it under your chin and cram the felt hat down over it.

We do customarily carry a wool toque, Scot's bonnet or Canadian cap in our packs for use in camp and while sleeping. As the hats have been in our packs all day, they are also dry when we need them most.

An alternative or addition to any of these hats is a hood. I find hoods that are permanently attached to a coat get in my way, getting tangled with pack straps and also make a wet coat more difficult to dry out. The Indians of the Northeast commonly used a separate hood with an attached flap that could be tucked under the coat or shirt collar to provide a better barrier for wind protection or left hanging out to prevent snow from going down the neck. These hoods are easy to make from wool scraps. They perform well and take up little room in your haversack when not in use.

MITTENS—Either knit or sewn mittens of blanketing work well, blanketing being the longest wearing and easiest to dry. These fit into greased leather outer mitts that are attached to each other by a five-foot "idiot string" that passes over the neck and prevents loss when a mitten is removed for work or to regulate heat. The leather outer mitts are usually greased to keep moisture out. At night we tend to sleep with our mittens on but take them out of the leather covers for this. Mittens add appreciably to your comfort at night when trying to sleep.

SCARVES—We use both silk and woolen. Silk is very good next to the skin and is light and compact. A wool scarf is the best for outerwear and is versatile. You can wear it around the neck, over the head as a hood, sit on it or use it for an extra layer under your shirt or for repairs to other clothing.

HALF-BLANKET—One way to travel light is to use a blanket instead of outer clothing. We use either a four-point medium-weight blanket that's torn in half (and therefore logically termed a half-blanket) or an extremely lightweight full-sized blanket. This blanket takes the place of extra clothing or a greatcoat and is compact enough to be carried rolled and tied on the haversack straps where it is easy to get at. A half-blanket is simple and versatile. It can be worn over the head and shoulders and belted around the waist as protection against snow or wind. You can sit on it when boiling up at a break, and it's handy at night for extra insulation around the head and shoulders or as a sleeping robe for your dog. In a pinch it can be used as a roof. You can even patch clothing with pieces of it, and it dries out easily when hung over the fire.

By comparison, a capote or greatcoat is bulky, heavy, confining, hard to dry and usually too hot to be worn on the march. Getting a coat on usually entails getting into your pack or at least much putting on and taking off of gear, whereas a half-blanket can be untied from your pack and donned in a few seconds.

The use of blankets as outer clothing is well-documented amongst the Indians. The English used them also, as Robert Rogers mentions in a March 1759 account of an incident near Ticonderoga. Rogers writes, "...the working parties were close to the banks of the lake, and opposite the fort, and were about forty in number; upon which we stripped off our blankets, and ran down upon them, took several prisoners, and destroyed most of the party..." (131).

When rigging the blanket as a cape, some people use a specially made metal pin for fastening it shut at the neck. Dan, who hates carrying extra trinkets, uses a wooden skewer that works just as well and can be made on the spot.

Try using a half-blanket in wintertime and you'll see why they were popular and common.

REGULATION OF HEAT

Regulation of heat while moving is as difficult as it is important. While on the march in winter, it's ironic that our main problem is not staying warm enough but trying to stay cool. A person snowshoeing, especially with a pack or toboggan, generates a tremendous amount of heat and sweating is almost impossible to avoid. As long as you're moving this is not a problem, but when you stop you're in trouble if your clothing has gotten wet from perspiration. Wool clothing helps by wicking away a lot of this moisture, but the obvious strategy should be to try not to get wet in the first place. There are several ways to prevent overheating. The first and most important is to under-dress. Dan always reminds us to "dress cold and walk warm." As cold as you might feel before leaving camp, a quarter of a mile out on the trail you will have worked up a good amount of body heat. Anticipate this by dressing lighter for marching than you would for a day in camp. Roll whatever extra clothing you have in your pack, where it will remain dry until you need it. Don't be afraid to strip off more clothing when you feel heat building up. This will be inconvenient, especially when you're in deep snow and have your pack and accoutrements strapped on, but always take the time to do it. You'll save considerable discomfort later and also won't have to spend time drying the wet clothing when you get into camp.

By limiting how much clothing you wear and by uncovering your head or hands in various combinations, it is possible to cool your body enough to prevent sweating. On the march I find I carry my hat as often as I wear it and nearly always have at least one mitten tucked up under my powder horn strap or belt.

EQUIPMENT

Clothes and equipment will vary according to preference, experience, the period of history and type of person you portray. For example on a trip with Mark Daiute we might go out as a civilian surveying party, for Mark is a surveyor by trade. For such a trip we might include surveying chains, notebooks and a surveying compass with its stand, and we would travel encumbered with a little more gear. We'd cover less ground because of the work of surveying and would want more comfortable camps. The following is a list of what we normally carry for gear on a snowshoe trip without sleds. Remember, this is how we've come to do it, but it is by no means the only way. We're still learning every time we go out.

ACCOUTREMENTS:
Musket—lock protected by greased leather cover and barrel plugged by tompion
Leather belt
Belt pouch—a small bag made of light vegetable-tanned leather, worn in front, containing birdshot, round ball, a few cartridges, wads, flints, musket tool, priming wire, extra char and compass

Sheath knife
Hatchet
Powder horn

BLANKET ROLL:
One medium-weight wool blanket, the larger the better
French knapsack for carrying gear and sleeping in
Catchall bag—light, of painted cotton, for storing gear in camp
Light- to medium-weight wool shirt, if not worn
Extra moccasins and liners
Food in bags
Leather blanket straps
Light ax, carried outside under the straps
Canvas or tarp, if carried

The weight of the packs varies according to the amount of food we bring. Before a recent ten-day trip, our haversacks each weighed in at fifteen pounds and the bedrolls at twenty-three pounds, food for men and dogs included.

HAVERSACK:
Size roughly 12 inches wide, 14 inches long and two inches

deep, with a wide cloth strap doubled for strength, waterproofed with milk paint, containing food enough for the day's march and these items:

Copper kettle (two quart)	Linen thread
Small notebook and pencil (lead)	Brass or copper wire
Cup	Small oil bottle
Fire makings in oiled bag	Salt horn
Pocket knife	Sharpening stone
Two hanks twine (about 100 feet)	Ice creepers
Maps (if any)	Small file
Two candles	Half-blanket (tied to haversack straps)
One pint rum flask (copper)	Two toothbrushes (teeth and musket)
Horn needle case	Horn spoon
Light pliers	Small thermometer

Fred Gowen carries a musket that is plugged with a tompion and its lock is protected with a leather lock cover—necessities of travel in winter.

Here's proof that 60 years old doesn't mean you're over the hill. This is Matt Bandella on the trail in winter. He also has a tompion in his muzzle and a leather cover on his lock. Also note his belt pouch.

PACKS

As people doing living history, we need to be concerned not only with ease of carriage but also with authenticity. My friends and I travel as New Englanders of the 1745-1765 period who are often civilians or at other times may be provincial militia from Massachusetts, serving at Lake George, Acadia, Number Four, perhaps in the East (Maine) or volunteering for ranging service. The Massachusetts militia of this period tended not to be uniformly clothed or equipped and this gives us some latitude for varying our clothing and gear within the confines of what was commonly available in New England at that time.

There are many historically correct methods of carrying your equipment. We've tried most of them and after much experimentation have settled on the use of a French-style knapsack in combination with a smaller common type haversack.

The French knapsack is a simple rectangular linen sack, finished size approximately 50 inches long and 32 inches wide with one 32-inch end being left as the opening. Two wide leather straps, one with a buckle attached to it, are sewn to opposite edges of the sack about halfway down. Once the sack is loaded and rolled, these leather straps are buckled together to make a carrying strap. Contemporary French references have the knapsack simply being gathered at the top and tied shut, then folded in half and loosely slung from the carrying strap. We vary this, having found that the pack carries better when tightly rolled and secured with small straps or rope.

This regulation-issue knapsack had its origins in Europe and was a way of both providing French soldiers a means of carrying their equipment and also saving the cost of issuing a blanket; the soldier was expected to sleep in the linen sack whilst on bivouac. These knapsacks were issued to troops at Louisbourg in 1747 and were probably not uncommon in the rest of Canada after that date, especially with the arrival of large numbers of French regulars in 1755 (Gallup 118).

These packs might have found their way onto the backs of New Englanders:

...Told us yt [that] He over Toock them & Fired on them Drove them off from some of their Packs Plunder &c Then we went & lockd [looked] round Where Ye scrimage was one of our Men found a Blanket.... (Fitch 5)

Capturing packs from a raiding party was not unusual. The incident Jabez Fitch describes occurred near Fort Edward on June 10, 1757, when Connecticut provincials under Phineas Lyman chased off a French and Indian raiding party that had ambushed the fort carpenters. Under most circumstances these captured packs would have been either the property of the men who captured them or been auctioned off within that unit.

Three times in three years (twice in 1746 and once in 1748) the packs of French and Indian raiding parties were captured by men from Fort Number Four and Fallstown (Northfield) on the Connecticut River. These packs were auctioned off to the public, one of the 1746 incidents at Number Four netting 45 pounds for the township (Burke; Hayward).

There seem to have been many opportunities for a French pack to come into the possession of a New Englander and perhaps even be copied if it worked well enough. And in fact these knapsacks do work well. We pack them by folding the blanket to fit inside. All other articles carried (shirt, food, moccasins) are put into a light catchall bag that is then placed inside atop the folded blanket. The knapsack is then rolled tightly and secured with two one-inch leather blanket straps with buckle closures. The carrying strap is then buckled, the

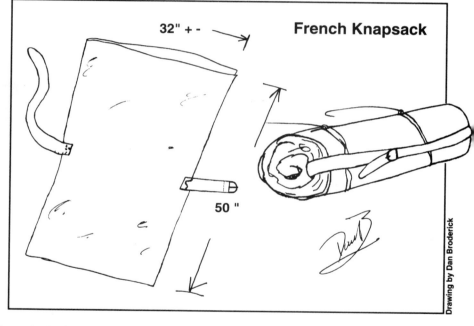

French Knapsack

32" + -

50 "

Drawing by Dan Broderick

ax slipped under the blanket straps, and you're ready to travel. The permanent strap allows the pack to be carried comfortably and can't be misplaced.

If a tarp is carried, it can either be rolled inside the knapsack or rolled around the outside and secured by the same blanket straps. When snowshoes need to be carried, we simply tie the pair together with the rope used for the squaw hitch, then use the blanket straps to both close the pack and secure the snowshoes.

When the knapsack is worn in combination with the haversack, as it usually is, both carrying straps go over the same shoulder and the knapsack rests on the top of the haversack. When you must rid yourself of the packs, you can remove both straps at the same time. A thumb or fingers slipped under both straps can easily relieve an aching shoulder while on the march. The sack itself protects anything placed inside it from the weather and in camp can be used to store all items not immediately in use, thus keeping things from getting lost under boughs or in the snow.

We also sleep in these knapsacks, which is how we can manage to get along without carrying heavier blankets. An average-sized person can get into the knapsack up to mid-chest. This, in combination with a medium-weight blanket provides much more warmth than a heavier blanket would by itself, keeping wind out and heat in. The sack also tends to keep your blanket in place all night in spite of any tossing and turning, thus further preventing accidental heat loss.

Despite our predilection for the French knapsack, there are other good methods for carrying gear that are historically accurate. The simplest and probably oldest is rolling up everything in a piece of canvas and using a tumpline to secure and carry it. I used this method for years and found it worked well when used in combination with a haversack. The drawback is less versatility and the awkwardness of attaching the tumpline as compared to buckling a permanently attached strap.

Snapsacks were another 18th century pack that would have been very common amongst the people we portray. A snapsack is a simple, kidney-shaped tube of varying length and width, usually with a drawstring closure at each end. A permanent strap was attached to each end, to one of which was sewn a buckle. Once the snapsack was loaded and closed, the straps were buckled together and thus provided a carrying sling. Although snapsacks were not generally large enough to accommodate a blanket inside, one could be rolled around the outside of the snapsack and either tied or strapped on. In combination with a haversack, this is a very usable system, but it leaves the blanket exposed to the weather (unless a tarp is wrapped around the blanket) and articles stored inside the pack are not easily accessible. In winter one of the important things to think about when choosing a pack is how easily it allows you to get at what's inside. When feet and fingers are cold, ease of packing and unpacking is important. Fumbling with frozen knots or unrolling your pack in a snowstorm and exposing many loose belongings to loss or moisture doesn't make sense. This is exactly why the French knapsack is superior to anything we've found so far that is historically appropriate.

TARPS & BIVOUACS

The Earl of Loudon describes in his letter a typical winter bivouac of any winter party of the French and Indian War. If boughs are available, this bivouac can't be beat for comfort; when there are no boughs, canvas becomes necessary. Several details should be added to Loudon's description however. Digging a hole in the snow was much more quickly and cut down drastically on the labor of getting settled in. If you're unfortunate enough to be caught by a thaw or rain, having a tarp can make the difference between comfort and suffering. Bougainville mentions the use of tarps by the Canadians on their 1757 winter expedition against Fort William Henry, stating that one tarpaulin was allotted for each

> *...I find that the people who attacked Fort William Henry last winter did not suffer as I expected; and by Lieut: Cols: Gage and Burton, who both marched out on that occasion and lay among the snow for many Nights without tents; that it is not so terrible a thing as they expected, and I find we had no men disabled by it.*
> *The method of lying on those occasions is: as soon as you take up your ground, they make Bush Tents of Pine Boughs, two opposite to each other, leaving a Space between them in which they make great Fires, and the men in each of the Tents lie with their Feet to the Fires in which Situation they are tolerably comfortable. (Loudon to Cumberland, New York, October 17, 1757; Pargellis 401)*

customary, as getting below the level of the snow cuts the wind and makes the fire more efficient. Also, brush lean-tos are only necessary during snow, sleet storms or periods of extreme cold. Normally, having a fire and a simple bed of boughs to keep you off the snow is sufficient. There is one other obvious thing Loudon forgot to mention, though I doubt it even occurred to him. Lieutenant Colonels Gage and Burton likely had a fine, easy time of it because they had enlisted men waiting on them hand and foot, doing all the work.

Tarps, or pieces of canvas, are trouble to carry. Even the lightest of them weighs too much and is bulky. The trouble is, they are very, very useful. On a snowshoe trip, having a tarp available at the end of the day means that you can get shelter

officer or four men. These people, however, were hauling sleds over lake ice nearly all the way and weight was less of a consideration (Bougainville 87).

Whether you bring canvas or not depends on where you go and who goes with you. On a journey by yourself there is no one to share the weight of equipment. Alone, only a small shelter is needed, and in country where boughs are abundant and you feel you can cut them, bringing a tarp adds unnecessarily to the weight of your pack; it's better to travel light or bring more food. However, in areas where boughs are not available, going without canvas is almost impossible to do without grievous suffering. Substitutes for boughs—leaves, reeds, grass—can sometimes be used, but finding these can never be depended upon.

On a trip with others, community gear like axes and tarps can be spread around. One tarp will shelter three or four men and will weigh down only one person's pack. A good size for a tarp for two or three men is eight by eight feet square. Eight feet by ten feet is better, although heavier.

Before every trip we usually debate whether to bring canvas or not, and lately we've tended to carry it. This probably is because we've run into severe weather often on recent trips and a tarp provides a quick, secure roof overhead. Erecting a good roof using brush requires a lot of labor and is time-consuming.

Tarps can be constructed of a variety of material, none of them absolutely satisfactory. Canvas and linen can be waterproofed after a fashion with oil, beeswax or paint. I've seen a variety of 18th century techniques described and have yet to find one that works the way I want it to and yet gives you a tarp light enough to be carried easily. To get very light tarps, we've used thin cotton and covered it with paint diluted with mineral spirits. These tarps worked fairly well for a couple of trips but were stiff, fragile and tore easily. They were eventually cut up and used as light food bags and still travel with us in that form today.

AXES

Traveling without an ax in winter is as smart as traveling barefoot. With an ax and fire makings, a person can survive in winter with little else. On our trips the weight we save by not packing extra clothes, shelter and blankets is only made possible by carrying an ax. The axes we use are light, having very light heads of about 1-1/2 pounds and helved with thin, straight 30-inch handles of hickory or ash. The ax's total weight is around 2-1/2 pounds and is worth every ounce. On a trip with three people we take two axes, thus always having a spare in case one breaks or is lost. Both axes find regular work. They're carried, as mentioned previously, under the straps of the knapsack where they're out of the way but easily seized.

Be sure to cover any ax with a sheath, even if it's only the toe of an old moccasin. This will spare accidental holes in equipment or body parts. A 1763 entry in Alexander Henry's *Travels and Adventures in Canada* illustrates a sheath's importance:

Another man, being on his wintering-ground, and from home, hunting beaver, was crossing a lake, covered with smooth ice, with two beavers on his back, when his foot slipped, and he fell. At his side, in his belt, was his axe, the blade of which came upon the joint of his wrist; and, the weight of his body coming upon the blade, his hand was completely separated from his arm, with the exception of a small piece of skin.

(122)

This man lived, after he walked back to his lodge and hacked off the rest of the hand with the same ax. This story is an argument not only for an ax sheath but also for ice creepers.

On this trip Mark carried one of the axes as well as a tarp. He is also using new, manufactured snowshoes that are longer than ideal in this terrain.

PROVISIONS

What you bring for food is a personal decision but needs to be limited by what was available to the persons in the historical time and situation you portray. Therefore on trips as civilians, we usually eat better than when going out as militia. The amount and types of food will also vary depending on the length of the trip you plan and whether you use sleds or pack everything on your back. Sleds make heavier loads possible, but not preferable. Bringing dogs, as we do, complicates things too.

If you read original journals you'll notice that parties that attempted long journeys on foot often began to run out of food after twelve to fourteen days on the trail unless the hunting was good. There is a simple reason for this. Carrying a greater amount of food would have weighed down the packs and made it impossible to march with any speed early in the trip when the packs were still heavy. A party overburdened with food would have eaten well early in the trip but traveled nowhere. Two weeks' provisions seems to be the heaviest burden that allows rapid traveling on foot.

We try to carry dried provisions (excluding rum, of course) because they're light. Here are some types of provisions that have worked well for us and are historically appropriate:

Corn (1 lb. dried = approx. 4 lbs. fresh corn)
Peas (1 lb. dried = approx. 3 lbs. fresh peas)
Oatmeal
Brown rice
Beans—nourishing but take a long time to cook
Potatoes—diced with skin on (1 lb. dry = 6 lbs. fresh)
Onions—dried and used to flavor stews (good dry-to-fresh ratio of about 1 to 12)
Dried fruit—raisins, apples, pears, etc.
Flour—whole wheat, used for trail bread and fried bread (mix flour with sugar and grease and deep fry)
Grease—lard or butter, lard being more useful (heavy but good for cooking partridge, hares and making bread); one pound goes a long way
Brown sugar
Tea—berry teas are excellent for noon boil-ups
Chocolate—popular in the 18th century and a good winter trail beverage
Coffee—Less commonly used in 18th century New England than tea or chocolate but without which there is no life
Beef—good for people and dogs (1 lb. dried = 2.5 lbs. fresh)
Rum—each of us carries a one-pint flask with either rum or mixture of rum and cream in a 1:1 ratio. This is carefully rationed into at least twelve servings; when the rum is gone we head for home.

For shorter trips:

Pork—precooked or salted, good greasy winter food but weighs too much for long trips
Ship's biscuit—the dogs love it; made from a dough of flour, salt, water and grease, rolled thin and baked. Too bulky and heavy for long trips.
Cheese—again, too heavy for long trips, freezes up in winter

Food consumption varies greatly according to the length of the trip, the difficulty of the route and what the weather is like. I'm constantly rethinking the amounts of food I carry. Here are two food lists, one of ours from a recent seven-day trip to feed one man and a dog for a week, the other list from Knox, for one soldier for one week.

Our list:

> 3.5 lbs. dried beef
> 1.5 lbs. dried corn
> 1.5 lbs. peas
> 1.0 lb. raisins
> 1.0 lb. lard
> 2.0 lbs. flour
> .5 lb. coffee
> .1 lb. tea
> 1.0 lb. sugar
> 1.5 lbs. flask of rum & cream

13.6 lbs. total including rum

Knox (garrison ration):

> 7.0 lbs. bread or flour
> 4.0 lbs. pork
> 1.0 lb. peas (3 pints)
> .4 lb. butter
> .5 lb. rice (1/2 pint)
> plus one gill (4 oz.) rum per day

12.9 lbs total plus rum

In another version Knox included suet, cheese, oatmeal and fruit (probably dried) replacing some of the butter and rice (2: 281-282). On this trip we portrayed civilians and ate well. On a longer trip, luxuries like raisins, flour and lard could be replaced by additional amounts of peas and corn, which are good, light traveling rations.

EATING TOOLS AND PROVISIONS

Horn Mug or Tin Cup

Small Kettle

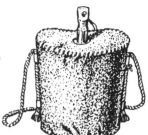

Canteen for Rum

Officer's Tin Rum Flask

Salt Horn

Tin Plate

Clasp Knife & Fork (Found on Rogers' Island)

Sheath Knife & Fork Set

Tin Spoon

Salt Beef

Salt Pork

Bologna Sausage

Potatoes

Onions

Parched Indian Corn

Peas

Rice

Beans

Ash Cakes

Biscuits

Chocolate

Ginger

Sugar

CONCLUSION

If you've read this far and still think winter trips are easy, then I haven't explained things very well. These journeys on snowshoes are the trips we absolutely enjoy the most but are very, very difficult. Absolutely nothing is easy in the winter and even little things, like fetching water or changing moccasins, get complicated when there's deep snow on the ground and the temperature is below zero. Several things need to be emphasized.

Never be afraid to alter plans while on a trip when unexpected weather or circumstances warrant it. Never be embarrassed about turning back if you feel conditions are getting dangerous. Many times parties comprised of experienced and tough woodsmen had trouble just dealing with the weather. In a letter to Colonel Haldiman from camp at Sabbath Day Point in March 1759, Rogers writes, "Two thirds of my detachment have froze their feet (the weather being so severe, that it is almost impossible to describe it) some of which we are obliged to carry" (133). In Rogers journal entry for January 17, 1757, he says, "The next morning, finding that some of the detachment had hurt themselves in the march the day before, as many were dismissed to return to the fort, as reduced our party to seventy-four men, officers included" (39).

Having good equipment is a necessity. If a part of your outfit is inadequate or breaks during a trip in warm weather, the consequences can usually be lived with. That's not true of winter. An old ax handle that breaks because you neglected to replace it can lead to trouble. Prepare ahead of time and be sure everything you have is in good condition. If you're still up the night before a trip sewing things together, then you haven't prepared properly.

Experience is important. If there is no one along who's made a winter trip of length before, be sure to go easy and not be too ambitious until you've gained experience. What seemed like ideal clothing and equipment at home often are a disappointment once out on the trail. It's also interesting how different covering ten miles on snowshoes feels as compared to walking the same ten miles on bare ground.

Being in good physical shape can't be emphasized enough. The best equipment and most extensive experience is of no use at all if you're too exhausted to tie on your snowshoes. The winter woods is a hard, unforgiving place for someone who's too soft, and it's dangerous. Fatigue leads to mental mistakes that bring serious consequences—hypothermia, frostbite, sloppy ax work, not checking for thin ice. Your being out of shape is not only dangerous for you but also for your partners. Anything you're unable to do, they will have to make up for. This will tax their energy, which is already severely taxed by the environment, and they'll have to work harder to make up for your deficiencies. It's a good idea to talk about things like this prior to a trip so that you can set realistic trip goals based on peoples' abilities or even question whether the party is really composed of people with whom you want to travel.

If you're not already in good shape, begin getting into condition months, not weeks, before a trip. Running, fast walking, snowshoeing, Nordic skiing— anything that exercises your heart, legs and lungs—is good and necessary preparation.

Age and gender need not be a consideration here. Most of us are on the backside of forty and plan to be doing snowshoe trips for the next few decades. Mark's twelve-year-old son, Jessie, has done very well on several trips, as has Matt Bandella, a sixty-year-old friend of ours who can out-walk many and out-wrestle all. Several years ago our friend Carol Neville was one of a party of eight of us and out-walked many of the men, even though she was encumbered by the heavy winter clothing of an 18th century woman. With preparation a snowshoe trip is within anyone's grasp, but don't fool yourself into thinking that conditioning can be ignored. Winter doesn't accept excuses or rationalizations about why you couldn't get your body prepared. Snowshoe trips are nothing but self-inflicted torture for people who are out of shape and don't belong there.

Getting preoccupied with large parties is a mistake. Being on trips with more than two or three companions can be enjoyable but is often confusing, harder work and the noise destroys the peace and solitude of the winter woods. When too many people have to be satisfied, agreeing on trip goals, determining routes, finding camping spots and most other decisions become overly complicated.

Parties of two to four persons seem to work well, with three (not counting dogs, of course) being what I consider an ideal number. Three or four people need only a small campsite but provide manpower enough to ease the labor of making camp, breaking trail and helping out if someone gets crippled up. Groups of three or four people make for easy conversation, yet also allow privacy and quiet.

Mark Daiute and son Jessie prepare to leave one of our brush camps. Jessie has been a good companion on several of our trips.

Three feet of fresh snow can halt a trek unless the members are in good condition. In soft powder Mark and Jessie follow their spaniel with Matt close behind.

A solo trip in winter is also a great experience but involves a considerable amount of work. Everything that has to be done—breaking trail, cutting brush, fetching water and wood, cooking—has to be done alone. On winter solos I often find that I cover less distance than when with others; breaking trail alone is tough and making camp takes longer. Also, caution is necessary in everything you do; if you carelessly get yourself into a tight spot, there is no one there to help you out of it.

Finally, choose your companions well. The difficulty of a winter trip brings out both the best and worst in a person's character. A person who is chronically exhausted, hungry and cold rarely holds feelings back and under this stress may conjure up petty grievances that are quite irrational. (Read the accounts of the British Antarctic expeditions of the early 1900s to see good examples of this behavior.) Large parties exacerbate this phenomena, so choose well. Again, it's a mistake to fall into the trap of assuming that having more people along is necessarily better.

I've been very lucky in this respect. The people mentioned in this piece are the best traveling companions anyone ever had. When you strap on your snowshoes and you're with people you like, trust and who are hard workers, you'll do well.

APPENDIX A: REFERENCES

Anderson, Fred. *A People's Army, Massachusetts Soldiers and Society in the Seven Years' War*. Chapel Hill: University of North Carolina Press, 1984.

Bonin, Charles. *Memoirs of a French and Indian War Soldier (Travels in New France by J.C.B., orig. title)*. Ed. Andrew Camp. 1941. Bowie, MD: Heritage Books, 1993.

Bougainville, Louis Antoine de. *Adventure in the Wilderness: The American Journals of Louis Antoine de Bougainville 1756-1760*. Ed. and trans. Edward P. Hamilton. Norman: University of Oklahoma Press, 1964.

Burke, John. Unpublished journal. 1746. Fort Number Four Museum, Charlestown, New Hampshire.

Drake, Samuel Adams. *The Border Wars of New England, Commonly Called King William's and Queen Anne's Wars*. Williamstown, MA: Corner House Publishers, 1973.

Fitch, Jabez. *The Diary of Jabez Fitch, Jr. in the French and Indian War, 1757*. Glen Falls, NY: Rogers Island Historical Association, 1968.

Gallup, Andrew, and Donald F. Shaffer. *La Marine: The French Colonial Soldier in Canada, 1745-1761*. Bowie, MD: Heritage Books, 1992.

Hayward, William. Unpublished journal. 1748. Fort Number Four Museum, Charlestown, New Hampshire.

Henry, Alexander. *Travels and Adventures in Canada and the Indian Territories between the years 1760 and 1776*. 1809. Readex Microprint, 1966.

Kalm, Peter. *Travels in North America, 1748-1751*. New York: Dover, 1987.

Knox, John. *An Historical Journal of the Campaigns in North America for the Years 1757, 1758, 1759, and 1760*. Ed. Arthur G. Doughty. Freeport, NY: Books for Libraries Press, 1970.

Montressor, John. *Journal of a March Undertaken in Winter on Snow-Shoes from Quebec the Capital of Canada to the First Settlements of New-England on the River Ammerascaegin Near Brunswick Fort, by Order of His Excellency Brigadier General Murray, Commanding His Majesty's Troops in Canada*. New England Historical and Genealogical Register, January, 1882.

Neumann, George C., and Frank J. Kravic. *Collector's Encyclopedia of the American Revolution*. Harrisburg, PA: Stackpole, 1975.

Pargellis, Stanley. *Military Affairs in North America, 1748-1765, Selected Documents from the Cumberland Papers in Windsor Castle*. Ed. Stanley Pargellis. Hamden, CT: Archon Books, 1969.

Rogers, Robert. *Journals of Major Robert Rogers*. Readex Microprint, 1966.

Stevens, Phineas. Unpublished letterbook. Fort Number Four Association, Charlestown, New Hampshire.

APPENDIX B: RECOMMENDED READING

I've found several books written in the early 1900s that contain valuable information on winter traveling. Until about 1930 the technology used for trappers and travelers in winter had not changed much from the 1750s; wool, canvas and leather were still the primary materials from which equipment was constructed. The books listed below contain a wealth of knowledge and were written by men who in most cases were recipients of knowledge that was passed on in an unending chain from 1750 to their time.

Kephart, Horace. *Camping and Woodcraft*. New York: MacMillan, 1928.

Kreps, E. *Camp and Trail Methods*. Columbus, OH: A. R. Harding, 1950.

—This is an excellent little book that describes winter camp and trail methods in good detail and has a very good section on snowshoe and toboggan construction.

Merrick, Elliott. *True North*. New York: Scribner's, 1935.

—A must-read for people who love the winter woods. The author traveled with Labrador trappers on their fall and spring hunts around 1930, using both canoe, snowshoe and toboggan. One of the most enjoyable and informative books I've ever read.

White, Stewart Edward. *The Forest*. New York: McLure, Phillips, 1903.

White, Stewart Edward. *The Works of Stewart Edward White, Camp and Trail*. Garden City, NY: Country Life Press, 1907.

—Author of The Long Rifle, White was one of the best-known woodsmen of the early 1900s. The Forest tells of White's experiences in the Ontario country east of Lake Huron. It is filled with information on outfits and woods lore. Camp and Trail was written by White as a guide to wilderness traveling and living after readers of The Forest demanded more details. Both are highly recommended.

Goods of the Trunk Maker & His Trade

by Steven M. Lalioff

Steven Lalioff's experience in recreating history began during high school when he worked as an interpreter at Connor Prairie, an open-air, agricultural folklore museum in Noblesville, Indiana. After four semesters at Indiana University studying history and folklore, Lalioff went to work for Colonial Williamsburg as an interpreter in the harness and saddle shop. He worked for Colonial Williamsburg from 1979 to 1981, and it was during this period that his interest in Colonial leatherwork developed.

Lalioff returned to Indiana in 1981 to pursue making authentic 18th century leather reproductions and has been enjoyably self-employed since. He makes a wide variety of historic reproductions, including trunks of all types, leather fire buckets and hunting pouches. The bulk of his current leatherwork is being produced for several major American museums to be used as display pieces representing the leatherwork once common to American material culture.

One of Lalioff's current projects is compiling data and photos for a book exploring and presenting many different historic leather artifacts, including early American hunting pouches. His hobbies include reconstructing original log cabins, 18th century hot air balloons, forestry and antique ironware. Lalioff lives in a reconstructed log home with his wife, Karen, and daughter, Hannah. He recently completed an addition to the house, and future plans include the purchase of a double-pen log barn to be erected next to their home for a leather workshop.

The trunks of the 18th century, once common and mundane, are now objects worthy of display in great museums. They are worthy not merely for their antiquity but for their artistry, craftsmanship and evocative mystique. It is hoped that this collection of period containers provides inspiration and reference for the living history reenactor as well as the museum professional. Comparing differences and commonalties between our contemporary artifacts and those of past generations, we may reflect upon the progress or regress of our craftsmanship.

The 1811 Dictionary of the Vulgar Tongue, defines a phrase "'Trunk-maker like'—more noise than work." Now I'm not exactly sure what the author was implying by that period colloquialism, perhaps it was meant as an offense, but I choose to believe what was implied was that a trunk maker makes a lot of noise relative to the size of the finished product. My family can probably attest to that fact, as my workshop is currently attached to our home. Hammering the hundreds of brass and iron tacks into a wooden box creates a loud drum-like noise. I try my best to schedule tack hammering around my family's nap time.

When I'm reproducing an artifact, I prefer to have the original artifact close at hand to insure accuracy in the reproduction. It strikes me as interesting that many of the specific details of construction are shared from one trunk to another, almost as if they have come from the same shop or that the makers had shared a common teacher. This is probably because of the fact that trunk makers repaired trunks that had been made years before and thousands of miles away. Since it is the very nature of a trunk to travel, so did trunk-making techniques and design. In essence I am learning the trade much in the same way my predecessors did, by copying what I see.

As a trunk maker of the 20th century, recreating wares from the past two centuries is a demanding task. The greatest difficulty is in obtaining the exact raw materials and components that were once a readily available commodity to my historic counterpart. Perhaps one of the most important components is leather. The reason for covering a box with leather goes beyond aesthetics. The leather or rawhide covering serves as reinforcement against the box coming apart when crammed full and subjected to the rigors of transport.

The types of trunks that I have presented in this article have their stylistic roots in medieval Europe and probably earlier. The examples of leather-bound trunks of medieval Europe that have survived are masterworks of construction and elaboration, preserved because of their quality and artistry. Unfortunately, more humble examples from this period seem not to have survived, or perhaps never even existed. Documentation on a simple leather-bound trunk from the medieval era would be a valuable find.

The survival rate of early leatherwork is so rare, and in constant danger of disintegrating, that great effort to preserve every artifact and explore its origins is a worthy pursuit. The historic leatherwork of the 18th and 19th century presented within this chapter will eventually be as rare as medieval artifacts and should be treated with due respect. However, first let us consider the trade of the trunk maker and then we will examine his goods.

TRUNK MAKERS & SIDE PRODUCTS

When a trunk has a label that advertises that the trunk maker also makes saddles, is that craftsman known professionally as a saddler or a trunk maker? I believe that any craftsman capable of making a quality saddle should be referred to first as a saddle maker and second as a trunk maker. Certainly, one with the skills necessary for saddle making could easily fashion a marketable trunk.

Whether a trunk maker or a saddler, both were leather craftsmen who by effort of their advertisements made many kinds of related side products. There were several reasons these leather workers made other products. Primarily, large quantities of scrap materials are generated in both trades, and leather scraps were and are too valuable to discard. These scraps were almost always rendered into smaller types of wares. Having reviewed several shop ledgers of leather craftsmen, I believe that even the wealthiest urban areas were unable to sustain either saddler or trunk maker at the business of making solely their most expensive wares at full production. This may have been because of competition or because their wares did not incorporate planned obsolescence. With reasonable care a trunk or saddle would last a lifetime.

The following list of the side products of trunk makers has been compiled from several different trunk makers' labels. A contemporary definition has been provided for those wares that are considered obsolete.

TRUNK MAKERS' PRODUCTS AS ADVERTISED ON TRUNK LABELS

Hair & Leather Traveling Trunks—Note that "hair" trunks are distinguished from "leather" trunks. "Hair" refers to untanned leather coverings that retain the natural fur of the animal.

Portmantua Trunks & Leather Portmantuas—A cylindrical bag or chest in which clothes are carried.

Carpet Baggs—A traveling bag made from carpet cloth, usually from good pieces of worn out carpeting. Common during the 18th and 19th centuries.

Covered Hampers—Typically, a hamper implied a large basket. It is uncertain what type of material construction is being offered.

Budgets & Trunks for Post Chaises—"Budget" in period dictionaries is defined as a pouch or bag with its contents; exactly what the contents might have been, in reference to a Post Chaise, is unclear to me. Budget is also a period term for a wallet, according to the *Dictionary of the Vulgar Tongue*. Post Chaise: a closed, four-wheeled coach drawn by "fast" horses, used to carry mail or for hire by passengers.

Sumpters—A horse of state, or a packhorse or packsaddle.

Saddle Bags—A pair of attached bags, designed to be secured in front of or behind a saddle.

Vallees for Bedding—An oval tube of leather large enough to accept a bedroll, usually designed to attach behind the saddle.

Fire Buckets—A heavy leather bucket with leather handle, made to hold sand or water and used to extinguish uncontrolled fires.

Jacks—A drinking vessel made of leather, lined with pitch or metal.

Powder Flasks—Usually of heavy, dense leather, affixed with a metal dispenser.

Harvest Bottle—A heavy leather vessel lined with pitch or wax, able to hold a quantity of liquid and having a plug or cork stopper.

Leather Baggs—Probably made to order to accommodate all manner of personal items, wares or tools.

Paper Trunks—Also known as bandboxes, usually of cardboard construction and overlaid with decorative printed papers.

Hat & Bonnet Boxes—Made either of solid leather construction or like paper trunks.

Peruke & Perriwigg Boxes—Boxes to keep men's and women's artificial hairpieces.

Cases for Plate, China, Glasses & Musical Instruments—Custom-made cases were made for very valuable possessions. Many were affixed with engraved brass name plates so as to identify ownership when stored in bank vaults.

Traveling Writing Desks—Usually a folding wooden lap-size box with a leather writing surface and various compartments to keep quill pens, ink, etc.

Guilded Nest of Trunks—"Gilded" refers to leather embossed with gold leaf. "Nest" may imply that all sizes are made or that they are made in matching sets that fit one inside another for storage.

Chains & Oil Case Covers—"Chains" refers to iron chains used to secure trunks to vehicles. Oil case covers were custom-fit canvases that were oil painted to turn rain when trunks were transported in open vehicles.

Clogs & Pattens—Clog: a shoe, usually with a wooden sole. Pattens: a clog with an iron ring attached to the bottom of the wooden sole, worn over good shoes to keep them out of the street mud.

Leather Caps—Perhaps referring to hard leather riding helmets.

Fire Hats—This reference is taken from a 1790s trunk label.

During this period both the "top hat" style and the jockey-style helmet with extended protective brim were in common use as fire-fighting garb.

Horsewhips—Whip making was usually a specialized trade. It is likely that some items like whips were retailed through the trunk makers store.

Walking Sticks—There are surviving examples of canes and walking sticks made of stacked leather discs over a thin iron rod. They are a perfect example of a product made from scraps.

Fire Hose—The hose used on 18th century fire engines was made of heavy, dense leather stitched down one side. This was also a specialized trade in large metropolitan areas that could sustain such a craft full-time.

These products and side products of the trunk maker are only some of the many types of leather wares available during the 18th and early 19th centuries. Aside from shoes, boots and bookbinding, the majority of leather products were made through the art and skills of the trunk maker.

COMPONENTS OF A TRUNK

Before we examine the trunk maker's goods, a discussion of the components of a trunk is in order. To begin, the typical wood used in the construction of 18th and 19th century trunks was termed "deal." "Deal" is an old term meaning a soft wood of undetermined species, usually fir, pine or spruce. The boards commonly used in trunk making were between 1/2- and 5/8-inch thick. The boards were usually left in the rough, having only the highest or roughest areas planed down.

Wooden pegs and hand-forged nails are found in the construction of most trunks dating prior 1790. After that time cut nails predominate construction methods. I have only found one leather-bound trunk that was assembled with dovetailing.

Perhaps the most prominent feature applied to early trunks is the brass domed-top tacks used to keep the leathers affixed to the wooden box. Aside from their function, the tacks were arranged to enhance the decorative appearance. Most of the tacks used were solid cast brass, however, I have found that iron tacks were also used during the 18th century. The brass tacks were lacquered when new to prevent tarnish. The iron tacks were tinplated to prevent rust.

The wooden lids of some 18th and early 19th century trunks were made by steam bending wide boards over forms or the partially completed trunk itself. I have found a few examples of dome-topped trunks that were not made of steam-bent boards but had the dome made of boards butted up tight and then planed to a smooth surface after they were applied. This method was inferior to solid bent wood tops, as in time the butted boards could warp in various directions.

Many varieties of leathers were applied to the exteriors of early trunks, but the most common types were rawhide horse and bark-tanned calfskins of various colors including reds, yellows, greens, browns and black. Decorative embellishments

of deed boxes were almost unlimited. Some techniques applied include embossed geometric patterns, hand-painted decorations and gold- or silver-leaf tooling also known as "gilding." The larger trunks with smooth, bark-tanned leathers were sometimes decorated in a manner like that of smaller trunks, but decorative applications primarily relied upon arrangements of strips of smooth leather and brass tacks.

Another common application to most trunks of all sizes is the "dust skirt." This skirt of leather was tacked to the bottom edge of the lid. Its function was to reduce the quantity of dirt and water that might otherwise invade the trunk's interior during travel. Typically, these dust skirts were decorated by having a scalloped edge applied with a cutting iron.

The hardware of a trunk includes some or all of the following components: lock, handles, hinges, and occasionally a brass nameplate. Some larger trunks have applied corner brackets of thin iron or brass known as "cramps." These cramps, applied to the exterior, provided additional strength to the wooden box.

Aside from the cloth and paper that was glued to the interior surface, trunk interiors often contained a thin rim of wood nailed to the top edge of the base. The function of this rim is the same as the dust skirt, providing yet another dirt barrier. The lids of the trunk were supported from falling backwards by the application of cloth tape nailed to either or both sides of the interior, stretching from the top of the base to the lid.

The finishes applied to the early trunks varied according to the function intended for the trunk. Those trunks of smooth, tanned leather intended to be used for travel were commonly coated with varnish or a thin tar substance that I believe to be asphaltum. Wax was also applied to prevent damage to trunk leathers, but the most prudent form of protection for traveling trunks was waterproof canvas slipcovers.

18TH CENTURY TRUNKS

Affixing approximate dates to trunks that haven't a maker's label or other documentable provenance is difficult to do with absolute certainty. I have made "educated guesses" by comparing commonalties of trunks that do have reliable dates, such as those that have dates applied in tacks, those lined with dated newspapers and those with makers' labels when the maker has been researched and it is known when he was in business.

The Museum of Early Southern Decorative Arts (MESDA) has compiled an extensive research data base of historic, Southern craftsmen. It includes over 60,000 artisans in 126 different trades. To date, MESDA has compiled 96 trunk makers working in the South. This progressive data base is an invaluable tool for identifying artifacts and their makers.

The photo at top right shows a campaign trunk, circa 1786, made by Drivers & Eyer that measures 36 inches long, 16 inches wide and 15 inches tall. Trunks similar to this were common styles made for both American and British military officers. A campaign trunk belonging to Gen. George Washington is on display at Mt. Vernon. This style of trunk was made from the late 17th century throughout the 18th.

On the front of this trunk, located between the lock and sides, were once wide leather keepers. These keepers were used to accept the strong leather straps or chains used to secure the trunk during transport. Note the cuts in the trunk leather to the right of the left keeper. Some insight into the source of these cuts may possibly by gained from the words of Peter Stockham. He wrote about "...robbers, who in and near the metropolis are ever on the watch to cut off trunks from coaches as they come in or go out of town" (82).

The enormous English trunk (circa 1779) pictured adjacent is so large that one person cannot reach both handles to pick it up. It measures 48 inches long, 25 inches wide and 20-1/2 inches tall. The exterior is of untanned horsehide that has been glued to the deal box. It is also affixed with hand-forged iron tacks. The iron tacks and the iron corner cramps were originally tinplated to prevent rust but the tinning has long since corroded away. So far, I have only found iron tacks on 18th century and earlier trunks. By the 19th century, only the cast brass tacks are to be found.

The circa 18th century trunk shown here is an enigma. I have found no other trunk that resembles it in construction, materials or hardware. The box is constructed from mahogany, is dovetailed and measures 28 inches long, 14-1/4 inches wide and 15-1/2 inches tall. It is bound in a parchment-like leather of undetermined species and tannage. It resembles rawhide coverings but was not intended to be hair-on. The tacks, cramps and handles are heavy solid brass. The handles resemble English styles of the 18th century but do not conform to any known examples in proportion or detail. It is possible that this trunk was made in the American Colonies.

Private Collection

Private Collection

Private Collection

The circa 18th century trunk illustrated to the right has folk-art stylizing typical of Pennsylvanian-Dutch artifacts. Even though it lacks a maker's label or written history, its style speaks so loudly that the provenance is unquestionable. The covering is hair-on horsehide. The tacks are hand-forged iron and were at one time tinplated. This Pennsylvanian trunk measures 34 inches long, 16 inches wide and 16 inches tall.

From the 17th to the mid-19th century, "hair-on" sealskin was a common covering for leather-bound trunks. Technically speaking, the "hair-on" skins applied to trunks should not be referred to as "leather" because the skins were not typically tanned, only cured by fleshing, cleaning, drying and perhaps salting. Therefore, this type of covering is known as rawhide or raw skin, rather than leather, which would have inferred a more costly commodity.

Illustrated below are four trunks from the first quarter of the 19th century and sealskin covered. When new they had all of their hair intact, but over time the hair or the epidermal layer of skin that held the hair in place has been eaten away by moth larva. Hair-on horsehide and calfskin were also common

period trunk coverings. Like sealskin, these other species of skins were usually left untanned. By using raw skins, the trunk maker could make trunks more affordable. The hair-on skins were attractive, but more importantly, they were more durable than smooth tanned leather coverings because they could not be easily scratched or scuffed when roughly handled during travels.

It has been interpreted by many that the hair-on trunks of the period were made so as to shed rainwater during travels. Having made many such trunks and also having had them rained upon, I can say with good authority that they do not shed water and in fact are like very large hairy sponges.

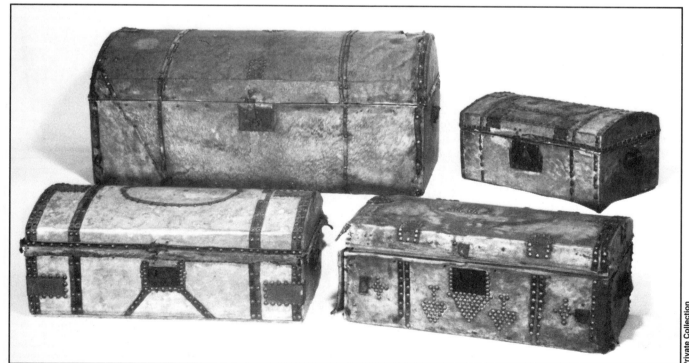

The saddleback trunk (circa 1790s-1840s) is known by its compartmentalized lid. The name "saddleback" comes from the comfortable seat that is formed when the lid's cavity is packed with bedding. Access to the cavity is by way of an interior trap door in the trunk's lid. I once thought that clothing was stored inside the cavity, however after all but ripping the buttons off of several garments in trying to remove them from the cavity, I came to the conclusion that bedding was a far more likely candidate.

Most modes of travel during the period offered few comforts. Having a saddleback trunk to rest upon would have been a welcome luxury, and sitting upon your trunk was a shrewd way to protect your possessions. This form of trunk would eventually evolve into the multi-compartmentalized trunks of the later Victorian era.

The dimensions of the Thomas Holmes trunk below, an original, Southern-made trunk, are very unusual: 10-1/4 inches tall, 11 inches wide, and 40-1/4 inches long. Certainly the product of a custom order, it was probably made to accommodate a specific need of the intended owner. I am eager to make a reproduction of this trunk for myself to discover what merit or practicality this oddly shaped trunk might have.

While the original contents remain a mystery, much is known about the maker. Glued to the inside of the trunk's lid is a handwritten maker's label. It reads, "Tho. Holmes/Maker/Broad Street/Charleston" (South Carolina). This is the first example I have found of a professional trunk maker using a handwritten label. The majority of original trunks bare no label at all. I find it curious that more makers didn't take this homespun approach.

Thomas Holmes is listed in the Charleston directory from the years 1790 to 1807. During the years 1790 and 1794, he

Private Collection

was listed as a saddle maker. It is likely this trunk was made during those years, as trunk making was a common sideline of saddlers. In the following years, Thomas Holmes was listed as a carpenter and then a custom house inspector. However, the only mention of his having a business on Broad Street is the label within this trunk. The trunk has descended from the family of William Alston of the Miles Brewton House, King Street, Charleston, South Carolina. The brass tacks on the trunk lid form the initials "W. A." and establish ownership to William Alston. One coincidence that may suggest the exact year of construction for this trunk is that Thomas Holmes also resided on King Street during the year 1790. William Alston lived on that street from 1790 to 1810.

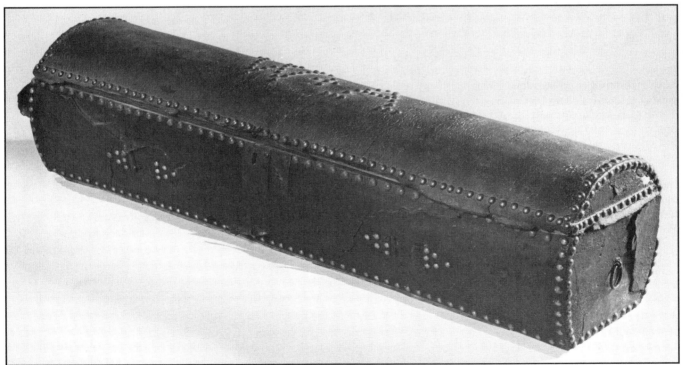

Photo courtesy of Museum of Early Southern Decorative Arts Research Files, Winston-Salem, North Carolina

Aside from the elaborate and costly trappings of this English trunk (circa 1751-1760), illustrated above, I have included it in this collection of originals because of its very practical, custom-made stand. I believe that many of the larger trunks had custom-made stands, because trunks not only served as containers for transport but as storage furniture in the home. There are many practical as well as aesthetic reasons for raising a large trunk off the floor. Those reasons may include air circulation to prevent mildew, protection from rodents and insects and reducing the strain of bending over the trunks' contents. I believe the rollers are not original to the stand, but are practical nonetheless.

The adjacent trunk illustrates the difficulty of dating period trunks. When was it made? Judging by the form and technique of construction, one might guess circa 1800. Fortunately, the trunk maker set the date across the lid in brass tacks—1678! Without the applied date, there would be no way to distinguish this trunk from those made 100 years later. It is unfortunate that this trunk is missing its lock and hasp, as the hardware mounted on trunks bear the strongest clues for appointing trunks to their appropriate time period.

DEED BOXES

Small leather-bound boxes were common items in many households, as tax records and estate records indicate from their inventories. Their function was to store records, money or valuable personal items. When traveling, they also served as toilet boxes containing articles such as razors, soaps and perfumes. Small leather-bound boxes were also popular trade items among native American Indians, as the remains of the iron and brass hardware have been recovered from occupation sites.

In the illustration below, the primitive box at top left was probably the product of a rural American maker who made do with what resources were available. I have dated the box circa 1820-1850, and it measures 10-1/4 inches long, 5-1/2 inches wide and 4-1/2 inches tall. It is possible that the leather and tacks used in this deed box were recycled from a larger trunk that was damaged. The locking method is simply two wire staples, one on the front and one on the lid. I believe it was merely tied shut with a cord. It was never lined, nor was great

care taken with the placement of the brass tacks. Nonetheless, it is one of my favorites.

In contrast to the first box, the deed box at the middle top, made by Willm. Jones, displays very refined craftsmanship. It has a domed lid of bent wood and is covered with costly bookbinding leather that has been finely tooled and gilded. The interior is lined with an English gentleman's magazine that is over-printed with a polka-dot design. The date 1795 appears in the printing. The box is quite small, measuring 10 inches long, 5-1/2 inches wide and 4-1/2 inches tall. The interior of the lid is almost entirely covered with the English maker's label.

Bound in red book-binders goatskin, the deed box (ca. 1780-1820) at top right possesses an English-manufactured brass pull and brass lock and hasp. This might lead one to assume an English provenance. However since hardware, leathers and styles of construction to be found in both England and America were similar, it is almost impossible to assign a

country or region of origin to trunks or deed boxes without a maker's label. This deed box measures 12 inches long, 5-1/2 inches wide and 4-1/4 inches tall.

Originally, the box on the lower left was covered with raw, hair-on horsehide, but the hair has long since fallen away. The patina that has been acquired by the exposed hide is even more attractive than the original condition of the hair-on covering probably was. The interior is lined with a New York State newspaper dated 1806 and another dated 1807, thus giving both a region and date to assign to this box. It measures 15 inches long, 8-1/2 inches wide and 8 inches tall.

The deed box in the middle front, region and maker unknown, is bound in black book-binders goatskin. Its interior is covered with grayish-blue paper (a common inexpensive paper of the 18th century, comparable to today's craft paper). Dated circa 1790-1810, the age of this deed box is determined from the style of brass pull and hasp lock.

The maker and region of origin of the deed box (circa 1800-1830) in the lower right of the illustration are unknown. It was collected in New Hampshire. The box is bound in vegetable-tanned calfskin, and stout iron handles are screwed into both ends. The interior is not lined but is finished very smoothly. It measures 22 inches long, 10 inches wide and 10 inches tall.

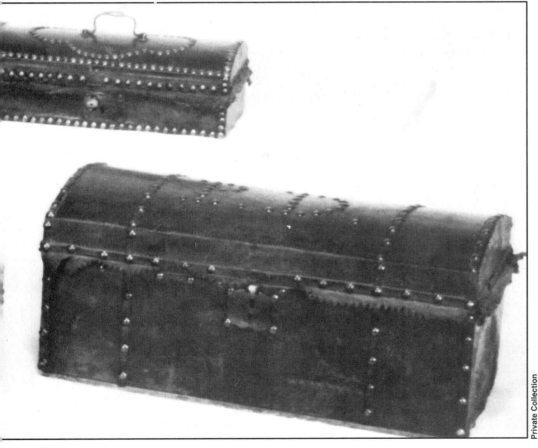

Private Collection

LOCKS, HANDLES & HINGES

A moment unattended...a small pry bar in hand and "snap," the hasp is broken and the trunk is open. The old adage, "locks only keep honest people out," describes perfectly the poor quality of most period trunk locks. Actually, a pry bar wasn't necessary, as most of the locks were only single ward mechanisms and were easily opened by a generic key. Keeping one's privacy seems to have been the primary object of the lock.

The locks, handles and hinges applied to trunks were not commonly the product of the local blacksmith but were obtained by the trunk maker through the exports of the mass production shops of England. Many period newspaper advertisements state, "Newly arrived [from England], thousands of locks and handles suitable for trunk making." The English production shops retained the majority of the American hardware market well into the 19th century. The mass production techniques applied by the English shops effectively retarded American production by out-producing and under-pricing.

One lock not produced by English hands is the beautiful one found on an 18th century trunk discovered in Pennsylvania. The foliated iron work suggests the effort of an artisan rather than a production shop. The style of work also suggests a Germanic influence.

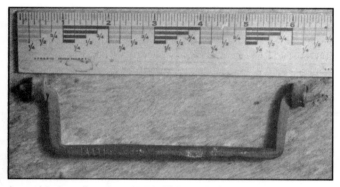

Iron side handle, circa 1779. This early form extends back to medieval period handle forms.

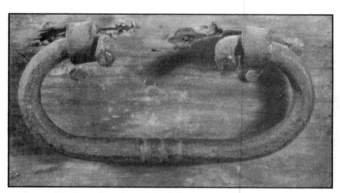

Iron side handle of a mid-18th century campaign trunk.

Iron side handle with kidney-shaped back plate, the most common variety, circa 1780s-1840s.

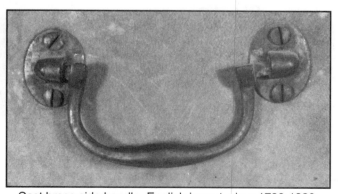

Cast brass side handle, English import, circa 1790-1820.

Iron side handle with simple back plate.
Pennsylvanian, circa 18th century.

Cast brass pull handle, English import, circa 1790-1810.

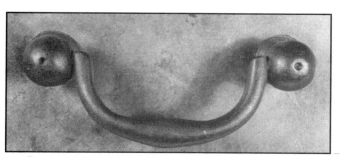

Bronze side handle, 18th century, possibly American.

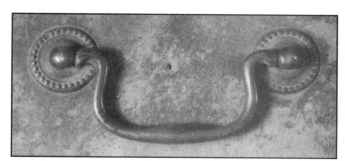

Cast brass pull handle, English import, circa 1806.

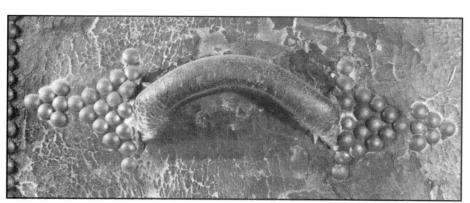

Solid leather handle, saddle maker-trunk maker
construction, circa 1790s-1840s.

Iron trunk hinge, mid-18th century, campaign trunk.
Many trunks used only simple leather hinges.
Amazingly, leather hinges survive intact and
functional more often than the crude iron hinges have.

TRUNK LOCK HASPS WITH APPROXIMATE DATES OF USAGE

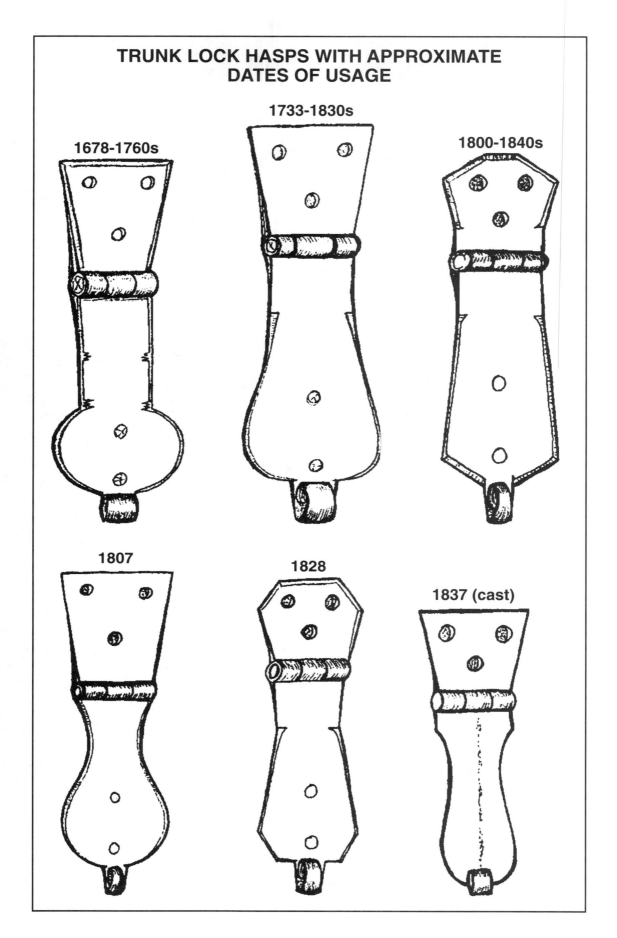

1733-1830s

1678-1760s

1800-1840s

1807

1828

1837 (cast)

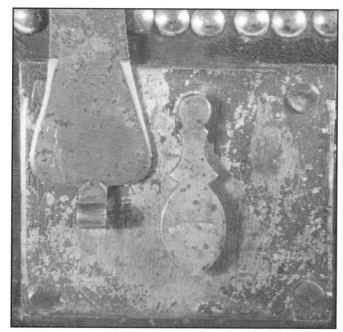

Hasp lock, circa 1790-1810,
English import. Such locks were typically
attached by very malleable clinch nails.

Hasp lock, circa 18th century,
Pennsylvanian. This lock is unique because
of its artistic workmanship and its
pewter-plated finish.

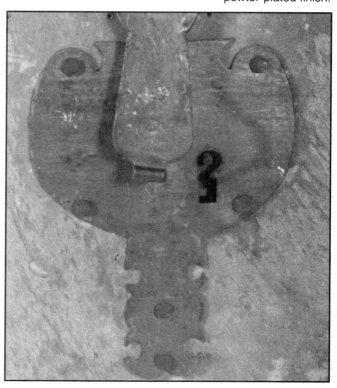

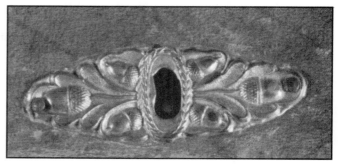

Internal "piano" type lock with
pressed brass escutcheon.
English manufacture, circa 1795.

Hasp lock, circa 1800-1840. Iron locks were typically coated with a
jappaned asphaultum finish to prevent tarnish and rust. This lock shows
how age has caused the asphaltum to bubble and crawl.

TRUNK INTERIORS

The interior treatments and linings of early trunks can be as interesting and educational as are the exterior embellishments. The wide range of fabrics and papers found glued to the interiors offers scholars an opportunity to examine textiles that are extremely rare and and otherwise exist only by description. By being glued to the interior of a trunk, many of the early textiles have been preserved from the damaging effects of the sun's ultraviolet rays and so give us accurate examples of period colors. In the following paragraph, I have given proper names to two of the cloth linings that I have found. I appointed those names by reviewing the descriptions and illustrations provided in Florence Montgomery's book, *Textiles in America*, and then by directly comparing the descriptions to the artifacts themselves. It is entirely possible that my conclusions are incorrect, as my experience with analyzing textiles is limited.

Other types of trunk linings included wallpapers, solid colored papers and marbleized paper. Seventeenth century trunks were most commonly lined with marbled papers or cloth.

Trunks were also sometimes left unlined. The difference between an unlined trunk and a trunk that has been stripped of its lining is that original unlined trunks were planed and scraped smooth on the inside to prevent splinters from snagging the cloth of garments. Many original trunks have been recently stripped of their linings to "clean them up." This is very unfortunate, for no matter how soiled or ragged, the linings hold the best clues to where and when these otherwise mysterious trunks were made.

The interior of the trunk just below has very early characteristics. The bottom half of the trunk appears to have

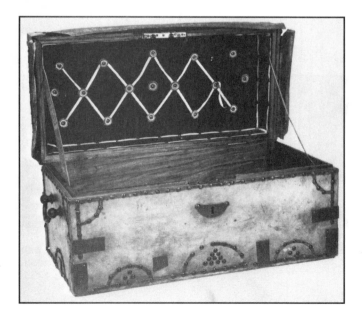

been left unlined to display the finely finished mahogany wood. The lid is lined with a thick, olive-colored, woolen cloth that resembles cloth described as "frieze" (Montgomery 243). Tacked to the lid's interior are cloth tape straps designed to be used as document or letter holders. Such crisscrossed tapes were also to be found tacked to the walls of 18th century homes and businesses as note boards.

The early 18th century campaign trunk whose interior is illustrated in the top photo has a coarse hemp-linen lining. It resembles fabrics described as "hessian," "ticklenburg," or "forfars" (Montgomery 242, 258, 363). This trunk also has remnants of a crisscrossed letter holder, the straps cut from leather calfskin. Unique to this trunk is a decorative **paper**

cutting aquatinted in a pale red and glued under the letter straps.

The photo at near left bottom shows a Pennsylvanian trunk lined with an oil-painted cloth stenciled in a floral pattern. The colors are bright burnt orange and indigo blue. At first glance it would appear to be lined with a woven coverlet.

The saddleback trunk shown above is lined with a copperplate-printed cloth in sepia color. Copperplate-printed cloth began in England in 1756 and continued into the first quarter of the 19th century. Eventually, this method was replaced by the more efficient copper roller printing that was invented in 1810 (Montgomery 203-205).

Many 18th and 19th century trunks were curiously lined with newspapers, magazines, print shop overruns and misprints. To enhance appearances the newsprint was then over-printed with block designs of floral or geometric patterns, as is the trunk shown below. Most trunks were lined because of the rough, unfinished interior surface of the wooden box. It amazes me that the buying public would have accepted such

crude newspaper linings but trunks were expensive and this was an inconspicuous way to reduce material costs.

An English campaign trunk lined with the pages of the London newspaper the *Evening Post*, printed in 1786, is shown directly below. Newspaper linings have proven to be the most valuable tool for accurately dating the time of manufacture. When using newspapers as a dating tool, keep in mind that in

the period, periodicals were often kept in circulation for a long time before finding their way into a trunk.

Of course, the maker's label provides invaluable information about a trunk. The label of the English campaign trunk, circa 1786, indicates that it was made in the shop of Driver & Eyre. Sir Ambrose Heal, in *The Signboards of Old London Shops*, lists the business of Driver & Eyre at the Kings Arms in Cockspur Street and at 70 Charing Cross in 1792 (172). It succeeded the firm of Chapman & Driver that was at

the same address in 1772. In 1797, Isaac Eyre was listed alone at the same address and sign.

Finding the label pictured below in the deed box made by Willm. Jones was rewarding for me, as it gives credence to my belief that trunks were often a joint effort of several craftsmen. The top left figure on the label shows the making of cardboard bandboxes, a side product of trunk makers. The top right figure is constructing the deal box that will become the core of the trunk. Bottom left, the figure is applying decorative tacks, "a monotonous task." The bottom right figure is pasting a wallpaper lining to the trunk's interior.

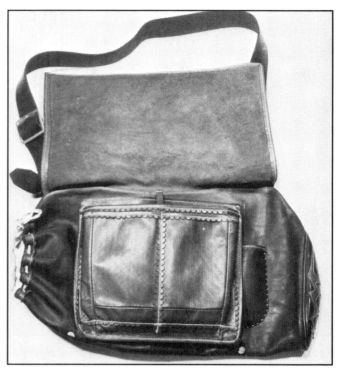

One final example of a personal container for storage and transportation is the leather traveler's pouch (circa 1750-1780) illustrated below. The pouch on the left is the original; on the above right, my reproduction. Made especially for long sojourns, this multiple compartmentalized pouch was very difficult to reproduce accurately. Because of the superior quality of the original workmanship and the complexity of the pattern, this certainly wasn't the first of its kind by the original maker, and certainly the owner paid handsomely for the quality of work and the quantity of calfskin.

There are six compartments total, the largest duffel bag-type compartment is drawn closed by a drawstring. This main compartment measures approximately twenty inches by twelve inches. There is a small pocket underneath the three larger top pockets. The smaller is difficult to access, requiring the top pockets to be unbuttoned. Perhaps this was a secret pocket for a money purse. Missing from the original is a long narrow pocke. Positioned half underneath the top pockets, this pocket would have accommodated a spectacle case quite nicely. The flap is raised for benefit of photography, but when down in position it completely protects the entire pouch's front. Note the remnant of strap under the buckle, the two slots cut through the strap correspond to two more slots cut into the strap on the opposite side. I believe these slots were to receive bed roll straps, thus securing the bedroll over the top of the pouch.

The original pouch was collected in southeastern Pennsylvania. Considering the region, the quality of workmanship and the "Austrian knot" decoration applied to the right end of the pouch, I believe the maker to have been of Germanic heritage. Whether the pouch was made in Germany or Pennsylvania is impossible to determine.

I have ascribed a possible date of 1750-1780 because of the style and manufacture of the buckle. It resembles many buckles retrieved from mid-18th century archaeological sites. Ascribing dates to artifacts based on such narrow evidence is certainly fallible, as numerous factors can taint the best guess of the historian. The most reliable dating technique is to document by period illustrations, and even then the objects found in artistic renderings are open to interpretation.

18TH CENTURY CARGO & STORAGE VESSELS

Leaving the examination of leather-bound trunks made for personal use, we now turn to commercial containers and boxes used for storage of trade goods and commerce. The following containers are presented as examples of the most common types used during the 18th and early 19th centuries.

It is the attention to small details that makes the difference between a quality reproduction and what is merely a prop. Those wishing to fashion historic reproductions of wooden cargo and storage containers will find the following designs to be easier projects to manage than trying to make an accurate copy of a leather-bound trunk. It would not have been uncommon for anyone during the period to have made personal use of these commercial type containers, therefore they make for a viable and less expensive alternative for the living history reenactor.

To begin with, the most rudimentary type of iron hinge, common for hundreds of years, is known as a snipe hinge. Basically, the hinge is made from two interlocking wires. One

Simple Snipe Hinge

"pin" is driven and clinched into the back, bottom edge of the lid. The other pin is driven and clinched into the back panel of the box. The diameter of the hinge wire is dependent upon the size and weight of lumber that the box is constructed from. For a box the scale of the shipping crate, a gauge of wire no less than 1/8-inch diameter is adequate. The points of the wires were usually hammered to a point and driven into a pre-drilled hole, the pre-drilled hole should be slightly undersized to the pin so as to hold the pin tight.

Barrels were the primary vessel for transporting and storing all manner of raw materials and finished goods. Almost every

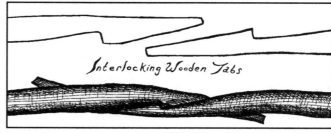

Interlocking Wooden Tabs

period illustration of street scenes and marketplaces is littered with barrels, sometimes even pressed into service as a makeshift table or market stall. Museums and living history reenactors might easily enhance the authentic appearance of early American daily life by cluttering up with barrels.

Not all barrels were made to be watertight. Many were rather quickly knocked together, needed only to ship wares such as shoes or other non-perishables. An inexpensive source of barrels for the reenactor would be the wooden nail kegs found in almost every country antique store. However, it is advisable to replace the wire bands with split sapling hoops like those illustrated. The wooden sapling bands are most easily bent when green and should be split in half to form easily. Interlocking tabs are whittled into the bands ends to secure the hoops in place.

It isn't certain if the type of box illustrated below was made for ship or wagon. It's doubtful if it ever tipped over in either case! All four corners are expertly dovetailed, a very difficult technique do because all four sides also taper inward to the top. The lid is held fast by a hand-forged iron hasp and staple while the hinge is simply a board nailed to the back of the box, keying the lid underneath. The absence of carrying handles may indicate that this box was intended to stay put rather than serve for transporting goods. Picking up this box when full would prove a challenge.

Photo courtesy of Colonial Williamsburg Foundation, Williamsburg, Virginia

The box above (circa 1750-1810) was collected in Brunswick County, Virginia. Its wood is southern pine and its measurements are: height 10-1/2 inches; base 19-1/2 inches by 15 inches; top 10-3/4 inches by 11 inches.

The common-style liquor bottle chest (circa 1750-1820) shown above was one of the traditional box forms that were made originally for the safekeeping of gin bottles. The sizes of these boxes varied according to the number of bottles to be held. Eight, nine, twelve, fifteen and sixteen were common. Certainly, these boxes were pressed into service for all manner of storage.

For living history reenactors in need of common boxes to hide anachronistic camp items like ice chests, this style of box would be an excellent choice. When constructing simple period boxes, a few important details should be observed, as follows:

1. Use a hand-held scrub plane on all wood surfaces to remove any and all modern saw marks.

2. Use only hand-forged or cut nails for assembly. Cut nails came into use by the 1790s, forged nails for all times prior.

3. Paint surfaces period colors to disguise any glued boards. Original boxes were made of very wide boards that are difficult to obtain today.

4. Don't shop for locks, hinges or handles at the local hardware store! Patronize the blacksmith that has knowledge of period style.

Scrub planes were widely used before the advent of modern machine planers. The blade of a scrub plane has a slight radius, so that when used for surfacing lumber it leaves a slight but distinctive hollow on the surface. Many scrub planes were homemade by taking a strait-bladed plane and re-filing the blade's profile.

The shipping crate illustrated below may be the only 18th century example of its kind to survive. Its form symbolized trade and commerce throughout England's Colonies. The crate is constructed from old-growth hardwood, possibly of red elm. Elm is an excellent choice of wood for a crate, as it is extremely strong and flexible, making it able to withstand the rigors of shipping. Both interior and exterior surfaces are scrub-planed smooth to an average thickness of 5/8 inch. All of the boards are full width, the widest being l5-1/2 inches.

Thirty-seven hand-forged, rose head nails were used in the construction of the shipping crate. Originally, the lid was hinged with wire snipe hinges. Having broken, they were replaced with leather straps that eventually wore out as well.

There is no evidence of carrying handles, but a hasp lock was used to secure the lid. The hasp lock is probably original to its manufacture, as there is no evidence of the lid having been nailed shut.

Another interesting and odd detail on the shipping crate is the translucent red paint that was applied only to the front board. Perhaps this was an effort by a merchant to fancy up its appearance for public display. The back board is deftly painted with a shipper's mark, "A." The "49" may be in reference to an invoice number. Smoking pipes were the likely contents, but certainly it might have shipped or displayed any product from buttons to sugar loaves.

CONCLUSION

It is my great pleasure to pursue the historic craft of trunk making. To study and reproduce historic wares has given me a sense of continuity and identity with the past. Apprenticing myself to the historic artifacts themselves has enabled me to "inherit" skills from craftsmen who have long since passed.

As a civilization, we have wasted more than we have made useful. In this era of exponential waste and diminishing resources, it is crucial that we stop incorporating obsolescence into our artifacts and instead render them with greater creativity, artistry and utility.

Special thanks are due the following institutions and people who have kindly provided me with information and materials: Colonial Williamsburg Foundation—Jay Gaynor, Kathy Grosfils, Richard Guthrie, John Sands; Conner Prairie Pioneer Museum—Bob Cottrell, Shirley Willoughby; Museum of Early Southern Decorative Arts—Johanna Metzgar and Martha W. Rowe; Old Barracks Museum—Larry Schmit; Rockhill Research—Trip Kahn; Winterthur—Donald L. Finnimore.

Great thanks go to my wife, Karen Abercrombie Lalioff, for her patience and professional photographic skills.

APPENDIX A: REFERENCES

The 1811 Dictionary of the Vulgar Tongue. Facsimile ed. London: Senate—Studio Editions, 1994.

Heal, Ambrose. *London Tradesmen's Cards of the XVIII Century.* New York: Dover, 1968.

—. *The Signboards of Old London Shops.* London, 1947.

Jones, Stephen. *Dictionary of the English Language.* Philadelphia: Bennet and Walton, 1806.

Little, Nina Fletcher. *Neat and Tidy.* New York: Dutton, 1977.

Montgomery, Florence M. *Textiles in America.* New York: Norton, 1984.

Nelson, Lee H. "Nail Chronology as an Aid to Dating Old Buildings." American Association for State and Local History Technical Leaflet 48. *History News* 24.11 (November 1968).

Neumann, George C., and Frank J. Kravic. *Collector's Encyclopedia of the American Revolution.* Secaucus, NJ: Castle Books, 1977.

Stockham, Peter. *Old-Time Crafts and Trades.* New York: Dover, 1992.

"Tack Manufacture." *Industrial America.* New York: Atlantic Publishing, 1876.

APPENDIX B: FOR MORE INFORMATION

Trenton's Old Barracks and Officers' House was one of five structures originally built in 1758 by New Jersey to relieve Colonists of having to quarter British troops in their houses. Opened to the public in 1902, the Old Barracks Museum interprets life in Colonial and Revolutionary New Jersey through living history programs, tours and special events. Washington's significant victory at the Battle of Trenton is commemorated annually in December. Restoration of this National Historic Landmark is expected to be completed by 1997. For more information, please contact the Old Barracks Museum, Barrack Street, Trenton, NJ, 08608; (609) 396-1776.

Conner Prairie, an open-air living history museum, features three historic areas that include 27 authentic, period buildings and a modern museum center. The circa 1836 village of Prairietown uses first-person interpretation to allow visitors to experience the unique lifestyles of first-generation settlers in central Indiana. For more information on Conner Prairie's many programs, events and services, call (317) 776-6000 or 1-800-966-1836.

Rockhill Research maintains a diverse collection of 17th and 18th century artifacts that are available for museum exhibit, publication, research and reproduction. For information contact Trip Kahn, c/o Rockhill Research, 403 East Walnut Street, North Wales, Pennsylvania 19454.

Tools & Techniques of Bark Tanning

by Mark Odle

An interest in the natural world combined with a love of history set Mark Odle onto the path his life has taken. Well-known in muzzleloading and reenacting circles for the quality powder horns and accoutrements he produces, Mark began developing his skills at an early age. To his mother's chagrin, Mark began bringing home animals, dead or alive, at about age eight. The live ones were returned to their habitats, but the dead ones were often skinned. Needing a way of preserving the hides, Mark began rudimentary tanning.

As Mark matured, his interest in history led him to research and test various tanning methods. Mark also began making top-quality powder horns and accoutrements. Sensing the possibilities of combining leather making with the production of accoutrements, he approached it with an eye to historical accuracy. Whether it be the leather or the powder horns he produces, Mark believes in a quality product. To this end he continues his research into the methods used by our forefathers.

Mark resides in West Virginia with his wife, Anna, and their daughter, Mairin.

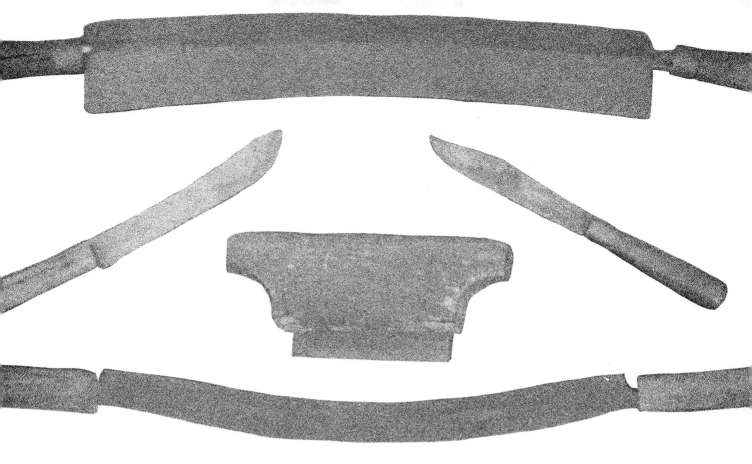

Hamlet: *How long will a man lie i' the earth ere he rot?*

1st Gravedigger: *"Faith, if he be not rotten before he die, as we have many pocky corpses now-a-days that will scarce hold the laying in, he will last you eight year, or nine year; a tanner will last you nine year.*

Hamlet: *Why he more than another?*

1st Gravedigger: *Why, sir, his hide is so tanned with his trade, that he will keep out water a great while, and your water is a sore decayer of your whoreson dead body.*

Hamlet, Act IV, Scene I

Shakespeare is believed to have written *Hamlet* in the year 1600. However the art of tanning was quite ancient long before the time of Shakespeare. Over the course of human history, leather has been absolutely indispensable. From earliest times the range of items made of leather has been practically endless. Shoes, clothing, bags, hats and household goods, including trunks, chair covers, wall-hangings and various types of covers and containers for both wet and dry storage have all been made of leather. Even the home itself may have been a leather tent or teepee. Agriculture and transportation would have been more limited if it were not for saddlery, harness and various parts of wagons and carriages. Man's creative and educational urges have been satisfied in part by leather-bound books and the parchments and vellum used to write and paint upon. Some musical instruments have utilized leather parts. If not for leather helmets, shields, quivers, gun cases and the like, man's darker pursuit of warfare would have been hindered.

Even as man became industrialized, dependence on leather did not decrease; it provided belting, parts for bellows and many other items. This is but a small fraction of what has been done with leather, all of it made possible by the tanner, whose life was generally a difficult one, from the odious nature of the materials he worked with, to the back-breaking labor required to produce the finished product: a high quality leather. Today, in the waning days of the 20th century where technology has supplanted many traditional leather items with synthetic substitutes, it can still be said, "There's nothing like leather."

Evidence that tanning is one of humankind's oldest arts can be seen in the artifacts recovered with the mummified remains of a man found in the Tyrolean Oetztaler Alps between Austria and Italy in 1991. Among the artifacts were deerskin clothing and a deerskin quiver that specialists have determined were tanned with some type of vegetable matter (Frity 47). Subsequent radiocarbon dating revealed that the man lived between 3500 to 3000 B.C. (Roberts 51). In other words here is one of the oldest known examples of vegetable or bark-tanned leather.

Two thousand years later, among the Egyptians tanning was a common occupation, one at which they were very skilled, as evidenced by articles recovered from Tutankamen's tomb. Beautiful pelts such as leopard were tanned with the hair on while less attractive hides were dehaired and made into leather. Exactly what the processes were is not known, but numerous heiroglyphics exist that clearly show many of the handworking processes, such as fleshing, soaking, breaking and softening with stone. Numerous leather objects have been found intact in ancient Egyptian tombs, leading one to believe that the leather was originally made in a firstrate manner (Austin 31). Not only Egyptians, but also Assyrians, Sumerians, Persians,

Phoenicians, Babylonians, Chinese and other Asian cultures were adept at producing quality leather goods.

Romans were also known for producing excellent leather. They took the methods of their conquered enemies and adapted them to their own use. The Roman writer Pliney describes a Greek, Tychios of Boetius, as being the originator of tanning, using various plants for that purpose. He is also mentioned in the *Iliad* and is thought to be the oldest known tanner, approximately 900 B.C. (Austin 33).

Greek literature has frequent references to the use of leather. The playwright Aristophanes wrote that tanning was well-established in Athens 500 years before the birth of Christ (Kellogg 11). The Bible also contains one of the earliest written records of the use of animal skins. The Old Testament states in Genesis 4:21, "And the Lord God made for Adam and for his wife garments of skins, and clothed them." Throughout the Bible are numerous references to the use of skins and leather.

As diverse and widespread as these cultures were, the methods of tanning were strikingly similar. Hides were physically prepared and manipulated in much the same way. The main differences were the solutions used for the actual tanning. The tools and their uses have remained practically unchanged since the days of the Romans, or before.

Even though leather became a vital component of civilization, tanners and tanneries were not generally highly thought of. Laws and restrictions were passed dictating everything from the tanyard's placement to the tanner's wages. The ancient Jews even stipulated that being a tanner could be grounds for divorce (Williams 33). Thus, the ancient art of tanning was carried forward through history, and when the New World was discovered, tanning of hides soon became an integral part of Colonial America using methods already centuries old.

THE NEW WORLD

The first Colonists to set foot on the shores of North America discovered an unspoiled world of seemingly limitless raw material and opportunity. Leather was an immediate necessity, but without established tanneries, the initial supply of leather was slow in coming and its quality was often poor. The Colonies were often without tanners and English law prohibited the exportation of articles made of English leather (Ford 7).

However, by 1620 leather was being made in Virginia at Jamestown (Hempel 15). The Plymouth Colony also boasted a tanner. Experience Miller came to the English Colony at Plymouth in 1623 and is probably the first known tanner in America (Fisher 10). In 1630 English Puritans founded Boston in Massachusetts and Francis Ingalls from Lincolnshire, England, built a tannery northeast of there at Lynn (Fisher 13-14).

The English were not the only Colonial power producing leather in America. In 1626 the Dutch West India Company Colony at New Amsterdam on the tip of Manhattan Island was mainly exporting fur pelts. However, sometime between then and 1633, Peter Minuit, the governor of New Netherland, directed the first bark mill in North America to be built. It was a stone mill powered by a horse and its creation caused a number of tanneries to begin operation in the area (Fisher 16).

Peter Stuyvesant and the Dutch colony surrendered to the English in 1664 and the city was renamed New York. Within a short time, the stench from the now abundant tanneries in the area caused their removal by order of Mayor Steenwyck. They were relocated to the area known as the Swamp near the Manhattan side of the Brooklyn Bridge and south of the present location of city hall. For the next 275 years, this area was to remain one of the most important tanning centers in America (Fisher 16).

In order for any industry to thrive, abundant raw materials are a necessity. It is therefore interesting to note that in 1649 in Virginia alone there were 20,000 head of cattle, 200 horses, 3,000 sheep, 5,000 goats and an abundance of hogs (Welsh 4). Bark from the clearing of forests for agricultural purposes was in great supply.

Even with a surplus of raw material, finished leather was usually in short supply. So much so that the Virginia assembly passed laws seven times between 1632 and 1682 prohibiting the export of, among other items, hides and skins (Ford 8). In 1680 Virginia also directed that each county build its own tanneries and have on hand tanners, curriers and cordwainers to make leather and shoes. Maryland also passed legislation in 1681 placing an export duty on leather in the hope that it would encourage domestic tanning (Welsh 4). However, southern Colonists preferred growing tobacco as it was more profitable and Colonial craftsmen preferred English leather as it was supposedly the best for superior work.

On the other hand, New England tanneries were flourishing. Bark mills and tanyards were being built in increasing numbers. Farther south in New Jersey, the increasing demand for food in New York and Philadelphia provided large quantities of raw hides. This, combined with a plentiful supply of bark, made New Jersey one of the most productive leather suppliers in the Colonies (Welsh 6).

Pennsylvania was well-suited to becoming a leader in the production of leather. The booming city of Philadelphia had six tanyards in operation by 1739 on Dock Creek (Welsh 7). William Penn wrote on several occasions of the abundant supply of hides and bark and of the usefulness of the Colony's tanners and leather workers.

The burgeoning demand for leather created its own set of problems, that of quality being foremost among them. Most of the Colonies eventually passed laws to guarantee the quality of leather being produced and to ban the sale of poorly tanned hides. Governmental control of many aspects of the tanning industry continued throughout the 18th century (Welsh 7).

After 1700 the demand for leather started to outstrip production and hides were imported from the West Indies, Lisbon, the Azores, the Canarie Islands and, after a time, South America (Welsh 9).

The American Revolution proved to be the impetus behind the building of many new tanneries and the increased production of leather. Isaac Starr, a resident of Wilmington, Delaware, familiar with the operation of a tannery wrote the following regarding the state of affairs just prior to the Revolution:

Although we abounded in every requisite material for making leather, yet very large quantities were imported from England; no power existed here to reject it and foster our own manufacture; a consequence was that when war came the country was bare of leather and suffered greatly. (Welsh 38)

The Moravians at Bethlehem, Pennsylvania, who had a tannery along with many other industries on Monocacy Creek, benefitted from the Revolution. They were producing 1000 to 2000 hides annually by the 1760s, with this number increasing dramatically during the Revolution. Not only was the supply from England cut off, but also the demand was compounded by the needs of the fledgling Continental Army (Litchfield et al. 14). The Moravians' original tannery was built in 1743, expanded in 1761, and proved to be one of their most lucrative endeavors. A note of interest was that their tanning facilities included a tanbark stamping mill. Typically barkmills utilized a large cylindrical stone that rolled in a circular trough and was powered by an ox or horse. The Moravians followed the German method of using a water-powered mill that used a series of lifter cams. These cams would alternately pick up and release four 18-foot stamping poles that had large iron heads with knives on the bottom. With this arrangement approximately 175 cords of bark were processed each year (Litchfield et al. 56).

The tanning industry in Delaware, able to make use of an abundant supply of local water, bark and hides, had also become strong and prosperous. By the mid-18th century, Wilmington became an industrial center with a fast-growing population and ready markets, especially Philadelphia. The year 1810 found ten tanneries operating in the Wilmington area alone.

The *Delaware Gazette* in 1817 describes one of the oldest tanneries, Thomas Smith's, in some detail:

A lot of ground on the corner of West and Second streets...on which is erected one large stone bark house, 60 feet by 31 feet, with a good cellar underneath; one handling house and drying loft, 20 feet by 15 feet; one mill house, 30 feet square; one stable, 30 feet by 12 feet; one bark shed, 67 feet long, with a pump; one stone lime house; one brick building, occupied as a counting house, 14 feet square; with 86 holes, which consists of 2 pools, 3 limes, 6 bates, 12 handlers, 6 latches, and 57 layaway vats, all in complete order. The pools, limes and bates draw off at the bottom. The whole lot is enclosed with a good stone and board fence. (Welsh 40)

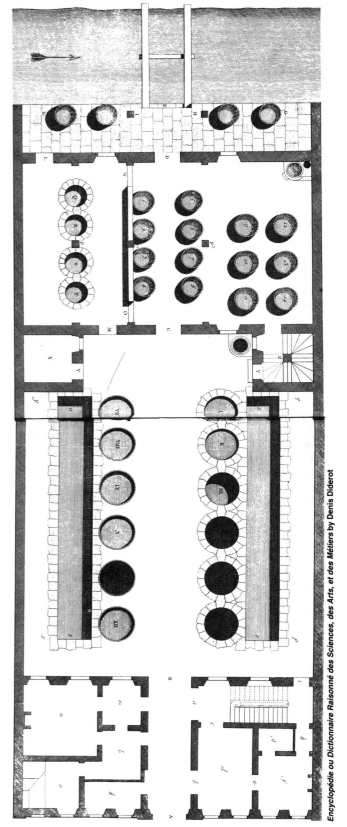

Encyclopédie ou Dictionnaire Raisonné des Sciences, des Arts, et des Métiers by Denis Diderot

This is the layout of a typical large 18th century tannery. The operation is divided into five main areas of work. At the top is the river with its washing platform. Moving down, at the left are four stone cisterns for liming, while to the right are fourteen tubs for rinsing and soaking. The central portion is an open courtyard containing twelve tanning vats. At bottom right are lofts for drying and rooms for oiling and finishing leathers. The master of the tannery lived at the lower left.

Even the famed black powder manufacturers, the duPonts, chaperoned a tannery along with their powder mills on the Brandywine. From 1815 to 1826, A. Cardon and Company ran the tannery that by 1821 was processing 3,000 hides and 350 cords of bark yearly (Welsh 62).

However, the boom times were drawing to a close for many tanneries along the Atlantic seaboard. The depression of 1819 made money tight, and by the 1820s bark was becoming scarce. Transportation and raw material costs rose and the price of leather fell. Large tanneries in the vast hemlock forests of western Pennsylvania and New York had drawn away much business. In addition there was a general neglect to adopt new methods and technologies (Welsh 50).

Up until this time, tanning had been a simple, slow and largely antiquated trade using methods centuries old. It was carried on as an appurtenance to a mostly agricultural society. Even so, the census of 1840 estimated some 8,229 tanneries in operation in the United States (Welsh 13). The industrial revolution brought unparalleled changes to the tanning industry. Methods and tools used for centuries were set aside for advances in technology, chemistry and mechanization. By the middle of the 19th century, there was a rejuvenation of the industry and an increasing demand for leather. This time the old, proven methods were slowly left behind.

At this point it may be of some interest to briefly examine two aspects of the North American hide trade. The fur trade is fairly well-documented and was operated in conjunction with the hide trade. To differentiate between the two, the fur trade dealt in peltries, in other words, fine furs such as beaver, otter, mink, fox, ermine and the like; the hide trade dealt with, according to the area of the country, hides of larger animals, for example deerskins in the Southeast and buffalo hides in the West. In the 18th century, trade was predominantly conducted east of the Mississippi. In the Southeast deerskins were traded by the thousands, so much so that the whitetail that is so prolific today was almost exterminated. From

Carolina and Virginia alone in 1699, approximately 87,166 deerskins were shipped to Great Britain. Roughly 153,000 hides were shipped from South Carolina in 1740 (Hanson 3). This continued for most of the 18th century. William Panton wrote in 1799, "Our annual exportation in deerskins only, for sixteen years back has never been less than 240,000 skins" (Hanson 3). While other items were traded for, the Southeastern trade was predominantly for deerskins. These were for the most part sent to Europe where they were tanned and processed.

In the West the trade in buffalo hides made the Southeastern deerskin market seem pale by comparison. While the peak years were fairly late, 1872 to 1874, the volume is staggering. It is estimated that some five million bison were killed, mainly on the Southern Plains, in this short period of time (Hanson 2).

Throughout the 19th century, a large portion of the raw hides had come to the tanning industry from South American sources. By 1870 this source was depleted. In the same year, a tannery in Pennsylvania had initial success with some raw buffalo hides it had received and ordered 2,000 more at three dollars per hide (Gilbert 1). In 1872 a prime bullhide sold for four dollars (Hanson 9). For many unemployed Civil War veterans, this was plenty of incentive. In November of 1872, the *Wichita Eagle* claimed that there were between one and two thousand hide hunters in the vicinity (Gilbert 2).

The slaughter of the American bison had begun. Until they were almost exterminated in some fifteen years, markets in the East and in Europe demanded buffalo leather and tanned robes. Households all across America had any number of items made from buffalo hides. The British Army used bison for its leather articles for twenty years (Gilbert 1).

The information on the hide trade in the Southeast and West has been included to show the tremendous demand for and the volume of leather used in the 18th and 19th centuries. Even today finely tanned leather is at a premium, as a quick look at any leather price list will attest.

STRUCTURE OF HIDES & LEATHER

In order to be successful at tanning, a basic knowledge of the structure of hides and skins is desirable. In this article all references will be to mammal skins unless otherwise noted. All mammals have skins or hides that follow a similar pattern and that consist of three distinct layers.

The outer section, or hair side, is composed of a thin epithelial layer of cells called the epidermis. The middle layer, the thickest, the strongest and the most important, is called the dermis or corium. The inside next to the flesh is the adipose or flesh layer. The corium is the only layer that is used to make leather; the other two are removed by fleshing and liming.

The surface of the corium just below the epidermis contains the grain membrane and hyaline layer. This, along with the distribution of hair follicles, gives each species of animal skin its distinctive grain pattern. The rest of the corium is composed of large collagen bundles. These bundles are interwoven in a three-dimensional network that gives the skin its strength ("Leather and Hides" 761).

Raw hides are made up of about 60 to 70 percent water by weight; 30 to 35 percent proteins; and less than four percent lipids, carbohydrates, mineral salts and pigments ("Leather and Hides" 761). From 90 to 95 percent of the solids in a hide

226

are both fibrous and non-fibrous proteins. Collagen, a fibrous protein, makes up over 85 percent of the corium. The non-fibrous proteins are either soluble in water, salt solutions or diluted alkalis and are removed before tanning ("Leather and Hides" 761).

This is very important to understand, as it is these soluble proteins that act as a glue and help cement the non-soluble fibers together. In fact by boiling a hide for a period of time, glue will be produced. H. Proctor stated:

The cause of the horny nature of dried skin is that the gelatinous and swollen fibres of which it is composed not merely stiffen on drying, but adhere to a homogenous mass, as is evidence by its translucence. If in some way we can prevent the adhesion of the fibres while drying, we shall have made a step in the desired direction, and this will be the more effective, the more perfectly we have split the fibre-bundles into their constituent fine fibrels, and removed the substance which cements them.

(Austin 45)

CROSS-SECTION SHOWING THE STRUCTURE OF A TYPICAL MAMMAL SKIN

Epidermis

Grain layer

Corium

Flesh layer

The grain layer contains hair follicles and both sebaceous and sweat glands. The collagen fibers in the grain are very fine.

In the corium the fibers become much larger. The strength of a hide is derived from the interwoven fiber bundles in the corium.

In the flesh layer, the fibers become fine again and run in a horizontal direction.

VARIOUS TYPES OF HIDES & THEIR USES

The hide of any mammal (also many birds, reptiles and fish) may be successfully tanned. However, not all hides are equal to every task or every type of tannage. Even the hides from animals of the same species are not always the same. The individual hide has strong and weak spots, thick and thin areas, and scars and other blemishes that may affect its suitability for certain uses. The quality of each hide has many variables including age, sex of the animal, time of year, health and the very environment in which it was raised. This does not even take into account the quality of the skinning and the hide's subsequent handling. In short it pays to be selective in choosing hides and to be careful in preparing them for tanning. Careless skinning or handling and indifferent tanning methods will all show up in the finished leather.

The size and weight of hides are also important factors in the production of leather. The larger, older animals will generally have heavier, thicker hides and, unless they are split, are better used for harness or sole leathers. This includes adult cattle, horses, moose and buffalo. These hides will weigh in excess of 60 pounds and will square 35 to 40 feet or better. They are often cut down the middle of the back for easier handling.

Medium-sized skins include those of deer, goats, calves and sheep. In this article it is this group that will be tanned.

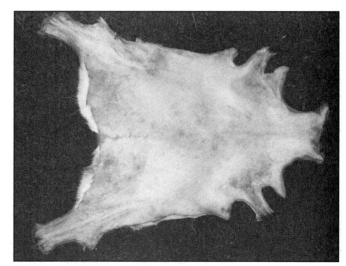

With the exception of natural scars, this is a perfect hide. It has no scores, has a good even trim and is completely clean. Providing the tanning process is completed in good order, it will make an excellent leather.

These hides will average from six to twelve square feet and are generally tanned whole. This medium-sized group is quite suitable for a wide range of finished products including shoe uppers, garment leathers, bags, upholstery, gloves and ornamental uses. Smaller hides may be tanned for leather. However, except for special cases, they are rarely worth the effort.

Occasionally, one will encounter hog or bear skins. They are very similar and have distinctive grain patterns. They are both very greasy and require careful attention in order to produce quality leather. Bearskin is especially worth the extra effort.

This is a close-up view of scores or knife marks. Such marks are the result of careless skinning, where the flesh side of a hide has been cut. Scores can be minor or may be severe enough to open up into holes as tanning progresses. They weaken the structure of a hide and are unneccessary.

Close-up showing the texture of three different tanned hides. From left to right: buffalo, hog and bear. Each one has also been curried.

Since skinning has been covered in other books and articles, it will not be covered here. There are a few points to keep in mind, however. It is much easier to skin an animal while the carcass is warm, the reason being that, after the opening cuts are made, the skin can very often be pulled off with little or no additional knife work. Doing this greatly reduces the chance of scoring or cutting the skin. Scores weaken the hide and often open up into actual holes. The skin should have a good trim. There should be no ragged, tattered edges. Poorly trimmed hides waste useable leather and increase the possibility of tears. In buying raw skins, choose only the best. Cannon-sized holes, poor trim and scores all add up and detract from the finished product no matter how good the efforts of the tanner. The best hides for making leather are generally taken in late summer and early fall while the skin is "full" and has not been depleted in making a winter coat of hair.

This an average-size buffalo hide, fleshed and dried in a frame and ready to be brain tanned. To show a size comparison, the author's brother is 6 foot 3 inches. The hide is approximately 40 square feet.

TOOLS & EQUIPMENT

For the small home or farm tannery, the tools used are quite simple. They are basically the same as have been used for centuries. A few good sharp knives are a must. Pattern and size will depend on the user's needs. Of equal importance are fleshing tools, as these will be what the tanner uses time and again during the tanning process. It is important to note that when fleshing a hide, especially a light skin, the flesh, fat and unwanted membrane is actually pushed off instead of being cut from the hide. In other words the fleshing knife does not need to be razor sharp. In fact it works better if it is well-formed but on the dull side. The handles should fit the hands well and be stout. Remember this tool is going to do a lot of work with you behind it. It pays to have one that will work well. The overall length is a matter of choice. Usually twenty to 24 inches will work for deer and calf-sized skins. The fleshing knives in the photo range from 20 to 29 inches.

The fleshing beam should be strong and made so as to be comfortable to use. The beam takes a lot of abuse from water, lime, abrasion and cuts. Hardwood is a wise choice. A slightly rounded surface makes working the hides easier.

It is strongly recommended that a good, strong pair of rubber gloves and a heavy rubber apron be used. It is best to be protected since lime can burn the skin and working with raw hides and skins can cause infections or disease. The tanks, tubs or barrels used are a matter of choice, although they should never be metal. Plastic, wood, fiberglass or masonry are all suitable. Large livestock watering troughs of high impact plastic are ideal and even come with drain plugs at the bottom.

A wooden paddle can be used for stirring solutions and removing hides from various tanks. A different paddle or stick should be used for each solution or tank to prevent contamination or weakening of the mixtures.

Other items that would be useful include a heavy scrub

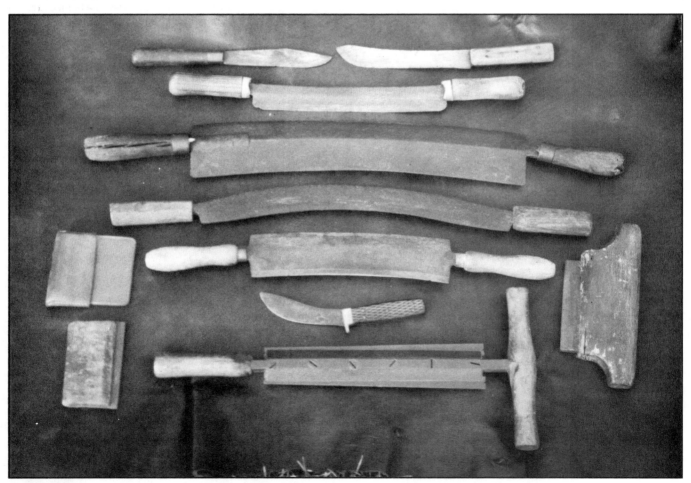

Selection of tanning tools, some of which are antique. From top to bottom: Handmade skinning knife; I. Wilson butcher knife; four fleshing knives, smallest 19-1/2 inches, largest 29 inches; Russell Green River skinner; currier's knife used for leveling or skivving the flesh side of tanned hides. On the left are two slickers. The top one has a glass blade and the lower one has metal. On the right is another slicker with a slate blade.

TWO TYPES OF FLESHING BEAMS

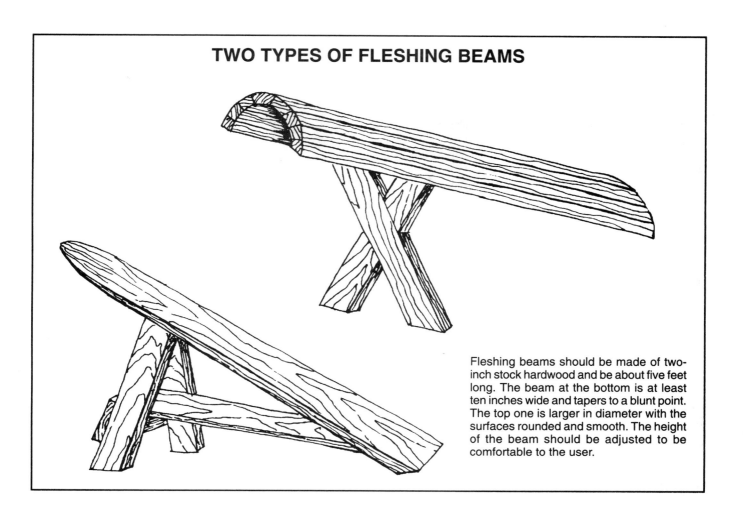

Fleshing beams should be made of two-inch stock hardwood and be about five feet long. The beam at the bottom is at least ten inches wide and tapers to a blunt point. The top one is larger in diameter with the surfaces rounded and smooth. The height of the beam should be adjusted to be comfortable to the user.

The author's beam and work area. This particular beam works well and the concrete slabs help in keeping the work area clean. The various containers are for liming, bating and soaking hides.

brush for cleaning finished hides and a slicker for removing water and for smoothing the hide's surface. A slicker may be wooden or may have a slate, brass, copper or heavy glass blade. Steel or iron is not a good choice because of rust. In fact the only time steel should come in contact with hides throughout the entire process is in cutting, trimming or fleshing.

For finishing leather, a skiving or paring knife is used for thinning but is not usually necessary. Also some method must be devised for softening or breaking some leathers. This may include a crutch knife, some type of stake or blade set in a vise or a heavy, copper ground cable attached to the top and the bottom of a stout post.

The working area should be well-drained and free of clutter and obstructions. Many old tanneries had their tanks or vats uncovered and out in the open. This leaves everything exposed to the elements. A small three-sided or an open shed like the one shown at right will work well. Covering the tanks will be helpful in keeping the hides in and unwanted things out. A concrete pad under the work area including the fleshing beam is nice but not essential as long as the area drains well.

Of final importance is water. A tannery needs an ample supply of clean, soft water free of chemicals that would retard or impede the work of the various solutions. Historically, tanneries have been located on rivers or streams because of the volume of water required.

Author's tanning shed. Heavy plastic stock watering tanks are ideal for holding the tanning solutions and for layering hides in bark. The simple shed helps keep the tanks out of most of the weather. The dark object hanging above the right tank is a large hog hide that has been tanned.

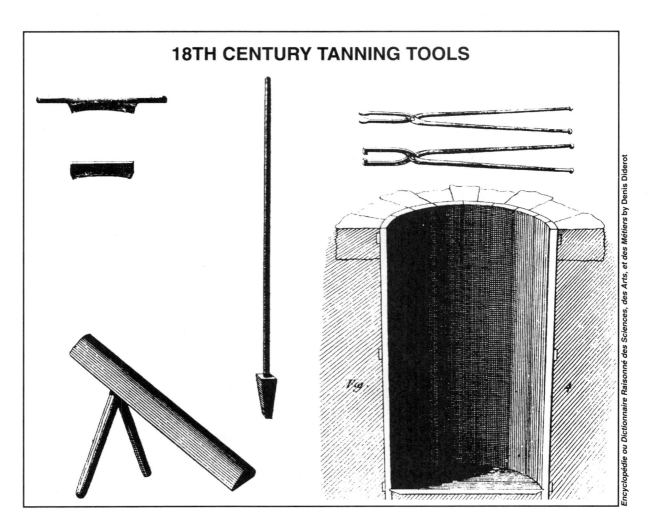

18TH CENTURY TANNING TOOLS

Encyclopédie ou Dictionnaire Raisonné des Sciences, des Arts, et des Métiers by Denis Diderot

PREPARING HIDES FOR TANNING

Before a hide or skin can be tanned with any degree of success by whatever method, it must be prepared correctly. It is likely that the biggest cause of failure in tanning lies in poor or inadequate hide preparation. This encompasses everything from thorough fleshing to complete removal of lime after dehairing. While experimentation can lead to new developments, the methods discussed here have been used for centuries. They are tried and true with known results, making it inadvisable for the novice to deviate from them. It should also be pointed out that period tanning (ie., without the aid of machinery or modern chemicals) is *work*. There are no magic elixers or secret solutions that will transform a raw hide into finished leather. It requires effort and knowing when to do what. If a tanner has any secret, it is in his or her experience. The reward of tanning is in taking a rawhide and by *your* efforts (and eventually your experience) transforming it into something useful and beautiful.

Encyclopédie ou Dictionnaire Raisonné des Sciences, des Arts, et des Métiers by Denis Diderot

This view shows the area next to the river where hides were initially brought from the slaughterhouse. Here they were washed clean of blood and filth. The vats were for soaking hides until ready for the liming process. The workman at the right is probably fleshing a hide. After liming, the hair and lime water was also removed here.

CURING

The first step in hide preparation is called curing. Once the hide or skin has been properly flayed off the carcass, it is generally allowed to cool. Simply folding the skin lengthwise down the middle of the back and laying on a concrete floor or suspending it over a pole for several hours, even overnight, will work. The flesh side should not be allowed to dry out. Keep in mind that dogs and other varmints would love to carry off the hide when it is in this condition.

The hide may be salted once it has been removed from the animal and allowed to cool. Spread out the hide flesh side up and remove all heavy pieces of meat and fat. Apply finely ground canning salt to the depth of at least 1/4 inch all over. (This is for calf-size hides; for cowhides one should use rock salt.) The hide should be slightly inclined so that the blood and moisture will drain off. Be sure the entire hide is covered, paying special attention to folds and thick areas. When the hide has drained for a day or so, depending on its size and type, the old salt can be shaken off. The hide may be processed now, another coat of salt may be applied or the hide can be salt-dried and processed later.

Some tanners prefer salt- or brine-cured hides as they feel the hides process faster and easier than hides that are not. At one time Argentina was known for a type of hide called "figorifico." These hides were washed clean of blood and

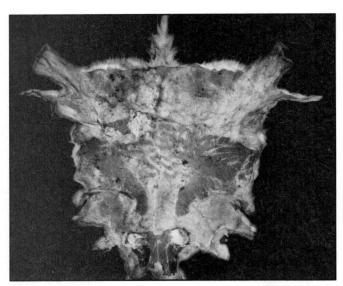

Fresh, raw deerskin. This hide is fresh from the deer and still covered with flesh and fat.

manure after slaughter and then fleshed. They were then soaked in a concentrated brine solution for two days. Once removed from the brine and drained, the hides were salted and dried. These hides by virtue of their curing were supposed to produce better leather (Theis 1628).

While salt can be used and is valuable in some instances, it is not necessary. According to Herman Moyer of Grantville, Pennsylvania, "Chestnut oak, or commonly called rock oak bark, was used by myself and other tanners...without salt." Mr. Moyer tanned with bark and supplied his area with leather during World War II when leather was in short supply. This is generally the method I use although I do experiment with others. I believe that a very simple method of bark tan without salt was what was primarily used on the frontier.

In western Virginia in 1778, salt cost six pounds sterling or about twenty dollars a bushel. The salt was brought from the sea coast of Maryland, where it was about eight dollars a bushel. In January 1779 salt prices rose to sixteen pounds or nearly fifty-three dollars a bushel in Pittsburg (Comstock 48). At these prices salt would not have been affordable to use in frontier tanneries.

If the hide is not to be worked immediately, it can be salt cured as described or it may be frozen. Still another treatment is flint drying: simply fleshing and drying the hide without special treatment. This is satisfactory for short periods or in cold weather. However, during warm weather insects will damage the hide when in this state. Flint drying also makes the hide more difficult to return to a soft, pliable state prior to resuming the tanning process. The hide must be alternately soaked and scraped until soft and rehydrated.

Regardless of how the hide has been handled up to this point, whether fresh, salt cured or dried, it must now be soaked and cleansed of blood, manure, salt and other debris. Soaking will relax and soften the hide, making it ready to flesh.

FLESHING OR BEAMING

Fleshing, the next step, is the removal of all traces of flesh, fat and membrane from the flesh side of a hide. This exposes the corium or dermis to the action of whatever solution in which it will be immersed. The grain membrane or hyaline layer is somewhat less porous, making it imperative that fleshing be completely done in order to permit the tanning solutions to penetrate the hide thoroughly. This is the stage that will very likely make the difference in the quality of leather produced.

A good fleshing knife and a beam of correct height and slope will more than pay for themselves. The workman holds or pinches the hide firmly between himself and the beam. The flesh, fat and so on is then pushed off. It is helpful to start a small patch in the middle of the hide and work outward toward the edges, pushing the unwanted material ahead of the knife. Rotate the hide and continue pushing toward the edge with the knife as seen in the photograph on the following page. Care should be exercised not to damage or score the hide, so a dull fleshing knife is preferable. Beaming, as this operation is

often called, continues until the last traces of membrane are removed and the clean, white corium is exposed.

At this stage the quality of the hide will be noticeable. A good healthy hide will have a smooth surface with a nice pattern of veins. The veins themselves are not there but there is often an impression of where they have been. This is an indication of a well-grown hide and one that has natural strength. Tanned leather can also be evaluated in the same way if it has not been split or otherwise reduced in thickness, thus eliminating that layer of leather.

Any scar, score, bullet hole, wrinkle or other defect can now be seen. These, plus the weight or thickness of the hide, determine the method of tannage to which the hide is subjected and the use of the future leather. For instance a light deerskin with a score running across the back would not be a good choice for straps. Straps must be heavy and the score would weaken them. A heavy bullhide would be suited for sole or harness leather, but not shoe uppers or bag leather.

The hide is now ready to be trimmed of ragged edges, tail

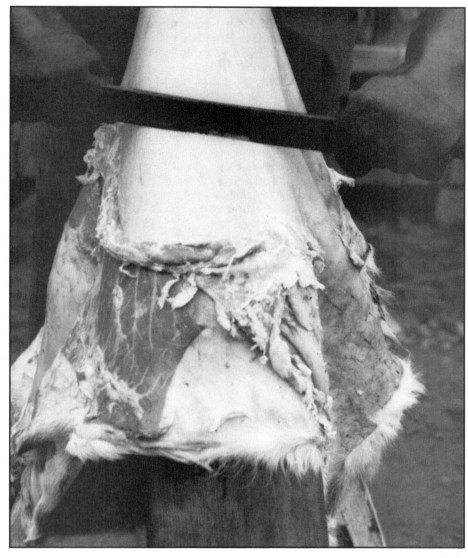

Fleshing a deer means all flesh, fat and membrane must be removed in order for tanning solutions to be effective. The skin above and just below the fleshing knife is completely clean. The author works from the center of a hide out to the edges.

and so forth and is graded using experience and those points previously discussed. The hide can now be soaked again for a short time and washed of any remaining blood and dirt.

With the skin's use and type of tannage decided, the process continues accordingly. The following information will mostly deal with bark or vegetable tanning. It should be

understood that this is the most basic method of tanning, and it is likely that this method or some form of it is how leather was produced on the frontier. The leather produced is meant to replicate early leather and to be used in making usable reproductions of early leather goods.

LIMING

The cleaned, soaked hide is now ready to be limed or dehaired. This is an essential part of preparing the hide for later tanning into leather. Not only does it remove the hair but also the epidermis. This layer contains the skin's pigment and will appear somewhat cheesy or curdled. The liming swells and conditions the fiber structure of the hides in addition to removing unwanted soluble proteins and fats ("Leather and Hides" 761). Once freed of these unwanted substances, the remainder is generally considered collagen,

the interwoven, fibrous net of non-soluble protein. This is what will be transformed into leather.

There seem to be many terms for or variations of lime. It is alternately referred to as caustic lime; milk of lime; lime water; burnt, slaked, lump or peppel lime. While there are differences in these various materials, they are all a form of alkali. For the average home tanner, hydrated lime is preferable. It is cheap, readily available and easy to use.

Stir about eight or ten pounds of hydrated lime into 40 or

50 gallons of water in a container used only for liming. Make sure there are no lumps and that the lime is fully in solution. It will precipitate out, and it will be necessary periodically to stir the hides and the solution to get a full even coverage. Plunge the wet hides into the solution being sure that the lime water comes in contact with the entire hide, hopefully down to the epidermis. It is important not to overload with too many hides because the solution will not make complete contact with all parts of each hide. The hides and solution should be stirred and the hides plunged in and out of the solution several times a day. The solution will work best if maintained at a temperature between 70 and 80 degrees.

The hide in the accompanying photos is a deerskin. Deer hair will "slip" very easily. Other types of hides may take longer. In warm weather it is possible to dehair a deerskin in two or three days. In cold weather it will take longer. The hair on the hides should be tested every day or so. At first the hair may be pulled out. However, when it is ready, the hair will slide off easily and in mass with very little effort. It is interesting to note that in early accounts of the tanning process, liming could take months or even up to a year or more. This was usually in reference to large, heavy cattle hides that were tanned for sole leather. Remember, the alkaline properties of lime help degrade and remove unwanted proteins from the skin. It is probably best not to leave deerskin or light calfskins in the lime any longer than is necessary to remove the hair and epidermis completely as otherwise it may damage the grain.

To remove the hair, use a wooden knife with a dull edge, the back of the fleshing tool or some suitable tool with an edge that will not cut or mar the hide's grain surface. Start in

This is the actual dehairing of a hide after it has soaked in the lime solution. The hair sloughs off easily with little effort required. It should be done with a dull edge. Here the back of a single-edged scraper is being used. The grayish area in the center is epidermis and must also be removed.

This is the liming area. Hides were initially put in cisterns of used, weak lime and progressively moved to stronger solutions. The workman at left is agitating the solution to ensure complete coverage. The men to the right are moving hides to a different vat.

Encyclopédie ou Dictionnaire Raisonné des Sciences, des Arts, et des Métiers by Denis Diderot

the center of the hide and push the hair and cheesy epidermis off, clear to the edges. The hide will be quite swollen and rubbery in texture. Completely remove all hair, epidermis and as much lime and water as possible. If patches of hair remain on the hide or if small fine hair is still evident, return the hide to the lime solution.

When the grain side is clean, turn the hide over and completely work the flesh side with the fleshing knife. There will be a small amount of tissue and lime that will be removed. This is important to do thoroughly. During this process remember that now with the hair gone, there is no padding or

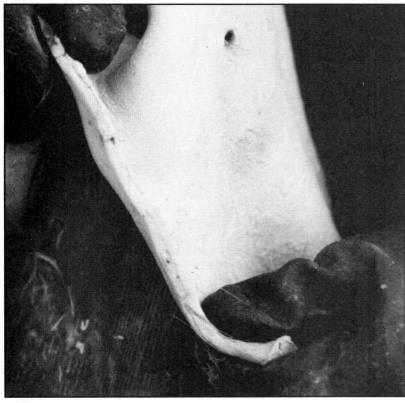

The hide becomes swollen and rubbery because of the penetration of the lime. This caustic lime residue is somewhat difficult to neutralize and remove from the hide. If it is not removed thoroughly, it will render the tan liquor ineffective and the tannins will not properly combine with the collagen in the hide (Welsh 19).

There are other methods of removing hair even though liming is considered the best and most practical for general use. Hair may be removed by the use of wood ash, lye or by sweating. Wood ash was probably used on the frontier as it was always available. If rendered it will produce the lye used

The skin when limed becomes swollen and rubbery. This is the neck of a large buckskin. At this point it is about 3/8-inch thick.

protection for the grain side so proceed with caution to prevent damaging the skin.

Some early tanneries used several vats in what was termed a raising series:

The vats are distinguished as dead, weak, and live vats. The dead vat is that which has been nearly exhausted of its strength; the weak is that which has only been used enough to deprive it of a portion of its force; and the fresh or live vat, is that which has not yet been worked. In the progress of operations, the live vat passes successively into the weak and the dead vat.
(Welsh 19)

Modern tanneries often use such a series. There are certain advantages in using older lime solutions, such as obtaining a smoother grain surface and a more rapid depilation of the hide. However, the old lime is less astringent and less uniform than the new sharp solution because of the dissolved and degraded proteins and the production of ammonia. By mixing half old solution with half new sharp lime, the qualities of both may be retained (Theis 1642).

Using lime to remove hair is not without its disadvantages.

in making soft soap. Wood ash may be applied in the form of a thick paste to the flesh side of a fleshed hide and the hide rolled up. The hide should not be allowed to dry out and should be checked periodically until the hair slips easily. It may be necessary to apply two or more coats of wet ash. Alternately the wood ash may be mixed with water and the hide immersed in the solution. If using either of these methods, simply continue processing as would be done with lime.

While pure lye mixed with water may be used to slip hair, extreme caution should be observed, as lye is very caustic and will cause severe burns. It is *not* recommended.

The process known as sweating was usually reserved for wool skins. This was done so as to save valuable wool and leave it undamaged by lime, etc. It is basically a method by which the epidermis is allowed to rot in a controlled situation. A closed room is saturated with moisture and controlled heat, often by using steam, and the epithilial layer of cells allowed to decay. The hair or wool is removed and the skin processed.

Even though lime has some disadvantages, it is by far the easiest, most thorough and most practical method of removing hair from hides and skins. The solution may be used agriculturally after it is spent and along with the hair will produce useful nutrients for soil.

BATING OR DELIMING

After the limed hide has been dipiliated and both sides thoroughly worked over, it should be washed and rinsed in clear, cool water. The hide should be soaked for several hours or even overnight. Agitate the hide periodically and change the water several times. It is important that as much lime be removed as possible.

The hide is called a "raised hide" after liming because of its swollen nature. This swollen, rubbery and hard texture is a result of the hide's highly alkaline state. This must be reduced and the pH of the hide returned to neutral or even a slightly acidic condition. In modern tanneries this is accomplished by the use of pancreatic enzymes. In Colonial and early American tanning, the process of bating hides was carried out by immersing cleaned, limed hides in a solution of water and manure. The dung most often mentioned is that of dogs or poultry. In trying to replicate the qualities found on old leather, one may wish to try this method. It is fairly simple and quite effective.

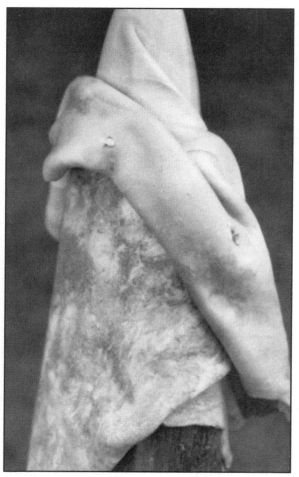

The neck area of the deerskin shown previously, which was swollen and rubbery. This view shows the bated skin and its now soft and flaccid condition. The flesh side has been worked one final time, and it is now ready to put in the tanning solutions.

The hide is taken from its cleansing bath of water and the flesh side lightly worked to open the pores and "scud" lime and remaining tissue from the hide. In the meantime a quantity of poultry manure is added to enough water to make a medium slurry type of solution. The hide is plunged into this solution making sure all parts are immersed and no folds or creases are allowed to be without contact. The solution and hide should be stirred and examined several times each day. When the hide is soft, smooth and flaccid (much as it was when it was removed from the carcass, only now without hair), it is taken out of the bate and thoroughly washed in clean water. This process will take several days depending on the strength of the solution, the air temperature and other factors. After the hide is rinsed, it is returned to the beam and once again the flesh side worked, after which it may again be washed. It is now ready to be placed in the actual tanning solution.

As disgusting as the previous process may be, it performs several chemical reactions within the hide. It is unlikely that the early tanners had any idea as to what was actually happening. They only knew that it worked and so it was used. Basically, acids and enzymes are present or are formed that act on the hide and any remaining lime. The hide is transformed into a state where it may be tanned successfully. The spent solution may also be used agriculturally.

Other methods of deliming the hide entail the use of acids or bran mixtures. Bran is frequently referred to in tanning literature. It is mixed in boiling water in a quantity sufficient to cover the hide. (Let cool before adding the hide.) As it ferments acids and enzymes, which act on the hide, are again formed. The process will take several days and the hide must be rinsed and worked as described previously.

Various acids have been used and include sulfuric (which may contribute to eventual red rot in the leather), lactic and acetic acid (vinegar). Lactic acid is used at the rate of three fluid ounces U.S.P. to 30 or 40 gallons water. One half to one gallon of sharp vinegar may also be used (Farnham 76). The hide is allowed to soak until soft and flaccid then removed, worked and washed as before.

These vats were for some of the various soaking operations required prior to the layering of the hides in the tanning pits.

Encyclopédie ou Dictionnaire by Denis Diderot

238

BASIC TANNAGES

ow that the hide is fully prepared the actual tanning process may begin. While the majority of work has been done, there is still much to do. Care and vigilance should be maintained.

The steps described so far have pertained for the most part to bark or vegetable tanning. However, historically, there have been three major types of tannage. These include oil, mineral, vegetable and various combinations of the three. Each method is suited to producing a certain type of leather, often from specific types of hides or skins. For example a heavy bullhide would be bark tanned for sole leather; while a sheepskin would be shamoyed or oil tanned. A fine pelt such as leopard would likely be alum tanned, possibly in combination with oil. These various methods would take anywhere from approximately two years for the bullhide to as short as a couple of months for an oil-tanned lambskin.

The standard definition of leather is "...animal skin, which on soaking in water and subsequent drying does not become hard and tinny, but remains soft and flexible; which does not decay in the presence of cold water; and does not yield any gelatine on boiling with water" (Austin 46).

This definition covers both vegetable and oil tannages. However, mineral or alum tan is more properly termed "tawing" and is more suited for pelts with the hair left on or for very light leathers. Alum and salt are the principal ingredients and may be washed or soaked out of the skin. Upon drying, the skin is left hard and somewhat brittle.

Oil tanning, shamoying, chamoising and brain tan are all part of the oldest form of tannage, which is the use of various oils, both animal and vegetable, to produce leather or treated skins that are largely unaffected by water and are resistant to decay. In the simplest, more primitive form, animal brains or some form of animal fat are manipulated into a skin by physically pulling and stretching the skin until all water has evaporated. The physical manipulation and the introduction of a lubricant prevent the hide's fibers from adhering to one another upon drying. Smoking makes the hide water-resistant and more permanent.

In a later version of this method, sheepskins are coated with some form of a drying oil. The oil is mechanically worked into the skin, and it is then hung up in a warm room. The process is repeated until the skin is sufficiently tanned. The drying oils oxidize forming various chemicals among which are aldehydes. These chemicals aid in the tanning process.

Drying oils are different than those termed finishing oils. Finishing oils only act as waterproofing and softening agents. They do not have the ability actually to tan a hide or affect that type of change within the hide's fibers. These include both

A view of the main courtyard showing the various operations involved in the actual tanning process. Workmen are carrying in hides and ground bark from the left. The men in the vats are variously layering hides and bark and removing tanned hides and spent bark.

Encyclopedie ou Dictionnaire Raisonne des Sciences, des Arts, et des Metiers by Denis Diderot

animal and vegetable oils. Tallow, lard, neatsfoot oil and butter are non-drying animal fats or oils. Among the vegetable oils in this class are cottonseed, castor, olive and coconut oils. Mineral oils are petroleum distillates and may be used only as a finishing agent (Austin 59-60).

In true oil tanning, the fats or oils actually seem to combine with the hide and its fibers. This combination is permanent (Austin 59). Some of the various drying oils include cod-liver, seal and whale oils (Austin 60). Safflower, rape seed and sardine oils are also in this category. Cod-liver oil has historically been the most preferred of these drying oils and was used in the manufacture of chamois leather ("Leather and Hides" 762).

While oil and mineral tannages are probably older, the discovery of vegetable extracts or tannins and their ability to convert raw hides into quality, long-lasting leather was of monumental importance. Vegetable-tanned leather is strong, durable and unaffected by water, heat or cold. This makes any number of applications possible, from shoe soles to leather harness and saddlery, to mention but a few.

Cultures of the Old World adapted vegetable tanning to their own situations and to the various plant materials found in their geographical regions that contained the necessary tannins. It is curious to note that the indigenous peoples of the New World, both North and South America, did not seem to practice vegetable tanning prior to its introduction by Europeans. Even then, while they traded for bark-tanned leathers, they still "tanned" their own hides and skins by variations of the oil tan method, i. e. brain tan. (Author's note: I am not aware of definitive proof of vegetable tanning being conducted by people in the New World prior to European contact.)

As most fibrous plants contain tannins, it was by experimentation that those plants which were most effective and which had the best quality tannins were found. Various parts of individual plants (leaves, fruit, wood, bark and roots) contain greater or lesser quantities of tannin. The following

While vegetable tanning is not specifically suited to hair-on tanning, it can be done. This is a calf knee to be used for a lock cover.

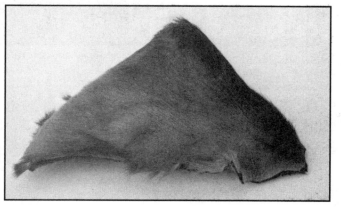

These are oak galls. While they have not been used to any extent in North America, they have been used in other parts of the world. The two on the left were picked "green," while the other two reached maturity. Galls are the result of insect parasites.

are a few of the characteristics of tannins that are of interest to tanners, although there are more:

1. *Tannins are astringent.*
2. *Tannins react with ferric salts and produce colors, for example, driving an iron nail into a wet, oak board will make a blue-black stain. The iron has reacted with the tannins in the oak.*
3. *Tannins are generally amorphous or formless.*
4. *Alkaloids, which are found in plants, will precipitate tannins out of solutions. There are other chemicals that will do this as well.*
5. *Tannins will precipitate gelatine. This is a leather-making characteristic.*
6. *Tannins are soluble in hot water. Colloidal sols are formed. These are tiny gelatinous particles in suspension in the water.* (Theis 1665)

There are two types of tannins: pyrogallol and catechol. While two different species of plants may contain the same tannin, the leather made with them may be quite different. There are also insoluble tannins called "reds," which can impart some useful qualities to the tanned leather, such as the firmness found in sole leather (Theis 1665). It is interesting to note that while science has certainly made progress in understanding these substances and the way they work, there are still processes that are unexplained.

While tannins are found throughout most plants, there is usually one specific part that is utilized. It may be the bark of hemlocks or it may be the leaves of sumac. Each species or variety of plant will produce a leather with its own characteristics. Sometimes tannins from several sources are mixed to produce particular qualities in leather.

The intention of this article is to show how leather may be produced much in the same way and using the same materials as did our ancestors. There are many different species of plant material that can be used and probably as many methods of using them as there are tanners. Even though there are sources of tannin the world over, many of which are used in quantity for commercial tanning, this article will concern the use of the bark of oaks and that of hemlocks. The barks of these trees were the primary sources of tannin in early and Colonial America. They are available today and, if used correctly, will produce leather that is essentially the same as that produced by our forefathers.

While wood contains tannins and has sometimes been used, it is the bark that contains tannins in quantities most

readily accessible. An older tree has more tannin than a younger one, and the lower parts of the tree contain a higher concentration of tannin than the top parts.

The stately American chestnut once provided a large portion of the raw materials used for bark tanning. The chestnut blight has since ended that source. Even so, it was predominantly the hemlock in the North and various species of oak in the southern regions that were commonly utilized. The hemlock forests in the Eastern United States and Canada were all but eliminated by the demand for tanbark. Literally thousands of square miles of virgin hemlock forest were cut to obtain tanbark.

The air-dried bark generally contains about ten percent tannin by weight and is of the catechol group. The liquors are bright red and full of acid-forming sugars. It is well-suited to producing various leathers, both heavy sole as well as light, fancy leather (Theis 1667-1668).

The different white, red or black species of oak are all rich in tannins and have been successfully used. Chestnut oak, also called rock oak, is classified as a white oak. It is among the highest in tannin content with about ten percent by dried weight. It is also rich in acid-forming sugars and is of the catechol group. It is among the most desirable of barks for tanning (Theis 1667). In my home area of West Virginia, it is called tan oak or tanbark oak by some older people. Chestnut oak bark was used by the commercial tanneries and private individuals in central Pennsylvania in the early years of this century. According to Herman Moyer who bark tanned in the Hershey, Pennsylvania area, "There were very many large logs lying in the mountains at that time, in the 1920s, which were cut down just for the bark."

Whatever bark is used, it is collected in the spring when the sap starts to rise in the trees. About the time corn is planted and the leaves are just coming out on the trees, bark will peel easily. For about one month, the bark would be stripped from trees in large sections and left to dry for a period of time. When at least partially dry and much lighter in weight, it would be

hauled to the tanneries. If kept dry, bark could be stored indefinitely without losing its effectiveness.

In order to utilize the tannins properly, the bark must be ground or crushed into fairly small pieces or into a coarse powder. The bark must be dry in order to do this easily. Typically the bark was crushed using a large stone wheel much like a millstone. It was powered by an ox or horse and rolled in a circular trough like a wheel. Different mills were developed using water power to grind, crush or pound bark into the necessary coarse powder. Eventually a cone mill came to be used almost exclusively (Theis 1669).

The bark, once ground, is variously described as being the size or consistency of shelled or cracked corn, wheat grains or of a coarse powder. Today, large sawmills very often use a debarker before logs are sawn. This is to protect expensive sawblades from dirt and other foreign matter that may be on the logs. The machine strips and coarsely shreds the bark from the log. The bark is then sold as mulch. This bark is entirely suitable for use in tanning provided the tannins have not leached out by exposure to the weather. Of course, it must be a species that has sufficient tannin to be worthwhile. This bark mulch is the consistency of coarse shredded wheat with small bits and pieces of bark. It is usually cheap and available in quantity. In general it takes about twice the weight of the hide in bark to effect a good tan.

Once the bark has been acquired and is the right consistency, there are many different ways to use it. Before going further, it should be noted that fresh, strong bark liquor

In order to leach the tannings from bark effectively, the bark must be reduced to as fine a state as possible. This bark came from a local sawmill. Before the log is sawed, the bark is removed by machine. This is the end result and is sold for mulch.

This is the process of rendering bark liquor. The raw bark is to the right. It is heated with water in the drum. When the liquor is sufficiently strong, it is poured through a screen and allowed to cool. It is then transferred to the tanks in the tanning shed to the left.

is *not* suitable to tan fresh hides. It is too astringent and will "case harden" the skin. The outer surfaces will tan and shrink preventing the movement of the tannins into the center of the corium, leaving a raw streak. Typically liquors are lined up in a series from new, fresh solutions to older, spent ones. The hides, once prepared, are started in the spent liquors, left for a period of time and moved into progressively stronger solutions as the tanner deemed them ready. A tanner's most valuable, effective tool was and is his experience. Knowing what to do and when to do it; what a hide is supposed to look like; how strong solutions are supposed to be and how to use them; plus a host of other items all make up a tanner's mental tool chest. If you know how, hides can be tanned in many ways with very little in the way of equipment.

Large commercial tanneries will often extract tannins using hot water and a series of gravity fed tanks. A moderate heat is used because higher temperatures will turn the extract dark through oxidation. Dark extract will produce a dark leather. For light-colored leather, the extract is often leached using cool water (Theis 1669). This cold method takes longer and is probably the method most used historically. Steam and pressure are also used to obtain extract.

To produce a uniform product, tanneries clarify or de-colorize the extract. The leathers are also bleached. While this makes for a standardized, uniform, pinkish leather that is easily dyed, this is not what was historically produced. Thoughtful, caring tanners of earlier times tried to produce an even, good quality leather but color was not necessarily uniform. The quality and texture were probably more important than the color, especially in a frontier setting. This is not to say leather was not dyed; it was, in a variety of colors. It was also blackened for heavy leathers, harnesses and so forth.

In order that the tanning process may be continued without delay and risk of damage to the prepared hides, the bark should be leached in advance and ready when the hides are.

The first method of tanning I will discuss is one used by Herman Moyer. One needs several wooden or plastic barrels. Metal is unacceptable. Fit one barrel with a false bottom, screen or something that will permit liquid through and keep bark out. The barrel needs a spigot or drain below the false bottom. Fill the barrel with ground bark and cover with rain water or some chemical-free soft water. Let this set for two days and at

the end of the second day drain the bark liquor from the bottom and reserve in another container. This liquor is too strong initially to start tanning a hide. Fill the barrel again with water and let set. After two days drain the liquor again and reserve in yet another container. Repeat the process once more and use this third liquor to start the tanning process. The hide can be suspended on sticks so that it is entirely in contact with the solution. It should be stirred several times each day so that all parts of the hide have fresh liquor over them. Be sure to watch for folds or creases that could prevent contact. If this is done out-of-doors, the process is at the mercy of the weather. The temperature will definitely affect how fast the tanning proceeds. The warmer the temperature the faster the process. Cold

A 100-gallon tank layered with bark and hides. Alternate layers of bark and hides are placed in the tan vat. The vat is filled with water and the tanner lets time and nature run its course. This process seems well-suited to heavy leather.

weather and frozen tan troughs certainly delay the procedure.

Provided the weather is warm the hides may be moved to the second run of liquor in a week or ten days. It is important to stir and check the hides daily. The hides will change in both color and texture. The color will deepen from the pale creamy white of the prepared skin through reddish browns. The texture will change from somewhat slippery to a firmer, rougher grain. The pores and grain will become quite distinct as the tan progresses. At no time after the actual tanning process is started should the hide become slick, slippery or slimy. If a sulfurous smell is noted, it indicates spoilage. The liquor, or ooze as it is called, should have a somewhat pleasant fermented or vinegar-like smell.

After an additional week or ten days, the hide may be moved into the first liquor or ooze. The same procedure is followed as before.

The hides are now ready to be placed into a concentrated ooze. To prepare (this should be done in advance) arrange three barrels in a series. They should have the false bottoms and drains described earlier. Fill each barrel with bark but put water only on the first one. In two days drain the water and place it on the second barrel's bark. Fill the first barrel with water again. In another couple of days drain the liquor from the second barrel and pour into the third and again drain the water from the first barrel and pour over the bark in the second barrel. Continue in this manner until the first barrel has had ten changes of water. As the liquor is drawn off the third barrel, put it into a storage container for later use.

When the hides have progressed through the three changes of weaker ooze, they are placed into this concentrated ooze for at least a month or even longer. The heavier the hide the longer it should remain. Again, they must be checked and stirred frequently in order that the entire hide is subject to the action of the tannins. The hides will progressively look and feel more like wet leather, which is what they are becoming.

The hides may be layered after the successful completion of the previous steps. The hides are removed from the concentrated ooze. Place a couple of inches of ground bark in the bottom of a large clean tank. Lay a hide on the bark being sure that folds and creases are kept to a minimum. Place another layer of bark on the hide. Do this until the hides are buried in layers of bark. The tank is filled with clean water and the hides are left until they are fully tanned. This will depend on the temperature and the size and weight of the hides. A heavy bullhide could remain in the layers for several months or even up to a year. This would be up to the discretion of the tanner. His experience and knowledge would ultimately determine when the leather is to be removed.

There are several methods used to determine when a hide is tanned. The best is probably to cut a small sample from the heaviest part of the neck and place it in boiling water for several minutes. If it remains relatively unchanged, the leather is ready. If the piece becomes rubbery, hard and curled, it is not ready to be removed. Another good visual test is when the thickest part of the hide (the neck) is cut, it should be uniformly colored throughout. If a white, raw streak remains in the middle, obviously the hide needs more time in the tan. As one gains experience it becomes more evident when each tanning phase is complete. If unsure about when to remove the hides, it would be better to allow them to remain in the tan rather than to remove them prematurely. In general the best leather is produced using successively stronger solutions in which the hides remain for an extended time.

In another method light skins are sewn into a bag or bottle

This deerskin has just been removed from the tan vat. Even though it is technically "tanned," it must still be curried or finished before it can be used. Note the pronounced grain.

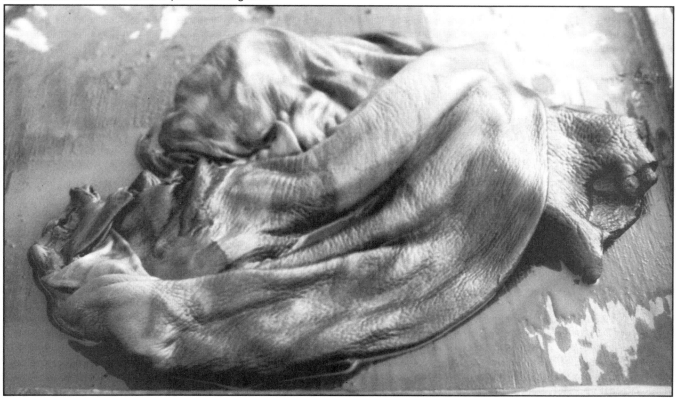

243

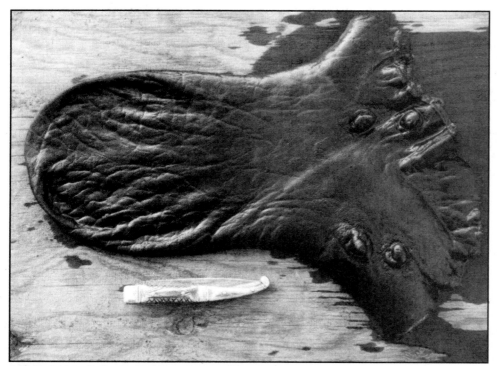

A bull scrotum just removed from the tan. There is evidence that scrotums have been used for centuries to make bags. They are well-suited to the task and make an attractive and useful item. The knife is 4-1/2 inches long.

in this solution for six weeks, stirring occasionally. At the end of six weeks remove the hides, empty half the solution, stir well and replace the hides. Fill with fresh bark and leave the hides for another two months. Keep the solution stirred and add water and bark as necessary to keep the hides covered. At the end of the two months the hides should be ready. Test as mentioned before, and if they are not finished, return the hides to the bark until they are.

According to Farnham, sole or heavy leathers require two extra months in the tan, for a total of about 6-1/2 months.

As mentioned before each tanner has his own method and combination of techniques. There are any number of ways to utilize vegetable tannins. The only hard and fast rule would be the initial treatment of the hides in a weak solution and the progression through a series of stronger baths.

It should be noted here that while bark or vegetable tanning is primarily suited to the production of leather, it can on occasion be adapted to the tanning of hair-on skins or hides. This entails a combination tan and will work with a fair degree of success on short haired hides such as summer deer, calf and the like. Hair slippage is a problem as well as is the staining of light-colored hair. Delicate fur skins are definitely not candidates for this process. Since there are better methods for tanning hair-on hides, it is recommended that one master vegetable tanning leather before attempting this.

The tanning process I use is primarily for deer- and calfskins. Even so, it has been successfully applied to hog, bear, goat, cattle and buffalo hides as well as numerous smaller skins.

For my tanning process, I obtain the bark from a local sawmill in the form of a finely shredded mulch. It is exclusively oak bark procured in the spring when the acid-forming sugars are at their highest. Care is taken to get bark that has been freshly removed from logs and has not been exposed to the weather, which would leach out valuable tannins.

Once the bark is secured, a fire pit is prepared. A 50-gallon drum or other suitable, large kettle is placed over the fire and filled with bark and water. The mixture is heated continuously for three or four hours and is periodically stirred. The extract will be dark as a result of the heat and probably to some degree the contact with the metal drum. A dark leather is desired so this color is not objectionable. If a lighter leather is preferred, then the leach system should be used.

The fire is kept burning at a moderate rate (enough to thoroughly heat the contents of the barrel). Water is added as needed to keep the container full. Every four hours or so the liquid, which is dark, opaque and has a deep, rich smell, is drawn off and poured through a fine screen into a tub and allowed to cool. When cool the tan liquor is transferred into

shape, suspended, and the tan liquor is poured in. The tannins are diffused through the skin by osmosis. (Although this method is mentioned in tanning literature frequently, I have no firsthand knowledge of this method.)

In his book, *Home Tanning and Leather Making Guide*, A. B. Farnham describes another method for tanning with bark. Start preparing this solution fifteen or twenty days before it is needed. Put 30 or 40 pounds of ground bark in a barrel and pour twenty gallons of boiling water over it. Keep covered and stir periodically until needed. When the hides are ready, strain the ooze into a clean barrel. Pour ten gallons of water over the bark and stir thoroughly. Strain this into the clean barrel with the other liquor. Add two quarts of vinegar and stir well. The solution is ready to be used and the hides may be hung in it. Be sure to agitate the hides periodically to get thorough coverage. (Author's note: I question this initial tan solution as perhaps too strong to place fresh hides, as explained previously. However, not having used this method I don't know. Proceed with caution.)

Prepare a second bark liquor at this time using the same proportions as before.

After the hides have been in the first solution ten or fifteen days, draw off five gallons of the first liquor and replace it with five gallons of the fresh, second solution. Add two quarts of vinegar and stir well. Every five days add five gallons of the fresh solution but not any vinegar until the second solution is gone.

Thirty-five days after the tanning was started, prepare the following: Put forty pounds of ground bark in a suitable container and add just enough hot water to moisten it. Remove the hides from the tanning barrel and add the moist bark. Retain all the old solution possible and mix well. Replace the hides in the barrel, completely burying them. Leave the hides buried various tan vats or holding tanks. The spent bark is removed from the drum and a fresh supply of bark and water is added. This process is continued until the required amount of tan liquor is obtained. The spent bark is used as mulch around gardens and shrubs.

There is a fair amount of sediment, which has the consistency of fine mud, in the solution. The sediment appears to be a fine bark powder and is used along with the rest of the solution. It precipitates out of the solution and must be stirred occasionally, which can be done as part of the regular stirring anyway. It probably adds somewhat to the solution and does not seem to cause harm.

If heavy leather is to be tanned, a quantity of unprocessed bark should be retained for later use in layering. For hides and skins that are the weight and size of a deer and also smaller calves, the tan liquor is sufficient to effect a thorough tan. However these skins may be layered if so desired.

Once the tannery is established, spent and partially spent ooze will be available in which to start hides. However at this point, since you are just getting started, some of the newly made strong solution can be diluted or a quantity of bark can be leached as previously described. The fresh tan liquor should be diluted by half with water for beginning the tan process. The initial bath should be stirred several times a day and the hides plunged about. These first baths or solutions are called handlers. The hides can just be thrown in as long as they are moved frequently and are not crowded in the tan vat, but suspension is probably best.

After six or eight days (depending on the temperature and other factors), the hides may be moved to another vat of stronger solution or a portion of the original liquor may drawn off and fresh added.

Continue stirring the liquors and moving the hides frequently. Every week or ten days the hides are moved into a stronger solution. If the tanner will stagger his production, hides may be in different tan vats and in different stages all the time. In other words when hides are moved from one vat, there are new ones to take their place. This has worked efficiently for me.

A calfskin and a summer, or red, deerskin. In order to tan hair-on hides with bark, they must first be pickled or pre-tanned. This sets the hair and reduces hair slippage.

When the hides have been in the progression of tan liquors for five or six weeks, the liquor may be used full strength. At this time the tanner may wish to add vinegar to the solution. This will acidify and strengthen the solution. It is added at the rate of three or four gallons to 80 or 100 gallons of ooze. This is not an exact science and with experience the tanner will probably develop his or her own method. Remember that hides in successively stronger tan liquors over a longer period of time seem to produce better leathers. Of course the liquors must be strong enough to prevent spoilage and have a positive tanning effect.

The tanner should check the hide's progress at least once a day for the first few weeks. It won't take long to notice a change in the hide's appearance. The grain will become prominent and somewhat rougher in texture. The flesh side will look coarser and fuller, and the color will deepen. Cuts in the edge of the hide will reveal the tan's progress into the corium. Later when taken from the tank as it becomes more fully tanned, the hide will seem to drain rapidly and the surface will appear slightly damp as opposed to wet.

Any change in the odor from a rich ferment to a foul, sulfurous smell indicates spoilage. The smell should be strong but not putrid or malodorous. The grain should not feel "slick" or fall away in patches or strips. On occasion lighter hides or the belly areas on deerskins will have damage to the grain as a result of the physical operations of fleshing and dehairing. This is different from the grain sloughing off. In extreme cases the hide will literally fall to pieces.

If the hides being tanned are deerskin-size, they should remain in a full strength ooze for three or four months in moderate temperatures. If the temperature is cold and the vats are frozen, the process should be lengthened correspondingly. Testing will show when the hides are fully tanned.

When tanning heavy hides such as cattle or buffalo, it will be necessary for the hides to remain in a strong ooze for at least five or six months. This is followed by layering in bark as described before. Lighter skins may be layered if so desired, however this process seems better suited to heavier hides. Layering seems to make a full leather and may also improve the color. Hides on the bottom of the pack will be subject to a stronger action than those on top, so it would be advisable to put thicker, heavier hides on the bottom and the lighter ones toward the top. The pack may be reversed halfway through the process by changing the hides on the bottom to the top and those on the top to the bottom. This will cause more even results. Very heavy hides may benefit from a change of bark after several months, also. As can be seen, this method of tanning is not particularly complicated. It is work, hard work. One must be diligent and perform operations as the hides are ready. Delays and indifferent methods will most certainly be seen in the end result.

When the tanning process is deemed complete, the hides are removed from the tan vat, rinsed in clean water, and the flesh side is worked over once more with the fleshing knife. The hide is then thoroughly washed in clean water and both sides scrubbed with a heavy brush. One now has leather, although the process is not complete. The leather may be slowly dried and stored or the finishing process may be continued and the leather made fit to use.

CURRYING

The final step in making useable leather is called finishing or currying. Currying tanned leathers was sometimes done by the tanners themselves. However, in more urban areas, the currier was a separate trade or skill. Currying is defined as "the preparation of tanned skins for the purpose of imparting to them the necessary smoothness, color, lustre and suppleness" (Kennedy 167).

The operations involved might include skiving or shaving, dyeing, dubbing, stuffing, fat liquoring, oiling, breaking and softening. There is a host of terms and processes for the currying of raw leather into equally numerous groups of finished leathers. The type of finished product is dependent on the type of skin or hide, the tanning process, as well as the way it is curried.

To describe each finishing technique and the resultant leather would require a book of its own. Therefore, only a basic currying operation will be covered.

New leather will dry stiff and some will crack if it is not curried. As with the tanning process, currying is best done slowly and with care in order to produce the best results. The principle ingredients required are tallow or some type of finishing oil and plenty of "elbow grease." In order to proceed, the hide must be damp but not soaking wet. If dry, the hide may be placed in a tub of clean, cool water until it becomes pliable in the thickest, heaviest areas. Stretching and pulling will help the process.

Traditionally, once the hide was damp it would be shaved. This was to level and even the flesh side. The thickness could be determined by this method also. For deer- and light calfskins this is rarely necessary. It should be noted that it took a skilled operator with a lot of experience and practice to level a hide successfully with the currier's knife.

Curriers often employed a marble or another type stone slab for a beam. This made a hard, unyielding surface that would aid in compressing the leather's fibers to produce a firm leather. It was also unaffected by water and oils. A table with the top slanting away from the workman was also used.

The hide is now worked on both sides with a slicker. All excess water is expelled and the hide is stretched in every direction. Plenty of pressure and muscle is put into this operation. When thoroughly worked the hide is ready for oil or tallow. The oil is spread evenly on the grain side, and the hide is hung up or tacked down to dry slowly. As the hide dries, the water is replaced by the oil. The hide should not be subject to excessive heat at any point in the currying process especially when wet or damp. A good rule of thumb: If it is too hot for you to tolerate comfortably, it is probably too hot for the leather. This applies to the temperature when drying as well as when spreading heated oil or tallow.

When the hide is dry, it should be lightly dampened or "damped back." The process is repeated for the flesh side: working, oiling, drying. When the hide has dried, any surplus oil or tallow is removed with a clean rag. This is one very basic method of finishing a hide. There are innumerable others.

Light skins may be softened by drawing them across a dull edge or wire as described in the section on tools. They are

When hides were removed from the tanning vats, they were still not ready for use. This view is of the finishing or currier's shop. Shown here are some of the many finishing operations that were employed. Leather was finished in many different ways according to its final use.

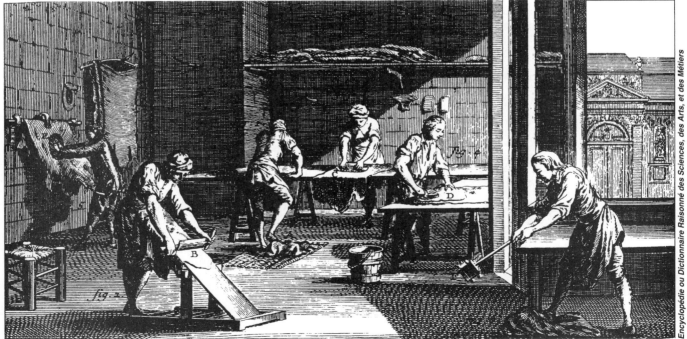

Encyclopédie ou Dictionnaire Raisonné des Sciences, des Arts, et des Métiers

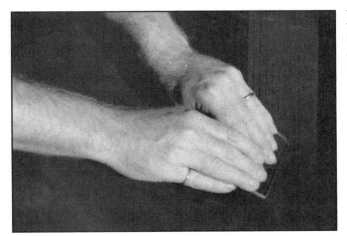

The final process in leather production is currying. There are numerous ways to finish leather. Here a buffalo hide is gone over with a glass slicker. This compresses the leather and makes a firm, dense material ideal for items such as shoe soles.

also pulled and stretched by hand as they slowly dry. Sole and other heavy leathers are not softened but are instead heavily oiled or greased and worked out flat. They are also beaten, rolled, pressed or otherwise worked in order to make as firm and dense a leather as is possible. There is at least as much effort and skill employed in currying leather as there is in tanning it. It is beyond the scope of this article to detail all the various ways leather may be finished. It is possible to experiment and with patience find acceptable methods to achieve the desired result.

HEALTH & SAFETY

This article would not be complete without a brief mention of some health and safety concerns that the tanner should know. While tanning is not a particularly dangerous occupation, there are potential hazards. Because humans and the animals whose hides are tanned are both warm-blooded, there are a number of debilitating and potentially fatal diseases that can be transmitted by the unsafe handling of carcasses and hides. Some of these diseases are rabies, anthrax, tularemia, brucellosis, ringworm and Rocky Mountain spotted fever. There are quite a few others. It is therefore *strongly* recommended that rubber gloves and aprons be used. Also, be selective about the hides with which you work. Know the source of your hides and don't be tempted to handle hides from diseased animals. Besides the health risks, the quality of a hide from a sick animal is very often poor compared to one that is in good health. There are far too many good hides and skins thrown away to make the risk necessary.

Historically, tanneries were considered noxious and filthy places. Very often they were. There was little attention paid to cleanliness or general maintenance. It takes relatively little to keep one's tannery clear of fleshings and scraps that attract vermin and breed disease. Occurring near Miles City, Montana, during the buffalo slaughter, the following anecdote is an example of how unsafe and unhealthy conditions can result in a near fatal infection. Remember, every hide was considered money in the bank, and on occasion the buffalo skinners would come across a buffalo that had been dead for some time but whose hide was still thought to be good. Happening upon one of these, a fellow went to work and while skinning the beast, he wiped his hand across his mouth, which had an already cracked lip. By the next morning his lip was swollen, and by that afternoon both lips were badly swollen. The next day his eyes were closed and his nose was three times larger than normal. His head was described as resembling "a battered pumpkin." For five days the man could not eat and was consumed by fever. All those involved thought he would die (Gilbert 193-194). The man did recover but most certainly paid a hefty price for his carelessness. In short—it pays to be careful.

These leathers were all tanned using bark by the author. They were finished by several methods. Included from the bottom, counterclockwise, are bear, hog, buffalo, calf, goat and the black hide is deer. The small shiny, dark hide in the center is kidskin.

CONCLUSION

The art of tanning is just that—an art. While it can be complicated, it does not necessarily have to be. Modern commercial tanneries have a great deal of complex and expensive machinery and rely on a vast array of chemical knowledge to accomplish an impressive number of tasks. The art of the tanner is based on personal knowledge gained by experience. This applies to the tanner in charge of a complex modern tannery as well as to one who emulates our ancestors and uses the traditional methods handed down for centuries. This article is directed to those who are interested in duplicating the old processes and, by doing so, recreating the type of leather that was used historically. Granted, it is a slow, time-consuming task that involves a tremendous amount of work. However, the first time one successfully turns a raw, messy hide into finished leather with a beautiful color, grain and texture, there will be a sense of satisfaction that will be beyond compare.

On a personal level, I deplore the wanton waste and destruction of natural resources, whether it is the cutting of trees only for tanbark or killing a deer only for the hide. I urge all who wish to pursue tanning to obtain their materials in an ethical manner. Another note is that the materials used in this type of tanning are non-toxic if used as directed. The lime and manure used in dehairing and bating are useful in building up poor soils. The spent tan liquor can be recycled and is non-toxic. Even though streams and creeks are black with tannic acid in the fall, one should never dump any by-product of the tanning process into any body of water. Done properly, tanning is a process that can be accomplished in conjunction with nature.

The methods that have been described here are meant to be a primer. As mentioned there are numerous ways to tan. The leather made by these procedures is not a standardized, uniform product but has variations in color, texture and thickness. This leather can be used to recreate articles that would have been common on the frontier. It should be understood that a master tanner in the 18th century with a well-equipped facility could make leather as good as any found today. With time and practice, it can be done again.

Finally, I would be remiss if I did not thank those involved for their help and encouragement. I thank Bill Scurlock for giving me this opportunity. My thanks to Steven, Tom and Gary for their suggestions and support over the years. I would especially like to thank my wife, Anna, without whose help I would not be able to work at what I truly enjoy.

APPENDIX A: WORKS CITED

Austin, William E. *Principles and Practices of Fur Dressing and Fur Dyeing*. New York: Van Nostrand, 1922.

Comstock, Jim, ed. *Hardesty's Early West Virginia: The West Virginia Heritage Encyclopedia*. Vol. 1. Richwood, WV: Comstock, 1974.

Farnham, A.B. *Home Tanning and Leather Making Guide*. Columbus, OH: Harding Publishing, 1950.

Fisher, Leonard Everett. *Colonial American Craftsmen: The Tanners*. New York: Franklin Watts, 1966.

Ford, Thomas K. *The Leatherworker in Eighteenth Century Williamsburg*. Williamsburg, VA.: Colonial Williamsburg Publications, 1967.

Frity, Sandy. "Who was the Iceman?" *Popular Science* Feb. 1993: 46-50+.

Gilbert, Miles. *Getting a Stand*. Union City, TN: Pioneer Press, 1986.

Hanson, Charles E., Jr. "The Greatest Years of Hide Hunting." *The Museum of the Fur Trade Quarterly* 13.2 (1977): 2-10.

___. "The Southern Fur Trade." *The Museum of the Fur Trade Quarterly* 22.1 (1986): 1-9.

Hempel, Edward H. *The Economics of Chemical Industries*. New York: John Wiley and Sons, 1939.

Kellogg, Kathy. *Home Tanning and Leathercraft Simplified*. Charlotte, VT: Williamson Publishing, 1984.

Kennedy, David H. *The Art of Tanning Leather*. New York: Baker and Godwin, 1857.

"Leather and Hides." *Encyclopedia Britannica*. 15th ed. 1975.

Litchfield, Carter, et al. *The Bethlehem Oil Mill 1745-1934, German Technology in Early Pennsylvania*. Olearius Editions.

Moyer, Herman. Personal interview. Feb. 1993.

Roberts, David. "The Iceman: Lone Voyager from the Copper Age." *National Geographic* June 1993: 36-67.

Theis, Edwin R. "Leather." *Rogers Industrial Chemistry*. New York: Van Nostrand, 1943.

Welsh, Peter C. *Tanning in the United States to 1850*. Washington, D.C.: Smithsonian Institution, 1964.

Williams, Trevor I. *The History of Invention*. New York: Facts on File, 1987.